A Michael Hamburger Reader

Michael Hamburger was born in Berlin in 1924 and moved to Britain in 1933. In addition to his many books of poetry, he published several collections of essays, a study of modernist poetry since Baudelaire, *The Truth of Poetry*, and an autobiography. He translated from, among others, Goethe, Hölderlin, Rilke and Celan. His awards included the German Federal Republic's Goethe Medal for services to German literature and the European Community's first European Translation Prize for *Poems of Paul Celan*, now in its third edition. He died at home in Suffolk in 2007.

Dennis O'Driscoll was born in Thurles, Co. Tipperary in 1954. His publications include nine collections of poetry, a book of essays, two collections of literary quotations and the much admired *Stepping Stones: Interviews with Seamus Heaney* (2008). He received a Lannan Literary Award in 1999. As well as this book, he had completed a second collection of essays, *The Outnumbered Poet*, before his death during the Christmas holiday, 2012. He received numerous honours and awards both in Ireland and the USA. He worked for almost forty years in Ireland's Revenue and Customs service.

By Dennis O'Driscoll

POETRY

Kist
Hidden Extras
Long Story Short
Quality Time
Weather Permitting
Exemplary Damages
New and Selected Poems
Reality Check
Dear Life

ESSAYS

Troubled Thoughts, Majestic Dreams
The Outnumbered Poet

INTERVIEWS

Stepping Stones: Interviews with Seamus Heaney

AS EDITOR

The Bloodaxe Book of Poetry Quotations
Quote Poet Unquote

A MICHAEL HAMBURGER READER

Edited by

Dennis O'Driscoll

CARCANET

First published in Great Britain in 2017 by

Carcanet Press Limited
Alliance House
Cross Street
Manchester M2 7AQ
www.carcanet.co.uk

We welcome your feedback: info@carcanet.co.uk

A CIP catalogue record for this book is available
from the British Library, ISBN 978 1 78410 515 0

The publisher acknowledges financial assistance
from Arts Council England

Set in Monotype Ehrhardt by Anvil
Printed and bound in England by SRP Ltd, Exeter

for Anne Beresford

Note

Asterisks indicate section divisions in the original editions, while a row of dots indicates omissions in this selection, as do bracketed ellipses at the end of paragraphs or of sections. Quoted texts are separated from their translations by a short row of dots.

CONTENTS

Introduction

MICHAEL HAMBURGER'S birth, in Berlin on 22 March 1924, coincided with the anniversary of the death of Goethe. Hamburger's death, at his Suffolk home on 7 June 2007, occurred on the anniversary of Hölderlin's death. Poet, translator, critic, essayist and memoirist, he was the quintessential 'man of letters': the creature whose own death, like that of the 'general reader', is perennially mourned but who, fortunately, proves as imperishable as he is irrepressible.

Goethe and Hölderlin were among the writers – German principally – whom Hamburger would translate: Hugo von Hofmannsthal, Paul Celan, Hans Magnus Enzensberger, Bertolt Brecht, Gottfried Benn, Peter Huchel, W. G. Sebald and many others. His lifelong Goethe translations are collected in *Roman Elegies and Other Poems* (1996); Goethe features extensively in Hamburger's criticism also. Hamburger's engagement with the work of Friedrich Hölderlin – the central translation project of his life – culminated in the 2004 edition of the great poet's *Poems and Fragments*, sixty years after *Poems of Hölderlin*, published before Hamburger was twenty. One of his earliest 'persona' poems, 'Hölderlin', dating from 1941, was 'the first poem I published after my contributions to the school magazine'.

His translations from Hölderlin and other German poets served to bridge two lives in two languages. Along with his parents and three siblings, he moved from Berlin to Edinburgh in 1933, after his Jewish father – a distinguished paediatrician and professor – had been dismissed from his post by the National Socialist authorities. While English became his everyday language, Hamburger never lost touch with his native German; he read German and French for his Modern Languages degree at Oxford. Indeed, in later years, he frequently observed that his work – his poetry in particular – received greater acclaim in Germany than in England: a literary repatriation about which he was markedly ambivalent, clearly hankering for more appreciation in his long-adopted homeland. He bemoaned the fact that 'The nearest thing to general assessments of a writer's work now appears in obituary columns. If the better newspapers were interested in extending that privilege to writers who have withstood neglect and are still kicking, they would have to give that amount of space and care to people who are only candidates for death . . .'

I hope this book will help to gain for his work the recognition it has long-merited in the English-speaking world. My intention has been to let the poet speak for himself, with minimal editorial intrusion. It is because his work is so various that aspects of it have long been underestimated or overlooked; and it is precisely that same multifarious nature which demands a miscellany such as this, if even a semblance of justice to his complete oeuvre is to be done. Known as a translator, and as author of the classic *The Truth of Poetry*, other facets of his work have been largely ignored, and his writings as a whole urgently need revival and revivification. I trust that the excerpts presented here will act as pointers to the wider hinterland of texts from which they derive. Aimed as they were at a general, rather than specialist, audience, Michael Hamburger's books – other than his Hölderlin (equipped with 'minimal and selective' annotation) – were published without textual notes; this practice has been followed here. I regret, however, that in giving priority to Michael Hamburger's work, insufficient space remained to follow his practice of presenting translations and original texts *en face*. Happily, the critical essays are themselves mini-anthologies, in which the originals are included.

The present compilation (arbitrary and personal though any selection must be) is, I trust, not just a tribute and memorial, but a vibrant collection of writings that will introduce new readers to the breadth and intellectual vigour of Hamburger's work, remind more seasoned Hamburger readers of the key texts of his oeuvre, and allow his prose works to inform and illuminate contemporary critical debates: debates in which they can still hold their own with a freshness, originality, erudition and even radicalism that is both stimulating and challenging. He subjected every critical assumption to scrutiny, questioned every orthodoxy, refused to take poets at their own word. An invariably courteous critic, eschewing the cheap jibe, he was nonetheless an uncompromising one, determined to identify and champion the very best that has been written: 'Discrimination is needed. Without it, art succumbs to the randomness of commercialism, in which the shoddy product can displace the well-made and durable simply by being more effectively marketed.' Disdainful of the anti-

'élitism' of the age, he 'could never understand why it should be thought undemocratic to prefer the best to the second-rate or worse'.

As is evident from his book-length 'conversation' with Peter Dale, he would have welcomed the fact that this miscellany does not assume his translations to be his principal achievement: 'The parrot cry raised to brush aside my poems again and again, *ad nauseam*, is 'better known as a translator' – as though it made the slightest difference what a writer is best known for . . . For me, translation is a humble activity, a service to works I care about, not a surrogate for productions of my own.' He added that 'I think of my translations as a middle ground between reading and writing, not a home ground shared by my own poems.'

As the writer whom Christopher Middleton dubbed 'Gloomburger', and who was lugubrious enough, yet playful enough, to adopt the persona 'Mr Littlejoy' in some poems, it may, at first, seem surprising that he believed that 'all poetry, whatever its theme, affirms life; it does so because form itself is the progeny of the marriage of mind and matter. Only the unformed poem, the bad poem, can be negative'. But the subtle refinement of thought characteristic of this unusually well-read and intellectually-brilliant man animates his writings, rendering them as unpredictable as they are insightful. In a letter to me, he remarked, 'I always try to get through to essences, so that my realism isn't an end in itself. What I aim at are very simple words, images, situations that are somehow transparent, so that the complexity remains below the surface. People who look only at the surface find banality in my verse. That is a risk I take.'

'Friendships, including those with fellow poets, have always been of utmost importance to me', Hamburger attested. He was himself the most generous of friends, sacrificing large tranches of his scarce time to correspondents from all over the world, and ever-ready to appraise and encourage the work of even the most callow young poets. Those of us privileged to have known him well will recall him with gratitude and loyalty of the kind that, in his memoir, *String of Beginnings*, he directs towards similarly unfashionable poets like Vernon Watkins and Edwin Muir. When he depicts Watkins as possessing 'an integrity and a steadfastness that I never ceased to admire' and as 'one of the most admirable and lovable men it has been my good fortune to know', I want to borrow every one of those words and apply them directly to Hamburger himself.

An equally good fit are the characteristics he attributed to Muir: 'Edwin Muir's heroism was not of the swashbuckling, his diction not of the word-rattling, kind. As a poet, as a critic and as a man he was equally unassuming; and his utter lack of pretensions was due to a wholeness, an integrity... that has become so rare as to be incomprehensible to many... His humility was neither an attitude nor a virtue in any conventional sense, but simply an aspect of his self-knowledge or – this comes down to the same thing – of his humanity.'

In conclusion, some votes of thanks. I gratefully acknowledge the support of Goethe-Institut Dublin for my editorial work; in this regard, I wish to extend particular thanks to Ms Monika Schlenger. That I have been allowed to present some of Michael Hamburger's finest writings – work of immense clarity, sagacity and incisiveness, banged out to the end of his life on ramshackle manual typewriters – is a privilege I owe to his family: to his widow, the poet Anne Beresford, and his son and literary executor, Richard Hamburger, in particular. Their forbearance with my tardy progress towards completion of the project was matched by that of Peter Jay of Anvil Press Poetry. Peter was hearteningly enthusiastic about my endeavour from the very start. I hope, for the sake of the estimable work presented here, that his ardent and inspiriting enthusiasm will prove infectious.

DENNIS O'DRISCOLL

June 2012

1 *The Man*

Autobiographical Essay

From *Contemporary Authors: Autobiography Series* Vol. 4 (1986)

THERE WAS a time, in my teens and twenties, when nothing came more easily to me than writing about myself. All those long letters I used to write my friends about what I felt, thought, believed about this and that! Autobiography, though, is something different. One is supposed to write it in retrospect, as near the end of one's life as possible, out of an awareness of the totality of a life and in the knowledge of what mattered in it, what did not. Yet the older I have grown, the harder it has been for me to write about myself let alone sum up that totality or be sure what in my life was mine, what was anyone's, what I made of my life, and what life made of me.

I came up against some of those difficulties when, before the age of fifty, I wrote a book of 'intermittent memoirs' called *A Mug's Game*. The memoirs were intermittent because, even then, my memory was selective, 'like a sieve'; and the meshes in that sieve have grown larger since. Even then, too, it became clear to me that recollection is inseparable from imagination – and so from invention. Mnemosyne, Memory, was the Mother of the Muses. Whether we like it or not, autobiography – as distinct from merely factual chronicles – is a kind of fiction. Since I had no wish to write fiction about myself, I made my book of memoirs as drily factual as I could make it, incorporating diary entries and assorted documents that had no emotive or literary appeal, because they gave no scope to imagination. This procedure may have been forced on me by a puritanism or purism that has inhibited me throughout my life. In the book of memoirs I traced it to my upbringing, and especially to the character of my father, a scientist – paediatrician and professor of medicine – in whom moral intransigence and extreme conscientiousness were combined with strong artistic leanings which, most of the time, he had to sacrifice to his many obligations. Strict truthfulness was one of the demands my father made on himself and on his children.

A Mug's Game dealt with my life only up to the age of thirty. In spite of that it could not tell the whole truth, and not only because one doesn't know the whole truth about oneself but because what I did know of the truth about myself involved other people whose private affairs I had no business to make public. Despite the reticence imposed by that restriction, I had to conceal the identity of several persons, and omit all reference to events or relationships that were part of my life. Yet the writing of that book precipitated a break with one of my oldest and closest friends, whose memory or imagination contradicted my version of our earliest meetings and of his circumstances at the time.

Ever since, I have wished to write a complement to that book of memoirs; not a chronological sequel, though, on the same documentary lines. Not only have I ceased to keep a diary of events and meetings which, without one, I can no longer place in any sequence, but later experience has set up new misgivings about the decency and usefulness of chronicling my own life.

I took the title for my book of memoirs from this remark by T. S. Eliot: 'As things are, and as fundamentally they must always be, poetry is not a career but a mug's game. No honest poet can ever feel quite sure of the permanent value of what he has written: he may have wasted his time and messed up his life for nothing.' By the time he wrote these words, Eliot had received ample confirmation from others that what he had written was of 'permanent value'; but, because a poet can place no reliance at all on how other people judge his work at any one moment – even if those judgments amount to a consensus, and they rarely do – that remark struck me not as a personal confession of Eliot's, or gesture of humility on his part, but as a general and incontrovertible truth about being a poet.

If I tell the story of my life, though, without wishing to write fiction, I assume that either my life was representative enough for others to identify with my experiences, or that my life was so exceptional as to be of interest to others for that reason. The second assumption would rest on the belief that my work is of 'permanent value'. If it isn't – and I have no means of knowing whether it is or not – that would leave only the career I never wanted and succeeded very well in warding or breaking off before it could carry me away.

Well, my life has been representative in some ways, in that I had to undergo an education, serve as a soldier in a war, earn my living in various ways, worry about those I loved, work very hard to keep up the mug's game of my choice; and it was exceptional or freakish in at least one regard, that I was born in Germany into a German-speaking family, uprooted at the age of nine, but began nonetheless at the age of fifteen to turn into a British poet. That oddity must have been my main incentive to write a book of memoirs; to explain it to myself, in the first place, by retracing the stages; though clearly in the hope – not confirmed by the immediate reception or sales of the book – that the story might be of use or interest to others.

That work has been done, and need not be done again except for a few improvements, corrections, and excisions I should like to make if and when the book is reprinted. The complement I have in mind now is no more a reiteration than a sequel. It has to do not with the facts of my life and work – which can be found in reference books like *Who's Who* – but with themes pushed out of *A Mug's Game* by its linear and austerely factual structure. One reason why the facts and events of my life are receding from my awareness now is that I care less and less about what I have done or failed to do, more and more about the conditions in which those things were done or not done. Drastic changes in the world at large, and in my own country, have called in question even the ambition of 'permanent value' that has always underlain the poetic mug's game, where it wasn't played only out of vanity. In the present state of affairs 'permanent' has become too big a word. I prefer the word 'durable'; but even durability, in products of any kind other than those made for the very rich to remind them that they are different, is no longer a value in the societies I know. Built-in obsolescence and instant consumption have replaced it. If that seems inapplicable to the arts, every sort of 'pop' or 'camp' art proves that it isn't. So do the personality cult and the cult of instant success, with their built-in obsolescence. These are exact counterparts and concomitants of the ethos of salesmanship that has replaced the value of durability.

As for any of the careers that were open to me, they have come to look like a luxury and a self-indulgence, when the most I can wish those I care about is survival in an environment worth surviving in, and employment of any kind. In the thirteen years or so that have passed since the writing of my memoirs, these have become the realities that confront my three children and await my four grandchildren, if they are allowed to grow up.

This much had to be said before I could set out on any new ego-trip or only re-exhibit some of the data brought back from the first. To dig up and set down those data once was an exploration. To string them together once more – as one is asked to do again and again for the obligatory biographical and bibliographical notes in periodicals and anthologies – is a tedious chore, if only because an unwritten law forbids writers to repeat themselves. Up to the age of thirty, the data I can exhibit here are the same as before, though I shall have to reduce them to their bare bones. If anything has changed, it is the perspective and the presentation.

I WAS born in Berlin just after the runaway inflation that was like an economic prelude to the political monstrosities that followed a decade later, and part of the destabilization brought about by Germany's defeat in the First World War, in which my father had served as a medical officer, winning the Iron Gross for some act of gallantry he never talked about. Both my father's and my mother's families were of Jewish descent, but had become culturally assimilated for at least three generations before mine. Of my grandparents, only my father's mother, who was born in Poland, went to a synagogue, which she called 'the Temple' – but never once took us four children there. We grew up in complete ignorance of the Jewish religion and of Jewish traditions. One of my great-uncles, an industrial manager and 'gentleman' show jumper, had taken assimilation to the point of marrying a non-Jewish wife of the Junker class. I have an edition of the works of Klopstock – the 'German Milton' and author of *The Messiah* – published in 1782 and stolen by my mother in girlhood from the library of a grandmother she disliked; and a Latin text, a Sallust, studied by a maternal great-grandfather, Ludwig or Louis Hamburg, Jr., at the Gymnasium of Mainz in 1847. On my father's side, his grandfather N. Hamburger received his royal licence as a teacher in the Prussian educational system in 1835 at Oppeln in Silesia. His son, my grandfather Leopold, was a writer, sometimes under the anagram Burghammer, who was in touch with Alphonse Daudet and Émile Zola in Paris, where he wrote literary criticism for German periodicals before moving to Poland, marrying there, then settling in Berlin. Like my father after him, that grandfather had to give up the occupation of his choice for a career. He died broken-hearted and bankrupt soon after my birth, and had ceased to speak or write in his last years. A family tree drawn up for my maternal grand-father suggests that his family came to Mainz from Spain in the seventeenth century. Other documents suggest that Hamburger and

Hamburg, my father's and my mother's surnames, were only variants of one name – and a certain degree of inbreeding in my descent. My mother's mother came from a village in Baden-Württemberg that has since been incorporated into the city of Heidelberg.

My father was an agnostic. My mother became a Quaker after his early death. They had met shortly after the end of the First World War, at the Berlin hospital where my father worked as a doctor, my mother as a temporary nurse, though her family, unlike my father's, was rich enough for her to have no need to work. Some years before our emigration we had come to divide our time between our apartment in central Berlin and a house in the village of Kladow, on the river Havel, that my mother's father had had built for his extended family. This country place, rather than the seaside holidays we had taken in earlier years on the Baltic coast, established the preference for rural surroundings that made me a 'nature poet' amongst other things. Music, which both my parents played and my father would have liked to make his mug's game, and animals were my first loves, though even before the age of nine I had fallen in love with at least one little girl. In early childhood, too, I became a voracious reader, mainly of natural history; so much so that my parents thought I was sure to turn into a naturalist of some sort. (That I should not turn into a musician became apparent when I gave up my violin studies as soon as school work gave me an excuse, while at my prep school in London. I continued to improvise by ear on the piano, harmonium, and other instruments, as my father did before me and my son after me.)

My extreme introversion in childhood, even before the trauma of the months before our emigration, is explained in *A Mug's Game* – in so far as it can be explained – as a reaction to the regimenting by a governess the four of us suffered from infancy, because my father was kept too busy by his duties as a hospital consultant, teacher, and family doctor, my mother by her ministrations to my father's domestic and secretarial needs, for more than minimal attention to ours. It was not till the harm was done, in his last London years, that my father took up psychology, in response to a lack he had come to feel in his work as a physician, but also, I think, out of a realization of what had gone wrong in his own home. His mentor was Alfred Adler, whom I remember seeing and having to kiss, not Freud – though we were also friendly with Freud's son Ernst, his daughter-in-law Lucy, and their three sons, who were patients of my father's. I call my introversion extreme – though I could come out of it when the coast was clear – because it could turn into trance-like states of withdrawal, in one of which I almost died by drowning when I lost my balance on our Kladow landing-stage, dropped into the water like a stone, and made no attempt to swim, though I was a strong swimmer. I was rescued by a governess who, unlike her predecessor, was not strict but sadistic, and whose power over us had almost certainly driven me into that state.

Almost immediately after the National Socialist victory early in 1933 my father decided to leave for Edinburgh, where he had to qualify once more as a doctor, in a foreign language, so as to be allowed to practise in Britain. It was in the next few months, before we were removed from school and went to live at Kladow while my father made preparations for the family to join him in Edinburgh in November, that our lost Jewishness came home to me with a vengeance at school, as a threat and a curse, by the shock of being suddenly picked on, segregated, and having the separateness rubbed in, physically at times, by teachers and fellow pupils. When my best friend's big brother whipped me with a length of wire on the way home we had always shared, the physical pain hurt me less than the betrayal. Yet when my father gave up his consultantship and professorship at the hospital, the Charité, members of his nursing staff burst into tears and implored him to stay.

Despite the uprooting and the parting from relatives and friends, especially from my father's widowed mother, who felt too old, ailing, and set in her ways to begin a new life, but survived long enough to be murdered in an extermination camp – and the confiscation, at the English port, of my grandfather's two pet budgerigars, which I loved – I must have come out of those traumatic shocks with a new competitiveness and self-assertiveness. For the first time in a city – after escapes at Kladow from supervision and outbursts there of our repressed energies – we were left to our own devices – even on what I think was the very first day, when my younger brother and I had to make our way to a new school through streets we did not know, vainly asking for directions in a language we had not yet learned to speak. My brother was in tears by the time we found a schoolmistress from that school, George Watson's, who showed us to our classrooms. My father, under pressures of every kind and much more deeply shattered than his children had the capacity to be, scarcely left his room while preparing for the examinations – special ones set up for immigrant doctors – that would permit him to set up a new practice in London within a mere year and a half, while living on borrowed money. My mother, as ever, supported him by learning to cope with domestic chores that had previously been left to servants. She had never so much as cooked, though she soon did so excellently, let alone laid a coal fire or cleaned a grate. Within a term or so at school, I won a book prize for an English essay, established my standing by what looked like feats of daring in the swimming pool, but were nothing but my familiarity with water, and was even invited to join a gang of classmates who roamed the streets for ritualized fights with boys wearing the uniforms of other, rival, schools. This kind of aggressiveness and pugnaciousness was to be needed until almost the end of my school years in England, though only in rare emergencies later, when, outside the boxing-ring, I resorted to it only when attacked, taunted, or challenged. My face is still scarred by an injury received when two Westminster enemies ambushed me on my bicycle, seized the handlebars, and made me dive off head first on to a tarmac road. What astonishes me now, though, is how little time it took me to adapt to and feel more or less at ease in all the successive institutions – from George Watson's in Edinburgh, the Brighton and Hove Grammar School (briefly), The Hall, Hampstead (my prep school in London), Westminster School, Christ Church, Oxford, to the British Army – in which I spent most of my working life from the age of nine to the age of twenty-four.

The next blow was my father's death in 1940, after hard years of struggle in London, where paediatricians rarely practised as family doctors, as in Germany, and no major hospital appointment was forthcoming, notice from the International Red Cross of his mother's transportation, and the damage done to his practice when he was ordered to leave London to await bombing casualties at Hitchin, Hertfordshire. (We had become British subjects before the outbreak of war.) By then, at the age of sixteen and at the third of the successive places to which Westminster School had been evacuated from London, so that day-boys like myself became boarders, I had begun to write and translate poems consistently enough to think of myself as a writer. The loss of my father, with whom I shared most of my interests and who read my early literary attempts, at once desolated me and propelled me to action once more, by putting a sudden end to my adolescence. I persuaded my mother, guardian, and headmaster to let me leave school early, won an Exhibition to Christ Church, Oxford – but for which any further education would have been more than my mother could afford – and managed to get to Christ Church when I was barely seventeen.

The relative freedom of my first stay at Oxford – a mere four terms – gave me time to write poems and do the translations of poems by Hölderlin, with their long and rambling introduction, that became my first book, finished by the time I was eighteen and published when I was nineteen, in 1943. The book appeared when I had just become an infantryman or foot-slogger. Through the English Club at Oxford I had come to know a good many eminent writers, who talked or read there, and some of them became my friends, as well as fellow under-graduate poets like Sidney Keyes – who was to die soon after as an officer in the same regiment I joined – and Philip Larkin. Other poet friends made at Oxford were John Heath-Stubbs and David Wright, both of whom also frequented the Soho pubs that became my 'second university' when in London – most regularly while I was waiting for my call-up from the late summer of 1942 to the early summer of 1943. Dylan Thomas, whose host I had been at Oxford, narrowly missing being 'sent down' in consequence, was the centre of attrac-tion in those pubs. It was there, too, that I met my first publisher, Tambimuttu of *Poetry London*. A few early poems appeared in miscellanies of Oxford and Cambridge writing in those years, so that I started out as an insider, becoming an outsider later, when I was an 'established' writer – more and more so over the decades.

From 1943 to 1947, my army years, I published very little, but managed to work on another little book of translations, from Baudelaire's French in 1944, while stationed in the Shetland Islands, a wild outpost and garrison where regular army routine, with its 'square-bashing' and 'fatigues' and 'bullshit', was suddenly in abeyance, and boredom also drove me to getting myself the job of braving the high winds on the moors to walk from camp to camp with a portable gramophone, 'entertaining' my fellow soldiers with classi-cal music very few of them wanted to hear. There, too, I fell in love with a married woman, a pianist from London staying at Lerwick with her Shetland relatives while her husband was serving abroad. The poems I wrote about that and other things remained unpublished at the time. Very few of them got into my first collection.

It was not until 1945 that I succeeded in being sent overseas, and that only by having myself downgraded medically so that I could be transferred from my infantry regiment to another occupation – that of interpreter. As such I was posted to Naples – though I had only begun to teach myself Italian with a bilingual Dante small enough to carry about in my kitbag. After having all my personal possessions, other than the Dante, stolen while I was in my hammock on the troopship, my papers also proved to have been lost at the transit camp in Naples. Since I received no pay for the extraordinary fatigues I did there, I was reduced to selling part of my cigarette ration on the black market. The 'fraternization' that let me in for helped to make my Italian slightly more up to date than Dante's. In the course of moving by stages through Italy to Austria I contracted hepatitis and almost died of it, by drinking myself into a coma with a bottle of Italian cognac given to me by the ambulance driver who was to have taken me from hospital to a convalescent home, but chucked me out on to the roadside when I had lost consciousness. My punishment for this breach of medical orders was not the disciplinary action that ought to have been taken by the Commandant of my new unit in Austria, but abstinence from alcohol for the rest of my life.

The climate, landscapes, and cities of Italy were a powerful experience of that period, since we had never travelled beyond the British Isles before the war. In Austria it was the alpine scenery of my first posting, Lienz in the Dolomites, but also the impact of the collapse of a civilized order – already felt while roaming the streets and alleys of Naples. These experiences went into my sequence of poems 'From the Notebook of a European Tramp', though soon all leisure and privacy for writing became so scarce that I did not finish the sequence until after my demobilization and brief return to Oxford.

At Lienz I worked with German prisoners of war employed in my unit, a store or 'dump' of captured enemy equipment, some of which they found a way of smuggling out to civilians for cash over the barbed wire fence. An investigation of that smuggling ring, with cross-examinations I had to interpret, was one of my more unpleasant, but revealing, duties. Another was the murder trial of a British soldier, involving his Austrian girl friend. A German groom taught me to ride horses there, some of which had been captured from the Cossack Army that fought on the German side. The method was simple, on the same principle as teaching someone to swim by throwing him into the water, and within minutes I had learned to keep my seat. To that initiation I owed my long solitary rides through the mountainside woods on my favourite Cossack mare (which I could have bought when the unit was dissolved, but had to leave behind).

No longer needed as an interpreter, when the prisoners were repatriated, I joined the Royal Army Education Corps, taught at an Army school for British soldiers in Carinthia as a sergeant, suddenly received an 'emergency commission' and was posted to the GHQ in Graz as an educational staff officer. When both the city and the office work proved uncongenial to me, I returned to the Carinthian lakes to find myself appointed headmaster of a coeducational boarding school for the children of military and civilian administrators in the British occupation zone of Austria. That proved to be the most exacting responsibility I have taken on in my life, and one that was too much for me at the age of twenty two. When my seven-day-a-week, all-day work was also subverted by the opposition of members of the staff to my unconventional notions of how a school should be run – by persuasion, not coercion or punishment – I developed a fever that was the alternative to a nervous breakdown, and was given a short leave in England. When I returned it was as 'second master' to an older, more experienced, and less libertarian head, a schoolteacher in civilian life, who also had the advantage of higher military rank in his dealings with our remote controllers at HQ. The school, an unprecedented experiment and showpiece for the Army, was inspected by Field-Marshal Montgomery amongst others.

It was during my last months there that I was given leave, but no official passes, for a very brief trip to Berlin, to visit my surviving relatives. It was a strenuous and exciting journey across the different occupation zones, helped by a dress uniform, complete with campaign ribbons and insignia, lent to me by the new headmaster, Captain Murphy, in place of my battledress and lieutenant's pips. Despite or because of that imposture, there were no hitches. I found my relatives – two great-uncles and their families – in the ruins of West Berlin, was able to deliver the gifts of food I was carrying, and even managed to make my way back to Carinthia before my leave had expired.

I was demobilized in the summer of 1947. Concessions to returning ex-servicemen enabled me to pack my remaining degree course at

Oxford into one year. I duly graduated in Modern Languages, German and French, but was too impatient to get out at last into the 'real', uninstitutionalized world to stay on for a doctorate and likely appointment at Oxford. In the vacations, and for some time after that, I lived at my mother's house in London, where for the next four years I earned a living of sorts as a free-lance writer and odd-job man, contributing poems and book reviews to periodicals like the *New Statesman* and the *Times Literary Supplement*, writing occasional broadcasts for the Third Programme of the BBC, but also tutoring for an agency, teaching French at Pentonville Prison, or conducting parties of foreign visitors on tours of London for the British Council. My earnings from all these activities became just enough to pay for a one-room apartment, at a time when the rent was one pound a week, with something left over for very rough travels in Italy and France out of which I concocted the one novel I ever wrote, but had the sense to withdraw before my agent had placed it. At the same period I wrote a stage play that was also spared publication and performance. I made short stories out of parts of the novel, and had to reprint them twenty years later in my book of memoirs, because the fictions had overlaid the realities on which they were based. What I remembered were the fictions, not the facts; and my documentary rigour could not undo that process.

After marrying in 1951, and with a first child on the way, I had to look for a more secure income, and was offered an assistant lecture-ship at University a College, London. We were able to move again, from two-room flat in Hampstead to three or four rooms on two floors near Holland Park. After three years there and the birth of a second child, I moved to a lectureship at Reading and we acquired our first house in the then still rural outskirts – the former servants' quarters of a large Victorian mansion that had been divided into three parts, still leaving more land for us than I had ever dreamed of owning. There I began to garden in earnest, grew fruit and vegetables, and became a specialist in apples, thanks to a fine old orchard that belonged to our plot.

There, too, our three children spent their formative years – much happier and freer ones, we did our best to insure, than those of their parents, though at the end my son contracted an illness that crippled him for a year and changed his character. After nine years at Westwood Lodge, our home, and at the university, my wife, the actress, musician, and poet Anne Beresford, became so unhappy there that I decided to give up my Readership, move back to London and put an end to the full-time teaching that should have been my career, but had begun to clash more and more with my writing projects and commitments. Bought as a 'country house' by a speculator, our home was demolished and the garden bulldozed, all the work I had put into that in nine years utterly erased. That was in 1964, when I was forty.

A Bollingen Foundation fellowship helped me to work on my book *The Truth of Poetry*, prepared over a period of ten years out of reading that went far beyond my specialization in the German literature I had taught. Between 1965 and 1977 I also spent a great deal of time in America, as a visiting professor at various universities and colleges, never for longer than one semester at a time, so that I could return to my writing in between, or on tours that took me from New Hampshire to southern California, from South Carolina to Montana. America became the setting or theme of quite a few of my poems, including parts of the long sequence *Travelling* written between 1968 and 1976.

The strain of family life in unfamiliar surroundings at Mount Holyoke College and my frequent absences on tour during my semester there, while Anne had to cope with our unsettled and disturbed children, led to the break-up of our marriage after our return to London in 1967. We were separated or divorced for seven years – years of acute loneliness for me, bungled new relationships, and one intense new passion 'begotten by Despair / Upon Impossibility'. At the worst times I was on the verge of collapse through undernourishment, not because I couldn't afford to buy food but because I couldn't be bothered to buy or cook it. In fact our bonds proved stronger than our differences, and Anne never moved far from our South London house, even when the children had gone to live with her. After wretched muddles and complications, involving others, we entered into a second marriage on my fiftieth birthday.

I now wish that I had kept a diary of my comings and goings, adventures, encounters, impressions, and discoveries in those critical and troubled years. Since I didn't, and have lost all sense of chronological sequence, I cannot recapitulate them other than as fiction without laborious researches and reconstructions from scattered documents and tatters of recollection. Only a few of them come back to me from poems of those years.

In 1976 – with the children grown up and Anne now prepared for a life away from London – we moved to Suffolk in East Anglia, one of the most 'backward', least industrialized parts of England, into a house that began more than four centuries ago as a cottage and is so far from being practical after its last enlargement and conversion in 1920 that 'only a madman would have bought it', as a former village rector was tactful enough to tell us. As I write this, my fingers are numb with February east winds coming in from the North Sea, blowing right through the flimsy walls of the newer parts of the house and the warped window-frames. Snow has dislodged a pane glass from the top of our unheated lean-to greenhouse, threatening the plants I grew from seed collected in Mexico, Colorado, California, and the State of Washington, on trips in 1981 and 1984. As I type this, water has poured through a ceiling on to a bookcase, drenching the books. Here Anne directs an amateur drama group and puts on plays for the villagers, amongst other occupations; I divide my time between my writing-table and cultivating our three-and-a-half acres, though half of them remains wild marshland reserved for the local flora and fauna. Pheasants, partridges, moorhens, and mallard ducks breed there. Herons, snipe, kestrels, a marsh harrier, and a barn owl are among the visitors. On the other half I have planted flowers, shrubs, many kinds of trees, including the New England hemlock, vegetables, soft fruit, and a second orchard of mainly obsolescent varieties of apples.

Two of our children with their families have chosen to settle near us. Until her recent death at the age of ninety, Anne's mother lived with us, writing her first book, published when she was eighty-eight, and devotedly nursed after that by her daughter Jane, who still shares the house with us. My mother, too, lived to see the first of her great-grandchildren, though she could visit us only once – and that against doctor's orders – before her death in London at the age of nearly ninety-three. For a time, four generations could be brought together under the four roofs, built over four centuries, of our conglomerate house, most of whose worst leaks, most of the time, we have been able to stop over the years.

So much for the bare bones of a life. These bare bones were fleshed by the thousand things around them, bound up with persons and places, scenes and situations, moments and continuities of which my factual account has stripped them. It is because the bare bones of biography are dead and meaningless that one takes up the mug's game of writing poems. Compared to narrative fictions, lyrical poems may be a sort of shorthand, but they can catch the live moments. Put together, they can also trace the continuities both of an individual life and of human life generally. So if my real and essential life is registered anywhere, it is in my poems. I write 'if', because of what Eliot wrote about the mug's game; and because, when I put together my collected poems for my sixtieth birthday, I had to reject most of those in my first and second collections. Those were poems that did not catch the live moments; and the reason is that I was literarily precocious long before I was anything like emotionally mature. Since I could not know that at the time, I published too soon, though a single marginal comment in the script of early poems of mine that Eliot himself was patient enough to read became a pointer to my worst failings at the time – bombast and generalization. 'What kind of birds?', Eliot wrote against one of the symbolic or apocalyptic creatures that filled my lines. In my introversion I had not yet learned to trust my senses, least of all my eyes.

As for 'messing up' one's life for the sake of the poems that may or may not have grown good enough, I did that too, inevitably, though not perhaps in the spectacular way that would make me posthumously attractive to the biography-reading public. Even my close escapes from death – and I had as many lives as a cat, the animal so dear and near to me that it would be hard for me to live without one – were private and unsensational, as when I swam back to my wife and small daughter on a Bay of Biscay beach in a gale, against a back-tow so strong that I progressed by inches, and thought I wasn't progressing at all; or the series of motor accidents that began when the army driver of a jeep I was in ran head-on into a rock escarpment in Austria at 50 mph or more. No, the messing-up was that of the monomania one needs to keep up the writing of poems for a lifetime – at the expense of everyone and everything else, one's 'human' self and its needs included; while for others that occupation is a harmless hobby at best, a 'career' only in retrospect, at best, when all the prices have been paid and the messed-up life is over. Not that I regret the price I paid, or the things I might have done instead. That was my choice from the start, and I have been able to stick to it much of the time for forty-five years. What hurts is the price that those I love have had to pay.

The first book I published was a book of translations – so inade-
quate, too, that I had to spend another thirty years and more on the
same poet, Hölderlin, trying to improve my translations and adding
to them. As I found out much later, even that inadequate juvenile
attempt was of some use to others, by providing a first key to a
difficult and incomparable poet. My early need to translate must have
sprung from my own translation from one country, one language, to
another. Ever since, translation has been so much part of my work
that for long stretches it displaced my own writing, and I have trans-
lated far more poems than I have written poems of my own. In the
minds of many readers, too, my translations have displaced my
poems. The bearing of this anomaly on the mug's game is that, with
rare exceptions, translations can have only a very limited life span, so
that for them not even the possibility of 'permanent value' can be
entertained. Part of their value, then, must lie in their being useful;
and being useful, of service, is also the only good reason I know for
having a career. Translating and the critical writing which, for me,
was akin to translating in being a form of mediation, made up for the
career the writing of poetry could not be.

Unlike Eliot's work as a publisher or the jobs most poets have to
do to subsidize their work, these occupations of mine were hardly
more remunerative than the mug's game itself. So they, too, had to be
subsidized – by teaching, lecture and reading tours, and the like.
Translating was also the next best thing to writing poems of my own,
since it involved a related grappling with the same medium, language,
a related search for the right word, right rhythm, right image in the
right place. Because a translation called for all my concentration, once
I was immersed in it, I made a principle of not accepting commissions
to translate long works, like novels, except in the few instances where
the commissions coincided with plans and preferences of my own – as
with Beethoven's letters or the Goethe verse plays that cost me a full
year's daily work as recently as 1982. The writing of even the shortest
poem takes much more time than most people think; not so much
because that poem may go through many drafts before its is finished –
most of my later poems do not – but because the poem cannot get
through at all in the first place if the writer's mind is preoccupied
with matters that compete with it, as it has to be when translating.
Idleness of a sort, though not physical idleness, is a prerequisite for
the writing of poems. Outdoor labour, on the other hand, was not

only congenial to me in its own right – because I am an introverted outdoor man – but the sustenance of many of my poems. Walking, sculling, swimming, or horse-riding took the place of physical labour when I had no plot to cultivate, but was exempt from the team games and other sports – football, cricket, tennis, boxing, and rowing – compulsory in my school years.

Strangely enough it is an indoor game I had played only once or twice in my adolescence, in blacked-out London during the war, at the house of a friend, that gave me the imagery for one of the early poems I could and did salvage from my first book of 1950, because there was something in it beyond its literariness, even a prediction that came true:

A Poet's Progress

Like snooker balls thrown on the table's faded green,
Rare ivory and weighted with his best ambitions,
At first his words are launched: not certain what they mean,
He loves to see them roll, rebound, assume positions
Which – since not he – some power beyond him has assigned.
But now the game begins: dead players, living critics
Are watching him – and suddenly one eye goes blind,
The hand that holds the cue shakes like a paralytic's,
Till every thudding, every clinking sound portends
New failure, new defeat. Amazed, he finds that still
It is not he who guides his missiles to their ends
But an unkind geometry that mocks his will.

If he persists, for years he'll practise patiently,
Lock all the doors, learn all the tricks, keep noises out,
Though he may pick a ghost or two for company
Or pierce the room's inhuman silence with a shout.
More often silence wins; then soon the green felt seems
An evil playground, lawless, lost to time, forsaken,
And he a fool caught in the water weeds of dreams
Whom only death or frantic effort can awaken.

At last, a master player, he can face applause,
Looks for a fit opponent, former friends, emerges;
But no one knows him now. He questions his own cause,

And has forgotten why he yielded to those urges,
Took up a wooden cue to strike a coloured ball.
Wise now, he goes on playing; both his house and heart
Unguarded solitudes, hospitable to all
Who can endure the cold intensity of art.

I wrote that poem in 1949, when I was twenty-four or twenty-five, an age by which some poets have done their best work. For me, with at least two cultures to bridge before I began to write, then cluttered with more book learning than I could digest – not to mention skills like telegraphy, radio, semaphore, morse, and cable-laying I had to acquire when I became an infantry signalman, on top of rifle, hand grenade, machine-gun, assault course, bayonet, and other training – the hardest thing was to work my way through to directness, plainness, and immediacy. Those came later, if they came at all. Yet this poem's house and heart that are unguarded solitudes remain valid for me now that I have indeed withdrawn from the London-based literary life so important to me in youth and middle age, shedding even the 'best ambitions' of that poem. These have been driven out by concern about all the other games being played outside, on a playground far more evil and lawless than that snooker-table. To do my own thing to the best of my ability is still a self-evident requirement; but I now know that my mug's game could turn out to have been a waste of time not because I wasn't good enough at it, but because there will be no one left to invite into my 'hospitable' solitude, even if it hasn't vanished without a trace like our house and garden at Tilehurst.

Those concerns are most explicit in poems that are not my best – those I have called 'owls' pellets, gobbets of matter so coarse that they couldn't be assimilated poetically, only regurgitated' – about the madness of our automatized and automated technologies, industrial, commercial, and military. Less directly they also inform my critical writings, because literature, however autonomous that may try to be, cannot be sealed off from the things going on around it. My special interest in German literature – though I have also translated from the French, Italian, and some other languages-springs not only from what remains of my German roots but from what can be learned from the violent extremes that have clashed or interlocked in German life and writing. My latest critical book, to be published in 1986, comes closer than earlier ones to being a sort of history, of the postwar period. Out of the same concerns I have translated work by the most diverse German-language writers of this century, West German, Austrian, Swiss, and East German. It is the last of these, and the poets above all, whose individual voices and needs have been brought up against the tightest corporative restrictions – and prevailed against them in many cases.

A British anthologist placed my poems in a section allotted to 'Influences from Abroad', meaning not that the poets in that section were influences from abroad but that they were open to such influences. In a note on my work he wrote: 'Curiously enough, his own poetry remains more "English" in flavour than that of some of his collaborators, such as Christopher Middleton' – meaning those born in Britain, but represented in the same section. My early poems were influenced more by French poets – Baudelaire and the Symbolists – than by German ones, except for Hölderlin, a contemporary and coeval of Wordsworth, and perhaps Rilke and Trakl. Later it was American poetry, above all, that shook me out of the rhymed stanzaic forms of my early verse. If my poems did remain 'English in flavour', it must have been because I adapted so thoroughly to British assumptions and ways – possibly with the excessive fervour for which converts are notorious. Someone who had experienced only the little I experienced of Nazism could respond to British civility with an appreciation more keen than that of people who had taken it for granted from birth.

Before the erosion of that civility, rapid and conspicuous in the past ten years, I had no reason not to take my assimilation for granted; least of all during my army years, when my German name and birth were never so much as alluded to by a single fellow soldier, any more than differences of race or class, though I spoke the English of the public schools and of Oxford in barrack-rooms shared with working-class men. My oddities and awkwardnesses at first were not only tolerated, but accommodated with a delicacy and helpfulness I shall never forget. In the first weeks of intensive infantry training I was marched into the Company Commander's office for what I thought must be a reprimand or punishment for inefficiency. It turned out that he had received a letter from the Poetry Society in London asking me to give a reading and talk to celebrate my newly published Hölderlin translations. Never having done such a thing before, and too conscious of the incompatibility of those two worlds, I asked to be excused, but he ordered me to 'represent the regiment' at that celebration of a German poet in the midst of a war against Germany. This was the British civility, British magnanimity, which often went with a seeming innocence or ingenuousness, I thought worth fighting for, and dying for, if it came to that. The reason why it did not come to that may well be that the same authorities kept me out of the fighting as a special case. I never found out why I was not drafted to Burma with other soldiers in my regiment and intake, most of whom did die there, and posted instead to a battalion on home duty in Lancashire.

The same British civility and magnanimity may have made the country uncompetitive in the postwar world, after the loss of empire and the wealth that empire had brought. Because, to me, the civility and magnanimity are incomparably more precious than success in the international power and money arenas – and even that success has not come with the monetarist brutalities that are destroying the old decencies of the nation – it is in the last years that I have been beset by the most acute doubts and difficulties as a writer, often to the point of feeling that it is time for me to give up. Yet, as I wrote somewhere, 'the poem knows better than the poet . . .' Somehow or other, the poems still get through my worst despondencies, demanding to be written. Even translations, a few, still demand to be done – as from Paul Celan, whose poems were wrested from a deeper trauma than any I have suffered – though in the end it pulled him down into the death by drowning from which I was saved in childhood. So does the prose I write to bear witness to those things or get closer to an understanding of the conflicts and tensions out of which all imaginative work is produced.

Thanks to the vanishing civilities and magnanimities, as well as my father's prescience more than half a century ago, only one member of my family fell victim to the combination of ideological atavism and technical efficiency that was National Socialism. Since my maternal grandparents emigrated when we did and died in England, and two great-uncles and their families survived in Germany, it was easier for me than for many others to recover from childhood traumas and build those bridges without which I could not have functioned as the poet, translator, and critic I became. For a few years, at school before the outbreak of war, all things German were almost lost to me, and I was reluctant to speak the language. In a satirical sketch we performed at Westminster I took the part of Hitler, published a political sonnet –

about the annexation of Czechoslovakia – in a school magazine and, at the age of fifteen, sent my first submission to a national magazine in the form of an allegorical story with an anti-Nazi moral. Yet I could not hate the Germans as a whole without falling into the very racism to which some, not all, of them had succumbed; and a return to Judaism, when I had had no grounding in it at any time and only racial descent was left of that heritage, would have come up against the same interdict, besides demanding an immense effort of deliberate reclamation for which I had no opportunity and no time, either at a school attached to Westminster Abbey or a college attached to the Cathedral of Oxford. Though theology and nature study – not biology – were the two poles of my earliest concerns, and all the others flickered in between, I chose to remain outside all the religious communities – a pagan or a heathen, outwardly and officially at least.

That choice, too, goes back to my school years, I think, beginning with the Creed that is part of the Church of England liturgy. Faith, it seemed to me, is something other than belief. My beliefs could be shaken by experience or knowledge, and they changed over the years. My faith did not change, because it lay beyond experience and beyond reason. That Creed worried me, for it seemed to have less to do with worship than with religion in its most literal sense – a binding together, and a binding together *again*, implying that there had been a separation; and that separation did indeed take place as soon as people were not at church. In that sense, religion was a closing of ranks. I could not reconcile that with the lone voices of prophets or the Passion of Christ.

In later years another stumbling block was the anthropocentric fixation of the same religious tradition, Jewish as much as Christian. Had Noah saved the animals for their own sake, or only because we need them, or some of them? Unlike Greek pantheism, some of the Far Eastern religions, and most 'primitive' ones, our theological tradition seemed to posit a world made only for human use. St. Francis of Assisi was the one glorious exception known to me – and I always wondered how he had escaped excommunication as a heretic. When Christianity was secularized, in the so-called Enlightenment of the eighteenth century, so was this emphasis on the utilization and exploitation of the non-human world. Not content with the botching of our own earth, the twentieth century has carried the same processes into outer space.

Not that I longed for any regression to a stud farm or gut tribalism, when the Third Reich had taught me that every merely biological or racial classification of human beings is barbarous and pernicious. City and countryside, civilization and culture, were prototypes, also going back to antiquity, to which my poems returned again and again, before I had found a third paradigm, wilderness, and all three of them had to meet and clash. I have tried not to falsify the hardships and cruelties of any of these orders, whatever my personal preferences. In interhuman affairs, both experience and faith convince me, gentleness is stronger than assertiveness, mercy and magnanimity are stronger than retribution. Yet when the long-suffering, exploited, and oppressed are exasperated into violence, I am on their side.

WHAT I have almost left out of my account are the loves and friendships that meant quite as much to me throughout my life as anything I could write about here. A few of them are recorded in my book of memoirs, and other tributes or recollections will follow in another book. In some cases friendships impinged on my translating and critical work, too, though I have tried to keep them out of essays and book reviews, and made a principle early on of not writing about the work of British fellow poets in their lifetime, just as I kept out of groups, movements, and cliques of every sort, for related reasons. If the same prohibition didn't apply to foreign writers, including a few American ones who were friends, it was because I was in less danger of getting entangled in their literary politics, and friendships did not conflict with the job of mediation that was part of my work. Though I have written few 'love poems', all poetry is love poetry, no matter what it is about; even the ugly or harsh verse I called 'observations, ironies, unpleasantries', about things opposed to my loves and loyalties, which are implicit in my rejection of those things. (Robert Graves called the two kinds 'poems of the right hand' and 'poems of the left hand', aware that the same force moves both hands.)

Nor can I attach enough importance to the occasional gratifications and persistent setbacks of my professional life to write about them. Parts of my work have been kept in print for thirty or even forty years, and that is as much as a writer can hope for, short of 'permanent value'. The rest has been an unremitting struggle against pressures and frustrations, with help at times in the shape of awards or prizes. Holidays became a habit we had to break when I dropped out of full-time teaching, but invitations to read, lecture, take part in poetry festivals or the regular sessions of the three German academies of which I am a member have provided me with as much travelling as I can cope with, now that I have come to hate tourism, hotels, and airports. The walks I owe to some of these events, and meetings with friends I could never have expected to see again otherwise – even at airports in some instances, or in hotels – were the rewards of those travels in many parts of Europe and America.

It is to America mainly that I owe my discovery of wilderness, as distinct from the cultivated countryside in most of Europe. Very early one morning I wandered from Antioch College into a small valley where every step I took was a revelation; and that was only one of more such 'epiphanies' than I can list or place. The wild animals, birds, and wildflowers of America are as much a part of me now as those I grew up with or those around my house. That goes back to my first stay in Massachusetts. It was there, much later, that my friend Peter Viereck told us that, as far as he was concerned, there are 'three kinds of birds – big birds, little birds, and seagulls.' Near Austin, Texas, where I stayed with my friend Christopher Middleton, we counted more than fifty kinds of birds at his feeder – mainly little ones, down to the hummingbirds – and I got so close to an armadillo that I could have grabbed it. On a South Carolina island racoons took food from my hand. The chickadees that did the same for Robert Francis outside his hermit's cabin at Amherst went into a poem I wrote for him and into the title of an interim collection of poems; but images from Brooklyn – my very first American scene – Manhattan and Boston had to counterpoint those near-idylls, as did the first supermarket I had seen in my life, before shopping in supermarkets had become as inescapable and unremarkable a thing in England as it was in America by the mid-sixties.

That kind of naïvety – a sense of wonder that can also turn into a sense of outrage – seems to be a characteristic of poets, and a condition for their persistence in the mug's game. This naïvety can go with a good deal of sophistication and worldly wisdom, though not, I think, with a cynical accommodation to things as they are. If the wonderment and the outrage dry up, so does – or should – the poet. To many, therefore, poets are freaks who would become formidable monsters if they were ever taken seriously; and they could be taken seriously because such a core of naïvety, even of childishness, lies hidden in most people, however mature they think themselves and are taken to be – very much as an old cat, grown staid and dignified, will revert to kittenish play from time to time. That would be one reason why the lonely mug's game of poetry, played for no calculable audience in a world obsessed with other matters, is not the obsolete pursuit which, sociologically, it was judged to be long ago.

As a poet, though, it is not my business to ask why or how I go on, how or why my work appeals or does not appeal to those who read such work – a tiny minority at the best of times – whether or not it will prove to have been worth the price paid for doing it. My business is to remain true to the wonderment and outrage as long as they recur, always unexpectedly, always in a way I can neither plan nor choose; and to keep quiet when there is nothing that wants to use me to make itself heard.

From Michael Hamburger in Conversation with Peter Dale (1998)

WHAT FOLLOWS is part interview, part 'printerview'. Michael Hamburger answered initial questions on the phone but asked for questions to be printed and sent if they required detail from, or reference to, his papers and large bibliography. Once these questions were typed and answered, a visit to his home was made for final questions, clarifications, and last minute reflections. The conversation was recorded on 11 May 1998, a magnificent summer's day, in the Hamburgers' meadowy garden in Suffolk after a thorough inspection of Michael's orchard of rare and endangered apple trees. – PETER DALE

You left Germany as a child around the time of Hitler's election. You fought for the Allies in the Second World War. After the war, you lectured and began translating Hölderlin, Goethe, Rilke, Celan and the emerging East German poets. You have taught in America and written many poems about it. You have lived your life through the tragedy of Europe in the twentieth century. As a writer, have you any further reflections or points you would like to share on these experiences?

Yes, most of my family left Germany immediately after Hitler's election – my father for Edinburgh, before the rest of the family, to start on a crash course that would qualify him in Britain to continue work as a paediatrician. My mother and her four children followed later in that year, 1933.

I served, but did not fight, in the war. For reasons I could not understand at the time, I was not allowed to go abroad until the war was over – and then only after much agitation and complicated formalities that entailed medical down-grading. Now I am sure it was because of my German birth, though we had been naturalized before the outbreak of war. I'd begun to translate poems, before my army service, at school and university – probably impelled to it by my traumatic translation from one country, one language, to another, but also by my specialization in modern languages at school and university. (I translated from the French also, managing to produce my second book of translations, prose poems by Baudelaire, while serving as an infantryman in the Shetlands.) My first book, *Poems of Hölderlin*, had been finished before my joining-up and appeared in 1943, when I was nineteen and in the most intensive stage of my infantry training. That book, translations of a German poet barely known then, was reviewed in *Punch*! And it won me my first invitation to read in public, at the Poetry Society. I refused that reading, but was ordered by my Company Commander to accept and represent the regiment there, the Royal West Kents. I reiterate these circumstances, because they are minders of a past era in British life. I think I mentioned in my memoirs that I did far more fighting at my prep and public schools, both in and outside the boxing ring, than I did in my four years of army service.

My later activities as a translator and critic – mainly, but not exclusively, of German texts – are too multifarious to be summarized here, though I may return to one or the other. My teaching in America followed a brief academic career in Britain, from 1955 to 1964, taken up when it was clear that I could not support a family on my literary earnings, helped out by a succession of casual non-literary jobs. America enabled me to split the year between a visiting, one-semester professorship and sustained work on my writing in London. Some of the poems I wrote in the USA are responses to my discoveries of wilderness and wild life, on the walks that were my main compensation for enforced absence from home, others to the civilization that has become ours also, since American monetarist and free market ideology were imported by Margaret Thatcher. In both respects my American experiences became formative for all I have written since the mid-sixties, when the visits began. They fizzled out, with reading tours only, in the early eighties.

In an early poem you wrote, admittedly in persona:

As for my heart, it broke some time ago
When, in the towns of Europe, I still tried
To live like other men and not to know
That all we lived for had already died.

(*Collected Poems*, p. 13)

And later you wrote on the Eichmann case:

And yet and yet I would not have him die

. . .

But show him pity now for pity's sake
And for their sake who died for lack of pity

(Collected Poems, p. 112)

That indicates an immense leap of experience and imagination. Have you any reflections or points to make about this? For example, have Jewish people been upset with your position on this? (Many people have been upset even by the hostile picture of Nazis given by Snodgrass in his "The Führer Bunker".)

'The tragedy of Europe' is what I tried to render in that sequence 'From the Note-Book of a European Tramp', from which you quote; but I should have excluded it from my *Collected Poems* if I hadn't felt it necessary to salvage something from that early phase. The fact is that I joined the army with my head – and kit-bag – full of literature, and with delusions of civic decency and fair play partly inculcated by my education in London and Oxford. That is why I needed a persona for that sequence. My own person or persons, military or civilian, and my own poetic equipment at the time couldn't register the shock given to me by the misery and demoralization I saw in Naples, while working as an interpreter with German prisoners of war in Austrian Displaced Persons camps, among the civilian population in Austria and on a brief unofficial and unauthorized trip from Carinthia to Berlin, to see my surviving relatives there. But my tramp figure couldn't do it either, because of the same residual romanticism and bookishness. To find my own voice as a poet, as I hardly did before my late twenties, I had to rid myself of that second-hand clutter. My tramp persona may have been the outsider I have remained through-out my later life, but his diction was still too bland and conventional – even after years of my having roughed it as a private soldier. The only tramp I'd ever known well enough to visit him in a dosshouse, in my Soho days or nights, was in fact gentle and genteel, a former lawyer who had chosen or been pushed into that alternative way of life. At a later period my friend Philip O'Connor became a part-time, amateur tramp and wrote his excellent study *Vagrancy* out of his experiences. On his tramps he would drop in at our Berkshire home in the early hours of the morning.

As long as I was in the army I could be an amateur poet at best. I wrote most of that sequence while serving abroad, but not in conditions conducive to the writing of anything; often with no table to write on, not even a bedstead to sit on, but a palliasse on the floor, in a barrack-room full of my fellow soldiers – to whose unfailing friendliness and consideration I owe such verse as I was able to write at that period, in Britain and abroad. But privacy was the last thing available to a private soldier. Soon after my sudden commissioning 'in the field', in Austria, I found myself in charge of a co-educational boarding school for British children – the first of its kind ever to be set up by the Army. Then I had an office and even a bedroom, but never a moment's respite from my daily duties and responsibilities, which never ended until late at night. I think I finished some of the tramp poems on a brief home leave granted to me only because I was in a state of nervous exhaustion that made me temporarily unfit for that engrossing but more than full-time job; and may still have been working on the sequence after my release, back at Oxford.

The Eichmann poem from which you quote, 'In a Cold Season', was written in 1961 – a freak among my poems, both because I never again resorted to the dead-beat, unbroken and unpunctuated iambics of three of its sections – contrasted with the free-verse sections, one an ironically bureaucratic summary of Eichmann's career, the other of my grandmother's life and her death in the Third Reich – and because it was the closest thing to a public poem I ever wrote. It appeared immediately in the magazine *Encounter* and was promptly translated into Hebrew for an Israeli newspaper. I think that only the conclusion, from which you quote, was controversial, though, for me, it followed naturally and inevitably from the data. Since I have no Hebrew, either ancient or modern, I never knew what was said or written about the poem in Israel; but someone told me: that only Martin Buber had come out in its defence. No public controversy reached me from Britain or America either. What I do remember is an objection to the poem by A. Alvarez, who thought that my plea for mercy to Eichmann was an instance of soft liberalism. In retrospect I still believe that mercy is harder than retribution. Mercy breaks the dismal chain of cause and effect, by asserting our freedom, even where that freedom entails a risk. The alternative, the tit-for-tat of retributive justice, perpetuates the evils it is intended to curb; and it leaves no room for the *metanoia* that might have come of the

Eichmann trial. I don't like paraphrasing a poem – the surest way to neutralize it, as Eichmann was neutralized in Jerusalem when his case was settled, filed and put away, so that new horrors could follow; but since you've asked the question, and I've never commented on that poem, I may as well do so now. It was one thing to bring Eichmann to trial, so as to establish and commemorate the nature of his part in the atrocities, quite another to suppose for a moment that his conviction and punishment could bear any relation to what he had done to others. Even on the principle of 'an eye for an eye, a tooth for a tooth' – a principle quite unacceptable to me – there were simply far too; many eyes, too many teeth, in that equation. What concerned me in the poem was the character not of Eichmann or his function – he had very: little character outside his function – but of twentieth-century mechanized murderous bureaucracy anywhere, of any kind. The alternative to that monstrosity was to let Eichmann go; and only the paradox of his gratuitous acquittal could have jolted Eichmann himself to the faintest awareness of his guilt.

Perhaps I need to explain that I was not brought up as a Jew, though of unmixed Jewish descent. Of my grandparents only the grandmother of the poem was a practising Jew, and she was born in Poland, not Germany, where emancipation after Napoleon was granted on the condition that Jews were to cease to regard themselves as different from the majority of non-Jews. My father remained an agnostic humanist, but read Kierkegaard in the last year of his life. My mother became a Quaker. It must have been on the grounds of her Polish birth that my father's mother was deported from Berlin before the mass extermination of Jews was implemented; and she was the only member of my family who died in that way, though two of my great-uncles did not emigrate, and the non-Jewish ('Aryan') wife of one of them was murdered in Berlin after the war, for non-political reasons, by a mugger.

Because there is a persistent confusion among Jews and non-Jews about what constitutes Jewishness, whether race or religion and culture, I have had poems in anthologies both of Christian and of Jewish verse. If I'd succeeded in getting myself killed in the war, I should have been buried as a member of the C. of E., as my identity disc described me, for the simple reason that I'd never worshipped anywhere but in the Church of England, though I'd been no more baptized than circumcised, and it was beyond me to identify myself as anything else, when I was far from being an Atheist, and carried Jeremy Taylor's *Holy Dying* around in my army kit. In fact I was never to become a professed and outward member of any religion, sect or community. This left me free to test my most deep-rooted convictions against experience and doubt.

For the benefit of any potential undertaker or exhumer of my poetic corpus, I must confess again that two long poems in which the pieties of my youth became monstrously explicit, did find their way into print. One was the pamphlet *Later Hogarth* of 1945, in fact called 'London Nights' by me but cosmetically laid out by one of the weirdest and disastrously adventurous of my Oxford friends, Edward Haliburton (later Lord Haliburton, self-styled) with a fictionalized 'biography' and a change even in the spelling of my name. I managed to get the pamphlet pulped, while serving abroad, but a few copies must have escaped. I have kept only one into which I scrawled my furious corrections. The other long poem was, 'Profane Dying'(!) published by Tambimuttu in his book-size *Poetry London* X, of 1944, so solidly bound, in real cloth still, that many copies of it will have outlasted the war. Other rejected shorter juvenilia, less theological than these, appeared in the anthologies *Oxford Poetry* for 1942–3 and 1948.

Paradox has been at the root of my life, as a poet and otherwise. That may be why it's as difficult for me to make sense of what I've been or done as it's proved for other people.

I suppose when we come directly to literary history it is the position of Pound which tangles all these issues together. Have you any further reflections on this?

Paradoxically, again, it was the Christianity and self-discipline of another anti-Semite, T. S. Eliot, that I contrasted with Ezra Pound's muddle, when I reviewed his *Pisan Cantos* on their appearance in Britain. Like many poets of my generation, I fell under the influence of Eliot's prose writings – his poems could be parodied but not imitated – in my adolescence. I never reprinted that review, and it's best forgotten. I did reprint an early essay on Eliot, but found it necessary to add a later one, written when I'd outgrown the influence of his opinions and critical manner. All I can say now is that I've made my peace with parts of both Pound's and Eliot's works, in the teeth of their opinions and stances, because good poetry is always more and other than the opinions that went into it or can be read out of it.

. . . .

Michael Schmidt says, in his discussion of The Truth of Poetry *in* Agenda *35.3, that your 'securest reputation is as a critic [and that your] poetry has never had its due.' He goes on to say that 'the time is ripe for a reversal' of this assessment, predicting that the translations will be supplanted – 'there are now other Hölderlins, other Goethes, other Hofmannsthals, other Brechts … [Hamburger's] originality was in giving us a stable point of departure – that the criticism will last a lot longer, and that 'the poems will in time be recognized as [your] securest achievement.' What is your response to this prediction?*

It seems ironic to me that my 'secured reputation' should be 'as a critic', when it's criticism that I've given up in the present climate, and all but one of my critical books are out of print in English, if not in Italian, Spanish, and German. Whether or not my 'poetry has never had its due' isn't for me to say or comment on, other than with thanks to Michael Schmidt for sticking out his neck. All I can say is that for me the writing of my poems has become my main occupation and preoccupation, beside the manual work m my garden and orchard inextricably bound up with much of now. The parrot cry raised to brush aside my poems again and again, *ad nauseam*, is 'better known as a translator' – as though it made the slightest difference what a writer is best known for. It could just as easily have been the apples I was asked to exhibit at Covent Garden for Apple Day, but couldn't that year, because I had to go to Belgrade at the time, and it happened to be a bad year for the many kinds of apples I've grown. Reputations are part of the brand advertising that goes with our totalitarianism of commerce and finance. A tabloid newspaper that doesn't give a damn for anyone's poems or translations telephoned me about my apples, asking for a visit to photograph them on and off the trees, but promptly dropped me as an unsuitable subject for its publicity. That would have made me 'better known' in a flash than all the many book I've published in fifty-five years.

I agree that very few translations can establish themselves as 'classics or need or deserve to. For me translation is a humble activity, a service to works I care about, not a surrogate for productions of my own. I am astonished that some of my earliest translations have lasted as long as they have – more than half a century in some cases, like my Hölderlin and Baudelaire, nearly half a century in the case of the Beethoven *Letters, Journals & Conversations* I put together and tried in vain to correct in proof on our honeymoon in 1951 for its first printing. Others, later on, were scarcely noticed, in the present climate, like the Goethe verse plays I translated for the 1982 anniversary. One of these, his *Pandora*, a play never previously translated and hardly ever staged even in German, is the most metrically complex text I have ever attempted; and, as usual, I grappled with that complexity, instead of naturalizing the verse in sloppy up-to-date prosody, introducing new metres into English in the process, as Goethe had into German. Not a word reached me about that work, not one response to the sheer virtuosity and artistry I did my best to imitate and convey. Most translations that do outlive their translators do so out of interest in the distinction of those translators as writers, rather than that of their texts, which will be retranslated again and again. For reasons already intimated, I cannot predict whether any translation of mine is likely to survive me, even if literature as such is not made redundant by technology and the 'soundbites' that are destroying concentration.

From *String of Beginnings* (1991)

ON AUGUST 1st 1914, before leaving Berlin for the Eastern front, my father wrote a letter to his parents, brothers and sister, intended as a testament in case of his death in action. After apologizing for early laziness at school and occasional 'impetuosity, unfairness and lack of understanding, all-too-human outbursts of emotion' in later years, he continued: 'To take leave of life is not hard for me, only the separation from you, and the thought of no longer being able to help and please you. My disposition, deep down, was too inward, too much fixed on certain relations to the natural and beautiful, to derive pleasure from what is usually called life. My character is too primitive and pure not to have suffered by the compromises it imposes. I made such great demands on myself that I could never be satisfied; and so I was rarely happy. I always felt a peculiar urge towards the natural, the pure and the noble, and my aim was to work for the improvement and true cultivation of the human race. This gave rise to inner conflicts that did not allow me to be quite happy. If I can write about this without self-consciousness and with frankness, it is because this conception of life existed in me quite independently of my physical being, involuntarily, and ruled me completely, so that I could observe this mainspring of my life quite impartially, as though in an experiment.' He asked them to apply themselves to an enlightenment that would make 'later generations exempt from the barbarism of war', and went on to express hopes or wishes for the future of his brothers and sister individually. He begged his brother Freddy 'to steel his will and learn to work in a more purposeful and fruitful way'. His sister Katy, when she was older and wiser, would 'remember our family tradition' and act accordingly. As for his twin brothers Ernest and Paul, he thought that they were on the right path and would go on to even better things.

At the age of not quite thirty, and in his father's lifetime, my father felt morally responsible for the conduct and welfare of his family; but his wishes were not to be fulfilled. Ten years later, his brother Alfred was still an inveterate bohemian never capable for long of earning his living and partly dependent on my father's charity, as he remained until my father could no longer subsidize him, so that he gave up being a violinist, painter and generally 'artistic' drifter and settled for a mere craft at which he was more than competent, book-binding. His sister Kate had been married and divorced, as she was to be a second, time, without ever becoming a mother of that happier and better generation to which the testament looks forward. Worst of all, his father was bankrupt and heart-broken because the promising twins had run off to America with funds held in trust for their father's clients. A major scandal and legal prosecution were avoided only with the help of my other grandfather, but my father's father never recovered from the blow to his honour and affections, fell into a brooding melancholia and died soon after.

He had been born in Upper Silesia, where his father was a school-teacher in the small town Myslowitz. In early life he had been a journalist, a correspondent in Paris, then in Poland, for German literary reviews. Though Myslowitz was part of Prussia, the Polish connection was close, and it was in Poland that my grandfather Leopold met and married his wife, Antonina, and that my father was born. Since all my grandfather's effects were lost when she was transported to an extermination camp from her flat in Berlin, most probably dying in her native country, the only record I have of my grandfather's literary career are notes to him from Émile Zola and Alphonse Daudet and a long letter from the German novelist Friedrich Spielhagen, kept by my father. From these it appears that my grandfather was trying to introduce French Naturalism to German readers about a decade before it established itself in Germany as a literary movement. In notes dated 1878 and 1880, Daudet apologized for being unable to write the requested study of Zola but offered three 'portraits contemporains' instead, one of them on Rochefort, and asked my grandfather to translate them 'without changing anything'. Zola's undated note asked him to call at the office of the periodical *Voltaire* to collect a copy of an article on Victor Hugo. It is to the editors of Zola's letters that I owe a little more information about my grandfather's brief literary career: they discovered that between 1878 and 1886 he published articles on French writers and their works, sometimes under the pseudonym or anagram L. Burghammer. I assume that it was in 1886, shortly after my father's birth, that my grandfather settled in Berlin and was forced to go into business as a merchant banker, with little inclination or success even before the disaster.

My father, too, was drawn to the arts and would have liked best to be a musician, but he studied medicine at Rostock and Berlin. Together with his Polish cousin Casimir Funk – the inventor of the word vitamin' and an eminent scientist at one time – he did research on the dietary causes of rickets. I know this because, as a child, I came across the manuscript of their paper on the subject, which included photographs of dogs whose rickety legs made them look like dachs-hunds, though they were not, but had been reduced to that state by dietary experiments. The shock of seeing those photographs made them unforgettable. After his war service in the German medical corps, my father worked in Berlin as a paediatrician, both in private practice and at the Charité, where he was a consultant and teacher. It was there, in 1919, that he met my mother, who was a ward sister. She had taken up nursing during the war as a volunteer and found the work more satisfying than the pastimes of her pre-war years: the tennis club for which she played in tournaments, winning several trophies, her accomplished piano playing and the social round of parties and excursions. Unlike my father's family, hers was well-off, if not rich. Her father, Bertrand Hamburg, also a merchant banker, had moved from Mainz to Frankfurt, where my mother was born, then settled in Berlin. This grandfather's forenames, Louis Bertrand, must go back to the francophilia among German Jews since the Napoleonic era, because it was to the *Code Napoléon* that they owed their emancipation from the ghetto. For related reasons, perhaps to do with the Dreyfus affair, this grandfather, too, was a reader of Zola's novels, several of which, in their crumbling paper bindings or rebound, were among the few possessions he kept by him when he emigrated to England in his old age. My mother's mother, Regina (née Münzesheimer) was born in the village of Rohrbach near Sinsheim in Baden-Württemberg. My mother first saw my father standing by a window at the hospital with a newborn baby laid across one outstretched hand – a procedure peculiar to him that must have impressed her, since she recalled it half a century later. When she married my father, after a brief engagement, she gave up hospital work.

My father's cello had to be put aside for decades, until his last years in London, when we had chamber music sessions in our house; but he could also extemporize on the piano or harmonium – as I did after him and my son did after me – at any odd moment snatched from his professional life. I remember seeing him do so with tears in his eyes when he had heard of the death of a close friend, and slipping out as quickly and quietly as I could after that intrusion. The disposition of which he wrote in the testament made it difficult for him to relax. Even when he was on holiday from Berlin, in Scandinavia, Switzerland or Austria, he would treat any case that came his way, and I recall various peasant artefacts given to him by the grateful parents of such patients. On one occasion someone from a circus came to see him in Berlin with a sick chimpanzee, and this chimpanzee, too, was accepted as a patient, though the animal died. On another occasion he was summoned to a Junker estate in Pomerania and asked to treat not only the son and heir of the family but the pigs – whether only the piglets and sucklings, because he was a paediatrician, I am not sure. A difficult case would worry and upset him to a degree hardly conceivable now that medicine tends to be practised rather like a motor mechanic's skill. Most of the families of my father's patients became personal friends, and so did many of the young doctors who were his students at the: hospital, including several from Japan, who would turn up at our flat with gifts that could be woodcuts or exotic sweetmeats which we children found more interesting than palatable. There was no end to my father's professional involvements. Though he had been a good oarsman, horseman and swimmer – twice winning medals for saving people from drowning – he had no time to keep up any sport. Even when he had become a professor and his practice was flourishing – before our emigration – money pressures were often acute, with four children and a widowed mother to support, not to mention his brother Alfred, or other beneficiaries of whom we had no knowledge. Up to his early death my father remained hard on himself, while growing less hard on those who did not or could not live up to his expectations of them. Yet the effects his purism had had on some of those closest to him could not be undone – and he knew it before the end.

A LIFE doesn't begin with birth, and I have sketched in a few antecedents, mainly on my father's side, because I inherited not only my father's pocket watch, which kept me more than punctual for some thirty years after his death, but his intransigent super-ego. About this part of my inheritance I can be sure, knowing it by the damage it has done. What is more, when I came to look at some of my father's letters and manuscripts, and used a magnifying glass because his script was so minute, I suddenly noticed that, magnified, his handwriting was almost indistinguishable from mine. Having dabbled in graphology at times, I could no longer doubt that essentially I was very much a chip off the old block, for all the differences between our outward lives and occupations. If nature and beauty – in my father's Schillerian and idealistic German they are one and the same, 'das Natürlich-Schöne' – have more to do with Groddeck's 'It' than with the humanitarian ideals to which my father wanted to couple them, that contradiction, too, is significant. In art and science perhaps, his kind of super-ego can be harnessed to the unknowable ends of the It. In social life it cannot, since the society in which my grandfather, father or I functioned or failed to function demands those compromises which the super-ego refuses, preferring death to compromise. A super-ego that is socially conditioned makes for conformism, renouncing its 'purity' and 'primitiveness', its commitment to the It. This was my father's dilemma, and it came to be mine. Most probably it was my paternal grandfather's too, judging by what seems to have been his total renunciation of literature in later life; but I have been unable to discover more about him than the few bare facts I have recorded.

All the same, I was born; and what is more, with alacrity – so I am told – in the small hours, at the crack of spring, and impatient for it. Impatience, Kafka said, is the primal sin. I was guilty of it, in early years at least. It was the month of the year when Kafka left Berlin to die. It was the day, March 22nd, of Goethe's death and his cry for more light. The year, 1924, was one of relative stabilization after the failure of a Hitler-Ludendorff 'putsch' and the success of Schacht's measures against an inflation so extreme that it had turned most Germans into undernourished millionaires.

The place was Berlin, Charlottenburg, Lietzenburgerstrasse 8A, not far from the Kurfürstendamm, to which the street runs parallel. The block of flats, astonishingly enough, is still there, after the bombing, like all the buildings connected with my family in early childhood years. Kafka's few publications were not among the books in the heavy glass-fronted mahogany cases, which also outlasted all the upheavals, removals and disasters. Goethe's copious works were there, leather-bound and uniform, with duplications and supplements in other shapes and sizes, cheap Reclam paperbacks dating from my father's youth – though his favourite German poet was

Schiller – *de luxe* editions from my mother's library, volumes of letters, biographies, even scholarly yearbooks of the Goethe Society, to which my mother had subscribed for a time. Not that I suffer from total recall where books are concerned, or started to read the moment I was born; but most of those books, including the eighteenth-century edition of Klopstock's works 'borrowed' by my mother in girl-hood from a grandmother she disliked, were reassembled in London, in the same glass-covered cases. Not the old Bechstein grand, though, which was left behind like the gilt rococo chairs in the best room and the austere Biedermeier portraits of great-grand-parents on my mother's side.

Of the three or four reception rooms in our gloomy, but fairly spacious flat, the one I liked best was the one used as a waiting room for my father's patients, because it contained a tank of tropical fish – one of the earliest points of convergence between my father's inter-ests and mine. More than a decade later he and I would meet in South Molton Street, when I had finished school and he had finished work at his Upper Wimpole Street consulting room, to choose tropical fish at a shop there and take them home. I can still see and smell the two little tubular tins of fish-food that provided a varied diet for those first ones. Somewhere, I think in the dining room, there was a canary, too, in a cage covered at night with an embroidered cloth.

A dark passage led to our bedroom and nursery, perhaps also to the kitchen and servants' room shared by the cook and the house-maid, just as the four of us had to share a room. From time to time we would creep along that passage at night when our parents were entertaining, to catch a whiff or snatch of the incredible freedoms of the adult world, at the risk of being intercepted. Once or twice the cook would connive by giving us a taste of the splendid fare she had prepared for such feasts – grave offence though that was against the discipline imposed on us by our East Prussian governess. Our diet was more strictly regulated than that of the fish, with daily doses of molasses and cod liver oil. Coffee and tea were forbidden. Instead we drank an innocuous substitute called 'malt coffee'. Theatre and cinema were forbidden. Instead we were taken to the planetarium, which was educational and so utterly tedious to me at the time that it left me with a life-long indifference to stars and astronomy.

When decades – ages – later I revisited that block of flats amid the ruins of Berlin, with its marble and stucco that had grown more pathetic than pretentious in the meantime, I thought I recognized the very spot where my perambulator had been parked in the entrance hall. It transmitted wave after wave of tedium, greyness, frustration – the wages of the sin of impatience, of boyish impulses systematically suppressed and repressed. Of Berlin itself memory has made a perpetual winter. It can't be only that part of the first summers were spent in Mecklenburg and Pomerania, most of them at a seaside resort on the Baltic, Heringsdorf, the later ones by the river Havel, at my maternal grandparents' villa. At one time my family rented a tiny city garden that must have registered spring, summer and autumn, since there was a tree to be climbed. At times we were even taken there by our parents or by my father's mother, whom I adored, because she was childlike and did not care about rules and prohibitions. When she took us out she bought us ice-cream, against the rules, I am sure, and gave us sweets from a small silver box she carried in her handbag, secretly, because she was diabetic and had been forbidden to eat them. For once it was we children who had to promise not to give a grown-up away. In her tiny flat in the Kanststrasse she kept an urn containing the ashes of my grandfather Leopold, and a stuffed French bull-dog, a pet of hers that had been run over, but she seemed to live happily enough with those relics, because she was truly primitive. My father told me that she had reared her five children on the general principle that if they were too ill to get out of bed, they were too ill to eat, and that this had led to miraculous recoveries. We were less fond of her tiny lapdogs, which were spoilt, possessive, and inclined to snap at us if we competed with them. She also kept a bowl of goldfish, one of which was hump-backed, and took them out each day to wash them under the kitchen tap. Like her children, they flourished because or in spite of such treatment. Among the entertainments she offered us in her flat was a crystal set with earphones – a magical toy to us, when our parents kept no wireless of any sort.

Exercise was part of our regimen. There were afternoon walks to one of the three little squares or parks in Charlottenburg or Wilmersdorf where we played, always under the supervision of our governess, though contact with other children could not be wholly avoided. Marbles and hide-and-seek and hoops are some of the games I remember. In winter we learned to skate on the lakes or on the tennis courts converted to ice-rinks in hard frosts – one way of avoiding constant supervision, if only in the shed where skates were screwed on and off and one warmed one's hands against a barrack-room stove. Fresh air was obligatory, too, for our after-lunch siestas on the balcony, where we could be watched through a window and ordered to sleep if we moved, talked or so much as opened our eyes. The sound of traffic and motor horns, like other noises drifting up from the street was inexhaustibly mysterious to me. I longed to know what it was all about, what the city was for, where everyone was going in such a hurry, and why. No one told us anything about it. We were marched to this place and that, for our health; and we did indoor exercises, too, involving a ladder that was supposed to prevent flat feet.

For educational, hygienic and administrative purposes we were treated as a unit – my two older sisters, myself and my younger brother. Our clothes were made for us by the governess, poor woman, and those I remember – more from photographs than from life – were uniform, except that the girls' frocks were shortened to boys' tunics and their knickers lengthened to boys' mini-shorts. Those were the ceremonial outfit, wholly unfunctional, to be kept as spotless as a soldier's ceremonial dress. If we had rougher clothes, not of embroidered silk, for everyday use before we went to school, these were unfit to be recorded: on the early group photographs. As for modifications when we went to school, I recall only the acute shame of having to wear long stockings in winter – winter again! – clipped to a sort of undergarment called combinations. Long trousers were ruled out as the prerogative of men.

We were pampered and deprived. Pampered for the sake of hygiene and decorum, deprived of individual attention, simply because my parents were too busy and had not yet begun to question the conventions that relegated middle-class children to a separate world. Our governess, Maria Baensch, was an upright, efficient, hard-working person who did what she thought it was her duty to do. She was a devout Roman Catholic, and ended her life in an old people's home run by nuns. She never lost her temper with us, never broke down under the strain of her self-denial. If she felt anything about us – and I believe she did, because she kept in touch with my mother for decades after she had left us – felt anything for us or against us as individuals, we never knew it. I remember seeing my mother wince when she uttered some sudden command or reprimand at table; but that was her function, and she performed it with the dedicated austerity of a nun. When, around 1931, she left us for friends of my parents with only one daughter, her successor gave us cause to appreciate her reliability and impartial fairness.

Claustrophobia is what has stuck, making it difficult for me to enjoy any large city, live in a flat, or endure the kind of temperature our central heating provided. (There was a hot water pipe behind the wallpaper of the corner in which I had to stand as a punishment.) Of breaks, treats, remissions I remember little, other than Christmas and birthdays, when the routine was suspended, and at least one illness serious enough to turn me into a person in my own right, fussed over by my mother and father. Eva, the younger of my two sisters and I did have a special place for rougher games which we called the 'romping carpet'. There were children's parties in similar flats with bookcases, antique furniture and grand pianos, the flats of our parents' friends, but our attendance there was also rigorously supervised and timed. Another kind of excursion involved only my mother and myself – perhaps because it belongs to a period when my sisters had started school and my brother was too young. This was shopping, at an outdoor market, one of the large department stores, or in smaller shops to one of which – a hardware shop and laundry – I responded with a loathing close to nausea. To this day I recall its barrels of soft soap and some kind of incomprehensible wooden machine in perpetual motion whose creaking evoked a peculiar horror. All the dreariness of domesticity seemed to be concentrated in that place. Since my grandfather Bertrand would send his Buick limousine for some of these outings, they were also a rare opportunity for relaxed and intimate conversation with my mother. It was in the car that I asked her why my aunt Kate, who was married and beautiful, had no children, and received the puzzling reply that people have children only if they love each other. (I knew far too little about Aunt Kate at the time to do so much as guess what might lie behind that answer. She was one of the family's black sheep – a loose woman, always surrounded by admirers in and out of her marriages; and remained so even in her old age.) Other positive pleasures came from those department stores, like a free drinking fountain of lemonade, and the danger of getting lost in the crowd, as I did at least once.

In Berlin, in the late twenties, in a family like mine, any separation of a child from his escorts was feared as an acute danger, one of many that turned our flat into a fortress, hence into a prison. The front door was not only bolted, chained and locked in a variety of ways, but metal-plated on the inside. The criminal underworld whose threat was felt to demand such measures began in the building itself, in the back-building flats on the other side of the bare, forbidding and forbidden courtyard. (In fact it began even nearer home, with skeletons in the family cupboard like our absconded uncles or Aunt Kate's love life, but we had no knowledge of those until much later.) If we heard screams or shrieks through the hygienically open windows at night, they were attributed to the tenants of those unhygienic parts of the building, drunken lesbians, sadistic pimps and the like. These invisible bogies got mixed up in our imaginations with real people we met on our walks, innocuous eccentrics who wanted to talk to us, like the lady we called 'the man-woman', because she was large and gruff and wore a man's hat, or another we called 'die Frau mit dem Wauwau', 'the woman with the woof-woof.' There was no end to the scares about kidnappers, confidence tricksters, thieves, perverts and murderers. A few knick-knacks were stolen from the waiting-room by someone who got in as a patient or parent of patients, and the rings of anxiety spread as far as our nursery. Not that there wasn't plenty of crime in Berlin in those days. When, a few years before we left, my father learned to drive and bought a small Mercedes, the car was stolen or stripped so many times within months that it had to be fitted with an elaborate alarm. I remember hearing it go off.

That, at least, was an event and a thrill for us, unlike the anxiety that made us feel embattled, threatened and walled in, because everything beyond the front door was felt to be dangerous and hostile. Even if it was, it would have been better for us to know more about it, before the really traumatic experiences hit us. Very early on I had seen a runaway cab horse clatter down the street and a man stop it by stepping in front of it with outstretched arms. From the window I had seen a man with a dancing bear on a chain, and heard the music of barrel organs, a sound that affected me strangely when I heard it again some forty years later in the same and utterly different city, on a lecture tour. Because I never went out alone in Berlin – at least before the age of eight or nine, and then only to go to school and back – I have no recollection of the city as such or of any district of it as a whole; and developed no sense of direction or topography, because we were always taken wherever we went. When I came to revisit the city after the war, my explorations had to be guided by something altogether different, altogether less conscious than topography, a sort of somnambulism that led me to one or two rediscoveries of places and; landmarks of which I had no conscious memory at all. What I never found again was the second and last school I attended there, wholly erased even from my unconscious memory, probably because it was there that the traumatic blows were struck.

In the country I hardly ever lose my way; and I think the reason is that outside Berlin we were allowed to walk about on our own, so that my sense of direction and habit of observation did develop there, though they still don't function very well in cities. In the late sixties I was staying with friends in New Jersey. I went on a long exploratory ramble through fields and woods without paths, in a part of the country completely unknown to me and completely wild, because the small farmers who had cultivated it had been forced to abandon their land by the industrialization and commercialization of agriculture. When I was almost back at the house I noticed that I'd lost my wallet, containing all my money, air tickets and other indispensable documents. I worked out that it was most likely to have dropped from my jacket, which I was carrying, when I jumped over a stream; but miles away, somewhere in the undergrowth lining the length of that woodland stream. Though, as usual, I had paid more attention to details of flora and fauna than to the lie of the land, I not only found the stream again but the exact place of my crossing – and the wallet. In a city I should have panicked and taken a wrong turning, thanks to my childhood in Berlin.

What I recognized on later walks through the city was the landmarks of my dreams and nightmares – the blank, windowless walls of tenant blocks known in Berlin as 'fire-walls'. The heaviness of those late nineteenth-century façades with their muscular caryatids and lions' heads – as though a Prussian's house must be his ministry; a heaviness carried over into the interior, too, in my childhood, into the mahogany furniture, like the massive desk I inherited from my father and still use to store documents, though no longer to work at, and reception rooms kept more like museums than as living-rooms. Some of the apartments, like my maternal grandfather's (the address of which, in Bleibtreustrasse, found its way into Joyce's *Ulysses*, because Joyce must have picked up the address from a bizarre newspaper advertisement put out by my grandfather) seemed endless to a child, as awe-inspiring as the suites and passages that we saw in the palace of

Sanssouci at Potsdam. Most probably we were never allowed to see the whole of that extensive flat. That made the palace more comprehensible, for one could get an idea of its structure from the outside, from the park, and that made it finite at least, less sealed off from the light of day and the weather.

By drifting with a current deeper than conscious memory I could find some traces of my childhood even among the ruins of Berlin when I first returned there in 1947, but might not have recognized the building I was born in or the one in which my grandparents lived without the guidance of my surviving relations, two great-uncles who had stayed behind in Germany. Recognition took time, because memory had been overlaid with so much disparate experience and the discontinuity had been so abrupt, that my childhood seemed that of a person who could only be formally identified with the man I had become. It was not till a later visit that I found those little rented gardens, 'Schrebergärten', in one of which I had made the acquaintance of climbable trees; and, well beyond those gardens, a park that had been our playground in the earliest years. On an even later visit memory stabbed me like a knife. I had taken a bus to Grunewald and heard the conductor call out 'Hasensprung'. All at once that name brought back a parapet and a stone hare, the vertigo that had overcome me when I was balancing on the parapet on a walk with my father, and his calling me 'Angsthase', which means a rabbit, chicken or funk. That must have been one of my earliest traumas. The vertigo stayed with me and hit me again on the landing-stage near my grandfather's house on the river Havel, making me drop into the water like a stone. It came back some fifteen years later on an infantry assault course, when we had to walk a narrow plank on the top of high scaffolding with all our equipment on, then cross a gap in the plank, and I knew that I should drop again if I didn't hold on to something; got down on my knees and funked it, with the result that I was sent on a special toughening-up course, scaling chalk cliffs on the Kent coast, doing monkey walks on two wires strung across a river, winning a long distance walking race, swinging on ropes across chasms, but never once having to repeat the one thing I couldn't do when the vertigo threatened, balance without something to grip with my fingers. If my father had taken up psychology earlier than he did, I might well have got over that vertigo very much sooner, as over other irrational fears.

Less than a year before our emigration we moved into a new flat, in Schlüterstrasse, and discarded some of the heaviest lumber. For his consulting and waiting rooms, now transferred to a private clinic, my father went to the opposite extreme, going modern with unstained half-panelling, cork floors, steel tube furniture and a set of miniature tables and chairs for small children, all designed for him by Ernst Freud, son of the psychologist and father of Stephen, Lucian and Clement, who were our friends. It must have been about that time that my father took me with him on a car journey to the estate, somewhere in Brandenburg or Pomerania, of one of the aristocratic, landowning families among his patients – an experience memorable because it was the beginning of a new understanding between my father and me, because it took me out of the city into a way of life quite unknown to me, and because I was given a special family bed, perhaps a canopied four-poster, whose ornate antiquity seemed like something out of a fairy-tale. Only one earlier trip had left a related impression. It was a visit to a country estate in Thuringia where my great-uncle Paul hunted and fished, kept his pointer dogs and showed me a badger in a cage. I also watched a fishing ritual on a lake, involving boats and drag-nets. That caged badger and the hunting trophies on the walls aroused less pity in me at the time then wonderment and associations with the same fairy-tale world of forests and foresters, hunting lodges and huntsmen, a world of pure romance as different as could be from Berlin. It is to an earlier phase of my childhood that I attribute my claustrophobic aversion to large cities, as recurrent in later life as the urge to escape from them into open spaces less confined than gardens or parks; but I should have forgotten those two excursions, as I must have forgotten many others, if they had not made me more aware that there were other ways of living than ours in Berlin.

At about the same time, in the early thirties, my father did take up psychology, having learnt that most of his patients' illnesses were their parents' neuroses, though his mentor was not Ernst Freud's father but Alfred Adler, whom I remember meeting once or twice, though I think it was later, in London. Adler's visits, my sister Eva reminds me, failed to initiate a new era of spontaneity and liberation in our household. On the contrary, we had to kiss the old man when he arrived, and no one asked us whether our libido inclined that way. It did not. Perhaps that is why my sister became a Jungian analyst and

I never bothered to purloin any of Adler's books, though these were available at home, like a few of Freud's.

My father, meanwhile, had become a professor at the Charité, and he had become eminent enough in his profession to be asked to give a radio talk. I forget the subject, but remember the great occasion of listening to him and hearing his voice through a box – a radiogram – that seemed hardly less magical than my paternal grandmother's earphones. At home we still kept no radio, only a portable gramophone that was brought out on my birthdays, when I had the privilege of being awakened by my favourite record, a military march for fifes and drums; but that ceremony, too, and the preference belong to my earliest years, since those military predilections did not outlast my sixth or seventh year. There were other records, mainly of popular classics, before the London years, when I started collecting my own, as well as borrowing my parents.

At the age of about five I had begun to play the violin, taking lessons from a Dutch teacher. Although I could play 'classical' tunes at an early age, like an arrangement of a song by Beethoven and similar arrangements of songs by Schubert, the violin never suited me as an instrument, probably because it was not self-sufficient unless one was a virtuoso and could play unaccompanied works of Bach. If I had started on a keyboard instrument instead, and learnt to read music for it as I could for the violin, I might have developed as a musician. As it was, I'm not aware of having made any progress on the violin since the earliest years, though I liked my teacher and his wife. Yet music was my first art; and my love for it was not diminished by my dissatisfaction with the violin or my failure to master it. I did make one attempt, in adolescence, to learn the piano; but that was thwarted by my sin of impatience. I could not be bothered with the beginners' exercises set me by the teacher, but wanted to plunge straight into the kind of music I should have liked to play. So it came to nothing and I continued to strum by ear on pianos, harmoniums, church organs or harpsichords when I had the chance and was moved to do so, without the technique and practice needed to make such playing more than a self-indulgence.

At a time when one either made music at home or went to concerts – and my parents did both – those gramophone records must have served mainly as a treat for us children. For those records I do have total recall, not only because in my early childhood I lived more by ear than by eye, but also because I knew those pieces by heart and developed a special loathing for them in later years. The records included the overtures to 'Der Freischütz' and the 'Cavalleria Rusticana' and – my pet aversion – parts of the 'Nutcracker Suite'. There were also Viennese waltzes like 'The Blue Danube' and these, too, came to be associated for me with a sentimentally escapist bourgeois culture that had blighted my childhood. Fortunately there were also records of satirical pieces in the Berlin dialect by the comedian Paul Graetz – who ended his life in Hollywood exile – and some sort of peculiar cabaret song that was a coarse skit on my father's profession, and relished for that. It began:

> Ich bin der Dr. Eisenbart –
> Wiedewiedewit bum bum –
> Kurier die Leut nach meiner Art –
> Wiedewiedewit bum bum ...

> (My name is Dr. Eisenbart,
> Wiedewiedewit bum bum
> I cure 'em my way from the start ...)

and continued with horrors of quackery that have slipped my mind some sixty years later. No visual impression has remained with me from all those early childhood years with a clarity that would allow me to reproduce it in my account. My early seeing was immediately translated into fantasy or day-dream, and I may have been incapable of taking in the pictures in our flat, just as I was totally incapable of drawing with merely childish competence. Seeing and looking were later acquisitions, developed by my interest in natural phenomena long before I learned to look at pictures.

Recollection of my first reading is also somewhat vague. There will have been the usual fairy tales, mainly Grimm and Andersen, though there were collections of others in my parents' library, reserved for adults, to judge by the state of those books. I am pretty sure that my mother had little or no time to read from them to any of us at bedtime. Like many German wives and mothers of that era, she was wholly dedicated to her husband's domestic and professional needs. Besides administering the household, though with the help of servants, she acted as my father's secretary and typist. A good-night kiss must have been the extent of her attention to us in the evenings, when we were not ill, since more often than not in those Berlin years my parents either went out or entertained guests at home. During the day my mother must have found time to keep up her piano practice and her reading, especially of the new novels that accumulated in the bookcases throughout those years next to the collected editions of German and Scandinavian authors already 'classical' by then, and probably read by her more intensively before her relatively late marriage, in her thirties, and returned to in her long widowhood. We often sensed a frustration and moodiness in her she would never have admitted to feeling, least of all to us in her total devotion to my father. If my parents had any quarrels or any differences of opinion in those years, they were kept from us in the round of duties and conventions that ruled the family life.

Among the earliest books I recall were the cruelly cautionary tales of *Struwwelpeter*, and another German children's classic, only slightly less cruel but more deeply misanthropic, the rhymed tales of Wilhelm Busch, with his equally memorable drawings. Later one of my favourite books was a 'Berlin Fairytale' about a young devil and his grandmother, his excursions into and adventures in a recognizable human world. Then there were the adventure books of Karl May and those of James Fenimore Cooper, both much concerned with American Indians, a book about Arctic exploration by H. H. Houben, and the Dr Doolittle books of Hugh Lofting, devoured by me because they were full of animals, like a book about wolves by Richard and Cherry Kearton. Very soon these were joined or displaced by factual natural history books, like an abridged version for children of the twelve-volume work by Brehm, which my parents owned and I began to refer to at an early age. (I still have those twelve volumes and still find them most useful, though the edition goes back to 1922. If many animal species had not been discovered or studied by then, many more have become extinct or almost so in the meantime, including some I looked up because I knew them in my childhood – like the European tree frog I caught and kept at one time, butterflies like the swallowtail and the Camberwell Beauty or the storks that used to nest on rooftops even around Berlin.)

We heard my father's broadcast at Kladow, the village on the river Havel where my grandparents had had what was called a villa built for themselves, their married son Fritz and the four of us. I failed to notice or to remember that when my parents stayed in Kladow overnight they rented a room nearby; it was my mother who told me so in her old age. The so-called villa, too, was in a functional style, box-like and squat except for a terrace and balconies, quite unlike the fantastic *fin de siècle* follies in Grunewald, with their Gothic, Moorish or Palladian accretions. The flower garden seemed very large to us after the Berlin flat, though – like the house – it had shrunk to insignificance when I saw it after the war, so that I wondered whether some of it had been sold off by a later owner; but my grandfather had also bought a larger plot of land on the other side of the road, with a wooded slope down to the river, which my father had a little platform carved out for undisturbed work and rest among the pines. On the lower bank, close to the river which was so wide that I thought of it as a lake-and was corrected only after the first version of these memoirs – my grandfather grew vegetables and fruit. On the upper level we kept our rabbits and played our games, running wild, for once, like animals released from a cage. In the flower garden there was a special shrub to which my grandfather would attach bars of chocolate for us to pick. This did not prevent us from buying more sweets at the village shop, against my grandmother's orders. Though we would run for it if she happened to be coming that way, not even she, a formidable woman, or Fräulein Baensch's successor could now keep us from doing what we pleased most of the time, at least when we were at Kladow. We got up to all sorts of pranks and practical jokes. My brother and I rolled cigarettes out of the withered leaves of my grandfather's tobacco plants and bits of note-paper. (When, later, I started stealing my father's Russian cigarettes, he gave me a cigar that put me off smoking for several years. That must have been when he had taken up psychology.) My brother found a set of black-edged cards announcing the death, at least a decade earlier, of a great-grandmother, and dropped them through the mail slots all over the village. Thinking that my grandmother had died, several villagers called to express their condolences, to be met by the fury of my grandmother, who was very much alive and in the habit of doing early morning physical jerks in the nude at her open bedroom window, to our unfailing delight. Hygiene was one of her fads, women's libera-tion another. She had married, or been married off, too young, at the age of sixteen, and had revolted against that state of affairs long before we knew her. Though benevolent, her disposition needed to be resisted, as it was by my father, less so by my grandfather, least of all by her son Fritz, who remained emotionally tied to her until her death, and never grew up. Our white cat, which I loved more than some of my closest relatives, was not allowed to enter the house – perhaps because, at an earlier period, my grandfather had lavished too much love on a cat whose fastidious and expensive eating habits had exasperated her, but ostensibly because cats are unhygienic. We used to ask her if she would rescind the rule if we taught the cat to wipe her paws on the mat. Our grandmother took us on long country walks, during which she said her extempore prayers prompted by communion with nature and including poems like Wordsworth's 'I wandered lonely as a cloud'. At the dinner table she would have fierce political arguments with my father – what about I don't recall, only that she was a supporter of Count Coudenhove-Kalergi's Pan Europe movement. One of the last things she did before our emigration was to bury a tin box full of feminist or Pan-European literature in the wood behind the garden. If that wood has not been bulldozed, the box may still be there.

For us, liberation came too late, like my father's psychology. Early regimentation and rivalry for parental affection had driven us into conflicts among ourselves, suspended only when we had to close ranks against an adult. In that situation, as a gang, we could be cruel to people who meant well, as we were to a cousin of my mother's, Kurt, who tried to act as a sort of tutor to us when we ceased to attend school shortly before our emigration, or to a woman who tried as vainly to teach us English during our last summer at Kladow. Not only did we laugh at the funny new words and tease the teacher, but on one occasion we filled a whole sack with vegetables stolen from my grandfather's plot and watched her shoulder this burden obediently when she left, not so much because she could do with the vegetables as because she was too diffident and well-mannered to refuse the gift. My grandmother ran into her on the way to the bus and thought the poor woman had stolen the stuff.

This incident elicited one of my earliest literary works, written for my grandmother at Kladow as a sort of penance or – as I now see it – as an exercise in moral duplicity. My grandmother kept it till her death in England, and it came back to me with other papers she had kept. It was called 'English lesson as I should like it to be.' The correct spelling and rather stilted manner suggest the collaboration of my older sister Maria or, more probably, of our last governess Käte

Zellentin. 'I think it good if the English lesson proceeds like this: we don't sit down till the teacher has arrived. That way we learn for about an hour. Then we walk through the garden and through the rooms of the house and she explains everything in English. She needn't be so boring. Sometimes, too, she must tell us stories or read to us from an English book. My greatest pleasure is when we go with the teacher to our vegetable garden and she tells us the English name of every sort of cabbage and we secretly fill a whole sack with green stuff for her, which she then has to drag home with difficulty, but then either my grandmother or my uncle catch her and ask her what is in the sack. Then she says: the children took me to the vegetable garden and gave me a lot of vegetables. Then we get the scolding we deserve and the matter is done with.'

When not engaged in such perversities, I had grown so intro-verted and withdrawn that I would spend whole days and successions of days in daydreams which no outward reality could penetrate. Perhaps even the nasty trick played on the English teacher was a response to forebodings of an imminent upheaval that was not fully explained to us, when those English lessons were a preparation for our departure. I felt closer to animals and plants than to human beings. Walking through the village on my way to the pine and birch woods around Kladow and the solitary rambles I now preferred, I would pass a house guarded by a springer spaniel. Unlike most of the dogs in those parts – I had been bitten by a dachshund I tried to stroke, and my uncle had been savaged by an Alsatian trained to go for the throat – the spaniel was friendly and would join me through a hole in the fence every time I passed. We became so inseparable in the end that the owners realized they had lost their dog and offered to give it to me. I kept hedgehogs, white mice, tortoises, grass snakes, slow-worms, lizards, newts and fishes; even a baby wild rabbit, acquired when it ran into a ferreter's net. In the river I caught crayfish by prod-ding them with a stick and whipping it out when they clawed it. I caught butterflies, too, and beetles, because they fascinated me and I had begun to collect all sorts of natural history specimens. I caught birds in a trap made of a cigar box with horizontal and vertical sticks, which someone must have made for me, like the aviary in which I caged them until I learned that birds, too, suffer by being confined, and released those that hadn't died. One of our later governesses had tried to teach us handicrafts like carpentry; but too late, again, since we had begun to resist every sort of enforced activity, if only by apathy. When my brother or older sister provoked me in one of my trance-like states, I could fly into uncontrollable rages, attacking them with teeth and claws like an animal at bay.

It was in a daydream that I found myself on the landing-stage and compelled to go down, to undo the whole process of growing up, back to the moment of birth. If the new governess had not heard the splash and dived in to pull me out, I should not have moved a finger to save myself, though I was as unaware of a death-wish as of any other intention or desire.

Ironically enough, it may have been that new, young governess, who had reduced me to that extremity – treated as an accident by my parents, though the fact that I was a keen and strong swimmer must have made them wonder. Fräulein Baensch had been as strict with us as she was with herself. Her successor, a good-looking blonde in her twenties, resented her duties and showed that resentment – at least to me since the unit had broken up by now, and it was me whom she took every opportunity to torment and humiliate. That she once flogged me with a rope – knowing that she could count on my stubborn silence – mattered much less to me than more subtle humiliations, such as forcing me to go naked into some outdoor children's party where nudity was taboo. I think it was she who locked all four of us into a small room, with nothing to occupy us, while she went out with a lover, and there was no one about to hear our mountingly furious shouting and pounding. One of her admirers was our next-door neighbour at Kladow, a Bavarian who called her his 'golden pheasant' and once locked her into his large aviary for a lark. This neighbour was an early Nazi. When Hitler's speeches began to be broadcast he rigged up a loudspeaker in the garden, to make sure we should know which way the wind was blowing.

I knew it up to a point, because back in Berlin, at my second school, some teachers had begun to wear swastika badges. One of them started the day by ordering the Jewish boys to line up in front of the class for interrogation about such matters as their fathers' activities during the First World War. I went home and discovered that I was one of those who should have lined up. If we,had been brought up as Jews, as we were not, I should at least have had something to stand up for. I had heard my father's mother speak of going to the 'temple', but that might have been a Greek one for all it meant to us, who had never been inside a synagogue, learnt no Hebrew and grown up in total ignorance of Jewish tradition. No other member of our family had so much as mentioned anything to do with the Jewish faith. Our Catholic governess had taught us some childish prayers connected with no particular creed, and that was all – except for my other grandmother's outdoor devotions.

It is only lately that I have come to guess that her husband Bertrand never forgot Jerusalem, though neither he nor anyone else ever spoke of Zionism in my family and my grandfather kept quiet about his sympathies, as he tended to do about almost everything, having been cowed by my grandmother's militant intellectual superiority. Certainly he was proud of his Jewish antecedents, had a family tree drawn up back to the seventeenth century when his forebears came to Germany from Spain, and kept a history of the Jewish community in Mainz that listed all the families, including his. From this I gathered that my father's and my mother's surnames had once been interchangeable and could also have derived from the city of Homburg in Hessen rather than from Hamburg, the Hanseatic city. Not only the advertisement taken over by James Joyce, but a collection of ancient coins and glassware dug up in Palestine, pointed to his support of the Jewish settlers there. These antiquities had been given to him as an acknowledgement of his benefactions, and someone told me that a street in Palestine had been named after him. Though in later years he bought the monumental two volumes of the English Bible illustrated by Doré, he also kept an edition of 1885 by Zunz of the Old Testament only, the Masoretic text. Because he was so reticent about his interests and allegiances it was not till long after his death that I saw these relics. The things he did show me were in line with the assimilation that had begun much earlier in both his and my father's families. Of the books owned by my great-grandparents on my mother's side I have only the four-volume Klopstock – known as the German Milton – stolen by my mother as a girl, and a Latin Sallust used by my great-grandfather Louis Hamburg in 1840 at the gymnasium in Mainz as a 'studiosus tertiae', inscribed and dated in Latin. On the other side of my family I have only one document, a letter of 1835 with the Royal Prussian seal certifying that the candidate N. Hamburger had passed the examination qualifying him for the 'educational service' ('Lehramt') in the district of Oppeln, Silesia. Unless such authorization was needed for teachers in Jewish institutions, I must assume that my great-grandfather was employed in the State system as a teacher in a secular capacity. It must have been my father, above all, who carried this secularization to the point that determined our upbringing. Yet, if he was an agnostic, he was not indifferent to religion. In his last years he contributed to a Quaker magazine and read a selection from the writings of Kierkegaard, with page references in pencil showing that certain passages were important enough to him to be noted for a book he was working on, but did not live to finish.

Suddenly, though, we were Jews – for that teacher's purposes, and others not yet clear to us. When the order was repeated, I duly lined up, but escaped the worst taunts because I had asked my father about his war record, and was able to report that he had won the Iron Cross for special gallantry while serving in the Medical Corps. What I did not say, and may have learnt of later, is that, patriotically, he had also put all his savings into war bonds that proved worthless after the war. When it came to games, a kind of handball called 'Völkerball', the teacher acting as referee divided us boys into an 'Aryan' and a Jewish team. That would have been acceptable, once the distinction had been driven home to those as unprepared for it as I was, if that master had not run with the 'Aryan' team cheering them on with the sort of expletives I was not to hear again until I did bayonet charges as part of my infantry training. Both of my best friends at that school happened to be non-Jewish; but after the indoctrination, when I was walking home from school with one of them, his older brother forbade him to have anything more to do with me, and finally went for me with a length of wire he had picked up in the street.

Those last memories of school in Berlin – a 'gymnasium', after a private preparatory school – have blotted out all earlier ones, except for some kind of solemn ceremony at the earlier school at which we had all sworn allegiance to the Fatherland – an oath I took seriously at the time, not knowing how soon I should be forced to break it. I remember the name of the first school, but not that of the later one, whose location I also failed to retrace on later visits to Berlin, though it was the one place there to which I had made my own way, unescorted. Nor do I know whether I liked or disliked my school work before that last Berlin year, when the same teacher set us extraordinary pieces of homework involving elaborate geographical charts and drawings that I couldn't begin to do, because I had no idea what they were about. Since that teacher, like others before him, ruled by mockery and intimidation, I was reduced to such despair that I could not go to sleep at night.

My father was beginning to be anxious about my state of mind, after the inexplicable 'accident' that almost drowned me; and when he found me awake and in tears one night, I broke my silence for once and told him what the school was doing to me. I think that soon after that we left school, living at Kladow and receiving (useless) private tuition there. He knew well enough, in any case, what was happening in Germany. One of his friends was a Minister in the Social-Democratic government of Prussia. As soon as the Nazis took over, this friend, Dr. Klepper, was on a black list. To escape arrest – his house had already been raided and ransacked while he and his family were out – the Kleppers went underground in the country and either stayed, or spent much of their time, at my grandparents' house, while preparing to emigrate. We saw a great deal of them and their children that summer of 1933, at Kladow, and we were warned not to mention their name to anyone in the village. That summer, too, my grandfather's chauffeur, Tietz, gave me a badge of the Social-Democratic Party. Though I had only the vaguest notions of politics at the time, I preferred the three arrows of the badge to the swastika, and pinned on the badge. When I returned from one of my walks through the village with that forbidden and provocative emblem I was told in no uncertain terms that I had endangered the whole family. Luckily, there were no repercussions. One Sunday, at lunchtime, two uniformed S. A. men came to the house. The new rulers had decreed a 'one-pot' meal for the day, and a compulsory collection for Party funds of the money saved by it. Since my grandparents had obeyed the order, an inspection of the kitchen revealed no irregularities and the S.A. men went off quietly with the money. Yet this intrusion into a private house was crass enough to serve as a warning of things to come.

I can't be sure of the sequence of events during that last year in Germany. One day I saw my uncle Fritz rush into the house, bellowing, one blood-oozing hand clapped to his face. He had been playing in the garden with the Kleppers' son, who had a toy aeroplane propelled by a catapult, and when my uncle was trying to catch it the sharp point pierced one of his eyes. I knew nothing about Oedipus or my uncle's mother fixation, which drew him to children and children's games, but the pity and terror of that moment has fused with other family scenes of that period, when my father had decided to emigrate well before the larger exodus of 'non-Aryans', and was trying to persuade other members of the family to take the same decision. Because my maternal grandparents had taken it – without telling us, as usual, the loss of my uncle's eye was inseparable in my mind from other calamities and forebodings of dissolution.

My other grandmother was too trusting and naïve, as well as too unassuming, to act on my father's warnings. She refused to leave with us; and by the time she was ready to leave, after the visible atrocities, no visa could be obtained for her. My father, who moved to Edinburgh many months before we followed him there, left her what little capital he could raise. Soon after the outbreak of war he received a postcard through the Red Cross informing him that his mother 'had gone on a journey' and he knew that she would not return from it.

The only other two relatives who stayed behind, old people also, survived the persecutions and the war; my great-uncle Paul as an itinerant farm labourer with false identity papers and no ration card, my great-uncle Martin, who had been the managing director of a large steel works and an amateur show-jumper, by an exemption he owed to the connections of his non-Jewish, aristocratic wife. Of their three children, the younger son, Tino, emigrated because he was a Socialist, joined the Foreign Legion and then lived as a jockey and chess-player in Casablanca. Their other son and daughter survived in Germany. When the girl wanted to marry during the war, her mother had to certify that she was the daughter not of her 'non-Aryan' husband but of a pure 'Aryan' lover.

At the age of nine, in that last year, I wrote a piece on 'Life at Kladow', probably also at my grandmother's request, since it was preserved among her papers: 'I get up at 7.30 in the morning. I get dressed and go downstairs. I play till about 9 and then eat my breakfast. After breakfast we have lessons till 12.30. Then we go out and play with our friends. In summer we swim from our landing-stage and lie about in the sun. Often we play cops and robbers on our plot of land. In winter we skate and toboggan. Skating is very fine because on the Havel you can skate all the way to Potsdam. There is a big hill for tobogganing. That's where all the children from Kladow go tobogganing. We always keep pets here, because it's a good place for them. We used to keep rabbits and hedgehogs, and now we keep birds and tortoises and cats. At first we had two kittens, but not for long unfortunately, for they belonged to other people. But soon we shall be getting a new one. In the autumn we go out looking for funguses and wild strawberries. That's great fun. Sometimes we go out on our bicycles or on a walk. Often we build tents and play Red Indians. In Berlin there is a lot of traffic, but at Kladow there isn't.

That's all.'

It was by no means all, only the shell of a normality whose brittleness everyone tried to conceal from us. I have no clear recollection of all the preparations and partings, the dissolution of the various households and all the practical arrangements that must have been made at the time, not even of my father's departure long before ours, though my attachment to my father was a deep one by that time. I do remember seeing my great-uncle Paul weep on his last visit to Kladow. As a bachelor until his late sixties, after our emigration, he was devoted to my mother and much involved with her parents and brother, so much so that he had a flat in Berlin adjoining my grandfather's, before buying a large detached house in Grunewald. When we paid a last visit to my grandparents' large, luxurious and mysterious flat, my grandfather told each of us to choose something among its contents as a keepsake. This something had to be small, so that the elaborate toys that had been brought out for us on earlier visits did not qualify. I chose a pair of tiny enamel dishes or trays ornamented with flowers. The things were duly packed and given to us later, in England. When we chose them, we did not know that the whole household was about to be dissolved, and that anything else in it not wanted by my parents would be sold or left behind. My grandparents were to spend the remainder of their lives in hotels or rented rooms, with no further use for their old furniture or anything but a few residual possessions, like my grandfather's various collections of prints, ancient glassware and coins, and a stamp collection I was to inherit and sell.

At Kladow, that last summer, I was wholly preoccupied with a love affair – the most passionate of a succession of them that had begun when I was three or four. The first, with a little girl called Beatrice, lasted quite a few years, and was renewed whenever our families met. This one was with a girl of about my own age who lived a few houses away from ours. Probably we had met while swimming in the lake. In some secluded place on the crowded slope above my grandfather's vegetable garden we built ourselves a hide-out, spending hours on end in an intense communion we felt to be a marriage. The enforced separation from that girl meant more to me than all the other partings. She stayed behind in Germany and I never heard from her again.

The third of our governesses, Käte Zellentin, came with us when we left in November 1933, though her functions had already become more domestic than educational and disciplinarian. The journey by train and boat to Edinburgh – where my father had already begun to work for his British medical degrees, in a language he was not fluent in and in branches of medicine he had not touched since his first student years – sticks in my mind only as a turmoil of perplexity and distress, brought to a head when, at Dover, H. M. Customs confiscated the pair of budgerigars my grandfather had kept. The male, reared and tamed by my grandfather, had not only talked – German – but spent most of its time out of its cage, perched on my grandfather's spectacles or rolling napkin rings across the dinner table. It had ceased to talk when it was given a mate. To lose those birds, with so many other partings behind us, brought us up against the whole monstrosity of changing countries. Although my uncle was to write countless letters in efforts to get them out of quarantine, we must have felt that this parting was final; and its suddenness gave me an intimation of how little we could take with us into the new life; how few habits, loyalties and affections; how little continuity with what had gone before. That much of this had been far from likeable or congenial to me, did not affect the realization.

· · · · · · · · · ·

FROM the moment we arrived in Edinburgh and moved into a small furnished house – stone-fronted, grey and cold – in Greenhill Place, we had to adapt to a way of life altogether new and strange. The struggle for survival began without transition or preparation when we were sent off to school, and two German-speaking boys wandered all over the buildings of what I believe was the largest boys' school in Britain, George Watson's College, and out again, looking for someone who could direct them to the right classrooms. By the time we found a woman teacher with a little German the younger of them was in tears. After too much custody and supervision we were suddenly on our own, at the very moment when we felt most helpless. My mother was preoccupied with the task of running a house in a foreign country, with no cook or housemaid for the first time in her life, with very little money and the same language difficulty that made us feel lost. As for my father, he hardly emerged from his study in that house, sitting from morning to late night over his textbooks and English dictionaries, so as to qualify as soon as possible for medical practice in Britain. His swotting was made harder for him by the cold. That winter he sat huddled over the small coal fire, wrapped in a blanket.

For us, at school, it was like learning to swim by being thrown into deep water; and it worked, in a way. This time I wanted to survive. Because I wanted to survive, my dreaminess and introspection had to be put away – at least for the duration of the struggle, until I could afford them again. Since English words were indispensable not only for school work but for what I needed most, the reassurance of being accepted as a member of the community, the words came with extraordinary speed. On my first day I stared in silent amazement at a curly-haired boy wearing a kilt, thinking that some incomprehensible custom required one girl to be admitted into every class. By the second day I had words enough to be put right about that, and to start making friends. Words, in any case, carried less weight than actions among those nine-year-old boys, and it was by an action that I won total acceptance with a suddenness I felt to be quite undeserved. It was as easy as walking off a plank – the plank being the highest of the diving-boards in the swimming-pool. No one else dared to use it. As I had been swimming since the age of four or five, quite apart from my special aptitude for falling, this feat meant nothing to me. Yet it established my prestige as no amount of fluent English or Scottish could have done, so much so that I was invited to join one of the gangs that prowled around Edinburgh after school, fighting boys from rival institutions like Heriot's and Fettes.

We spent less than a year in Edinburgh; and even though I roamed many different parts of the city with that gang or with individual friends, visiting their houses too, the city of which we had the freedom was still not that of adults, but a playground and battlefield. When I saw Edinburgh again as an adult I recognized nothing but the obvious sights and a tea-shop or two in Princes Street.

Since memory, once more, is defective, I shall translate some extracts from letters I wrote to my grandparents and uncle from Edinburgh. It goes without saying that these dutiful communications reveal only what I thought the recipients wanted to know; and what they wanted to know, above all, was that everything was going as well as could be.

December 14th 1933: '. . . How do you like the South of France? This letter is your Christmas present. I've settled down very well by now. At school it's really wonderful. I have so many friends, and such nice ones . . . Here, we have an awful lot of mice. We've already caught a few. We always have lunch at school, so that Mummy doesn't have to do so much cooking. At break-time we always play football on our school grounds. Our school has only been up for six months and is wonderful. There's a big swimming-pool in it. But we haven't started swimming in it.

March 10th 1934: '. . . This morning we played football. That was great fun. In form I'm in fifth place. On March 17th I'm having my birthday party, and I'm looking forward to that. I know you always like little pencils, so I'm sending you two. We now have two cats, one is only two weeks old and very small.'

March 25th 1934: 'Here the weather is wonderful now, so that we can walk about without overcoats. We spend the whole day in the garden, playing with our cats. I was very pleased with the chocolate biscuits. For my birthday I got 3 books, a big football, a pair of socks, a dozen crayons . . . At school it's very nice. Every Tuesday I have a violin lesson, but unfortunately it doesn't help much, since I'm asked to do exactly what my other teacher said I shouldn't, and it will take a long time for me to learn the new way. Eva gave me a little bedside clock which I like very much. Besides our two cats one always comes to our house. It doesn't belong to anybody. At this moment it's sitting on Maria's lap. Our big cat has an English name, Blacky, because it's completely black, our kitten is called Tiny, also an English name, because it's also a British cat.'

April 24th 1934: 'Now our holidays are over, this is our second day at school. Today another little German boy came to school, he's only four. We know him. He once came to Kladow with Frieda, one of our maids. This morning it rained, but now the sun is shining again. In the holidays I spent a lot of time with my friends. I'm in the tenth place at school. I thought I'd do better than that. It was only because of geography. I'm top in arithmetic. My report was good. Only in geography I got 32 out of 50, but that's very hard for me. In history I got 46 out of 50. In "progress" I got "excellent".'

'The violin lesson was always horrible. Once the teacher made me write out a rule 140 times. When I start he says: "If you play one note out of tune I'll kick you in the stomach." Today Daddy wrote a letter saying I was not to have violin lessons.'

June 6th 1934: 'Many thanks for the lovely stamps. It was a great pleasure to get them. I've already got more than 1,000 stamps, though I didn't bring any from Germany ... Here the weather is very fine now. A week ago a German couple came to see us and brought us a goldfish. I can't write more now because I want to stick in some stamps. I play a lot of cricket now, because it's too hot for soccer and rugger ...

6.30 Now I've stuck in all the stamps.'

Home life in Edinburgh was austere and severely restricted. My parents were much impressed by the courtesy calls of neighbours – a gesture almost inconceivable in Berlin – but in the circumstances these could have no sequel beyond a formal return of the call. The few people my father had time to talk to were refugee doctors in the same predicament as himself. It happened that there was a grand piano in the house, in a drawing-room known as 'the cold glory' and almost never used, because no one could cope with the coal fires. Neither my father nor my mother touched the piano while we were there, but a refugee called Adorno used to sit in that icy room, prac- tising. I don't think I ever spoke to him, but I invested him with all the romantic glamour that was missing in the new life, and would stand in the hall for hours to hear him play.

Most of the time the house was unnaturally quiet, because my father must not be distracted from the work on which our futures depended. That quietness dominates my recollections of Edinburgh, reinforced by the quietness in the streets on Sundays, when nothing at all was allowed to go on. I doubt that I should have seen the Castle, Arthur's Seat, Holyrood Palace or the Zoo, let alone the Forth Bridge and one or two places outside the city, if it hadn't been for a few acquaintances of my parents who would take one or more of us out for the day. It was they, too, who took us to the tea-shops in Princes Street.

The strain of more than a year's uninterrupted cramming in middle age may well have shortened my father's life, but I never heard him complain. I think he felt that it was a small price to pay for the hospitality that had been offered us and for the decencies of British life, which he never ceased to praise. Uneventful though it was, that interim period changed us all. Within half a year or so the four of us had begun to speak English among ourselves, and that meant more than progress in learning the language for which I was given a special prize at school. It meant a degree of identification with those who spoke the language, an adaptation easy for none of us and different for each one. For me, it meant a drastic shift not only from home life to school life and school friends but from introversion and fantasy to a boy's world of competitive toughness, uncomplicated alliances and relative independence. That, too, was an interim state, but a necessary one, since it healed some of the wounds inflicted by recent betrayals, rejections and losses.

For my mother, who was to survive my father by forty years, the change was far more drastic and difficult. That she began to develop practical skills which, from her childhood onwards, had been left to servants, was only the outward manifestation of the change; but it did not take her long to become as excellent a cook and confectioner as she had been a pianist, tennis-player, war-time nurse, secretarial factotum to my father and administrator of a professional household. In later years she added gardening to her accomplishments. During the next war she kept hens in London. Before the war, someone sent her one leaf of a pot plant widely grown in Germany, the Sparmannia Africana, in a letter. Not only do I still have the progeny of that leaf, more than half a century later, but it is to be found in paintings by Lucian Freud, who would call on my mother for replacements of the plant for his studio.

In her widowhood, after those war-time hens, my mother kept only dogs and cats. When her children no longer needed her full-time care, she took up social work for the Society of Friends, remaining active in it well into her eighties, even after an operation for cancer. My mother never spoke of her conversion to Quakerism, if it was a religious conversion rather than a congenial opening for good works beyond the family she never ceased to care for and care about, providing a base for reunions when everything made it centrifugal. I did touch on those questions with her at times, though as reticent as she was about matters of faith and belief. She seemed unaware of any breach between her Quakerism and the agnostic humanism that had left her children no more churched than synagogued. The identity disc I wore as a soldier bore the letters C. of E., because that was the church in which, belatedly, I had my religious education, though never christened in it nor confirmed. Had he lived, I could have talked with my father about that muddle. It wasn't in my mother's nature to discuss generalities or ideas, only to cope practically and indefatigably with every sort of hardship, muddle or conflict that might present itself. She could not have done so without a faith; but, as I was to learn also, faith is not the same thing as belief. My beliefs could be shaken by experience or knowledge, and they changed over the years. My faith did not change, because it lay beyond experience and beyond reason. From her mother, too, my mother had inherited a very strong will, though one less militant than her mother's, with far less need for opinions, certainties and causes. When she was almost ninety-three, confined to bed and kept alive only by constant medical attention, I announced a visit for after lunch, because I was driving over from Suffolk. I was astonished and shocked to find her sitting up at the table, with a meal prepared for me. By telling me a story about her youth and her hatred of leave-takings, she intimated to me that we should not be meeting again, did not answer the telephone after that, and concentrated her powerful will on dying.

My grandparents and uncle, meanwhile, had left France and set up a temporary household at Hove. In the summer or autumn of 1934 we went to live with them there, while my father worked for his examinations and my mother made arrangements for a permanent home in London. For a term or so I attended the Brighton and Hove Grammar School, getting on well enough to remember nothing about that institution. In Edinburgh I had watched a rugby match between Old Watsonians and a rival team. At Brighton it was county cricket, including an invitation to tea with a Lord Mayor whom my grandparents must have got to know. I never took to either game, as it happened, preferring soccer, rowing and boxing at school, swimming and riding in later years.

From Brighton Pier, where we spent our pocket money on slot machines and ice-cream, I did most of my fishing, though more often than not it was dogfish I caught, small spotted sharks which at that time had not been promoted to the dignity of 'rock salmon' and were either killed, with difficulty, to be cut up for bait, or thrown back. I respected the leathery strength of those streamlined predators and never killed them, but sometimes needed the help of old locals to get them off the hook.

It MUST have been towards the end of the year that we moved to an early Victorian semi-detached house in London, 45, St. John's Wood Park. When the lease expired during the war it remained empty and derelict for many years, before being demolished, like almost all the old houses in that street. Although my father also kept a consulting room in Upper Wimpole Street, certain patients came to the house, to a room that served him as bedroom, study and consulting room, with a small waiting-room adjoining it. Unlike later emigrants from Germany, my parents had been able to take their furniture and possessions – a strange assortment of the old and new, from the Berlin flat, the ultra-modern clinic and the functionally plain villa at Kladow. In the top-floor bedroom which I shared with my brother we slept on beds designed for Kladow – with hinges and collapsible legs, so that they could disappear behind curtains against the wall, giving us more room for the games we might have played if we had got on well enough together.

St. John's Wood Park was a triangular street, with a central island formed by large detached houses and their gardens. Motor traffic was minimal in those parts. Neither my family nor any of the close neighbours owned a car. Marlborough Road Station, later replaced by St. John's Wood, was only a street or two away from the house. There was so little noise that one could hear the lions roar in the Regent's Park Zoo. Another familiar sound, in the early mornings, was the clatter of horses' hooves when the soldiers from the barracks on Ordnance Hill rode out for exercise. There was something archaic even about the street musician we knew best in the street, an old harpist who sat there playing as though he enjoyed it and that pavement were the chosen setting for his art. We had many conversations with him, as with a pavement painter we passed on our way to school.

My father was no longer a professor, and his private practice, at first, was reduced to a few families, mainly of refugees, since in England it was unusual for paediatricians to function as family doctors. As he got to know more colleagues, who sent him patients, his practice grew, but there must have been no end of money pressures at the best of times, even when he had become a consultant at a London hospital. A cook and housemaid were still considered indispensable; and so were private schools for the four of us. Yet my father found time for some of his other interests. Not only did he and my mother take up music again but many eminent musicians played in our house – Feuermann, the cellist, Max Rostal and Franz Osborn, Lily Kraus and Szimon Goldberg are some of those I remember meeting. Marlene Dietrich brought her daughter as a patient, and I caught a glimpse of her. The Kordas were also among my father's patients. They invited me to their Denham studios, where I was initiated into the mysteries of film-making, such as the cutting of film tapes, and saw Rex Harrison and Merle Oberon at work. At the White City stadium, where my father took me, I saw Jesse Owens win a race.

My father's psychology books began to interest me, almost as much as the natural history books of which I had quite a library of my own. I used to borrow the odd volume of Freud and read it in the lavatory – though that must have been some years after we moved to London. I could now talk with my father about almost everything, but sexual matters were an exception. It was a residual puritanism in him, I suspect, that kept him faithful to Adler, for whom I had little use, even when my father became active in a child guidance clinic which he helped to found. Neither my own puritanism nor my innocence was much affected by early attempts to read Freud. I couldn't understand my parents' amusement at finding me in bed with the last of my childhood girl friends, Cornelia, when she was staying at our house. We were reading a book together, and we were comfortable there.

Reading, in fact, was more of an addiction than going to bed with girls. Even in my prep school years, at The Hall, Hampstead, I spent most of my pocket money on books, stopping at Miss Waterhouse's bookshop in the Arcade at Swiss Cottage, as I continued to do for many years to come. In addition I collected anything to do with nature: skeletons, skulls, a stuffed long-eared bat, snakes in bottles, a beautiful chain of Egyptian scarabs, a rose of Jericho – the miraculous plant that will sprout again years after its death, whenever placed in water – shells, rocks and crystals. Our next-door neighbour, an old man called Yeatman-Woolf, shared this mania and gave me many precious items from his collection, finally parting with a whole cabinet of tropical butterflies and beetles, which my father bought from him and gave me for a birthday. Yeatman-Woolf had also published one or two books of comic verse, and he had a large collection of gramophone records, some of which he passed on to me. I still have one or two of his original Caruso and Galli-Curci records, with one side of the heavy discs left blank.

The Hall, Hampstead, under its headmaster Wathen, was an efficient processing factory for potential public school boys. The buildings were drab, almost seedy, but the turnover was satisfactory. For games we were marched in crocodiles along the Finchley Road, to the playing fields or the old municipal swimming baths and gymnasium. I took up boxing, too, and was better at it than at most games. The Scottish boxing coach had a peculiar method. 'Punch me on the nose', he would invite us with disarming gentleness, and when we complied rather gingerly he would retaliate with a terrific whack on the chin, teaching us to keep our guard up.

There was much savagery and bullying at the school, especially in the small back yard that served as a playground between classes. For some strange reason old car tyres were provided for our exercise there, so that at any unwary moment one was likely to be hit by one of those formidable toys. The fighting there and in class-rooms was less clean than our street fights in Edinburgh, because it was more personal, the expression of real hatred and rivalries, exacerbated by the competitiveness of the whole school system. Bullying was against the rules and punishable by beatings with a gym shoe; but this didn't prevent some large lout from jerking a knee into one's groin, quite casually, in the back yard, and gloating over one's agonized contortions. Only a weakling would report such an incident. The code demanded reprisals, if practicable, or else a stoical acceptance. The Headmaster, who did the beating with gym shoes, had once been sued by a parent for victimization, but had been acquitted or rehabilitated. He seemed genial enough, a bit eccentric in his teaching – he taught us French syntax in rhythmic units repeated in chorus by the class, while he conducted the chanting – and otherwise conventional. This doesn't rule out the possibility that he derived pleasure from beating boys, or certain boys. Repressed homosexuality was part of the system, inherent in it.

I did well enough at that school and at the next, having learnt to stand up for myself, to get by, to do what was required of me while reserving more and more for my private pursuits, hobbies and friendships. One of my sparring partners, Timothy Hallinan, became my closest friend in those years. He was serious, especially about politics, inclined to priggishness like myself, and like me had two elder sisters and a younger brother. His family was Irish-American and his father a political journalist. His home in Belsize Park Gardens was congenial to me because the children were treated as persons with minds of their own. There was conversation about politics and ideas. Timothy's sisters became friends of my sisters, and his younger brother, at one time, a patient of my father's. In later years we drifted apart, not only because he went on to Gordonstoun, but because my increasingly aesthetic leanings struck him as somehow frivolous, lacking in moral and intellectual grit. Frivolity was what he could not abide. I remember defending the younger of his two sisters against his disapproval when he called her a 'social butterfly'; but that may have been because I found her attractive.

Another school friend, David Cairns, lived in our street. I spent a weekend with his family at their country house near Arundel, but got into trouble because we talked about rabbits. When he mentioned that his rabbits didn't breed as rabbits proverbially do, I explained to him that they couldn't, because the buck and the doe were in separate hutches. I supposed that this revelation of the so-called 'facts of life' was referred to his parents and that they thought I must be utterly corrupt to know them at my age. In any case I was never invited there again. My early acquaintance with country matters may have cost me the joy of another stay in the country, but the friendship was taken up again later.

My mother's parents and brother were still in close touch with us. When they were not in the South of France they lived near us, in a service flat in Fitzjohn's Avenue, then in Belsize Park Gardens, where my grandfather died. We were fond of him, though he was touchy, moody, and embittered by decades of conflict with his wife and son. To his grandchildren he was more than kind, but with a reserve bound up with the suspicion that we liked him more for his gifts than for what he was. He was deeply offended when in some skit my sister and I improvised for one of his birthdays there was a passing reference to an inheritance from a rich grandfather, a mere parroting of something we had heard or read. In his last years he had nothing to do but worry about his investments and buy the odd old stamp for his collection. I inherited a few books from him as well as a collection of old woodcuts and etchings, mainly Dutch and German – but I don't recall ever seeing him read a book. Not till many years after his death did I see the sketchbooks, of 1900 to 1911, that contain his impressions of landscapes visited on holiday, portraits of his friends, and painstaking copies of paintings and sculptures. The activity itself, like the execution of those pencil and crayon sketches, was conventional enough, but his delicate response to certain kinds of scenery, especially alpine, made me realize how little of himself my grandfather had been able to communicate to us in his old age. His collecting of paintings and engravings, too, seemed more essentially related to the man he was; and so did his solitary gardening under the wooded slope of his plot at Kladow. His very silences about what he thought and felt became something I could recognize and understand, for he had passed them on to my mother, and she had passed them on to me.

While he was alive we had spent part of each summer as our grandparents' guests, at Combe Martin, Bournemouth or Torquay, staying at hotels and passing the time much as we had done at Hove, except that we mixed more and more with other children and adults. My parents could not afford many holidays. They spent the summers in London, though once my mother went abroad, to meet her uncle Paul on neutral territory, at Karlsbad.

For a few years I kept up my violin practice and lessons, begun in Germany when I was five or six. My violin teacher, as it happened, moved to London at about the same time as we did. Much as I liked my teacher, a Dutchman, who became a psycho-analyst when a paralysing illness forced him to give up the violin, he could not arouse much enthusiasm in me for the instrument, and I gave it up as soon as pressure of school work provided an excuse. Ever since my early childhood in Berlin we had known a girl violinist, the daughter of a Russian émigré and former professor of music. Though at least ten years older than the oldest of us, she had climbed a tree in our little rented garden in Berlin. When we saw her again in London she was no longer merely tomboyish and odd, but gradually slipping into acute schizophrenia. She must have had a special attachment to my parents, for she would turn up at our house during her worst crises, frightening us with her incomprehensible behaviour and remarks. She had been a brilliant violinist. One day she started playing in the street, then gave her valuable violin to a passer-by. After a frontal lobotomy she fell into complete apathy, became quite unrelated to her past life, and finally killed herself. At about the same time we knew a boy virtuoso on the violin who disappeared into a mental home. I don't know whether these two acquaintances put me off the violin by association, or whether I simply wasn't good enough at it to get much satisfaction out of my playing. Later, when I was fifteen, I wanted to take up the piano and the organ. One of my friends at Westminster, Colin Turnbull, played the organ and had permission to practise in the Abbey. I sometimes joined him there and indulged in experimental strumming when he had finished. By that time my father could no longer afford lessons, and I was too busy trying to get through the School and Higher Certificates. For the rest of my life I have had to content myself with clumsy and barbarous improvisations on the piano. There were periods in my life when I had much more use for music than for literature, including poetry, and felt that words could never be more then pedestrian, beggarly aspirants to 'the condition of music'.

Compared to central Berlin, residential St. John's Wood seemed half-urban at the most, mainly because of the scarcity, at that time, of large blocks of flats. True, the working-class terraces in St. John's Wood were already being converted into fashionable and 'desirable' residences; but It was the war that made way for large-scale redevelopment. Perhaps it took old flat-dwellers like my family to appreciate the garden of our house, the wrought iron steps leading down to it from a conservatory, the sycamore tree as tall as the house, and the little pond in the garden. Just before we left Berlin my mother had turned her bedroom into a veritable birdhouse, with cages on the top of every wardrobe and every other suitable surface. In St. John's Wood we could keep a succession of cats and kittens, budgerigars and tropical fish in the conservatory, goldfish in the pond. To these I added whatever other aquatic and amphibian creatures I could catch in the country, though many of them, like the eel I brought back from a holiday, can hardly have felt at home in a London pond. By force-feeding with milk my father managed to save the life of a sick hedge-hog we had found.

I still hankered after the real country, for open spaces less knowable than Regent's Park, Primrose Hill, or even the plausible show of wilderness put up by Hampstead Heath. London had other kinds of wilderness to explore, but we hardly penetrated beyond the West End, with Kensington and Chelsea as our Far West. The City, the East End and the Docks – not to mention everything beyond the South Bank – remained almost unknown to me until the war had begun to transform them.

Some time before his death in 1936 my grandfather took us to our first opera – a performance of *La Bohème* that left me with the image of velvet jackets as emblems of the artistic life. The squalor and death by consumption that went with it didn't detract from its fascination, but heightened the appeal of living dangerously, amorously and melodiously to the end. The cinema was another belated discovery of those years, especially forbidden horror films like *Frankenstein* or *Dr. Mabuse*, with the early Tarzan films as close runners-up.

Our cook and housemaid at that time were Austrian, and one of them used to tell me stories about the depravities of Vienna night-life. It never occurred to me to ask whether they were based on first-hand experience or picked up from lurid magazines. To me they were as real and unreal as the case histories in Freud, the novels I read voraciously or the films I saw.

IN 1937 I left the Hall for Westminster School. My father, who could barely afford to send me there, had got me admitted after an interview with the departing Head Master, Costley-White. Luckily, the son of the German Ambassador, Ribbentrop, had also left before my first term. I was just tall enough not to have to wear the Eton jacket prescribed for shorter boys, and could begin as a fully-fledged gentleman in morning coat, striped trousers, top hat and obligatory umbrella or cane. That uniform – abolished during the war – must have been an effective means of inculcating the sense of superiority which public schools were intended to inculcate, combined with other qualities far less questionable. There were things one couldn't do in that garb. In fact there were precious few things one could do, if one was a day boy, except walk or ride to school and back with as unselfconscious a dignity as one could maintain in the face of stares, rude or sarcastic comments in tube trains, and the occasional stone aimed at the top hat by less privileged boys in the remaining working-class streets of St. John's Wood. Yet a silk hat is a very much tougher thing than it seems. Mine withstood several drenchings under the changing-room shower, being used as a football in Dean's Yard, being hit by missiles, being sat on, trodden on, bashed with umbrellas and sticks.

A feud began almost as soon as I went to the new school. A boy called Meyer, half German and half Scottish, went into the changing-room saying that anyone who opened the bathroom door while he was in it would be beaten up. I couldn't resist the challenge, opened the door and started a private war that lasted for years, in and out of the boxing ring, and ended only after an ambush that left my face permanently scarred – a moral victory for me, who had usually beaten him in straight fights, but a physical one for him and his assistant.

But this was a private war, and Westminster had nothing to do with the tensions that caused it. Relations between most boys at the school, and between most boys and me, were peaceable and easy-going. The only two older boys who threw their weight about in my House, Busby's, were a Yugoslav and an Iraqi, and even they were good-natured at heart, and could be dealt with if one stood up to them. The Yugoslav, Ivan Račic, used to order small boys to scrub his back under the shower, a privilege to which the strict rules of precedence didn't entitle him. He counted on the greater amenability of English boys, but would admit defeat if he was not obeyed. When he and the Iraqi, Ali Jawdat, taunted me about Germany and the Jews, what began as an attempt to brow-beat me turned into a political discussion that ended quite amicably. Even fagging proved less humiliating than I had feared, because the House Monitor whom, for a term or so, I had to serve in his study was too sensitive and decent to demand more than formal attendance.

At school I joined the Madrigal Society, singing in a performance of the St. Matthew Passion – not very well, because my voice had only recently broken and hadn't found its true range, and because my sight-reading was poor, so that I had difficulty in keeping to the right part. I also entered for an inter-House boxing tournament, though my liking for the sport had already cooled, and I had better things to do in my spare time than train in the gymnasium. I got as far as the Finals, nonetheless, only to suffer a bloody defeat. My opponent was a friend of mine, and he had asked me not to punch him too hard. By the time I resolved to go back on my promise it was too late, for he had winded me in the first round with a punch to the diaphragm, and proved too quick for me after that. The occasion mattered to me because my father was among the spectators, so that I felt ashamed of my poor performance and blood-stained vest. He and I were given a lift home by the father of my arch-enemy, Meyer, and that made it worse.

In the summer of 1938 we stayed at a farm in North Wales, near Betws-y-Coed, at the invitation of my grandmother and uncle. My father joined us there for a few days, my mother for a slightly longer stay. I got on well with the farmer's children and found their way of life so attractive that for a long time I wanted to be a farmer. About thirty years later the same thing happened to my son – in Teesdale – though his infatuation didn't last as long as mine. It was not till later visits to North Wales that I grew aware of the extreme hardships that beset the sheep farmers there. To play with the farmer's children in the hay loft or feed the poultry was one thing, quite another to make a living out of that land. On my walks I collected wildflowers and ferns, some of which my father planted in our London garden. This, too, became a habit, and I still grow wildflowers, much preferring them to most of the highly hybridized variants, and did so even when our garden was a city one.

Westminster School was close not only to the Abbey, where we attended morning services, but to the Houses of Parliament; and political passions were bound to penetrate into Dean's Yard even before the Czechoslovak crisis, when the school was briefly evacuated to Sussex. As far as I am aware, the sons of Labour MPs at school outnumbered those of Conservatives, even at that time, before the school's liberalism had become overt. Lively meetings of the Political Society were held at the houses of masters or parents, and these, too, tended towards the Left. I remember such meetings at the houses of Andrew Wordsworth, a master, and at the Wedgwood-Benns'. Another master, M. W. Blake, stood for election as a Labour candidate. In a school play written and produced by a later Head Master, J. D. Carleton, I played the part of Hitler. What may have been my first published poem appeared in our House magazine, *The College Street Clarion*, in April 1939; it was a pompous Petrarchan sonnet on the German annexation of Czechoslovakia, 'The Death of a Nation'. In the same magazine I published a very different piece of verse called 'The Science Master in Love'. I kept no copy of it, but found it again recently in a Digest of extracts from the *Clarion* for the years 1938–1948. The sonnet was produced in class as a verse-writing exercise. This piece was spontaneous and slap-dash, written for the fun of it:

> Thy sparkling eyes like manganese dioxide seem,
> Thy rosy mouth doth like acidic litmus gleam,
> Thy waving locks are of a fine sulphuric shade,
> Thy teeth like chalk (as that which in the lab. I made).
>
> The sight of thee, my dear beloved Felicity,
> By twelve per cent reduces my acidity,

The sound-waves of thy voice add sugar to thy charms,
With nine ergs' pressure I would lock thee in my arms.

Thy flowery breath hath strong ammonia's pungent smell,
Thy song resounds just like a chromium-plated bell,
Thy touch corrodes like H_2SO_4 (dilute),
To win thee I would give the leather of my boot.

O dear Felicity, consent to be my wife:
And lessen by a twenty-sixth my cost of life . . .
And when the calcium of my bones returns to soil,
And I have shuffled off this platinum wire coil,
When foul bacilli eat my decomposing flesh,
Then sodium chloride tears will be released afresh.

My grandmother, who kept copies of most of my early literary exercises, had no use for such frivolity. She did preserve the script of a speech I prepared for the school Political Society, opposing the motion that 'This House considers that the German nation should be annihilated after the war'. That must have been after the school's evacuation to Lancing College. The solemn high-mindedness of the speech was of the same order as that of the sonnet, which my grandmother also kept and translated into German. For a long time this sort of high-mindedness was to get in the way of my development as a writer, which demanded not generalities and commonplaces but a grasp of the particulars of experience, if only those picked up in the chemistry lab. At the same period I was obsessed with the rival claims of science and of poetry, or of 'progress' and nature, the subject of another piece of verse fustian written in 1939, 'The Beast's Farewell', and of several poems written over the next few years.

In the debate I said: 'The annihilation of the German nation would constitute a great loss to the culture of Europe. Germany has produced the majority of the great philosophers of the Western world. It is to Germany that Europe owes most of its finest music.' That was a mere Appendix, of course, to my main argument, summarized like this: 'A nation consists of individuals. Most men would hesitate to condemn individuals indiscriminately to death or misery, yet they are prepared thus to condemn a nation. As long as such a view prevails there can be no progress.' Yet it was through German culture that I tried to preserve some continuity with my own childhood. The earliest translation of a German poem I remember doing was of a sentimental piece by a minor nineteenth-century poet called Theodor Körner, and its theme was loyal friendship maintained in the teeth of separation. I did it in December 1939, describing it as a 'poetical translation', which seems appropriate:

Last Visit to the Brook

The boy sat near the water's edge
And listened to its murmuring sound.
He understood the whispered pledge
As words of one in friendship bound;
And while his brothers roamed o'er meadows wide
He watched the brook, sat silent by its side.

However, that boy feels 'deep longing surge and rise', and decides he cannot stay there for ever:

'The joys of peace no longer soothe my heart.
To seek the stormy world I must depart.

But should I see thee flowing fast,
Thy thundering passage onward wend,
In foaming waters rushing past,
I'll recognize my faithful friend.
Now we must part until another day.'
With one last glance he wandered far away.

The diction of that exercise points to the fact that my favourite English poet to date, before Shakespeare – three of whose plays I was to know almost by heart, because they were set as examination texts at various stages of my school career – was Thomas Gray, whose *Selected Poems*, vellum-clad and edited by Edmund Gosse in 1885, I bought in 1939. The next was Tennyson. In a waxed and glossy leather binding suitable for Victorian coffee tables, I acquired his *Collected Poems* at school, either buying it from a friend at Busby's or swapping it for something other than a book. It was Tennyson's 'Tithonus' and 'The Lotus-Eaters' that I learned by heart, attracted by their languid melancholia; and that influence was so apparent in my poem 'The Beast's Farewell' that my sophisticated friend Freddy laughed at its inflated and outmoded rhetoric.

The first translation was followed by others, rather less 'poetical' of Goethe's would-be Pindaric free verse poems 'Das Göttliche', 'Gesang der Geister über den Wassern' and 'Grenzen der Menschheit', to which I was drawn by their high-mindedness rather than by their superiority as verse to Körner's tear-jerker, though my father has intimated to me in a letter that Körner might not be the best of models for my own first efforts, and I had taken the hint to heart.

Another literary work I produced in 1939 was a short story called 'War Aims', which I had the cheek to submit to the magazine *Lilliput* – handwritten, on lined school exercise paper! Being rather more down-to-earth than my political speech, this war story was anti-pacifist and ironic. Its point was the difficulty of reconciling the kind of humanism I had expounded in the debate with the realities of war, as I imagined them at the time. The story was returned with a non-committal rejection slip, the first of many I was to receive.

By this time, at the age of fifteen, poetry was beginning to replace natural history, music and politics as my dominant concern. One of the more advanced of our masters had introduced the class to the work of T. S. Eliot, in an anthology, at a time when T. S. Eliot was far from being regarded as a pillar of the Establishment for educational purposes. Eliot's poem or poems made little conscious impression on me till some two or three years later, when I was won over not by 'The Waste Land' but by the earliest of the 'Four Quartets' to come my way. When I submitted something to Richard Wollheim at school for a very avant-garde magazine to be called 'Bogueur' he was planning to edit, he told me to read Dryden. Though the title alone was provocative under the reign of J. T. Christie, our Head Master, I am told that the magazine did materialize. Far from being ready to contribute – I was never to fit into any sort of smart set in literature or outside it – I must have missed that publication completely, because I thought it had never materialized until my friend Freddy told me he still had 'one, if not two issues' of it in 1977. Nor was I ready to take the sound advice about Dryden, who might well have knocked some of the maudlin romanticism out of my verse.

The ambiguous 'Bogueur' – it had to be French, because everything smart was French in those years, and much of that smartness was bogus – reminds me that homosexuality was the bugbear at that school, tolerant and liberal though it was in almost every other regard. Needless to say, the school was full of it, simply because most of the boys, even day boys, were either passing through a homo-erotic phase or leading lives that made contacts with girls impossible. The forbidden thing, therefore, was sexual and erotic need itself, since its existence was not acknowledged; and the more it was repressed, the more likely it was to break out in its most forbidden and generally abominated forms. The assumption was that decent boys do not know, and do not need to know, anything about sexuality. In practice, a good many boys at Westminster may have got through their school years without any sexual experience, though few of them can have avoided some sort of homo-erotic, sublimated hero-worshipping attachment. Those who could not resist physical contact – if only puppyish 'fun and games' – or were seduced into such common practices as mutual masturbation didn't necessarily become homosexuals in later life; but something of the surreptitiousness, 'filth' and 'shame' of those lapses was likely to stick to all sexual activity, with obvious consequences. What astonished me, when I was told about the later lives of some of the boys I had known at school, is how many of them have remained exclusively or sporadically homosexual; and how many more, with wives, children, and outwardly conventional careers, remained entangled in a social, ethical and emotional nexus set up in their school years. I doubt that in any country but Britain one can look at a prominent man, statesman or writer, and suddenly see the face of a prep school boy, a public school or grammar school boy, thinly masked by skin that has managed to wrinkle.

·   ·   ·   ·   ·   ·   ·   ·   ·   ·

THOUGH I published early, and had made literary connections even at this time, without being aware of looking for them, the only success I wanted was to write good poems – an end far more difficult to attain than Freddy's* Ivory Tower or the social acceptance he craved. It is easy enough in retrospect to see why it took me so long to write my *own* poems, good or bad. All my responses were exaggerated, inwardly over-dramatized, as it were, and utterly unstable, because I was trying out one stance, one identity, after another. The same Oxford acquaintance who disparaged my friends told me that I should

---

* Freddy Hurdis-Jones, a friend of Hamburger since their Westminster school days: 'a veteran and inveterate homosexual', admired for his 'precocity, eloquence and self-assurance'. – ED.

never write good poems because English had not been my first language. It may be that my linguistic transplantation at the age of nine has something to do with the distrust of verbal virtuosity that became acute in my later work. 'Word-scepticism', as Hofmannsthal called it, is as prevalent in twentieth-century poetry as its antipole, 'word-mysticism', – and much has been written about the aspiration of poetry not to the 'condition of music' but to the 'condition of silence'. Yet long before my word-scepticism became effective or explicit in my writing, I marked this passage in Jeremy Taylor's *Holy Dying*: 'We form our words with the breath of our nostrils, we have the less to live upon for every word we speak.' I can only wonder what made me mark that passage at the age of nineteen, when I had been far from sparing of words in my writing up to that time; but when I opened that book again at random, and re-read the marked passage, it struck me as a strange anticipation of the whole complex, word-scepticism and word-mysticism, that opposed the pull of silence to my writing in later years. To write in a language that is not one's first is to be at one remove from the seeming identity of word and thing. The gap made by that remove can be bridged by close adherence to convention – the over-assimilation to which 'naturalized' subjects are prone – as in my early verse, or it can be accepted, left open, explored, as in my later.

An even more daunting obstacle was something to which Freddy alluded when he wrote that I was less self-contained than he. For at least another decade my work was so variously influenced, apt to wander off in so many different directions, that I often despaired of finding my own way. Because of that uncertainty in myself I needed the response of friends and critics, yet could never be satisfied or reassured if that response was favourable. 'I know you want some recognition', X wrote in the June of 1941, 'You will grow to laugh at it.' And he was right. In poetry there were no ends, only new expeditions after every arrival. X was also right about my need, in youth, for heroes and mentors, due to the same uncertainty in myself and the early loss of my father. 'All men struggle for self-advancement', he wrote, 'and there is nothing more mutable than friendship. You are more likely to be hurt by this than most people. He who makes idols will always be picking up the pieces.'

For all my chronic dissatisfaction, I got a great deal out of my first stay at Oxford, becoming so deeply attached to the place and its surroundings that a decade later I would still go there whenever I could on visits, often returning with the nucleus of a poem. There was much about the university life that I disliked, since the war had not yet changed the social structure, and much of the would-be intellectual life struck me as distinctly decadent. Yet I was half-fascinated at first by the tall, stooping figure of Simon Asquith, who would recite poems in a booming voice after midnight as he crossed Peckwater Quad to the lavatory; even by the deathly white powdered face of another undergraduate who rose at noon, walked to some unknown destination, impeccably dressed, and never talked to anyone I knew on the way. The place was full of people putting all their energy into strenuous and futile efforts to be different. One of them described himself as a 'male lesbian' and made a fetish of the soiled bedclothes of his friends. There were parties attended by bizarre hangers-on of the university, like Professor Robert Sencourt, a friend of T. S. Eliot's, who molested me with invitations to dance with him until I had to run away and hide as the only alternative to knocking him down. He told me about his contacts in neutral countries that would soon bring the war to an end. In my own primitive fashion I, too, was an intellectual, and it seemed impossible to escape that sort of company if I was to have any social life at all. When I was in the army, Sencourt tried to pick up my friend X* in London.

On the whole, though, my puritanism and purism – priggishness, I'd call it now, but didn't and couldn't then, because I hadn't yet seen through the machinery that compelled me to live up to some idea of myself projected by my super-ego, my taskmaster – proved stronger than my curiosity and adventurousness. As soon as I was in danger of simply enjoying myself, the task-master rapped me over the knuckles. Any enjoyment more gross than that of literature, music, scenery, architecture, painting or theology wasn't good enough for him; and if it wasn't good enough for him, it mustn't be good enough for the encapsulated sensual man whom Freddy recognized in me, but couldn't help to liberate. My older or more mature friends knew perfectly well that my depressions were bound up with this repression, but nothing said or hinted at could make me admit as much to myself. In 1943, when I was in the army, Stephen Spender wrote

---

* A close friend, who 'has forbidden me to name him in these memoirs'.

about his impression of me at an earlier period: 'The trouble, I think, with you is that you let yourself get too depressed. Life is not so easy that one can stand being depressed by other people more than a certain amount, unless one is insensitive or unless one makes up one's mind to help the other person, and pay some price. I didn't feel that I could help you, so I didn't want to be depressed by you. On the whole I've developed a useful (to me) form of selfishness, which is not to see people when they're unhappy.

'If you could possibly see your way to being a little happier when you are with other people, you would get more out of them.

'Personally I don't think I could have borne to know Hölderlin – at all events not after he was 25. Our own romantics, Shelley, Keats, etc. were very cheerful and companionable people, when with each other. I hope our New Romantics will take note of this, and not be depressing Company.

'I don't in the least criticize you for being unhappy, but I think you ought to make up your mind to prevent its showing too much and too long; or it will affect your relations with your friends. A year or two of unhappiness will not do you any harm. But I hope that later you will find that you are able to develop a group personality which belies your sad solitary personality. I am all for the smile and grease-paint on the clown in company, and the broken heart when he is alone ... Forgive me for writing like this, but you raised the subject, and I feel you need a father, which I prematurely am in some lives ...'

Stephen Spender was quite right, of course, in terms of the accepted understanding of relations between writer and society in Britain, at a time when reputations trickled down from dominant social-cum-'cultural' sets into what one could still believe to be a general public. Although I came to see the necessity of good manners, as a regulator of formal transactions, including political ones, between individuals and groups, I never learnt to wear the mask or make-up that would have made me acceptable in such a system. If, for reasons of my own, I could not enter into a party game, I had no choice but to be a wet blanket and drop out. To try to become a poet at all was duplicity enough, where poetry could never fit easily into any order outside it or have any function in it that was more than decorative; and where one had to take on other functions to make a living and survive. That was a grim prospect, and if one did not face it grimly, the chances were that one would be diverted from it into one of the rôles – including the clown's, the charmer's and the shocker's – for which society did have a use.

Earlier, when I was at Oxford, Stephen Spender had also written to warn me of the dangers of hero-worship, and the burden placed on the hero by the worshipper; but I must have destroyed that letter because it came closer to the root of the trouble than the one I have quoted, and threatened the self-delusion by which I lived at that time. My hero-worship of Stephen Spender, in any case, was long behind me when he wrote his letter. For a father figure I needed someone as unapproachable, exacting and austere as T. S. Eliot, whose poems I could not imitate and whose pronouncements I could take to heart only to punish myself once more with demands of 'impersonality', classical rigour and ascetic spirituality; which reminds me that at Oxford I imposed long fasts on myself, only to test my will and prove to myself that I could do it.

During my first term I had made friends with a girl older than myself – the girl I planned to look up when I was at Torquay – but she had gone down in the summer and become an A. T. S. officer that year. I wrote to Joy at the vicarage her father had left twelve years earlier, and she begged me not to look for her there: 'Please may I ask you not to try to find me anywhere unless you have definitely heard from me that I shall be there at the appointed time', she wrote in October, also remarking very perceptively: 'You seem to flourish on wild goose chases, lost addresses and the like!' In September she had thanked me for writing her 'a reasonable letter' for once. I saw her from time to time over the next year or so, when she could London, and she was one of my few links at that period with a world less inbred than my Oxford or London circle of artists and intellectuals; and she was more intelligent than a good many of those intellectuals. 'In fact occasionally I am tempted to envy you your morbid preoccupations and to weary of the active energetic life which you presume is mine,' she wrote from Winchester in March 1942. At one time I almost involved her in a very different sort of life when I took her to a London night club to which I had been invited by the mother of an Oxford friend, and the mother decided it would be good for her son to see more of Joy; but she was too sensible to fall for the glamour of an aristocratic demi-monde. At the same time she urged me never to become a private soldier, a warning I could not obey, when it transpired that the Navy would not have me. 'You must have someone to laugh at you,

Michael,' she wrote in 1942, 'You take yourself so seriously. Nevertheless I am very sincere when I say that I am looking forward to reading your book.' If only I could have seen more of her, and hadn't lost touch with her entirely when I joined up, Joy could have done more than anyone I knew at that time to make me human. The 'someone' I needed to laugh at my absurdities had to be a woman.

The Oxford poets I knew at this time – Sidney Keyes, Drummond Allison, John Heath-Stubbs, David Wright and Philip Larkin – were far less outrageous in their behaviour, dress and way of life than the vaguely literary aesthetes of the smart set. Sidney Keyes came to see me at Christ Church and asked me to read the typescript of what was to be his first book of poems. He was also interested in German poetry and knew of my Hölderlin and Rilke translations, still unpublished at the time. We were fellow contributors to an anthology of Oxford and Cambridge writing that appeared in 1942, in which my very first published poem appeared; and to *Oxford Poetry 1942–1943*, another anthology. Though older, Sidney Keyes was only a little less shy than I was, and as serious about his work. I am sure that my comments on it were of little use to him; and it was his second, posthumous, book that impressed me more. Our acquaintance was very brief, since he left in 1941 and had been posted abroad by the time I joined his regiment. The one meeting with Drummond Allison I remember took place not at Oxford but in Soho, at the Swiss pub in Old Compton Street, where Allison's talk proved as vivacious as Dylan Thomas's.

Philip Larkin kindly acted as a go-between after I had gone down and was waiting in London for my call-up. John Lehmann had spent a Year or more 'considering' my Hölderlin translations and leading me to believe that he would publish them, but had asked J.B. Leishman, an established translator, to produce a book of Hölderlin translations instead. When I heard about this, belatedly, I found a new publisher for my work in Tambimuttu, at the same Soho haunt, and a ridiculous race began between the two publishers. Philip Larkin dropped a hint to Leishman over dinner: 'Perhaps I seemed rather rude', he wrote to me on October 2nd 1942, 'because having cheerfully embarked on the subject (I know a man whose life you have ruined) I was in an awkward position: I didn't want to appear holding a brief for you, yet I didn't want to suggest your versions were inferior in any way to his (or else the story would lose its point), nor did I feel like suggesting they were superior (not across the dinner table). Nor did I want to stress the only other aspect – that he'd got the job simply because of name etc. – So after a brief exchange on the difficulty of getting even German texts in these days the subject dropped uneasily among the salt-cellars.' It was an impossible undertaking, and my life wasn't ruined either. Tambimuttu won the race, it turned out, because I had been first in the field and he had a head start on Lehmann. Later I was to meet Leishman, as he suggested to Larkin I should, and the rivalry was forgotten.

· · · · · · · · · ·

. . . I WAS well on the way to becoming a professional writer, – partly, I now think, through unconscious pressures from the insecurity precipitated by my father's death – when I should have been learning to relax. Yet even by 1942 I had begun to submit my poems to older writers for criticism – to Stephen Spender, to Herbert Read, and to T. S. Eliot. To Eliot, more as a revered poet than as a Faber editor, I also sent my Hölderlin translations. He wrote about them on November 12th 1942: 'I am very sorry for the considerable delay over your Hölderlin translation. After a good deal of deliberation and consultation we have decided that such a book is a luxury for which we could not spare the paper at a time like this. While I admire Hölderlin's poetry and should like to see it more widely known in England, the sale for translations of poetry is always small. It is not a direction in which we feel justified in using our supplies at present. I hope very much that your admirable translations may be published by someone and, of course, if paper were unlimited, the ideal way would be to publish the text and translation on opposite pages. I think that the chief value of translations is for people who have some acquaintance with the language but cannot read an author of any difficulty with ease . . .' About my own juvenile verse, which he returned with a few annotations about a year later, he wrote to me:

'I have been a very long time over your poems and you may say that the result of my opinion is not valuable enough to justify it, but I do like to keep poems for a considerable time in order to lay them aside and reread them. I think I see what Herbert Read means by saying that this rhetoric and not poetry, though I should try myself to find other ways of putting it. I have made a few minor comments on the text, but those are not important. What I feel is that I do not find each poem to be a separate and distinct experience, and the general effect is of your being more interested in a persisting mood of your own than in the particular occasion. This helps to give a generality which partakes of what Read calls rhetoric, and a certain monotony out of which no specific sensations emerge. The actual writing is all right on the whole, though no word ever seems to be invested with a new life in the context. I don't know what will happen but I shall be glad to see the next stage . . .'

Of Eliot's comments, which I didn't preserve, I remember this one placed against the word 'bird': 'What sort of bird?' – and that question had the weight of pages of general criticism. I hadn't yet learnt to use my eyes, for reasons connected with Eliot's general strictures and my extreme introversion at this time. The things I saw evoked moods and sensations, but I wasn't interested enough in their quiddity. The real birds I had both observed and read about were not the birds I put into my poems.

It was in 1942 or 1943 that I first met Eliot – at the Spenders' flat in Maresfield Gardens, Hampstead. He had been to dinner there, together with E. M. Forster, Julian Huxley and Geoffrey Faber, and I arrived later, in time to hear Natasha Spender play a Beethoven sonata. I don't remember a word of what was said, only my awe at being in the presence of the living poet I admired more than any other. E. M. Forster, in fact, was far more inclined to be gracious, but I wasn't interested in him – a mere prose writer! Graciousness, in any case, was not to be expected of the High Priest of an austere, ascetic cult – who may well have been talking about wine or cheese. It was enough, much more than enough, to be in that room, breathing the same air.

While at Christ Church I had also begun to correspond with an earlier, and very different, hero of mine, Hermann Hesse, whose books I devoured at school, buying those not in my parents' library in Miss Waterhouse's shop or borrowing them from a fellow devotee, a childhood friend of my mother's recently turned psycho-analyst, Hannah Ries. At Oxford I wanted to translate *Der Steppenwolf*, my favourite, and wrote to Hesse in Switzerland. He replied that he could not grant me permission, since the rights were tied up with his German publishers, with whom he was not in communication, but he sent me a number of privately printed works. Later, he informed me that the novel I wanted to translate had already been published in

England before the war. He added: 'Certainly *Steppenwolf*, in exceptional cases, can be read by a very young person without damage – if the reader is a potential poet or has a related vocation.' The correspondence dribbled on into the fifties, but my admiration for Hesse's work hardly outlasted my adolescence, and I was never to translate his work. (The only exception, some lines of verse set by Richard Strauss in his *Four Last Songs*, doesn't count, because the translation was commissioned, and because translating words for music is a peculiar activity I have never felt happy about.)

'I LIKE your lines about him,' Herbert Read wrote to me on November 15th 1943, 'but I think it is frightfully difficult to be successfully elegiac. I mean that the very consciousness of the attitude or expression is somehow false. I feel this even about a poem like *Adonais*.' Herbert Read was commenting on a poem I had written for Sidney Keyes, who had been reported missing in North Africa and – as the same letter confirmed – almost certainly killed. I took the indirect stricture to heart and never published the poem.

When Herbert Read died I took his advice again, though no elegy I might have written for him could have been quite as inadequate as those early conventional lines, written for someone I liked and respected as a poet but had known only briefly as a friend. For more than a quarter of a century Herbert Read was a friend to me, and the words quoted are an example of the special kind of friendship he was generous enough to give a writer more than thirty years younger than himself. I don't remember how it came about that I got to know him when I was only seventeen. His earliest letter to me, of December 1941, suggests that I approached him at that time, sending him a poem. Possibly we had already met, either at Oxford or in London. What his letters bring home to me now is how much I owe to his advice and criticism in those early years. It is characteristic of the man, and of the rôle he adopted towards me, that his letters reveal more about my preoccupations over the years than of his. Herbert Read was shy, gentle and reticent; but he was also unassuming to the point of self-effacement. That is why he could take on young people like me without expecting any sort of allegiance, let alone idolatry or adulation. As he knew well enough, my supreme idol in those early years was T. S. Eliot, whose very remoteness as a person made him a better object of idolatry; but Herbert Read himself was devoted to

Eliot, and never tried to assert any kind of authority that might have counteracted the other. For the same reason there was never any need for me to revolt against Herbert Read's guidance, as I had to revolt against Eliot's authority before I could begin to be myself; and the simple human affection which I felt for Read from the first could grow without strain or disturbance.

Herbert Read's letters to me are a record of unselfishness in a thankless task – almost inevitably thankless, because I simply wasn't able to help him in the way he helped me – not, at least, until the last years of our friendship, and no letter records the meeting at which our rôles, for once, were reversed, and Herbert broke his reticence to tell me about the harrowing stresses and frustrations of his life. It was then that I urged him to reduce his public and professional commitments before it was too late, and to return to the kind of work which I had always considered his true vocation – the work that included his poetry, his novel *The Green Child*, the auto-biographical *Annals of Innocence and Experience*, essays on literature like those in his early book *The Sense of Glory*, and some of his writings on anarcho-syndicalism. Only his illness forced him into the partial retirement which he had desperately needed since his middle years, but thought he could not afford. It may have come too late, after all.

For a long time I took his kindness too much for granted; perhaps all the time, since it was the shock of his death that made me re-read his letters and discover the extent of his self-effacing furtherance of my work. If this sounds like conventional piety, as false as the elegiac sort, I must be specific here and confess a real sin of omission. It was Herbert Read who did more than anyone to bring about the publication of my *Hölderlin: Poems and Fragments*, a translation whose progress he had followed and encouraged since the beginning of our association. I cannot understand what made me dedicate the book not to him but to the memory of Arthur Waley, a man I never met or corresponded with. Was it a ghostly residue of Eliot's doctrine of 'impersonality', haunting me still? A temporary absence of mind or heart? A perverse kind of tribute to the unselfishness of Herbert Read's motives? Whatever the cause, I was taking his help for granted, long after I had learnt that his readiness to be bothered has always been rare among writers, and is becoming still rarer than it used to be.

In his own quiet and uncomplaining way, Herbert Read was one more victim of the philistinism that punishes British poets with more neglect and indifference than most of them can bear, while insidiously tempting each to become 'somebody', which means almost anybody other than a poet. Herbert Read preserved his innocence and his romanticism, but those very qualities proved detrimental to some of the activities – such as art criticism, sociology and psychology – into which he was drawn by genuine enthusiasms, only to find himself trapped in a variety of institutionalized functions. The elegy which I cannot and will not write was written by himself – in the form of a tribute to Hölderlin, the same poet who presided over our friendship, linking Herbert's last letters to his first. It is the poem 'A Gift for Scardanelli' from Herbert Read's *Moon Farm*:

> The clouds are unanchored: they might
> fall from the sky to cover you
> I have brought you a basket of figs
> and some fine linen
> but alas
> no white goat to slaughter
> and fingers have faltered
> that should have played the flute.

I wish I could be sure what poem I sent Herbert Read in November or December 1941, but I should think it was the persona poem 'Hölderlin', written at about that time, and the first poem I published after my contributions to the school magazine. Herbert Read wrote: 'I like it very much. I would like to read it again & perhaps I could say something more critical when we meet.' His letter was from his office at Routledge, but he gave me his home address in Buckinghamshire and suggested a meeting in London. Our earliest meetings were over tea at Yarners, near Broadcasting House, and once we were joined there by George Orwell, whose gaunt appearance and forthright manner impressed me, though I scarcely knew his work at the time. During those war years, too, Herbert Read once came to my mother's house to look at a collection of ancient glass phials and jars – Phoenician, he said – that had belonged to my grandfather. The visit stands out not only because it was an instance of Read's extraordinary kindness – such glassware, it turned out, was fairly common and of little archaeological interest to an expert – but because I recall only one later meeting on either's home ground, in the flat which the Reads occupied for a time in London. Most of our later meetings were over lunch at his London club – where he introduced me to tripe and onions, a plain demotic dish as incongruous with the menu of the Reform Club, even in war-time conditions, as Herbert Read himself was with London club society. From time to time we met in other people's homes or in wholly public places like the Institute of Contemporary Arts. In 1964 I was to have stayed with the Reads in Yorkshire, but the lecture that was taking me to York was postponed, and the new date clashed with an engagement of his elsewhere. Of our meetings all I can say is that all of them were a delight, since he bridged the thirty years' gap between us without effort or condescension. He never seemed bored or moody, though he had the habit of suddenly absenting himself inwardly from indifferent social gatherings. When there were silences between us, they were congenial to me, and as relaxed as our conversation.

Herbert Read's letters of 1942 are mainly concerned with my early Hölderlin versions, which he read in typescript but was unable to accept for Routledge, and to a surrealist fantasy by X which I also sent him. (This work – a prose poem rather than a novel – was declined 'chiefly because of its awkward length', and it has never been published.) In February of that year I invited Herbert Read to address the English Club at Oxford, but he replied: 'I only manage to get through my work by a strict rationing of such obligations, & I am afraid I have more than enough for the next six months.' I was too young and inexperienced to realize that he had more than enough for the next six years, or sixteen years; but the more I saw of him, the better I understood that business and busy-ness were his chronic affliction. 'I am really sorry to have missed you this time,' he wrote in April, 'but I have been so overwhelmed with work and business. I have to address two conferences next week, & have had to prepare the lectures, in addition to my usual work. And all kinds of engagements in town.

'I am returning your Hölderlin translations, after reading them again. I like them very much – they don't read at all 'literally', but at the same time they give such an exact rendering of the form and tone of the poems. I wish I could be more optimistic about publication, but I don't see much chance as long as the present conditions continue. But I think that when publication does become possible, you ought to make a substantial volume – a long introduction and all the best poems . . . I hope you will write about Blake. I would like to see a fresh point of view on a poet I am so devoted to.'

The really substantial volume had to wait another twenty-five years or so, and it was published by Routledge when Herbert had already left the firm. The long introduction, on the other hand, got written in time for the 1943 edition, packed with all my youthful pseudo-learning and miscellaneous references to almost any writer who preoccupied me at the time, including Blake. That long introduction had to be scrapped for later editions, and I was never able to replace it. The older I grew, the less expansive my writing became, and the less value I attached to opinions.

By October 1942 I must have begun to feel uneasy about burdening Read with my work and letters, but his answer was characteristically generous: 'The apology should be mine, for neglecting your letter. But you know how busy I am, & you must never feel conscience-stricken if I seem indifferent. I am always glad to hear from you and wish I could find more time to see you.

'I have read the poems with real interest, & do not find anything for definite criticism – but that rather implies, & it is true, that their virtues are rather negative. If only there were more lines like: 'To the soft tyranny of drums' – that gave me the authentic thrill. But mostly I find just the clever twist of rhetoric. It interests me, but it does not move me. The Hölderlin poem is surely the best.

'I am being honest with you, because that is my way of encouraging you. I don't want to dismiss you with conventional praise – I want you to press on, & show me more of your work in the future . . .'

No one could have done more for me than that. The 'clever twist of rhetoric' was not to be expunged for a longtime, because ideas remained more real to me than people, places and things. I could not act on Herbert Read's advice until that had changed – and it was a matter of learning to live, rather than to write. Yet at least I knew what was needed – thanks to that letter, and another, of April 15th 1943: 'The relatively leisurely intervals of a conference at Oxford give me a chance to catch up with my correspondence. I have, since I got your letter, read the poems three or four times. "Profane Dying" is an ambitious & on the whole successful effort. I think it is rhetorical rather than poetic – a distinction I am always in the habit of making. The images are apt, the expression forceful: but not essentially poetic. But this does not mean that it is not worth writing. Fine rhetoric, indeed, is an art we don't sufficiently practise these days & perhaps we have lost the tradition. It demands a high degree of technical "finish"

& in this respect I think your poem falls short. The rhythm is occasionally too staccato & there are awkward compressions and ellipses. But the force of your poem wins through.'

It wasn't Herbert Read's fault that I took this response to be ultimately favourable. My principle in later years was to ignore all favourable comments on my work and make what use I could of the unfavourable. What I took to be his approval in this case made me publish that poem sequence – written at fever heat while I was waiting in London for my call-up, over several days and nights of such intense absorption that I refused to talk to anyone and had to have food brought up to my room – only to freeze with embarrassment every time I was confronted with the printed text. Yet the point about rhetoric did sink in, leaving an irritation that made me look for a remedy.

.   .   .   .

OUR LAST meeting, over lunch at his London club, must have taken place before his retirement from Routledge, since it was then that I begged him to give up some of his many functions and commitments; but my unchronological memory tells me only that it began like earlier meetings, with Herbert as a quietly attentive adviser, before taking the turn I have mentioned. My only regret is that this did not happen sooner, and that we never met again. It had taken me too long to grow up and understand that being a father – literary or otherwise – is at least as hard as being a son.

In 1966, before leaving for America, I received this answer to a letter I had written Herbert about his recollections of T. S. Eliot: 'Thank you for writing about my T. S. E. Memoir. I am glad Wesleyan sent you a copy & that you enjoyed it. I did not know you had been to Wesleyan – we enjoyed our two visits there very much. I went to Mount Holyoke once to give a lecture & it seemed a very pleasant college. You should be happy there . . .

'I come to London as little as possible. I find it very exhausting. But I would like to see you again & will let you know when there is an opportunity. I am very sorry I missed you when you came to York, but I hope you will come again & then you must stay with us. I saw a little of the University & they were kind enough to give me one of their first honorary degrees.

'I always read your poems and reviews with pleasure when I come across them & hope you will always keep me in touch with your published work.'

I did so, and he read it carefully enough to point out one or two technical errors in *Hölderlin: Poems and Fragments* so serious that part of the edition had to be withdrawn and reset. His wing was over me almost to the end, for it was in his letter of February 26th 1967 that he did me this service. On January 23rd he had written: 'An advance copy of your noble Hölderlin volume reached me this morning, & I rejoice to see the fruition of so many years of labour. I shall spend many happy hours with your book, especially in my present invalidish state, which has reduced my extrovert activities to a minimum . . .'

Alarmed by this reference to his illness, of which I knew nothing, I wrote to ask him what it was. His reply gives precedence to the errors in the book. It continues: 'You ask what is wrong with me, so I will tell you – cancer of the tongue. It is accessible & therefore can be effectively treated, but I have had three separate manifestations. But at the moment it seems to be under control & I feel well enough. I hope to go to Portugal for a holiday in about four weeks' time.

'I am sorry you have had such an exhausting time. I did too much at your age & can only advise moderation.

'If you come this way we would love to see you, at any time – there is always room for a guest or two. Yours affectionately, Herbert.'

That was his last letter to me. If I wrote again, as I think I did, offering to take up his invitation, he did not reply; and I was half-reluctant, in any case, to intrude on him now that his illness had given him something like the leisure which he ought to have enjoyed throughout his active life. Yet I am sure that his illness did not change him, that he remained stoical and unselfish to the end. As late as 1962 he had written to me: 'I no longer understand poetic standards in this country. But I did enjoy an article by an unknown (to me) person called Falck in *The Review* – do you know anything about him?' I was able to tell him something about Colin Falck, and he returned to this in a later letter.

Sketchy and faint though it is, this record may have the negative merit of not falsifying that side of Herbert Read which he chose to reveal in letters to one of his many friends. His more essential self should be looked for in his works. For the greater part of his life Herbert Read was a neglected and misunderstood writer. His public honours were awarded to the public man he became out of a mixture of excessive modesty and a fatalism rooted in the trauma of his experiences in the First World War. The essential Herbert Read could have been honoured only by a realization of his vision, or at least by the kind of sympathy and concern with which he responded to the works of other men.

If I had presumed to write an elegy for him, it would have had to be as unassertive as the best of his own poems, with the quiet strength often concealed by his outward faltering; as unassertive too, as the man whose tragedy was of the distinctly modern kind recognized long ago by Hölderlin, when he wrote in 1801: 'For this is tragic among us, that we leave the realm of the living quite calmly, packed into a container, not that devoured by flames we atone for the flame which we could not master.' Hölderlin went on to write that this modern predicament was 'less imposing, but deeper' than that of the ancient tragic heroes; and that noble souls confronted with it will 'persevere in the teeth of exasperation'. Herbert Read was often exasperated and often isolated; but the constancy of his affections is one instance of his power to persevere.

WHEN I left Oxford to wait for my call-up papers – for nearly a year, it turned out – my mother had moved back to our bomb-damaged house in St. John's Wood. My sister Maria had moved into a flat of her own and was working in factories, my sister Eva had broken off her medical studies and joined the WAAF. My brother, I think, was still at his boarding-school. X was working at Miss Waterhouse's bookshop, where Freddy had stood in for him for a while before going up to Oxford.

In my morbid adolescent romanticism I took it as a certainty that I should die in the war. (Joy told me off for this assumption in a letter.) That may be one reason why the Introduction to my Hölderlin translations was so inordinately long: I had to put everything I thought I had to say into that one book, whether it was relevant to Hölderlin or not. Another reason was my extreme bookishness at this period, my still unshaken conviction that books were the chief repositories of the good, the true and the beautiful. That the essences each contained didn't always mix, but could well neutralize one another, was something that hadn't begun to disturb me. If an author excited me, no matter why or how, that author must be relevant in any context. The Introduction, though, was already finished, and I wasn't dead yet. So I got down to a study of John Donne and Metaphysical poetry, even working in the British Museum Library despite a library phobia that was to keep me out of it when my academic career demanded that I do 'research'. This study was completed before I joined up, and published in Stefan Schimanski's year-book *Transformation*. Like the earlier attempt at criticism it presented a great lump of unassimilated material – this time, material to which I had been led by T. S. Eliot's essays. For the next two years or so I concentrated on the Master's canon of sacred texts, packing my kit-bag with the works of countless minor Jacobean dramatists and filling my army diaries with notes on them. When I came to re-read the diaries I was so furious to find all those literary notes, instead of a record of my army experiences, that I tore up the lot and burned them.

Most evenings I went to Soho, to talk and listen over half-pints of bitter which I didn't particularly like. What I did like, from time to time, was to get really drunk on stronger stuff, which I couldn't afford. What drew me to the Soho pubs was that they broke down barriers of class and nationality. Though predominantly upper-middle class, or parasitical on the upper-middle class, the war-time and pre-war bohemia could accommodate the Welshness of Dylan Thomas, the Scottishness of W. S. Graham, of John Burns Singer and of the two Roberts, Colquhoun and MacBryde, the East End Jewishness of Willy Goldman. Paul Potts was a Canadian, Tambimuttu a Ceylonese. There was a very young Polish boy killed in an accident a year or two later. There were painters like John Banting already out of fashion; and others – like John Craxton, David Haughton, John Minton, Keith Vaughan, Lucian Freud or Francis Bacon recently established or not yet at the height of their reputation. Among the rarer visitors Bryan Howard – better known as a character than as a poet – was as affectedly and self-consciously elegant as Anna Wickham was negligent of her appearance, warm-hearted and bluff. If professional envy or competitiveness affected those drifting configurations, I wasn't aware of it. In many cases I didn't even know what those people did in the daytime – if they did anything at all. The youngest of the three Bernard brothers was said to be a boxer. Another familiar figure, Stephen Fothergill, said he was a lamp-lighter. I talked to Bill Belton for years before discovering that he was a painter. There were quarrels and fights, of course, but I don't think they had anything to do with the ambitions and intrigues that made me avoid literary groups in later years. The cult of success was still considered vulgar. There are other objections one could raise against the cult of failure deep in the hearts of quite a few of the Soho regulars of those years, but they didn't occur to me till much later; and even now I would rather fail on my own terms than succeed on other people's.

When the pubs closed we made our true descent into the underworld, in the form of a dive – that seems the right word – known as the Coffee An' (non-initiates called it the Café Anne, unaware that the An' stood for nameless amenities other than coffee, but not necessarily culinary). It was a large basement somewhere near St. Giles Circus. I never saw it in daylight, and never really asked myself whether it existed in daylight, let alone exactly where. One drifted there in small groups to sit at long tables, drink coffee and eat. The proprietor was a Greek Cypriot with a scarred face and a notorious readiness to draw a knife when provoked. At least one alsatian dog also belonged to the premises. I remember an occasion when Lucian Freud quarrelled with the proprietor and was chased round the tables; but fights were more likely to break out in the pubs or on our way through the streets, where there were gangs unfriendly to 'long-haired boys.' Dylan Thomas, I think, rarely got as far as the Coffee An', but either dropped out at the drinking stage or went on to more exclusive clubs to do more drinking. I recall only one meal with him, when an Oxford friend took us to a restaurant and Dylan was sober enough to compose parodies of Hardy, Housman, Auden and Spender on the back of the menu.

To some extent the Soho circle overlapped with my life outside it. John Heath-Stubbs and David Wright were two Oxford friends often to be found in the other place. David (at that time Anthony or Ricky) Sylvester – not yet an art critic but jazz musician, poet, literary critic and painter – could also materialize in broad daylight, in St. John's Wood, where we visited each other's homes. Tambimuttu, incredibly enough, was sometimes to be seen in a real office, in Manchester Square, when he had become the first of my many publishers. Philip O'Connor became a friend and correspondent for many years, with meetings in various parts of London, in Suffolk, in North Wales and in Berkshire.

With *Horizon* I felt less at ease than with the Soho drinkers, a few of whom contributed to it. Through Stephen Spender I had met

Cyril Connolly and Peter Watson, who financed the magazine, but something other than the circumstance that I wasn't good enough to contribute always kept me well beyond the periphery of this circle, with its adulation of whatever happened to be the latest thing in France. French literature had been my main subject at Oxford, and Baudelaire, Rimbaud and Mallarmé were among my poet heroes. Yet I had the feeling that the French orientation of so many British intellectuals of the inter-war and war years had less to do with literature or the arts than with a sophisticated life-style against which I had begun to react. When Peter Watson invited me to stay at his country house, Tickerage, during an early army leave, not even the presence there of David Gascoyne could induce me to accept, though Watson was a charming, intelligent and generous man. After a whole series of painfully ambiguous situations, not all of which I have mentioned, I had also grown wary of personal entanglements with any homosexual, however charming, intelligent and generous.

It was in war-time Soho that I first met Thomas Good, who remained a close friend until his death in 1970. Tom had been an actor in the Midlands, where he was born in 1901, then a High Anglican priest in the Society of the Sacred Mission. He fell in love with a girl met through his work in the Mission, lost his faith, was defrocked and put in a mental home. For a time he became a Nietzschean, and it was through him that I met Nietzsche's early translator and advocate, Oscar Levy, at Oxford. Tom Good had had contacts with the Orage circle and contributed one or two small pieces to Eliot's *Criterion*. In the forties he still published poems, criticism and translations in periodicals like *Poetry Quarterly*, and a book of his poems was published by the same short-lived Oxford press that produced Vera Leslie's Kafka book. By the fifties, he was almost unknown or forgotten. His marriage had broken up. Soon his only son was to die of diphtheria. He had prevailed on his doctors and psychologist to confirm that he must not live in England, ostensibly because of the climate, in reality because he could not face up to the disruption of his ties and aspirations there. When he lived in France with his wife before the war, he had a small private income. After the war, living abroad meant drudgery as a language teacher in France, Lebanon and Italy, year after year of solitude in furnished rooms, White Goddess celebrations of girl students and embarrassed visits to prostitutes. When he lost his last job in Italy, where a third book of poems had just been printed, he had to return to England with his meagre savings, no pension and no prospect of anything but an old people's home. In January 1970 he drowned himself in the Thames near Richmond, where he had been staying in a residential hotel. Six weeks after his disappearance from the hotel I had to identify his body.

Though Tom was old enough to be my father, he was not a father figure to me. In fact I was hardly aware of the difference in our ages, even when he had become officially old and economically 'redundant'. An unquenchable youthfulness was one of his troubles; one motive, too, for his suicide, when the alternative was to accept his official age and wait sedately for death. Like most of the inveterate outsiders I have known, he was connected by traceable lines of communication to the inside. In his own chirpy and mischievous way, he remained priestlike – not so much the bad or spoiled priest he sometimes accused himself of being as a naughty one. The actor and the priest combined when he entertained his friends with mock sermons, sang old musical hall songs or played Irish jigs on his tin whistle. Nor did he ever forget that he had been at Oxford, that an uncle had been an important person in Nottingham, that someone in his family had known Yeats and Yeats's sisters in Dublin, that someone else had borne the surname of a noble family. To the end he remained a student, filling exercise books with notes on his reading, sketches for works he never had the concentration or incentive to write, names and addresses of people likely to arrange the American lecture tour for which there was no demand. His old-fashioned manners didn't allow him to betray his acute depressions to his friends, though his manic cheerfulness and endless flow of disconnected reminiscences could be at least as hard to take. If he were alive now, his habit of living in the past – with unrealizable projections into the future – would have helped out my defective memory. He would amaze me by telling me what I said to him on such and such a day twenty-five years ago, when we were walking from this place to that, and he must have seemed what he always seemed, a man who didn't listen to anything or take anything in but perpetually trod the wheel of his own mind. But, no: once the thing said or seen was there, in his mind, it was there to stay, to be turned over with the rest as long as the wheel turned.

Tom Good's poems, and most of his prose, lacked incisiveness. That a poet can be dedicated for a lifetime to his craft or Muse, sincere within the limits of his self-knowledge, skilful within the limits of his sensibility, and yet remain not good enough (not Good enough?), is the most extraordinary of the risks entailed in the vocation to which Tom was committed. I, too, was committed to it by now, with no more certainty that my work would ever be adequate by standards nowhere defined, in no reliable or definitive relation to outward success or the absence of it. 'A mug's game', T. S. Eliot called it, aware of the risk he shared with those whose persistence was a blind obstinacy, a waste of themselves and of others. Or wasn't it – even at the worst? Where even the best is for ever being re-examined and re-assessed, where any new development could be a falling-off or a final defeat, mightn't it be enough to go on trying?

. . . .

As my demobilization approached I grew more and more restless, more and more dissatisfied with the writing I had been doing in recent years. 'Of course I see the difference between your position and mine,' I wrote to X in May, 'and realize that I've been unusually fortunate. If I'm depressed it's not because I think that I'm less successful than I deserve to be but because my work is not as good as I want it to be. If I believed firmly enough in the value of my poems I would not have asked you to give up circulating them. I had an easy start and must have thought that the rest would be a steady and comfortable ascent. But the real difficulties are yet to come.'

In April or May, I became a full Lieutenant. This made no difference to my status at the school, but must have incremented the gratuity I received on my release, and this meant a little more leisure to get on with my literary work. It was not till June, 1947, about six weeks before my release, that I took steps to clarify my position at Oxford, and found that I had gone through the army with false pretences, under the illusion that I had already obtained a wartime B.A., after four terms of residence! 'It's a curse,' I wrote to X, on being corrected about that, 'since I don't feel like studying philology. If I could begin again I would study a science, preferably zoology or psychology (but the latter is not scientific enough).' On June 26th, I wrote: 'As for me, I'm just hanging on till my return home. The other night the Muse paid me an unexpected visit and I was able to scribble down a verse or two. I'm busy making arrangements for the end of the school – setting & marking exam papers, preparing for the Sports Day (a great occasion, since the Commander-in-Chief will be there), etc. I've applied for leave to visit Berlin very briefly before my return home, but I don't think this will come off. Frankly, I'm not keen on the trip but promised my great-uncle that I'd visit him if I possibly can. Berlin has very powerful and terrible associations in my mind, and I'd rather keep away from it. Often I feel morbid enough as it is, without going back to the nursery of my neuroses.'

The trip did materialize, though no official leave or travel documents could be granted, since there was no official communication between the two armies, C.M.F. (Central Mediterranean Forces) and B.A.O.R. (British Army of the Rhine) Captain Murphy and the Colonel at H.Q. simply told me: 'You're free to absent yourself for seven days. Get there if you can, and good luck to you.' Captain Murphy also did more than that. He lent me his dress uniform – I had never bothered to acquire one, but was content to wear my old battledress or khaki drill outfit – complete with three pips and his campaign ribbons. This certainly helped me to get there, though it also made me feel an imposter as well as a stowaway. No conclusion to my army service could have been more bizarre than this trip without papers, in a borrowed uniform, to the heart of the former enemy's camp – on compassionate grounds, bearing gifts of tinned food. To me, it also meant a return to the birthplace I had left at the age of nine and almost expunged from my consciousness; and a meeting with relatives I had not seen since that time.

The trip was fairly straightforward as far as the American Zone of Austria. This could be done by civilian train. At Salzburg I had to obtain some kind of permit to cross over to Germany but, when I succeeded, found myself going not to Munich, the obvious place, but to Karlsruhe in Baden. I arrived there in the small hours of the morning – on July 6th – and wrote a note to X: 'I have been terrifically busy. I'm on my way to Berlin – at least I hope I am. At the moment I'm sitting in an American H.Q. waiting for somebody to arrive. (Everyone is still asleep.) I've got to get this permission to travel on an American train to Frankfurt; thence to Berlin. If they refuse I'm stuck here. Yesterday I had nothing to eat until 9.30 p.m. . . . And I've got to be back in Spittal by the 12th. If everything goes smoothly I can spend 2 days in Berlin and get back in time.' When a duty officer arrived I had quite a struggle to convince him of the pressing need to let me travel to Berlin; but, once convinced, he put me on the most luxurious train I ever saw the inside of, with a panelled sleeping compartment to myself. (I suspect that this was a train specially built by the Nazis for delegates to the Party Rally at Nuremberg.) I needed all the sleep I could get. At Frankfurt I had literally to barge my way on to one of the overcrowded civilian trains of those years. In the end my compartment was shared by only one German, and I stretched out again on the narrow wooden seat for more sleep, making a hard pillow of the provisions I was taking to my relatives.

I got to Berlin, and was directed to guest quarters in the former Olympic Games Stadium. Cars could be obtained immediately by telephoning for them, with no questions asked. My first visit was to my great-uncle Paul and his wife Ilse, whom I hadn't met, since they had married after our emigration. She had stood by her much older husband throughout the war, working with him as a casual farm labourer with false papers and moving on when there was a risk of detection. My great-uncle was now nearly eighty, and his time was spent in efforts to obtain restitution of his confiscated property, including a house in Grunewald. He was suffering from various ailments due to undernourishment and hardship – they had had no ration cards while living underground – but this didn't prevent him from acting as a guide to me through the ruins of the city. At first I recognized nothing – not even the street I was born in, or the block of flats I was born in, though it was almost unchanged. Even the old concierge, Herr Wolff, was still there, and I talked to him, naïvely asking him whether his tom-cat was still alive! (My great-uncle Paul and his wife were to stay with us in London before he died. He told us about the death of most of his Berlin friends, but wept when he came to the loss of the last of his pointer dogs, given up when he and his wife went underground. He got angry when somebody made a sweepingly anti-German remark, saying that he was a German still, and that he and his wife would not have survived if they hadn't been decently treated by many Germans during the war. He did not live to move back into his Grunewald house, which was returned to his widow.)

The visit was too brief and hectic for me to begin the long process of recognition among so much rubble and empty spaces. If some street corner or shop front did assert its familiarity, I passed by too fast to weigh up the assertion and await the confirmation of memory. This became clear to me as I walked down the Kurfürstendamm with my other great-uncle, Martin. Despite his short, slight, jockey-like figure and eighty-two years he moved at a speed with which I found it hard to keep up, though not many years before I had won a long-distance walking race! As though no time had passed, in the teeth of food shortage and rationing, my great-uncle Martin insisted on taking me out to lunch at one of the few restaurants functioning for civilians in those years. (We had seen little of him as children, and had found his tremendous extraverted nervous energy rather daunting when he did appear, with presents of chocolates. He had been the managing director of a large steel works and had lived a style too high for us in Düsseldorf, with coaches and outriders and the horses on which he won prizes as a show jumper. He had been given an honorary doctorate for his services to German industry, and had been protected during the war, though a 'non-Aryan', either by this record or by the connections of his aristocratic wife. One of his two sons – the other had emigrated – had been drafted for forced labour as a half-Jew, but only towards the end of the war.) His wife, my great-aunt Wanda, was in a suburban nursing-home, where I visited her and delivered my gifts of food. I remember the embarrassment of being treated as a sort of war-hero both by her and by the nurses at the home, including one who was memorably beautiful, and trying to tell them how little my borrowed campaign ribbons accorded with my utterly undistinguished war service.

A year or so later this great-aunt who had survived the bombing of Berlin and her marriage to a 'non-Aryan', was murdered in the street by a man wanting her handbag. In 1955, when my great-uncle celebrated his ninetieth birthday, my mother went to Berlin for the occasion, and his long-lost younger son returned from North Africa, where he had served in the Foreign Legion and then lived as a professional jockey at Casablanca. Soon after the birthday this son crossed over to East Berlin, to die in mysterious circumstances, seemingly by suicide. I last saw my great-uncle in 1956, when he was ninety-one and living in an old people's home at Nikolassee. 'No senile slip except one,' I noted then. 'His sight and hearing still keen. Showed me his diplomas, letters of congratulation from Vice-Chancellor of the Republic, etc., also from present owners of the industrial concern for which he had worked. But seemed to have forgotten about his wife and her death – and his conventional allusion to the suicide of his son Tino. Altogether, he seems to have no feelings or emotions. That's probably how he's managed to go on living for so long. He seems to have no values other than the outward ones of power and success – even at the age of 91 – living in a little room in a home for old men. He has a private room, of course, but downstairs the place is like a doss-house. Took him a bottle of claret and 2 grapefruits – he has a "passion" for grapefruit, as far as he has passions at all.' That impression may well have been superficial. I never got to know the man at all, perhaps because he didn't relate to people easily, certainly never to us when we were children or later. Nor could I ever understand people of his kind, dynamos activating something outside themselves or nothing.

My remaining relatives in Berlin were my great-uncle Martin's daughter Erika, her two young daughters, and her brother Kurt, who had once tried to act as tutor to us at Kladow but was now working in industry also. I had last seen Erika in London when she was a dancer in the Ballet Joos and was on tour. Of my father's family there were no survivors in Germany except a cousin living in Hamburg, with a non-Jewish wife. I had no time to revisit our house in Kladow, and there would have been no point in going there with no leisure for exploration.

As I travelled back to Carinthia I could make no sense of anything I had heard or seen in Berlin. What little I had known of the city was largely destroyed, and any pattern of relations set up in childhood with the persons revisited had been broken up by long estrangement and differences that would have become acute even if there had been no enforced separation. Only my great-uncle Paul had been close enough to me in childhood, and was bound to me still by an affection strong enough to have made the trip at all meaningful; and time had been too short for a real exchange of our disparate experiences. By the time I returned to Berlin and began to reorder all the jumbled fragments, he was dead.

AFTER that, nothing remained but to prepare to go home, wind up the school – with final group photographs for the record – say good-bye to my civilian friends, the employees at the school and a few other locals, and pay a last visit to Manya, whom I had met from time to time right up to the end of my stay. I never saw her again, but heard from her sporadically until she emigrated to somewhere in South America. Four years later I revisited those parts, on our honeymoon, and out of a perverse need I have always felt to keep my fingers on all the threads of a life lacking in any obvious or natural continuity, took my wife to see what was left of Manya's shack.

One sequel to my service in Austria suddenly arrived in 1988 in a letter not from Manya, but from another woman, received more than forty years after the events. One of the servants at the school, a maid-of-all-work, she called herself, was a very young girl with blonde pigtails of whom I had been especially fond, often talking with her and once asking her to go fishing with me on the lake – though that must have been considered fraternization at the time. When I was ill after my breakdown it was this girl, Steffi, who brought me food to the lodgings near the school to which I had moved.

Towards the end of 1988 I received a 24-page letter from her, going over our relations and life at the school with a minuteness quite beyond my selective memory, and with bitter reproaches to me for not returning her love for me and, worst of all, not saying goodbye to her when I left. She had traced me by way of a broadcast and of the publishers of books of mine translated into German. She was now married, a mother and grandmother. She enclosed a photograph of herself in 1946, as Steffi Feichter, probably at the age of sixteen and more child than woman still, and a group snapshot of staff and children from the school, including me, by a river. Later she sent delicate drawings by her husband of the small castle at Millstatt in which the school for soldiers had been housed, and of the lakeside road to it I had often travelled, passing a solitary little Gothic chapel on the mountainside.

'I fell in love with you at once', she wrote, 'You always had such a friendly smile for me if you happened to be looking into the scullery through the open sliding door from the dining-room at Seeboden and always called me "Cinderella". I was to have been engaged as a waitress, but Mr. Hull said at the interview, she looks like an innocent angel, so we will put her in the kitchen – and so I came to do the washing up.' She then went on to give an account of every meeting between us over the next year and a half, the removal from Seeboden to Millstatt, with the dog-roses in flower. She reminded me that I used to play the piano there – by ear, as always; and that I did say goodbye to her when I left for Graz, telling her to be good, and precipitating more tears than she had already shed over me. (She also knew that the British commandant of the unit was living with the sixteen-year-old daughter of another member of staff, the Austrian chef, who agreed to that arrangement in the hope of advantage to himself, 'selling his daughter', as she wrote.) At the place to which the children's school moved from Millstatt, a hotel at Spittal, Steffi asked to be taken out of the scullery and allowed to wait at table, a request I granted at once. Then came my failure to speak to her before I left the school. Probably, it was deliberate on my part, because I must have sensed something of her feeling for me; but though I dreamed about her once in one of my fevers, to me she had always remained a child, like the other adolescent girls under my charge, only one on the wrong side of the political and national divide. I made enquiries about her when I returned to those parts in Carinthia on our honeymoon, but did not know her married name and was unable to trace her.

Of my repatriation and release no detail has stuck in my mind, only having a choice between a number of civilian suits all of which were drab and badly cut, and being allowed to keep my old battle-dress, though it was issued to me before I was an officer, as well as my officer's trench and rain coats, which lasted me for at least another ten years. To this day I use the green canvas and leather hold-all that replaced my kit-bag when I was commissioned, and I still have the despatch rider's boots I wore for horse-riding in Austria, though the Cossack mares are a distant memory.

The temporary discharge certificate issued to me on July 22nd, 1946, when I received my Emergency Commission, describes my military conduct as 'exemplary'. On the back there is a Testimonial: 'A keen hard-working N.C.O. Honest, sober and reliable. A/n was employed as a Sergt./Inst. in Army Educational Corps from 16 March 1946, teaching German and English and running discussions in "Current Affairs". Knowledgeable and painstaking, he proved himself to be capable and efficient. He has a pleasant personality and is easy in his contact with both staff and students. He achieved his results by the sincerity of his approach and not by virtue of military rank or bearing. Completely loyal, he showed himself prepared to give of his best at all times. Discharged on appointment to an Emergency Commission.' My final discharge took place exactly one year later.

The document makes no mention of my years as a foot-slogger in the poor bloody infantry, or my near-suicide by drink, or of any of the peculiarities that made my military conduct far from exemplary during the greater part of my service. The Army, it seems, has a memory even more defective than mine. This is borne out, too, by the testimonial written for me by Col. Impson, Commandant of the Army College, Central Mediterranean, after my final release. Almost as over-generously as the other, it commends my work as 'Second Master at the Children's School', yet omits all reference to my Headmastership there, the most taxing responsibility ever thrust upon me not only in the course of my army years but at any time of my life – by none other than that same Colonel. The half-year elapsed since the leave that had terminated it was enough, apparently, to erase it from the record. If ever I 'gave of my best' – and there were long periods in my army service when I didn't and couldn't because no one wanted it – that headmastership was what I gave it to, holding so little of myself in reserve that the giving had to stop. Perhaps it was a good thing, after all, that among the books carried around with my kit I had studied the Bhagavad Gita, with its doctrine of work done for the work's sake; and writing poetry, that 'mug's game', was a discipline of the same order. Incidentally, I never made use of either testimonial in civilian life. The one thing I have never wanted is a career.

If I try to sum up what I owe to my four years in the British Army other than trench coat and riding boots – I should be defeated by the impossibility of knowing how I should have developed if I had spent the same years as a civilian. What I do know is that this highly authoritarian institution cured me of a whole complex of attitudes and prejudices bearing on authority, on social, moral and intellectual gradations, and on the rock bottom basis of communal life. I doubt that any other institution would have tested me in so many different ways, or imposed such contrasting conditions – from the barest servitude, with needs and expectations confined to little more than the minimal means of physical survival, to relative luxury, and responsibility for the welfare of a fair number of people, including some sixty children. The Army taught me that one can sleep on cold wet earth in the open air, suffering from a fever, on hard floorboards or a sack of straw, sitting on a bench in a railway station and even standing on one's feet in the corridor of a train, if only one is tired enough – or in the most expensive hotels in Europe; and that the difference isn't worth talking about. It taught me that I could live with the roughest, most ignorant of men, and find the company of more polished, well-educated men insufferable. It taught me to delight in sheer movement, without caring about the destination. It taught me more than I can begin to outline.

Above all, it rubbed in the ironies of outward experience, ironies inherent in the whole course of my life that have made me doubt nothing so much as the meaningfulness of given identity. That the Army found a use for me at all, after being wary of accepting a former enemy alien, is hardly less extraordinary than the use I was able to make of the Army, not only by setting up a 'progressive' boarding school under its authoritarian nose – and, in essence, getting away with it. Almost every condition and code the Army imposed on me could be turned into its very opposite, if the lesson drawn from it was the lesson I needed to learn. Admittedly, this would have been harder, or impossible, if I had found myself obliged to kill my fellow men rather than learn to live with them; but the fact, the irony, was that the Army spared me that obligation. I did much more fighting at my various schools than ever I did in the Army; and I ran an Army school in which boys felt no need to fight among themselves. I fell into the habit of swearing like a trooper – no sentence was complete or effective in a barrack-room if it didn't contain at least one of the obligatory boosters – only to find myself back among 'gentlemen' and among children. While serving as a soldier I wrote poems in the person of a tramp who was also one of the displaced persons of Europe. I was devoutly religious amidst profanities, and turned agnostic when it was incumbent on me to organize religious instruction and perfunctory devotions. Nothing was what it seemed or what it was meant to be; and later life confirmed that state of affairs, involving me in a long sequence of contradictions between what I did and what I thought I was doing, what I wanted to do and what I achieved in doing.

It is not the Army's fault that in those four years I didn't overcome my emotional inhibitions and inadequacies. To expect the most spartan of male institutions to undo the harm done to me by the other male institutions I had been 'privileged' to attend, would be asking too much of those ironies. Yet in the course of those four years I did get rid of the moral inhibitions, if not the emotional and psychic ones, that kept me in a state that makes me sorry in retrospect for every woman unlucky enough to get entangled with me. Another twenty years and more had to pass before I could write a love poem that wasn't 'impersonal' or metaphysical, and by then I was middle-aged, with children old enough to come up against erotic difficulties I couldn't even admit to myself at their age.

As for my writing, the Army provided me not only with spells of leisure for it but the material enough for novels, epics, plays or what have you. Again I wasn't ready; and the Army wouldn't have stopped me if I had been. Those disgusting Army diaries of mine, with their half-baked literary glosses and almost total lack of response to what was going on around me, are the proof – or were before I burned them. When I had outgrown that phase, by the time I went abroad, I ceased to keep diaries and preferred to ride my horse. So once more the material is missing. What I saw and heard and felt in Italy and Austria has been overlaid by the impressions of too many later travels. My first collection of poems – circulated in typescript by my friend until withdrawn at my request was called *Itinerary*. A book of my poems published more than twenty years later is called *Travelling*. This points to an obsession with travelling itself – every conceivable form of travelling, literal and symbolic – that has remained with me since my Army years, that tramp sequence and other, even earlier, poems in my first published collection.

So, in the end, I don't know what the Army did to my writing. Even the books I glossed in barrack-rooms did something to me, though I've forgotten what most of them were about. Everything I saw and heard and felt did something to me, though I've forgotten most of the details. That's one reason why one writes: sooner or later almost everything about a life is forgotten, by the person who lived it and by the others. The great mystery of the written word and its justification in the teeth of everything that people say about the 'media' – instant communication and instant blankness – lies in its power to oppose biological time, to create its own time dimension, the dimension that distinguishes human being from animals. A novelist may deal in biological time, or try to, and so may an autobiographer, but by doing so he inevitably shifts his material into the other dimension. If that shifting fails, the work will be neither here nor there. A poet knows that biological time can be nothing more than his complaint. If the things in his poems aren't at home in the other dimension, he's wasted his time putting them there. His material is what he doesn't know, what the other dimension demands. If anybody ever feels like taking the trouble to look at my poems in the light of the little I remember of my life – that is, if they're worth the effort – he or she will find superficial traces in them of my army experience; but the real sources, connections and developments are underground.

My guess about them would be no better than his or hers.

. . . .

AFTER going down from Oxford in December 1948 I continued to live at my mother's house for a year or so. Though writing was the only thing I wanted to do, I had made one dutiful attempt at Oxford to provide myself with a part-time job. When I went to the University Appointments Board I was told that they knew of no part-time job for literary men, but that a place in the Intelligence Corps could probably be obtained for me in the event of another war. I thanked them for that reassuring piece of advice and made no further use of their services.

The next step was to establish myself as a book reviewer. I had already published a few book reviews and longer critical pieces, and for another twenty years or so I reviewed pretty regularly – for the *Times Literary Supplement*, for the *New Statesman*, for *World Review*, while it lasted, then for *Encounter* and the *Spectator*, as well as little magazines in Britain, America and Germany. I think that I positively enjoyed this occupation until the mid-sixties, though often it clashed with my other writing and translating projects. I reviewed hundreds of books over the years. As long as I remained an avid reader of new and old works in several languages, it was a way of obtaining books I couldn't afford to buy. Destructive though it could be of long-term projects, the deadline attached to each piece was also stimulating. It made me do something when I might have moped or procrastinated. Yet it was a medium scarcely less ephemeral than broadcasting. If one ceased to review for some periodical to which one had contributed for a decade or more, hardly anyone so much as noticed the dropping-out. The columns were fed by someone else, just as radio or television transmitters are fed with one thing or another. In the end something in me revolted against that machinery. The instant judgements no longer presented themselves. The opening sentence, once thrown so readily across any dividing distance or depth, became an impassable barrier. Whatever skill I had acquired in long practice of writing to order simply fell away. I couldn't do it any more.

I remember feeling offended when a girl I knew said to me at a London party: 'Congratulations. I see you're writing for the *New Statesman* now,' referring to a poem I had published there. The idea that one could write poems for periodicals was more than I could stomach. Probably she meant no more than that my poems were appearing there, as they did rather frequently under Janet Adam-Smith's literary editorship, but the little word 'for' implied that she regarded my verse as a form of journalism. I shouldn't have taken that to heart but for the grain of truth in her remark. Living as a 'free-lance' writer meant the need to be paid for one's publications; and the odd guineas paid for poems by periodicals like the *New Statesman* were part of my wretched economy. Since books of poems brought in no money to speak of, without those odd guineas I should have been unable to write poems at all – as long as I remained a 'free-lance'. It was a vicious circle – how vicious, I didn't know until my friend Philip Rawson pulled my second collection of poems to pieces, and I had to admit to myself that economic pressure had made me publish too many poems too soon, with at least a dash of the journalist's promptness. Instead of the two years between my first collection and the second, six years passed before my third; and I became as wary of the sort of 'success' on which that girl had congratulated me as I had once been eager for it, under the delusion that to publish poems in periodicals with a relatively wide circulation was to communicate with more readers more effectively.

Nearly ten years earlier I had asked John Heath-Stubbs in the Swiss pub, Old Compton Street, whether he had ever had a poem in an anthology, other than the Oxford one of which I knew, and told him I thought that to be anthologized would be a true breakthrough for a poet – as though anthologies were compiled by recording angels for all eternity, and one's admission into one an assumption to a higher world! If I had begun with ambitions, they were deluded ones of that order. The anthologies did follow in due course: some two hundred of them by now, most of them wholly commercial commodities purveyed to readers who cannot find their own way through the bewildering superabundance of poetry, new and old; many of them put together by editors too busy, lazy or diffident to do more than rifle earlier anthologies for their fortuitous pickings, perpetuating those anthology pieces that are the kiss of death to living poets. A true anthology of contemporary verse would have to reduce its plurality by a daring reliance on personal judgement or only personal taste – an arrogant undertaking at a time when literary repu-tations tend to rest on a consensus as ephemeral and labile as opinion polls in politics. The merely 'representative' and 'comprehensive' anthology of contemporary verse re-registers that consensus or brings it up to date. It does not get to grips with the trouble acknowledged by Yeats long ago: that there are always too many poets at work and in print. Anthologized or not, for a living poet there were no certainties, no arrivals; only comings and goings like my travels of those years, searches for nothing to which I could have given a name.

Looking back at the four years between my going down from Oxford and my first university appointment, I can only wonder how I managed to persuade myself that I was 'free', when I had to take on almost any job of work that happened to come my way. These jobs included evening lectures for the Worker's Educational Association and for the London County Council; acting as a guide to foreign visitors for the British Council; coaching private pupils for an agency; teaching elementary French to convicts in Pentonville Prison; and adapting the libretto of the opera *Leonarda* by Else Headlam-Morley, who had been a pupil of Liszt, for its first and only performance in England, at the Chelsea Town Hall, on March 30th 1950.*

Yet between such jobs, book reviews and broadcasts, I did get on with my own writing and translating, no matter whether this work would find a publisher or not. However hard I worked, I couldn't scrape together more than an average income of £5 a week – still enough, in those days, to pay the rent for my first one-room flatlet, my second two-room flat, or my third of three, cover overheads like heating and telephone bills, and keep me fed after a fashion. What was left of my army gratuity paid for holidays abroad.

.   .   .   .

ONE OF my odd jobs in London, French lessons in Pentonville Prison, gave me trouble. When I started my teaching there – compulsory lessons probably instituted in the hope that some of the convicts would emigrate to the French-speaking part of Canada after their release – my pupils were marched into the classroom by a prison officer. I expected him to leave once the class was seated. He stayed, to watch them or protect me. Needless to say, I got no response at all from my pupils. I asked to be left alone with them on future occasions. The request was granted, and from then on I got all kinds of responses, few of which had anything to do with the work I was being

---

* The composer, unhappily, died a few weeks before the event, on February 25th, at the age of 84.

paid to do. There was one old lag out to sabotage the whole operation. He came into the class equipped with some antiquated textbook. If I was teaching conjugations he would read out some rule about verbs and nouns, shouting out: "'Ow about that, Guvnor?' I would then have to explain the difference between verbs and nouns, getting nowhere, until he threw in the next red herring. Another, older, man was more interested in ethics than grammar – only too understandably, in his situation. He had read a novel by Somerset Maugham and found a quotation from Pascal: 'The heart has its reasons, which reason knows nothing of.' That did have something to do with French – and with one of my favourite French authors, as it happened; but he brought it up because he had been thinking about his crime and punishment, and wanted me to confirm that a man can do things under a compulsion that absolves him from guilt. I, too, was more interested in the implications of his question than in teaching grammar to people who had no wish or reason to learn it. After a month or two I had to conclude that my assignment was a hopeless one. The more I came to care about those men and their needs, the less I could teach them elementary French. So I gave up.

My visits to Soho had almost ceased. One of the last friends I made there was Thomas Blackburn, of whom I saw a great deal over the following years, also going to Cornwall and North Wales with him more than once, to climb Snowdon again, reluctantly balance on ridges and even scale rock faces with a rope, but no passion like his for rock-climbing. He loved danger, and looked for it not only on mountains but in personal relations and humdrum things like driving a cat One night, when he was drunk after a party, he zigzagged from one side of the road to the other on our way through London to Putney. When I pointed out that sooner or later he would be colliding with another car, he said: 'You're my friend, aren't you? You don't mind dying with me, do you?' It was hard to answer those two rhetorical questions, except by telling him that at the moment I was not keen to die with anyone at all. Even in North Wales he would park his car with the back wheels just touching a ledge. Every personal relationship, too, had to be pushed to the verge of crisis, if not over the verge, so as to release the energies that went into his poems. In some ways this accorded with the Soho ethos, though few of my Soho acquaintances pushed dangerous living quite so far, so consistently; and Tom Blackburn was more than a Soho acquaintance to me, because I knew him in daytime also, and knew a good deal about his day-time work as a Grammar School teacher, then as a college lecturer, and his difficult family life, even before his family and mine shared a holiday cottage at Tintagel, where he worked a farmer and his wife into a state of psychic exposure and extremity they can never have thought themselves capable of. He had complained bitterly that nothing of the same order had occurred between my wife and me, no high tension, breakthrough or breakdown or conflict of the kind he needed to release his own demons and get down to the archetypes That is why the farmer and his wife, from whom we had rented the cottage, had to step in as media. Wholly unprepared, as they were, for what he wanted of them, they proved far more amenable than we were to his requirement. We could keep up that friendship only by being on our guard; and in later years, when Tom was destroying himself with a mixture of barbiturates and alcohol, it proved too much for my wife, who had grown up in fear of her father's drunken fits, and we saw less and less of Thomas. His second wife, Rosalie de Meric, and his daughter Julia have remained our friends.

Another of the late Soho acquaintances was Brian Higgins, whom I saw only rarely outside Soho but corresponded with, mainly about the 'loans' he asked for and I came to refuse on principle, having discovered that the people who regarded me mainly as a source of 'loans' ended by hating or despising either me or themselves for the gift. When Brian Higgins's need turned out to be genuine and acute for once, just before his early death, I hated and despised myself for having allowed those experiences to harden into a principle. Patrick Kavanagh was another poet I met in Soho when he was in London. I very much liked his poems and his novel *Tarry Flynn* – and was able to help towards the publication in England of a book of his poems – but had little communication with him beyond his requests for another whiskey.

The war-time Soho circle had disintegrated. Some of its members now went to the Anglo-French Club in St. John's Wood, where I spent evenings when I had nothing better to do. Many of the same people went to the annual Christmas party at the Phillips's house in Hampstead, an all-night festivity to which I had been introduced by John Mortimer. Though never invited to it – as one was meant to be – I became a repeated gate-crasher there, and was never turned away. It was a bohemian event in a style that proved what I had come to feel, that every bohemia is sustained by its dependence on the class it thinks it is in revolt against. When that class lost its privileges and wealth, the bohemia I had known had nothing to batten on and withered away. Its residual members were those who had been wholly formed by it, had no other resources or resorts, and no way of making other lives for themselves. Some of those continued to haunt Soho, more and more like ghosts, long after Soho had become a playground for very different sets.

One of the first things I had done after returning to London was to prepare a reading of selected poems by Edwin Muir, with introductory comments, for broadcasting, since Muir was still a neglected writer, better known for the criticism he wrote for a living and for his translations than for his poetry. On September 22nd 1950 he wrote to me from Newbattle Abbey, Dalkeith, the college that was to educate and sustain a great many younger Scottish writers whose prospects otherwise might have been as bleak as his own had been when he was young: 'I'm delighted you're thinking of getting together some of my poems for broadcasting. I like your selection very much, and have no criticism to make of it. You ask about my earlier work. Much of it I do not like very much, with an exception here and there. I think you yourself (for private reasons) might like a poem, "Hölderlin's Journey", from a small volume *Journeys and Places*, published by Dent at 2/6, I think.* But then you may not like it, for the same reasons. And if you don't please forget all about it, for it is your selection, not mine, and should follow your taste. "Merlin", I think, appeared in the one book I don't have a copy of, else I would have sent it. And probably (though I hope not) it may be out of print. I have written some poems recently which I like better than any of the others: but it would be inexpedient to touch them.

'I wish I had known earlier that you were in Italy, for I would have seen more of you. If you are in Scotland any time do come and see us and spend a night or two. This is a curious place, with lots of passages in which I got lost for the first week, and historical objects like Bruce's saddle and Mary Stuart's font (if genuine). I hope you're writing poetry.'

---

* This volume turned out to be still available in 1950, 13 years after publication. The price was now 3/-.

Edwin Muir, who developed late as a poet, was writing his best poems at the time – the best, I thought, that were being produced by a British poet. His 'delight' at an attention he should have been able to take for granted is characteristic both of his situation and of his response to decades of neglect.

In November he wrote again, apologizing for not writing sooner about my book of poems: 'I've been terribly busy, not only with starting the College (it's been going just for a month now) but with countless things which have turned up, indirectly connected with it. These will not recur (at least I hope so) and I should be having much more leisure in a short time. But I've really been having far too much to do during these last four weeks.

'I got the script of the poems and your commentary two days ago, and I should like to thank you very much indeed, and to say how much I like what you say about me. I'm very glad indeed to be introduced to the Third Programme audience in a way I like so much.'

Muir was sixty-three years old. His first book had appeared in 1918, since which time he had produced increasingly distinguished work in prose and verse, not to mention his early concern with writers almost unknown in England, such as Hölderlin and Kafka. Yet he could write without irony about being 'introduced to the Third Programme' by a man almost forty years his junior. A postscript to the letter refers to a review of my book of poems: 'Who is Mr. P. who was so supercilious to you and the other poets? And what right has he to be so lordly? What nonsense reviewing is.' Almost up to his death Edwin Muir had to turn out book reviews, since his own books provided no income to speak of. 'I do hope that the vein of poetry is running again with you,' he wrote in 1955; 'with me it turns itself off and on in the most disconcerting way, and generally when it comes on I have no leisure to deal with it. I have a few poems in my mind just now, but whether they will come to anything I do not know. I may find leisure in Harvard.'

I met Edwin Muir again in 1952, when he attended a small gathering at our London flat, meeting Kathleen Raine, G. S. Fraser and J. C. Hall there. 'I was pleased to meet some writing people again,' he commented: 'they really are the pleasantest people one can meet, I'm convinced, though others deny it.' In 1955 I attended a reading he gave in London, and in his last years I visited him more than once at Swaffham Prior, near Cambridge. After his death Willa

Muir remained a loyal friend.

Almost better than anyone else I knew, Edwin Muir understood the conflict in my early verse between preoccupations mainly ethical or 'philosophical' and the aesthetic demands of the medium. This had been his own problem, when metaphysical concerns tended to impoverish the sensuous and linguistic fabric of his poems. Though he was too gentle and considerate to censure the same shortcoming in my work, I drew my own conclusions from his remarks in a letter of 1952. 'Sincerity is a matter of degrees, and I feel sure a necessary quality of poetry, and it is in that sense (not the equivocal sense in which it is so often used by smart reviewers) that I'm speaking about it. Sincerity becomes grace (and not, again, a mere surface grace) when it is effortless, and not willed; and I think your poetry has that quality at its best. It's something that you have by nature, or have achieved: I find it difficult to tell which. In any case, if you are in doubt about your poetry (and who is not in doubt about his poetry?), it is a quality which you should respect and cherish. I am no good at discussing the technical points of verse; the word technique always gives me a slightly bewildered feeling; if I can translate it as skill I am more at home with it, for skill is always a quality of the thing that is being said or done, not a general thing at all. A thing asks to be said, but the only test is whether it is said well. You certainly have things to say of your own; and, from the enquiring, accepting spirit of these poems, I feel that there are many more things, of which just now you are probably not aware, which you still have to say: I go on my own experience . . .'

The comments on specific poems that followed – including one negative comment on a poem later picked out by a prominent actress for public readings and broadcasts that became an excruciating embarrassment to me – were helpful too; but it was the crux about sincerity that I really took to heart, knowing that mine had not yet become effortless, had not become 'grace'. Between the lines of Edwin Muir's approval I found an indication of the route I must take – towards 'negative capability'; and that indication was far more valuable to me than praise. It could have come only from a poet who had known related conflicts and perplexities.

In Conversation with Michael Schmidt

[*PN Review* 136, Volume 27 Number 2, November–December 2000]

MICHAEL SCHMIDT: *When* Ownerless Earth: New and Selected Poems *appeared in 1973, I seem to remember your referring to Theodore Roethke and his insistence that every new book should include what preceded it, making each volume in effect a new and selected poems, because the more recent work made sense only in terms of the earlier. This is what Umberto Saba wanted, too. In an ideal world, would you have wanted* Intersections *to come at the end of a relevant selection, and if so which earlier poems would have been most relevant to it?*

MICHAEL HAMBURGER: Though I don't recall what I wrote or said about Roethke's preference in 1975, I can still see the point of it, in relation to Roethke or Saba. But of course an author's concern with the wholeness of his or her work doesn't necessarily accord with the requirements of readers – quite especially now that every week at least one new poet is hailed and 'hyped' as the greatest of the living, and the most that can happen for an older or dead poet is that, almost fortuitously, a poem or two will be picked out for attention and briefly salvaged from the prevailing amnesia.

If a poet has more than one voice – and I believe I have – the matter becomes even more problematic. An eminent critic was utterly flummoxed by my first *Collected Poems*. I wonder whether that was because we have lost the notion of genres or kinds in poetry. At one time it was taken for granted that a poet would write differently for narrative (epic), dramatic, lyrical or satirical purposes – not to mention the countless sub-categories within the shorter kinds – ode, elegy, song, sonnet, epigram etc. etc. – and the hybrid possibilities. For the very few readers still prepared to grapple with my diversity, I still prefer the 'collected' – rather than 'new and selected' – form of presentation. An alternative is the division into kinds in small volumes. The main translator of my poems into German at present, Peter Waterhouse, has chosen to publish a series of selections called 'tree poems', 'dream poems', 'death poems', as well as separating my long sequences that cut across these thematic or generic divisions for other volumes. This seems to have met the readers' needs – saved them the perplexing endeavour to make sense of my diversity and gather up all the threads.

If there is continuity in my work, it's not that of a single voice but of development on different levels within the different kinds. Though it's obvious to me that my last longer poem, *Late*, connects with the earlier longer poems *Travelling* and *In Suffolk* – poems of the same kind, with a mobility denied to me in shorter poems – I couldn't make such connections myself among the shorter poems. You may remember that I found myself unable to do the selecting for the Carcanet *Selected Poems* and had to ask others to step in. The later additions to my 'Life and Art' series, for instance, strike me as a hybrid kind, somewhere between the classical kinds of elegy, epistle and satire. The new collection also contains a few songs that connect with my earliest lyrics, if they connect with anything. But it isn't for me to make such connections. Where I've learnt anything from critical studies of my work, it's where they hit on connections and continuities that had never occurred to me.

What I'm aware of is the diversity of my concerns and practices. For the period covered by *Intersections* I did get as far as separating both the long poem *Late* and the functional verse I published as a pamphlet called *Mr Littlejoy's Rattlebag for the New Millennium* from the shorter poems not of either kind. (I say 'published', but the pamphlet was never noticed anywhere, except in one reader's letter to a local paper, and the publisher was refused a subsidy on the grounds that it wasn't the poetry it was never meant to be; so 'functional' also calls for inverted commas, since my samizdat functional verse had little or no public function.) Again you may remember your difficulty with the verse I called 'Moralities' at the time – and published separately as a pamphlet with that title – or 'owl's pellets' or 'unpleasantries'. These and the dream poems at the other end of my range have proved unacceptable to many of my readers and critics. All I can say about both is that I found it necessary to write them; and that if a third *Collected Poems* were to materialize in my lifetime, I should include the contents of these separate publications with earlier poems of a related kind, for the sake of an ideal wholeness that may never become real for anyone.

I used to think that when your imagination wasn't responding to the visible world and memory, your instinct was to be an allegorist (in the dream poems for example), creating types and vertiginous narratives. In Late, *and now much more so in* Intersections *you seem to have integrated what before often felt like different threads or even genres in your work: literal vision and dream vision, the light of day and the lights flickering at night. Has the garden become more allegorical and the dream more a waking dream? Take a poem like 'Intersection, December'.*

I've never consciously aspired to the writing of allegory, but did find that my dream poems – and a single dream story written in later years – became allegories willy-nilly for those who could make any sense of them at all. There may have been a tension in all my work from the start between the Romantic-Symbolist premises with which I began and the realism that gradually took over. This dualism was acute in my collection *The Dual Site* of the 1950s. If this dualism has now become an equipoise, as you suggest, that is what I always hoped to achieve. I can't go into the psychological or metaphysical implications of the conflicts or their resolution. Nor can I interpret, 'explicate' or analyse any one poem of mine, such as the one you mention. Poetry, for me, comes out of what Yeats called 'heart mysteries'; and it happens that Yeats's later and last poems helped me to bridge the seemingly irreconcilable opposites.

The diction you use is often religious. In 'Intersection, December' you have Advent and Easter, a deliberate, ironized echo of the transcendent, Byzantine Yeats in the second line (it also suggests Plath's 'The Moon and the Yew Tree'!), Lent, grace, the sense not only, perhaps, of the transcendence of nature, but of another kind of transcendence. Is this a wilful over-reading? Or do the terms identify it in other than poetic terms? I get the same sense from other poems, especially extreme experiences like 'Surgical Case' for instance.

And Yeats happens to occur in your next question! Again, I must be reticent about the question of religion. This, too, has been a field of conflict for me, a battlefield, with ups and downs I can't begin to recapitulate here. Partly because I wasn't brought up in the faith of my Jewish forebears – with an agnostic-humanist father, a mother who became a Friend or Quaker – I was never able to commit myself to any outward profession of faith, let alone any denomination or sect. Poetry demanded openness above all. It was my poems – and the experience on which they drew – that intimated to me what I believed and did not believe at any stage of my life. And every new poem was a blind departure into the openness. The religious dimension has had to remain as open as all my other concerns; and the transcendence, too, now seems as indispensable and self-evident to me as the limited and restricted condition from which it takes off. On the biological level evolution may be nothing more than adaptation for survival. In human individuals and societies it becomes transcendence.

In short-lined poems or sections of poems, you seem to balance line to line in almost-couplets (rhythmically speaking), and in the longer lines time after time there is a strong caesura with half-line balancing half-line, giving a curiously still movement (it is movement, and moving, but tentative), something that has increased since Travelling. *Is this deliberate, this tentativeness, a kind of effacement before your subjects?*

I began with set forms, strictly metrical and rhymed verse, until I found these constricting. But even in my 'free verse' the ghosts of many different metres and rhythms continue to operate. From what I knew of classical metres – and my long work on Goethe and Hölderlin, who imitated or adapted them for a modern language – I also took over some of the rhythms, not metres, of Greek and Latin verse. As you have noticed, these haunt some of my more relaxed, conversational poems like the 'Life and Art' series, perhaps down to the odd caesura in long lines. Contrary to the general view, I don't think that the dominant iambic rhythm is more natural in English than any other. Truly popular English verse, like nursery rhymes or Blake's lyrics, tend toward a loose rhythm weighed by stresses rather than syllables. This may be a recondite link to the lost thing called 'quantity' in classical – Greek and Latin – verse. And something akin to that operates in so-called 'free verse' if it's more than chopped-up prose. In long and short lines I'm as much at home in dactyls and even spondees as in iambics. Recently I've found myself reverting at times to patterned rhythms in poems that called for them. The stillness or tentativeness you hear in my rhythms may have something to do with my overall avoidance of set metres – or set themes, for that matter; and old age is a preparation for stillness in any case. (This may be why

Peter Waterhouse called my more recent shorter poems *Todesgedichte*, death poems or poems of death.) Where the movement of my poems is hesitant, it could be because they are groping for a truth, rather than playing computer games with programmed ingredients.

There are several occasional pieces in the new book, the most curious occasion being the Bad Salzuflen commission. Can you discuss the circumstances of the poem 'Multiple Vistas, Mutable Light', and how you responded to the challenge of this commission?

In one sense all my poems are occasional poems, in that it is occasions that precipitate them – a coming together of some outward event, observation or 'epiphany' with my constant concerns. When I was asked to go to Germany to write a poem in response to one of ten locations in an area set aside for a conservationist project called 'Poetic Landscape' – each of the ten poets invited was to choose his or her spot in it – I refused at first, not being a landscape painter in words, and very shy of commissions also. I was then assured that if no poem materialized the organizers would accept a poem already written, and my misgivings were disarmed, especially since the project itself was congenial to me. The project turned out to be utopian, as a clever German critic called it; but I am convinced that utopianism is an essential leaven in any realistic enterprise, individual or corporative, worth our while. Without this leaven even the public realm lacks the magnanimity I have come to miss in it. This project was an ambitious and costly one, since each of the ten poems was to be exhibited in a small building designed for it by a prominent architect. When a CDU government was elected in that Westphalian region, the funds were withdrawn. A new area has now been chosen, and the poem I wrote has become as unhoused as all my other work. What made the writing of my poem possible at all, for me, was that it re-enacted all my doubts and reservations that counterpointed my positive response to the project. So the poem became much longer than I thought it would be; and I brought in the agricultural land that was part of the whole area and the motorcycle rallies for which part of it had been allocated. These uses of the area clashed with the utopian concept – and most probably helped to bring about its displacement. Nevertheless, the project has not been abandoned, as my poem has; and the poem remains a celebration of the possibility of bringing 'high' culture to 'ordinary' people, contrary to the world-wide trends, and art into nature. (The reason why the project remains possible in Germany, as it would not be in post-Thatcher Britain, is that it has the support of private patrons committed both to the 'high' culture and the conservation of landscapes.) Decidedly difficult poets, including the Danish poet Inger Christensen, the Chuvash-Russian poet Gennady Aygi and the English-Austrian poet Peter Waterhouse, were and remain among the invited ten. Yet these pavilions, if built, would not remain wholly unvisited by the pedestrians out for the landscapes more than for the poems.

You have developed the theme of 'Aging' from your previous book with three more 'Aging' poems (followed by a vivid suite of elegies), and 'Life and Art' which began in Observations and Ironies *(1969) is now a major sequence (you add VII–XXII in* Intersections*). Can you identify the continuities and the developments over thirty-odd years in this poem-barometer?*

Aging has become the precondition of the work I can still do; and an interest in old age other than my own has followed from that, just as the elegies have come out of the most painful of old age's realities, the loss of one friend and relative after another. Other concerns – like successive experiences with house martins, cats and a variety of animal and plant species – have run through my work for decades, recurring in short poems that are not sequences. I then tend to distinguish such poems by numbering only, rather than titles. (Titles, to me, are the least telling parts of a poem, except where they're part of the text, and I minimize them or leave them ambiguous.) The 'Life and Art' series began earlier than you say, in 1959, with a casual, ironic near-epigram, and has served me since for all sorts of ironic and sardonic reflections, not always obviously connected with what most people mean by art. More and more, art, to me, has become any productive work to which we apply ourselves, especially that which used to be distinguished as 'artisanship' – before artisans ceased to be a recognized class. Perhaps because I spend at least as much of my time on horticultural labour as at my writing-table, the two occupations have become inseparable in my mind. Where I resort to metaphor at all – and I prefer the plainest and barest of language even for the most complex of matters – the metaphors are likely to be drawn from my grapplings with the stuff of nature – through my periods of urban residence haven't vanished without trace in later poems.

It seems that you have, almost from the beginning when, as you report a critic saying, you were 'ghosting for the ghost of Yeats', had several long poems in mind. Sometimes they emerge, as in Travelling *and* Variations, *more or less together, though I remember you revisited, adjusted and enhanced them after the initial event. Other long poems thread through your books from the 1960s to the present. There is also your Mr Bones, called Mr Littlejoy, and here he is again in his anachronistic retirement. Is your work, from the perspective of your 76th year, unusually coherent? Is it right to see it as having a compelling clutch of themes, obsessions, concerns? How much of you is invested, ironically, in Mr Littlejoy? His new poem is devastatingly negative about the poetry scene. To what extent do you share Mr Littlejoy's view not only of the poetry scene today, but of the quality of the poetry that is being published?*

No, I never planned to write a long poem, though some early poems did fall into parts or sections, and one of the earliest made a sort of sequence, 'From the Notebook of a European Tramp'. (I was reminded of that juvenile sequence lately because, quite inappropriately, it was chosen as the title of an Italian selection from all my poems – most of which have long been those of a stick-in-the-mud.) *Travelling* began as a short poem – published as such in my Fulcrum Press book with that title. Suddenly, a year or two later, this poem opened out into a larger space, which I filled over a period of nine years in all. This particular kind of longer poem – with repetitions and modulations taken over from music – then became the model for my other longer poems, *In Suffolk* and *Late*. These soon turned into longer poems, though their nucleus may have been a short one, as soon as I needed a mobility of allusion in space and time which my plainness prohibited in most of my shorter poems.

As for Mr Littlejoy, he first appeared in 1973, when I felt I needed a persona – rather like the earlier European tramp, adopted when in fact I was serving as a soldier in Italy and Austria – for a voice different from that of other poems. The earlier, middle-aged Littlejoy was a self-caricature: accident-prone Gloomburger, as others saw him, therefore less a persona than a character. My publisher Stuart Montgomery had told me that my voice was marked by gentleness – a gentleness at odds with the brutality or wartiness recommended by Yeats and Bernard Spencer as a requisite for poets. Mr Littlejoy also favoured a diction more formal than that of most of my later verse. Though a socialist in politics, with a leaning towards an anarcho-syndicalist utopia of mutual aid, he was and is culturally conservative, simply because there can be no culture at all without the conservation of what remains sound and exemplary. This seeming paradox was inherent even in modernism, when there was still a sense of progress both in art and society. 'Make it new' could be the slogan, but the work of both Pound and Eliot is cluttered with miscellaneous and arbitrary pickings from the past. Now 'Modernize!' is the slogan of those who never think about the long-term effects of this modern- ization, which has become synonymous with short-term 'efficiency' and profiteering. Hence the desperation of Mr Littlejoy – if not of M.H., who has some sort of cryptic faith to pit against the despera- tion. Over the decades Mr Littlejoy, too, was transmuted. When his resistance to new trends became desperate, he became less urbane, less of a wag, having learnt that satire is not possible in a society with- out values. That made him cruder, too, so that it was to him that I came to attribute the polemics and invectives I collected for the pamphlet already mentioned. Perhaps it was only then he became a persona, a mouthpiece. I made an exception of 'Mr Littlejoy's Anachronistic Retirement', included in *Intersections*, feeling that the gravity of this poem was out of character with the earlier and later Mr Littlejoy. Incidentally, I killed off Mr Littlejoy in the pamphlet – which wouldn't prevent him from making a posthumous reappear- ance if that suited him.

I can only hope that my work is unusually coherent, despite the diver- sity of both form and tone – and the resort to such personae, only a little less drastic than Pessoa's self-divisions and heteronyms – and despite the developments or transformations. Much as I loathe dogmatic rigidity, in poetry or outside it, I'm aware of a core of immutable concerns in my work.

Is it fair to say that you have always been something of an elegist in the classical sense?

Classical elegy was not necessarily mournful, whereas my friend Christopher Middleton called me 'Gloomburger' some five decades ago. As one virtually condemned to death at the age of eight, subliminally drawn to death by drowning at an even younger age, and battered into adulthood in the course of a murderous war, I could hardly avoid a basic gloom, much as certain composers are most at home in minor keys. From the first I may have been obsessed by death, for one thing; but I shouldn't be here to answer you if such early wounds couldn't be healed. The closer I've come to my own natural death, after countless escapes from death by injury, accident or ideological decrees, the more joy I've been able to wrest from that closeness.

Your elegy for Ted Hughes is the most moving I have read. Can you comment on what his work meant to you?

But the death of friends and loved ones is another matter. Ted Hughes was a friend above all, though our meetings were rare over the decades. As a fellow poet I respected him and tried to understand that in his work which went against my grain – especially the hyperbole most grating to me in his Ovid versions. What was most congenial to me in his poetry was his searching concern with and knowledge of the things of creation (or evolution, if that word is preferred). His too early death was a blow to me. Into a spontaneous elegy, written immediately after hearing of his death, I tried to put the understanding of the self-contradictions and conflicts that generate all poetry – in his case those between a celebration of raw energy often seen as peculiarly masculine, if not 'macho', and a great tenderness and delicacy in human relationships. I could never forget his telling me after the death of his first wife that he felt he was growing breasts, in relation to his children. If that was hyperbole, too, it pointed to a truth, just as understatement and ellipse can point to a truth in others. And Ted Hughes had a magnanimity that I now miss in public and private affairs.

Which of your many translations, from the perspective of today, has been of most use to you as a writer, and which do you think is the most durable?

Most probably the translations of most use to me as a poet have been those on which I spent half a century, off and on, those of Hölderlin.

I might not have hit on the structure of my longer poems without the precedent of Hölderlin's later poems, his so called 'hymns' in seemingly free verse. As I've written elsewhere, what influenced me in Hölderlin was his long breath, his overflowing or encapsulated syntax and sudden ellipses – perhaps also what he called the 'naïve' tone, which he deliberately modulated with other tones within one poem, rather as a composer changes his tempi within one work. Yet Hölderlin's breath had been schooled by his reading and translating of Pindar – whose poems are inaccessible to me in the original. But I scarcely ask myself what I have absorbed from the many diverse texts I have translated – and don't even know whether I could learn anything from my later translating of Celan. I translated poets in many languages, some of which I knew very little or not at all. To me, translation is not the appropriation of this or that in the poets translated, but a losing of myself in that work. Quite recently I was asked to do a free adaptation of a poem by Leopardi. I began by trying to transpose Leopardi's poem, 'L'lnfinito', into my own terms – even from Southern Italy to Suffolk, his hill to my marshes and heathland! – but gave up the attempt as an absurd and impertinent travesty – something I shouldn't much like to be done to a poem of mine. Instead, I did a version as nearly literal as my language allowed, retracing the almost philosophical dialectic of that very personal and confessional poem. If this exercise didn't accord with the request and can't be used, it was a small addition to the translating work I've now reduced to a residual minimum; and the work gave me pleasure.

As for the durability of any translation, that is a matter beyond my control. A few of my translations have remained in print for some fifty years or more, others vanished almost as soon as published – and not because they are inferior as translations, but because there was and is no demand for that poet's or prose writer's work. It's best for me not to think at all about the question of durability, but continue to write what I'm moved to write and do what little I can for the work of those I have translated.

I always ask my students to read The Truth of Poetry, *and though it was published originally in 1969, it retains much of its force. If you had the inclination, and energy and time to 'bring it up to date', what would you add; and in retrospect, what would you change now that we are no longer in the wildly promising 1960s?*

Because I have no inclination whatever to 'up-date' *The Truth of Poetry* and didn't have even when it was reprinted by Carcanet and Methuen before I'd given up criticism – your question is unanswerable. The preliminary work on that book goes back to the 1950s. And I've come to see that I shouldn't have written it at all – as the only book-length critical work I ever produced – if it hadn't been one way of getting to grips with my own most intimate conflicts as a poet. It was never a history of modern or modernist poetry, but a study of tensions, of the extremities of poetic practice in the directions both of 'purity' or autonomy and of the opposite, the usefulness and prose-like intelligibility to which Brecht aspired. These tensions were my own, and I've fought them out, once and for all, both within and outside my poems. What has happened in or to poetry since 1969 is a subject for the historian I never was and the critic I've ceased to be. All I was able to add was afterthoughts in little prose pieces that have grown shorter and shorter over the years – mostly prefaces, introductions and afterwords to books. These later pieces remain uncollected, since the Carcanet *Testimonies* marked the end of my function as a critic and 'man of letters' – another anachronism, of course, where literature is no longer a republic but a supermarket.

Your poetry has never been an adjunct to your critical writing in the way that, say, Empson's and Davie's were; but there must be some feedback or feed forward from one to the other. Can you identify things you have done in your poems as a result of things you have done in your prose?

As I've indicated, my criticism was bound up with my own poems, but also with my translating work. All the essays in my first critical book, *Reason and Energy*, for instance, were on writers I had begun to translate, with the single exception of Heine, extracts from whose work I translated only for my essay on his verse and prose. I never thought of myself as a literary scholar, and did only one little job of research even when I was an academic. I wrote not for my peers or colleagues, but for what one could still think of as the common or general reader, so making it possible to be a 'man of letters'. This general public was already beginning to dwindle away, even in the 1950s.

Outside and before my academic specialization I published an essay on 'John Donne and Metaphysical Poetry' – always a special interest of mine – and a good many on French writers important to me for one reason or another. Leonard Forster, Professor of German at UCL when I was an assistant lecturer there on probation, introduced me at a party as a journalist, because I was a prolific book reviewer at the time. Scholar that he was, he was right, by his standards, not to give me tenure at UCL, although late he came to see that jobbing critics may also have their educational use. Though I doubted it in my case, my students confirmed it when I dropped out of regular teaching. Very briefly, I also reviewed living English-language poets, but soon found that this involved the literary politics I have always done my best to keep out of. Some of my last reviews were of ecological books, when these issues had become more urgent for me than the endless introduction and re-introduction of foreign writers, and the interpretation of poems had lost its attraction for me – too much aware by then that the meaning of poems is received only from the text itself, often only after repeated readings, which may change them utterly.

William Empson and Donald Davie may have found it easier as teachers to get away with their extra-disciplinary affairs. In the 1950s I wrote a piece of comparative criticism – on Milton and Hölderlin – without ever having encountered such a discipline as comparative literature in a university. When I proposed some lectures on Nietzsche at UCL, my own department banned him as a philosopher, while the Philosophy Department – dominated by the logical positivist school – didn't think much of Nietzsche's logic and wouldn't have the lectures either. So there were no Nietzsche lectures, when I was grappling with his work, not caring a rap whether he was classified as a rhapsodist, aphorist, essayist, poet or thinker. Yet Empson and Davie were poet-critics above all, and the rare curiosity and passion they brought to their dual identity may now make them irreplaceable, as Donald Davie is for me both as an occasional sparring partner and as a constant friend both to me and to my work. But I became an academic because I couldn't make a living for my family as a writer – or as the odd-job man I was before I was an academic, or as a gardener and grower of mainly obsolescent apple varieties in later years.

Book by book it can seem that the hold that the two cultures, German and English, had on you has loosened and that now you are very much a writer in the English tradition and largely in an English landscape. Yet you have not succumbed to the mandatory irony of the age or to the demands of performance poetry. What does German culture still provide?

Contrary to appearances – the number of my translations from the German – it was more than two cultures that had a hold on me. At one time French models were at least as formative for me as German ones, and during my military service in Italy I extended my interest to Italian. Several other literatures entered into *The Truth of Poetry*, and in Portugal I was welcomed as the discoverer of Pessoa for Britain – to my embarrassment, when I could only just make out the written language and couldn't speak a word of it. German, of course, was a special case, because it had been my first language – overlaid within a year by the English learnt in Edinburgh. It's possible that I should never have started translating in my adolescence if that hadn't been a bridge to a culture lost to me in every other regard. But it is the once uprooted who have the greatest need for a single home and habitation. That's why it was out of the question for me to settle in America when I worked there as a visiting professor and was offered all sorts of inducements to accept a permanent appointment there; and this although certain modes of American poetry had also been among my concerns and it was in America that I had my first experiences of virgin wilderness. Most of my conscious and formative life was spent in Britain, beginning with very British institutions like a prep school, a public school, an Oxford college and the Army. The last of these was the most formative of all, since it uprooted me again – from the class system, as well as from my home – and made it impossible for me ever again to seek security in membership of a class, club, clique or clan.

Judgements differ as to whether my poems are in the English tradition. I may now have more readers in German translation than the originals have in Britain, and in the USA my poems have vanished. My work has also received more thorough critical attention in Germany than it has here. Those in Britain who dislike my work call it 'rootless cosmopolitan' or German. Those in America who disliked my work called it too British. Most of the Eng. Lit. establishment, whether scholarly or journalistic, has ignored it.

So, once more, I leave it to others to place me here, there – or nowhere. What's certain is that since our removal twenty-four years ago from the cosmopolitan metropolis to the edge of a Suffolk village, most of my poems have drawn on my immediate environment, with only memories or tourist impressions of other places, other ways of life.

Christopher Middleton also told me that I have a 'literal imagination' – perhaps implying that I have no imagination at all, relying, as I do, on experience rather than fantasy, whim or word-play. This could be the very reason why I had to write dream poems, availing myself of an order of experience that confounds and obliterates the confines of space and time. This is part of the dialectic of opposites I believe to have run through everything I have written.

Situated in Suffolk in your 76th year, with a sometimes rather bleak perspective on the political and the poetic scene, I wonder if you could idealize for a moment and suggest what you feel might re-invigorate poetry – reading and writing – and whether this has any bearing at all on the political world we inhabit?

Well, I don't believe that 'poetry makes nothing happen' – a rather misleading statement outside its context, since it makes no distinction between the fallacy of political commitment or *engagement* and the subliminal effect on us of anything to which we respond. Anyone who doesn't look away and turn off the sound for television commercials will be brainwashed by those as surely as others were by the indoctrination devised by totalitarian régimes. If that weren't so, the advertisers would be wasting their money, and the whole economy would collapse. 'Oh,' people will reply, 'they're just fun'. Yes, and political propaganda – a word taken over by Goebbels from commercial advertising – is so reassuring, makes you feel so good. Because culture is what we have forgotten, and we are shaped and sustained by everything that has been absorbed by us and gone through us, like food and drink, the current political and cultural correctness is as fallacious as the conscious commitments once demanded of poets. Our endless talk about racism, sexism, classism, ageism merely rubs in the differences and perpetuates them. The Welfare State rested on a consensus of heart and head among civilized people at the centre, Left and moderate Right, and it effected a revolution that was more than slogans and chatter. Civilized people were those who took the differences for granted and proved their rising above them by not talking about them. Nor can programmes, legislation and bureaucracy level out these differences exacerbated by gut (and herd) reactions to the harping on them.

What's true is that poetry can't be geared to political action, because politics has to do with power, poetry with rightness – also known as beauty – and truth. A poet can, and usually does, have a vision of what a good society might be like, but he or she is taken in and trapped when that vision is hitched to any political ideology or faction. All he or she can do as a citizen to make anything happen politically is 'defend the bad against the worse' – to quote another of the poets once regarded as politically engaged. As a poet, though, he or she can remain true to the vision – in whatever circumstances and the hope alone of contributing something to the leaven essential to any civilization or culture. In the poetry itself this leaven may be invisible, implicit rather than explicit; and it can be active even in satire and polemic, as the invisible positive pole of a negative current.

Where something of that sort happens, poetry is invigorated. It is not re-invigorated by the mere re-enactment in words of kitchen sink realities – the verse equivalent of the nightly sit. com. – even if some wit or invention goes into the re-enactment. This is where the transcendence you ascribe to me comes in. But I must leave it at that, because this question of yours calls for the book-length answer I shall not now produce. In condensed and elliptic form, it could be implicit in my new book of poems.

2 *The Poet*

Poems selected by Michael Hamburger

[*PN Review* 100, Volume 21 Number 2, November–December 1994]

WHEN ASKED to select one of my poems for the anthology *Poet's Choice* (The Dial Press, New York, 1962), I chose one of three poems recently written, because I was excited about the belated breakthrough into what I felt to be a new freedom in the writing of those poems. For the same anthology Philip Larkin chose his 'Absences' 'because I fancy it sounds like a different, better poet than myself. The last line, for instance, sounds like a slightly-unconvincing translation from a French symbolist. I wish I could write like this more often.' That was before the persona Larkin adopted became a permanent fixture. I find the – slightly tongue-in-cheek – statement interesting because he chose what he thought his least characteristic poem; and because I'm incapable of recognizing any single persona, let alone 'image', of myself as poet, in my work as a whole.

Even when asked to put together a *Selected Poems* for Carcanet six years ago, I came up against this difficulty and had to ask four friends and relatives to do the choosing, decided by proportional representation. Here, too, I've been guided in part by the choice of Anne Beresford, my wife, and Michael Schmidt, to both of whom I'm most grateful for helping me out.

For reasons of space I had to discard several of their choices; and an extract from my two sequences, which many regard as my best work, was out of the question for me. Being 'variations', as I called them, they must stand or fall as longer poems.

After more than fifty years of writing and publication I know only that I've tried to do very many different things in verse – something that would be taken for granted if we still had the notion of kind or 'genre' in poetry, instead of the notion of a 'voice', a 'personality' or, most recently, a brand name. Because I care most about the people, things or phenomena I write about, and these are necessarily various, every poem I write is an attempt to do justice in the appropriate words and shape to a particular experience of one of these. The dreams I include among the phenomena demands an ordering quite different from that demanded by the phenomena of waking life, which may also be as single and clear-cut as a specific animal or tree or composite and complex.

The few poems picked out here cannot possibly represent the diversity or range of which I'm much more aware than of the unity that critics have found – or failed to find – in my work.

It has to be said, too, that I am not a reader or critic of my own work, except that becomes unavoidable for purposes of selection. Such critical faculties as one has ought to be operative in the process of writing itself. But it's for others to decide whether the product was well or badly finished – and whether the choice I have made leaves them more or less inclined than before to grapple with the heterogeneous whole.

BIRTHDAY

A shovel scrapes over stone or concrete.
Cars drone. A child's voice rises
Above the hubbub of nameless play.

An afternoon in August. I lie drowsing
On the garden bench. Fifty years melt
In the hot air that transmits
The sounds of happenings whose place and nature
Hang there, hover. That's how it was
For the baby laid down on a balcony
At siesta time in a distant city;
And is here, now. The known and the seen
Fall away. A space opens,
Fills with the hum, the thrumming of what
I am not; the screams, too, the screeching;
Becomes the sum of my life, a home
I cannot inhabit – with the sparrows even
Mute this month, all commotion human.

Elsewhere, my mother at eighty-eight
Lies on a deck chair, drowning
In that same space. Were my father alive
Today he'd be ninety, the tissue
Undone in him larger by thirty-five years;
But the sounds and the silence round him
The same; here, to receive him, the space.

A train rattles by. A drill, far off,
Throbs. A cup falls, shatters.

MAD LOVER, DEAD LADY

Oh, my Diotima.
Is it not my Diotima you are speaking of?
Thirteen sons she bore me, one of them is Pope,
Sultan the next, the third is the Czar of Russia.
And do you know how it went with her?
Crazy, that's what she went, crazy, crazy, crazy.

Thirteen funerals they gave me when I died.
But she was not there. Locked up in a tower.
That's how it goes: round the bend
Out of the garden where lovers meet,
Walking, talking together. Over the wall.
No one there. Till you visitors come:
Will the corpse write a poem today
About his mad lady?

But I'll tell you a secret: we meet.
Round the bend, on the other side of the wall
Our garden is always there,
Easy, with every season's flowers.
Each from a dark street we come
And the sun shines.
She laughs when I tell her
What it's like to be dead.
I laugh when she gives me
News of our crazy children
Who've made their way in the world.

No poem today, sir.
Go home. In a dream you'll see
How they remove themselves, your dead
Into madness. And seem to forget
Their loved ones, each in his own dark street.
How your mad loved ones
Seem to forget their dead.

That's how it goes. No one there.
Oh, my Diotima.
Waiting for me in the garden.

MORNINGS

String of beginnings, a lifetime long,
So thin, so strong, it's outlasted the bulk it bound,
Whenever light out of haze lifted
Scarred masonry, marred wood
As a mother her child from the cot,
To strip, to wash, to dress again,
And the cities even were innocent.
In winter too, if the sun glinted
On ice, on snow,
Early air was the more unbreathed
For being cold, the factory smoke
Straighter, compact, not lingering, mingling.

I look at the river. It shines, it shines
As though the banks were not littered
With bottles, cans, rags
Nor lapped by detergents, by sewage,
Only the light were true.
I look at light: but for them, mornings,
Every rising's not-yet,
Little remains now to wait for, wish for,
To praise, once the shapes have set;
And whatever the end of my days, to the last
It will hold, the string of beginnings,
Light that was, that will be, that is new.

GARDEN, WILDERNESS

Green fingers, green hand, by now green man
All through, with sap for blood,
Menial to it, gross nature,
And governor of a green tribe
No law can tame, no equity can bend
From the sole need of each, to feed and seed,
Unless, refined beyond resistance to a blight
More grasping than their greed,
Rare shoots evade the keeper's pampering.

He goes to referee
A clinch of lupin, bindweed, common cleavers
And stinging nettle – each with a right to be
Where if one thrives the other three must weaken;
And with his green hand, kin to tendril, root,
Tugs at the wrestlers, to save, to separate
Although his green heart knows:
While sun and rain connive,
Such will the game remain, such his and their estate.

More rain than sunshine: his green lungs inhale
Air thick with mare's-tail spore,
Grass pollen; his legs trail
Trains of torn herbage, dragging through swollen growth
Twined, tangled with decay.
For his green food he gropes,
To taste his share, bonus of fruit and berry,
Tribute for regency,
Sweet compensation for defeated hopes
Or dole despite the drudgery, the waste.

A garden of the mind,
Pure order, equipoise and paradigm
His lord, long far away and silent, had designed,
With bodies, never his, indifferent machines
To impose it and maintain
Against the clinging strand, the clogging slime;

And best invisible, as now that lord's become
Whose ghost the green man serves; that contemplated flower
Whose day of stillness filled all space, all time.

THE STREET, DECEMBER

for Charles Causley

By inane innuendo he and she converse,
She and she, he and he, run into each other,
Exchanging as ever the message already familiar,
Safe in littleness, tucked away in discretions
And devious, devious, lest two raw wounds touch;
By local cryptograms of health, prices and weather
Conveying the constants, the universals of care.

May the Goodness that knows, the Lord that loves a duck
Keep it so, keep them so, never let them bumble
Into extinction, as bustard will, dodo did
In gun weather, knife weather, and worse to come
With prices too cruel for health.
May the drabbest, dumbest of birds and their words get through,
Zigzagging clear of on-target missiles.

MR LITTLEJOY'S PRAYER

Logos, one Word before the world was peopled,
Take back your progeny of words, words, words
Whose babbling intercourse, proliferation
Makes counterworlds, more packed than tube trains are
When offices close, with some not even sure
Of a mere dosshouse bed; and with no Malthus

To warn, far less to legislate, against
Their polymorphous promiscuity.
Oh, and immortal, thanks to tablet, paper,
Translator, necromancer, necrophile
For whom the living are not good enough,
Too mixed, too lax, too ugly or too blank.
In ever-growing graveyards, libraries,
Once more they copulate and grossly breed,
Dead with the dead or living with the dead.
Contain them, Logos, curb the lexic mob.

If now I speak, it is to clear a space
Where things are things, grow nameless in your name.

Be in that narrow silence, Word, and fill it.

ENDLESS

It began as a couch grass root,
Stringy and white,
Straggling, to no end,
Branching out, breaking
For procreation.

Traced and pulled, it became
A bramble shoot that climbed
Through leafage of shrub, tree
With a root at its tip, for plunging.

I pulled at it, pulled,
Miles of the thing came away,
More and more.

I pulled and pulled until
I saw that now

Straight up it had risen
With its end in space,
With a root in heaven.

RETURN

Making today for the hill track,
The rock-riven slopes, the grottoes,
Water's hard course to the sea,
Tree-root's to water, light's
Through the trees, and the light broken
By brushstrokes of wind and cloud
Over contours, colours themselves mutated
By growth, erosion, decay,
I was halted: to the horizon sprawled
A flat surface, fenced off.
And in garish letters on boards I read:
Memorial Park. Through the palings
Glimpsed a single sheep penned,
One cow, one goat farther off,
Last, a pinkness that could be one pig –
Exhibits, I took it, memorials
Indeed to forgotten breeds
Never seen here, homestead for herons,
Pasture for wild geese in passage,
And both for wandering senses,
Minds that in motion found rest.

At a roped gap in the fence
A Minister loitered, chatting
With local officials dressed up
For the Park's inauguration.
'Welcome!' he called to me, smiling,
'In your keenness you've come a bit early,
The cashbox is not yet in place.'

Late, I thought, much too late –
But early if I could return,
Man, woman, child could be here
For the land's reopening,
For the resurrection of hills.

CONVERSATION WITH A BLACKBIRD

'Will you please, will you please, will you please'
He begins, and I wait for more
Which comes, indistinct, unemphatic.
'Keep away' I think I make out
Or 'let things be'
May or may not have heard:
The vowels are blurred,
The consonants missing.
Oh, and the rhythm is free
After that courteous request.

Translated, my answering whistle says:
'Be more explicit. Our kind can't endure
Things unsure, songs open-ended.
To be kept guessing is more
Than we can bear for long.'

Does he laugh? 'Please, please, please, please, please'
Is the reply. Then coloratura, among it these phrases:
'We repeat, don't complete.
Mysteries, mysteries.
Improvise, weather-wise.
Now I dip, now I rise.
Vary it. Don't care a bit
If it's indefinite.
Now I sit, twitter. Now I flit.'

From *Collected Poems 1941–1994*

LIFE AND ART I

for Denis Lowson

'A cell,' I reply when visitors remark
On the small high windows of the room I work in,
A room without a view. 'Exactly what I need,
Daylight enough – no more – to push a pen by,
And no distractions. Even the two great elms
With their congregations, race riots and social conflicts,
Endless commotion of squirrels, jackdaws and owls
Not to be seen, and only seldom heard.'

You dropped in one morning and sketched the garden,
All blue and black with the bulk and shade of those elms.
At once I longed to possess it. (The garden, the sketch?)
And above my desk I pinned up the silence extracted
From the endless commotion of squirrels, jackdaws and owls.
My garden hangs on the wall – and no distractions.

TIDES

To wake without fail when milk bottles shake in their racks,
Scrape one's face in the morning, every morning,
Take the same route to work and say 'good morning'
To the same row of scraped or powdered faces –
I cursed the roundness of this earth, I raged
At every self-perpetuating motion,
Hated the sea, that basher of dumb rock,
For all her factory of weeds and fishes,

The thumps, the thuds, the great reverberations –
Too much in rhythm; jarring, but by rote.

The metronome it was in my own head
That ticked and ticked; caged cricket in my head
That chirped and chirped until I had no ear
For syncopation, counterpoint of stillness
Beating against all music – of the sea,
Of birds and men, of season and machine,
Even of cricket and of metronome.
In silence I learned to listen; in the dark to look.

And unrepeatable now each morning's light
Modulates, shuffles, probes the daily faces
Often too suddenly different, like the street,
This weathered wall re-pointed, that new one cracked,
Apple-trees that I prune while I forget
The shape of last year's boughs, cankered or grown,
And where that stump is, one that died in blossom;
Forget the hill's curve under the aerial masts.

No, wheels, grind on; seasons, repeat yourselves,
Milk bottles, rattle; familiars, gabble 'good morning';
Breed, hatch, digest your weeds and fishes, sea,
Omit no beat, nor rise to tidal waves.
Various enough the silences cut in
Between the rock cave's boom and the small wader's cry.

SECURITY

1

So he's got there at last, been received as a partner –
In a firm going bankrupt;
Found the right place (walled garden), arranged for a mortgage –
But they're pulling the house down
To make room for traffic.

Worse winds are rising. He takes out new policies
For his furniture, for his life,
At a higher premium
Against more limited risks.

2

Who can face the winds, till the panes crack in their frames?
And if a man faced them, what in the end could he do
But look for shelter like all the rest?
The winds too are afraid, and blow from fear.

3

I hear my children at play
And recall that one branch of the elm-tree looks dead;
Also that twenty years ago now I could have been parchment
Cured and stretched for a lampshade,
Who now have children, a lampshade
And the fear of those winds.

I saw off the elm-tree branch
To find that the wood was sound;
Mend the fences yet again,
Knowing they'll keep out no one,
Let alone the winds.
For still my children play
And shall tomorrow, if the weather holds.

IN A COLD SEASON

I

Words cannot reach him in his prison of words
Whose words killed men because those men were words
Women and children who to him were numbers
And still are numbers though reiterated
Launched into air to circle out of hearing
And drop unseen, their metal shells not broken.
Words cannot reach him though I spend more words
On words reporting words reiterated
When in his cage of words he answered words
That told how with his words he murdered men
Women and children who were words and numbers
And he remembered or could not remember
The words and numbers they reiterated
To trap in words the man who killed with words.
Words cannot reach the children, women, men
Who were not words or numbers till they died
Because ice-packed in terror shrunk minds clung
To numbers words that did not sob or whimper
As children do when packed in trucks to die
That did not die two deaths as mothers do
Who see their children packed in trucks to die.

II

Yet, Muse of the IN-trays, OUT-trays,
Shall he be left uncelebrated
For lack of resonant numbers calculated
To denote your hero, and our abstract age?
Rather in the appropriate vocabulary
Let a memorandum now be drawn up –
Carbon copies to all whom it may concern –
A monument in kind, a testimonial
To be filed for further reference
And to circulate as required.
Adolf Eichmann, civil servant (retired):

A mild man, meticulous in his ways,
As distinctly averse to violence
As to all other irregularities
Perpetrated in his presence,
Rudeness of speech or deportment,
Infringements of etiquette
Or downright incompetence, the gravest offence;
With a head for figures, a stable family life,
No abnormalities.

Never lost his temper on duty
Even with subordinates, even with elements earmarked
For liquidation;
Never once guilty of exceeding his authority
But careful always to confine his ambitions
Within the limits laid down for personnel of his grade.
Never, of course, a maker of policy,
But in its implementation at office level,
Down to the detailed directive, completely reliable;
Never, perhaps, indispensable,
Yet difficult to replace
Once he had mastered the formalities
Of his particular department
And familiarized himself with his responsibilities
As a specialist in the organization
Of the transport and disposal of human material –
In short, an exemplary career.

III

Words words his words – and half his truth perhaps
If blinking, numb in moonlight and astray
A man can map the landmarks trace the shapes
That may be mountains icebergs or his tears
And he whose only zeal was to convert
Real women children men to words and numbers
Added to be subtracted leaving nothing
But aggregates and multiples of nothing
Can know what made him adept in not knowing

Feel what it was he could not would not feel –
And caged in words between their death his death
No place no time for memory to unfreeze
The single face that would belie his words
The single cry that proved his numbers wrong.

Probing his words with their words my words fail.
Cold cold with words I cannot break the shell
And almost dare not lest his whole truth be
To have no core but unreality.

IV

I heard no cry, nor saw her dying face,
Have never known the place, the day,
Whether by bullet, gas or deprivation
They finished her off who was old and ill enough
To die before long in her own good time;
Only that when they came to march her out of her human world,
Creaking leather couch, mementoes, widow's urn,
They made her write a postcard to her son in England.
'Am going on a journey'; and that all those years
She had refused to travel even to save her life.
Too little I know of her life, her death,
Forget my last visit to her at the age of nine,
The goodbye like any other that was the last,
Only recall that she, mother of five, grandmother,
Freely could share with a child all her little realm;
Recall her lapdog who trembled and snapped up cheese –
Did they kill her lapdog also, or drive him away? –
And the bigger dog before that, a French bulldog, stuffed
To keep her company still after his early death.
Three goldfishes I recall, one with a hump on his back
That lived for years though daily she brushed her fishes
Under the kitchen tap to keep them healthy and clean;
And how she conspired with us children,
Bribed us with sweets if we promised not to tell
Our father that she, who was diabetic,
Kept a pillbox of sweets in her handbag

To eat like a child in secret –
When neither could guess that sweets would not cause her death.
A wireless set with earphones was part of the magic
She commanded and freely dispensed,
Being childlike herself and guileless and wise . . .

Too little I know of her wisdom, her life,
Only that, guileless, she died deprived
Of her lapdog even, stuffed bulldog and pillbox of sweets.

V

And yet and yet I would not have him die
Caged in his words their words – one deadly word
Setting the seal on unreality
Adding one number to the millions dead
Subtracting nothing from death dividing nothing
Silencing him who murdered words with words
Not one shell broken, not one word made flesh.
Nor in my hatred would imprison him
Who never free in fear and hatred served
Another's hatred which again was fear
So little life in him he dared not pity
Or if he pitied dared not act on pity;
But show him pity now for pity's sake
And for their sake who died for lack of pity;
Break from the husk at last one naked grain
That still may grow where the massed carrion lay
Bones piled on bones their only mourners bones
The inconceivable aggregate of the dead
Beyond all power to mourn or to avenge;
See man in him spare woman child in him
Though in the end he neither saw nor spared –
Peel off the husk for once and heed the grain,
Plant it though he sowed nothing poisoned growth;
Dare break one word and words may yet be whole.

WORDS

'A writer you call yourself? And sit there tongue-tied
While others talk about books?
Jolted, answer in monosyllables, non-committal at that.
Are you shy, then, or sly? Superior or plain dim-witted?
Do we bore you, or aren't you there?'

'A bit of all these. But words are the root of the trouble.
Because I can't speak – what I can't speak – I write.
Words? Yes, words. I can't do without them.
But I hate them as lovers hate them
When it's time for bodies to speak;
As an acrobat would,
Asked to tell how he leaps, why he leaps, when he's leaping.
A curious trade, I admit:
Turning a thing into words so that words will render the thing;
Setting a movement to words so that words will render the
       movement.
But words about words about things? I can do without them.
Look: the arc-lamp's game with the plane-tree's windblown
       branches.
Listen: an owl. And those voices – closing-time down the street.
And smell: the coffee boiled over two minutes ago.'

TWO PHOTOGRAPHS

           I

At an outdoor table of the Café Heck
In the Munich Hofgarten
Six gentlemen in suits
And stiff white collars
Are sitting over coffee,

Earnestly talking.
The one with a half-moustache
Wears a trilby hat.
The others have hung up theirs,
With their overcoats, on hooks
Clamped to a tree.
The season looks like spring.
The year could be '26.

On a hook otherwise bare
Hangs a dogwhip.

No dog appears in the picture –

An ordinary scene.
Of all the clients
At adjoining tables
None bothers to stare.

2

The year is '33.
The gentleman in a trilby
Is about to board a train.
Behind him stand
Four men in black uniforms.
'For his personal protection'
The Chancellor of the Reich
Carries a dogwhip.

No dog appears in the picture.

VARIATIONS I: TRAVELLING

I

Mountains, lakes. I have been here before
And on other mountains, wooded
Or rocky, smelling of thyme.
Lakes from whose beds they pulled
The giant catfish, for food,
Larger, deeper lakes that washed up
Dead carp and mussel shells, pearly or pink.
Forests where, after rain,
Salamanders lay, looped the dark moss with gold.
High up, in a glade,
Bells clanged, the cowherd boy
Was carving a pipe.

And I moved on, to learn
One of the million histories,
One weather, one dialect
Of herbs, one habitat
After migration, displacement,
With greedy lore to pounce
On a place and possess it,
With the mind's weapons, words,
While between land and water
Yellow vultures, mewing,
Looped empty air
Once filled with the hundred names
Of the nameless, or swooped
To the rocks, for carrion.

Enough now, of grabbing, holding,
The wars fought for peace,
Great loads of equipment lugged
To the borders of bogland, dumped,
So that empty-handed, empty-minded,
A few stragglers could stagger home.

And my baggage – those tags, the stickers
That brag of a Grand Hotel
Requisitioned for troops, then demolished,
Of a tropical island converted
Into a golf course;
The specimens, photographs, notes –
The heavier it grew, the less it was needed,
The longer it strayed, misdirected,
The less it was missed.

Mountains. A lake.
One of a famous number.
I see these birds, they dip over wavelets,
Looping, martins or swallows,
Their flight is enough.
The lake is enough,
To be here, forgetful,
In a boat, on water.
The famous dead have been here.
They saw and named what I see,
They went and forgot.

I climb a mountainside, soggy.
Then springy with heather.
The clouds are low,
The shaggy sheep have a name,
Old, less old than the breed
Less old than the rock
And I smell hot thyme
That grows in another country,
Through gaps in the Roman wall
A cold wind carries it here,

Through gaps in the mind,
Its fortifications, names:
Name that a Roman gave
To a camp on the moor

Where a sheep's jawbone lies
And buzzards, mewing, loop
Air between woods and water
Long empty of his gods;

Name of the yellow poppy
Drooping, after rain,
Or the flash, golden,
From wings in flight –
Greenfinch or yellowhammer –

Of this mountain, this lake. I move on.

II

A hybrid region. I walk half seeing,
Half hearing the mourning dove,
The mockingbird's range of innate
And of mimed music, jumbled.
Here the dogwood grows wild, and here
It was planted, flowering pink
Above gaudy azaleas, in gardens
Carved out of hillside and forest.

Red clay. White sand. Meagre pines.
If no copperhead basked
On trails a Cherokee cut, no tortoise
Lurched over fallen branches
I might be back where I started.
Three thousand miles back. And colder.

Thirty years back. Three hundred.
It's the same earth,
With beer-can openers lying
Inches away from arrowheads,
Flint, and fossils barely covered.
The sameness confuses. If now
A rabbit screamed I'd be elsewhere,

By Thames or Windrush or Taw,
Moving as now I move
Through one death to the next.

On the one bank of the Bea,
Oak, beech, thickly bunched,
I half see, on the other
Spruce, larch, for pit props,
Their thin trunks planted, with gaps
For a black light.
Over both buzzards loop.

By the Yare I called
On my father thirty years dead
In a city. From his bombed house
He'd retired, into a shack
With holes in the roof, gaps
In the board walls. Alone,
He was rapt, absorbed
In his new profession of nothingness,
And needed no calls, no concern;
Had forgotten so much,
I could not speak, looked on,
Looked around and left, quietly.

Still those words rot in my mouth
Which I did not speak, and others,
Unspoken, spoken, of caring,
For ever mocked as I stepped
Out of indifference fulfilled
Into a street, path, track
From which time peeled away
And yesterday's name had been swept
Together with yesterday's paper.

And yet I speak to you, love,
Write words for you. Can you read them?

Can you bear them, bear with me there
Or here, anywhere?
Can you keep them from falling, hold them
In a place become yours, real?

It's the same earth we walk,
Variously lost,
You from the dogwood, white-flowering,
I from the thin pines,
With many rivers between us,
Ocean between us, one.
To meet you I move on,
Sorting, throwing out words
Only so that the one
May prove sound, yours,

One place contains us, a whole year,
Our spring and fall, our growth and our dying
Be like your breath when you stand
Arrested, your eyes
Darkening, widening to reflect
And draw in, drown what's around them;

Wholly to see, hear again
And be here, there, wholly.
For that alone I walk
The named and nameless roads
Through tame and wild woods,
Along the banks of so many rivers
Too much the same till we meet.

III

No, it's over, our summer,
Part of a summer, you gone
Across the Channel with too much luggage,
Making your way back
To dogwood, red-berried now,

To nights warm still and loud
With whip-poor-will, crickets,
And I about to go
Where maples begin to turn,
In half-sleep katiedid, katiedid
Grates out a brainless reminder
Of what and what, meet you, will not.

The sun has come out again
Here, in the same garden
That's turning too, never the same
One whole day, one whole hour.
Gales have snapped off
The last early pear
And, darkening, the goldenrod withers.
Over there it's budding, wild,
Like phlox, long withered here,
But without you where am I?
Neither here nor there, and the names
Dissolve, garden and meadow float
Out of my reach together,
Different, the same, both remote.

You move on, looking,
Finding something to feel
Here or there, anywhere,
Collect and lose, recollect
And like the more for the losing
That makes it more your own.
How you rush through Rome
In a morning, to see, to see,
To have seen, to have been
Where the names tell you you were,
Then, moving still, gather
What the names will not hold.

You got it home, your too heavy luggage,
Unpacked, and put away

Our summer, part of a summer,
Left again and for lodging chose
A trailer. You hinted:
An alias now was the name
That loving had learnt you by.

My travels, true, are unlearning,
An unloading of this piece and that,
Shedding of names, needs.
But the last have the pull of earth,
Of the earth we walk, our foothold.
Break them, and we fly or go under.

Almost the lightness came,
Almost the bareness in which
'The worst turns to laughter'.
I wait. The days drag,
Heavy, and long, long.
The laughter I hear is not mine,
My lightness no more than the weight
It was driven away from, a drifting
Between indifferent shores
Through this autumn now hot, now cold,
With the sky clouding over, clearing,
As if there could be no end,
Only the turning, clinging of leaves to stalk,
Of flesh to bone,

Though for hunger I needed your tongue,
For wanting to touch, your fingers,
For wanting, wanting you,
For looking, your hungry eyes,
For rest, their drowsing, their closing,
For bare words, your listening,
For destination, you,

Not here, not there, not anywhere
To be reached now,
So fast you rush on, away from
The place that, holding you still,
Could fill and affirm your name,

As I pack again, off at last,
For a while yet to travel,
Go and return, unlearning.

At their lightest the leaves fall,
At their lightest glide on the wind.

But enough now. More than enough
Of pressing into words
What sense, cluttered or stripped,
And mind leave behind them:
Mountains, lakes, rivers,
Too many, and you,
One, but moved on,
Nameless to me because named
You'd evade the name.

Here, in the same garden,
Branches are barer,
The late pears ripe.
No frost yet. Heavy
The grass droops, damp.
I wait, learning to stay.

IV

In winter light, walled
With glass too thin to hold
Any motion but memory's
That displaces no bulk, breaks
No surface, fills

No space, leaves no trace,
Litter or wake,

Travelling, stay
As Earth does, fixed,
And staying travel
As Earth does, revolving.

Earth. That must be the name
Still. Light. Air.
Walking the city I noted
That men live on light, air
Still, even here, unless
Filtering eyes or lungs
Fail, and waste clogs them,
Killing. The sun gets through
Still, the luckier poor can sit
On doorsteps, look up and see
A strip of sky they could almost
Feel to be common property.
A wind in those parts can cross
The river, cold, but bringing
Air nearly as good as new,
As nearly pure as the water
Rich people buy, canned.

Where am I? Bare trees
On a slope. Between the trunks,
Forked or single, islands of green,
Moss-green brighter than snow
Against leaf-brown, and evergreen,
Glossily dark, of laurel and
Rhododendron. Between shrieks,
A bluejay's, one call recurs,
High, low, low, low, the fall
Chromatic, moan of the
Mourning dove.

America,
East, with a little voice
Unfolding an emptiness, huge,
Though trucks roar through it, sirens,
Foghorns defy, define it.

And you? How near
In space, and more deaf
To me than my dead are.
So that now if I speak
It is of the emptiness, in a voice
Damped as the dove's in winter,
Of the emptiness only. But there,
If anywhere, you are listening,

Part of it, never more
Than half-born into place,
Time, from a region
Watery, leafy, dreamed
Before the cities were built.

Too late I take back
Those words and names
Of place, time, spoken
To bind you, to bend you
Awake. A mending, you said,
And left and hid from me. Where?
Awake? Or lost now,
The next quarter of birth
Too sudden, a wrenching, a rending
Away from the shapes of conch,
Pebble, tendril and frond
That moulded your mind?
Not to know, your need now,
To creep into what remains
Of sleep, not to be known?

Enough of grabbing, holding,
Of our fidgety greed,
Clutter that men dump
On to Earth, into Earth
Until no cure will work
But beyond herself
To unload, explode her.

Last of my needs, you
I'll unlearn, relinquish
If that was love. Too late,
Let you go, return, stay
And move on. Let you be,
Nameless.

Begin again, saying:
Mountain. Lake. Light.
Earth. Water. Air.
You. Nothing more. No one's.

V

Now or before, when the dogwood flowered
And you came walking out of no street or house
Known to me, with a gift
So much more than itself that the promise
Could not be kept. But the loan
Was mine, to consume like the air
Of that 'sweete and most healthfullest climate',
Yours while you walk there, changed,
Breathing its loan of air,
And the dogwood flowers
Where other trees grew,
'Great, tall, soft, light,
And yet tough enough I think to be fitte
Also for masts of shippes'
Of the kind sunk by sandbanks,

Battered by hurricanes there,
At the wild cape.

Gone, lost, the trees and the ships,
The possession and hope of possession;
Found, through the giving up,
Where I'm not, on the white sands,
A shell in her hand, she, 'for ever fair'.

I move on, closer now to the end
That is no end as long as
One mountain remains, one lake,
One river, one forest
Yet to be named, possessed,
Relinquished, forgotten, left
For Earth to renew. Move on
To no end but of 'I', 'you'
And the linking words, love's,
Though love has no end,
Though words, when the link is broken,
Move on beyond 'I' and 'you',

As do his, who forsook the place,
His traffic island where love
Set up house and raised orphans,
Tenderly taught them to till
The hardest rock. Yet, after so much,
Gave in, to his blood's revolt
Against veins, against the heart
Pushing its dope, pumping
And pumping hope
Out into limbs that had learnt,
From things touched, to be still.
Could not eat now, the new bread
That tasted of flesh left unburied
Decades, frontiers ago,
Could not drink now, the new wine

That tasted of salt,
From a dry sea,
From a blinded eye,

And, slowly, began to go
Where he must, where
His poems had gone before him,
Into silence now, silence,
Water at last, water
Which, unclean, could wash
All it flows over, fills,
Even his mouth, of last words,
And move on.

Slowly, detained by love,
He went, but never
Slowly enough for Earth
In her long slow dream
That has not finished yet
With the gestation of man,
The breaker of her dream,
And has not finished
Digesting the teeth and bones
Of her dinosaurs.

Making and breaking words,
For slowness,
He opened gaps, for a pulse
Less awake, less impatient
Than his, who longed
To be dreamed again,
Out of pulverized rock,
Out of humus,
Bones, anthropoid, saurian,
And the plumage of orioles;
Cleared a space, for the poems
That Earth might compose
'On the other side

Of mankind'
And our quick ears
Could not hear.

Gone. Lost. Half-forgotten already
What quick eyes took in,
Quick hands felt the shape of, tongue
Touched with a name. Half-forgotten
The oriole's drab call
High up, on the crest of a flowering pear-tree,
A month or two back, not here,
Not in the city garden
Where from a drabber throat
A thrush luxuriantly warbles and foxgloves
Find a wood, though the woods were felled.

VI

Autumn again. Heavy and hot
Between rain. With a flowering still,
Belladonna, hibiscus, honeysuckle
While the leaves turn.
Around noon
From treeless pavements the sun
Hits back. All over them lie
Cicada, locust, moth
And butterfly, dying.
Neither frost nor gale
Hurt them. Their end
Was inside them, always.

But even on grey mornings now
It is birdsong I hear, and the dove's call,
Dark, not heard when I woke
To the slant of rays on to branches
Or brick. In all seasons,
All weathers, the first light,
Though less than the straight, lifts

A weight from foliage, from roofs,
From dew-wet grass, from
Those who slept.

There will be a second warbling
Before dusk, of thrush or mockingbird,
No matter now which, when the day's dregs,
Business half-done, half-botched
Beyond undoing, yes and no knotted,
Clutter ears as they settle,
To rise once more in dream,
Wildly churned, swirling,

Each particle a body, a face,
Now near, now receding, dissolved
Into flux and reconstituted
Only for more dissolution,
Mad dance within the mind
On a floor that spins, drops
And shoots up,
Till the hand held, become
The hand about to stab,
Plunging back too far, too fast,
Punctures the membrane wall.

Hardly one name was contained
In the dream fluid
Which, draining out, washes.
True, the awakening gives
Names to the shapes
Already gone,
In a silence nothing
Worse than owl's cry,
Train's rumble breaks.
Yet night belittles those dancers
'I', 'you', so that morning too
Is emptier, cleansed,

And at last it comes, the lightness,
Freedom to move or stay,
Be here and there, wholly,
Rid of the luggage left
In airports, railway stations
And locked up there, unclaimed,
With labels that peel, fade;
Forgetting to ask what woods are these,
What spider weaves the thread
Stretched from high branch to low
Across the path;
Felt on the skin, too fine to be fingered.

Knowing less and less, knowing
That to walk is enough
On the one, the various earth,
To see is enough,
The less lumbered with names,
The more filled with the sight,
With the light that's nobody's yet,
New, after all it has fallen on,
New, wherever it falls;

Needing less, knowing
That at last a rightness must come
Of so much unlearnt.

    VII

So much forgotten. Care:
A furniture carefully kept,
Lovingly dusted, a houseful of it,
And passed on, in perfect condition,
For the heir to care about, care for
And leave to his heir undiminished.
A garden of it, endangered
By one week of neglect.

So much forgotten. As leaves fall
To make room for buds,
Food for the root that remembers
Leaf-shape, leaf-texture
When boughs are bare, sap lies
Low and rests.

Number, name alone
Are lost, reduced, fused
In humus. But seed
Remembers its kind.

Somewhere she walks, forgetting,
And the dogwood, scarlet here,
Where she walks is green.

No season now.
On the autumn, the spring bough
A mockingbird sings.
When rain comes down,
Wind rattles, wind soughs
It is winter. A dry stalk cracks.
And the bird rising
Flies into stillness.
If then a tree stirs
Wind has shifted, before
Snow blots it all.

Any season now.
When sun breaks through
It is summer.
There's a whirr, faint,
Intermittent, of grasshopper, cricket.
Sunbeams, through haze, draw
Copper, bronze, brass tints
From the wooded hills;
Green again, too. The air blends

Fragrance of sweet fern
With hemlock's, juniper's harshness.

I move on, I stop.
The chipmunk that shot for cover
Between rocks, creeps out
And sits, exposed.
We meet, eye to eye,
Where we can, in a stillness,
A suspense of ourselves in stillness,
Breathing, both of us, in a stillness taut
As breath held.

I break it, walk on
Or back, into rain, snow
That conceals and holds
Every colour, shape;
And without looking know
The buds on bare boughs.

Where am I? Here and there,
In a place my own
And no one's. The seasons whirl,
Halt. I question the air
And hear not one dove moan.

Let the rains wash
What they will; and snow fall
On all, over all.

Clouds bunch. A cold wind blows.
On the leafless tree
A mockingbird sings.

VIII

Or here, in the city garden,
Thinly, a wren,
Wintry piccolo minims,
Icicle tinkle, heard
From the house that was
Home. Or a robin
Twittering seasonless, thinly.

That much remains. While the walls crack,
Tiles come sliding down from the roof
And rot reduces doors
To a brittle screen, just holding.

Time to begin to think
Not of staying, there's none,
But of letting wheels roll,
Bow thrust, turbine suck in
Any air whatever, wherever.

With hope, fear? Not much.
Listening, looking still,
Not too shocked by the lurch
That fails to alarm, mocks:
To fall is one way of moving.

March. A swirl of snow
On to crocus, daffodil, primrose,
In earnest, it seems, for an hour,
As though come to stay, cover
Blossom proved rash and wrong,
To soak it, if not to freeze.
The sun breaks through; and flakes whirl
Single, slow, like petals
To which fumbling bees have clung.

That much remains:
Spring again, for an hour,
In the city that was
Home, but now forbids
A sense of return:
The remembered doorway
Different, the new
Indifferent. Both estranged.

Earth. Water. Air.
And fire, the sun's that sustains
Or fission's that sears, blasts
When other energy fails –
These remain, while Earth is stripped,
Ripped and chipped by steel,
Rain forests felled, even the sea's bed
Pierced, whole mountains levelled, lakes
Poisoned or drained.

Not for long will a bird circle
The place where the treetop was
And the nest. Once released
From the need, never again
May breed, but in his kind's unmaking
Only find rest –

Light now, light indeed
From such unlearning,
With earth to rot into,
Water to wash, dissolve,
Air to fall through
And fire, to burn in.

Estranged. By those global routes,
All curved now, all leading back

Not to the starting-point
But through it, beyond it, out again,
Back again, out. As the globe rotates
So does the traveller, giddy with turning, turning
And no return but for more departure,
No departure that's not a return.
To what? To a home beyond home,
Beyond difference, indifference, sameness;
Beyond himself, who is here and there,
Who is nowhere, everywhere, in a season endlessly turning.

IX

Together we've walked, and apart,
Over mountains, by lakes,
On seashores, of sand, pebble, rock,
Moorland or marshland, on cliffs
Overgrown or sheer, through woods
Dark with leafage or dense
With bramble, scrub, bracken;
Down streets of how many cities,
On cobbles, on brick, on slabs
Always dabbed with old blood or new;
To look, to listen, to take in
And discard the dialects, histories,
To discover, uncover, a bareness
More lastingly ours; to return
And, dying a little, become
Less than we were, and more
By the loss, by the giving back;
If not moving, moved on,
Out of ourselves, beyond
'I', 'you', and there
Brought to a meeting again
After difference, barer;
Hardly daring to speak
The other's name or the word
Of sameness in otherness, love;

To name a thing or a place,
Lest the name stick to a husk,
To a stump, to the gateway left
When a house was demolished.
                                    No,
Let the light record it, the seedling
That rises once more to the light
Where the parent's taproot was cut;
Or love's element only,
Fire, the last and first –
Let it blast, consume, reduce,
Propel, transmute; and create
Again, out of glowing rock-mash, an island,
Out of loose, mad atoms a planet.

For a while, though, yet
It's the wind, the sky's colour
That will bring us news. Today
Blackish clouds, blown, merge
And fray; their shadows race
Along pavement, lawn, chasing
Break-away sunbeams. A hint
Of hyacinth now; stronger,
The odour of soil roused
By showers, with last year's leaves
And wood-ash being rendered,
Washed down, mixed in, still,

Whether or not we see them, mountains, lakes,
The forgotten, the unknown, breathing
Heather or thyme, blossom of lemon or laurel,
Pine tang, salt tang or tar or dust;
Trusting the name, seek out
A roadside changed, grown strange,
Or await the turn and recurrence
Of mind's, of blood's weather,

Fragrances that a breeze
Blew where we walked, blew beyond us
And blows to someone, to no one;
Stop here, move on.

REAL ESTATE

for Anne

1

Weary we came to it, weary
With advertisement's weary verbiage
And all those inglenooks, plastic antiquities,
The cocktail bar cottage,
The swimming-pool farmhouse,
The concreted paddocks, the pink mirrors lining
That bathroom suite in the Georgian mansion,
All the stuff that, bought at a steep price,
We could never afford to get rid of, by de-converting.

2

'For sale by auction: The Rectory,
Standing in well-timbered grounds
In this unspoilt village.
A fine period house requiring
Improvement and restoration.
A range of Outbuildings.' Yes.
'A Garage'. Noted.

3

We went. And there it stood,
Plain, white, right,
Austere, but with gables, bow front
('A later addition'), hint
Of indulgence in curves, dips.
Large, but not grand, compact.
Too sure of itself to be showy.
So real, it amazed, overwhelmed you.
So self-sufficient, you wanted it.

4

For sale by auction, at a low reserve,
After Easter, the powerful temptation
Of realness, every inch of the house honest –
With the rendering brutally stripped
Here and there, to reveal
Rot of beams, erosion, cracks
In brick, stone, the sliding,
Minute even now, and slow, slow,
Down into older dampness, of the foundations.

5

Settle there, could you, dare you,
On settlement? Settle ('subject to covenant'),
Bid for a place become
Pure idea of duration, dwelling
Among rook caws up in the black yews,
The taller pines, near graves,
Near enough to feel always
Held there, beyond dislodging –
If the floorboards, only a little aslant,
Hold, if the roof holds, if . . .

6

And the gardens, wilderness
Whose high walls keep intact
The pure idea, *hortus conclusus*,
Her who reigned with her lilies
Over wilderness trained, restrained –
Graveyard, no more, true
For bough, blossom, fruit
Gone down into older dampness,
To rise again, fleshed, if . . .

7

If not, the dead in their graves,
Near enough, will be heard laughing
At folk who need so much room,
Such an effort of warmed walls,
To make a home for themselves, a peace;
And on their treetops the rooks
Join in, with a raucous guffawing.

8

Let's go, let the place be:
Too real for us to meddle with, pure idea of dwelling.
Not for us will the rooks caw
Or the gardens bear again flowers and fruit;
Not at us will the rooks laugh.
But anywhere, miles from this burial-ground,
The wide-awake dead can tell us a thing or two
About making do with our real estate,
The for ever indifferently furnished, poorly maintained,
Defectively fenced or walled;
About how indifference grows on us, and the chores grow harder.

9

Let's go, and revisit those empty rooms,
Occupy them in dreams that restore without labour
Any house you have lost
Or lacked the means to acquire; improve it, too.
One look, and dream takes possession
Of all that the look took in; and will work wonders
With ruins, with rubble, with the bare site,
Instantly will rebuild, instantly raise the dead
For conversation with you, for communion;
And where no root is, no seed,
Break sunbeams for you with the blackness of full-grown pines.

WILLOW

Hard wood or soft?
It is light, startlingly,
Not close-grained, to last
As oak does; but makes up
In obstinate wiry toughness for that
With all its fibres.
From the barkless bough
My axe rebounds;
My handsaw bends,
From the sham death
Willow, by shamming, defies.

Pick any twig, dormant
Or wrenched off in a gale,
Stick it in moist earth,
And it makes a tree.
Leave a trunk, fallen
Or felled, sprawling
Across a stream,
And it lives on,
Sprouts from the hollow
Half-rotten stump or
Takes root from a dropped limb.

Chop up the dry remains,
Burn them: they'll spit.

BIRCH

Vestal she seems, ballerina
Of wildest, of waste places,
With an aspiration to whiteness
Fulfilled in America's North,
A papery peel so flawless,
It would shame the contagion of ink;
Yet rarely will attain
Her maturity's fulness,
Too often herself wasted,
Her bitter, her harsh timber
Stunted by what she favours,
Blizzards bending her limbs,
Long stillness under snow;
Will lie prone suddenly,
Crowded out, or as though felled
By a blow from her own boughs.
And proves brittle then, graceless:
Her wrapping of bark more lasting
Than the mouldered body within.

From *Late* (1997)

IV

IF NOW, a guest, I go back
To my native city,
What I see is not what I know
Who from certain death in childhood
Was removed for a second birth
In another city, another country,

And will not look again
At the buildings, all preserved,
Of the certified arrival,
Of the protracted departure, parting,
The many rooms two grandparents cleared
Of heirlooms, acquisitions
So that, lightened of that care,
In other countries, cities
They could lodge and die;
Nor the few rooms in which
The widowed grandmother left
Her heirlooms, her mementoes,
Dragged or driven east
Into her certain death,
Uncertified, nameless.

Will not look again even
At the village house, preserved,
By the river wide as a lake
Where my seeing began,
My knowing, rarely of cities.

SLOW CATHERINE WHEEL of a magpie's flight
Uncanny here, where repeatedly
Festive lights, on wings too heavy,
To the metallically plumed, the celebrants,
As to bare progeny snatched from mothering nests,
Divisive, carried destruction.

Coo of the collared dove, amplified
By windowless walls left standing
When those they were raised to defend from fire
Perished by fire or else by the blast
That cracked or burst façades,
Only concrete blank enough
To outlast the eras, dynasties.
Where the brickwork, the red, the ochre, the blackened
Remained, it grew archaic,
Became a monument overnight
With its caryatids, the stucco and marble,
Oaken doors so heavy, so thick
That homes were fortresses,
But a scavenging cat with luck could outlive
An order, a dynasty;
And the poplars' pollen puffs,
Wafted still down streets become frontiers,

NOT MINE ever again to cross,
Whether heavy, murderous,
Bureaucracy's barriers loomed there
Or bodily were demolished,
Known, if not seen, nonetheless
By those whom they fashioned,
Defended or shut out,
Released, delivered to
Another order not theirs.

The bordering blocks, while they stand,
The cobbled roads beyond,
Villas usurped, vacated
Palaces, too, again and again converted
To the complexions of power
By difference will remind them
Of histories that never could be growth.

ALIEN, SETTLER, traveller –
None in the flux, confusion
Looks long enough to tell
Which it is, was, will be –
For small continuities
Elsewhere I had to search,
Other light than the festive,
Intermittently found them.
Once in a city even,
At one time within a crowd
In whose hearts and heads
Civility prevailed
Over difference, real
Or projected, corporate,
A pervasive poison;
Over slyness so coarse that its lies,
Insistent, blunted the blade of wit
Till language itself was void.

NOT IN ANY city now
What I see is what I know.
For its business I lack true words
Unless a market, out in the open,
Or, subsisting, a shop
Offers produce, not numbers,
And artefacts, too,
Work of mere hands
Impelled by a heart and a head.
From the attrition, wear,
Murderous in the end,
Of manager and managed,
Of usurer and misused,
Waster and planet laid waste
Language itself rebounds.

Meanwhile here and there
From high window ledges, in trees
Collared doves not long ago
Removed from east to west
By a need beyond our knowing
Make their communal morning music
That, amplified or softer, more distant,
With a ritual of cadences, tones
To human ears transmit
Strange comfort, as of praise.
Here and there, slow Catherine wheels
Variously kindled in changing light,
A magpie's wings in flight,
Metallically plumed, are turning.

From *Intersections* (2000)

MIGRANTS IV

To the east a sickle moon glimmers,
From the west a low sun lights
With a radiance cleansed by lateness
Grasses beginning to droop,
Dandelion still open mixed with hawkweed that closes,
Colchicum heat-waves had forced,
Nerine also, paled by rugosa roses.
Mint, box, thyme blend their odours.
On the darker side evening primroses shine
With a noonday brightness deferred.
In breezes half-chill that whet them
Dragonflies whir and quiver,
More deeply butterflies drink.
On boughs shedding their foliage early
That bent when springs were milder
A few plums turn from purple to blue.

If swallows nested here still they'd be leaving,
A straggler or two be soaring once more, so high
That grounded senses must follow
And, failing, losing the trail, must acknowledge death,
By love rooted fast as the trees we planted.

Seed these may cast from the root that delved and reached out,
But are not the seed or the sapling,
Dislodged, cannot home like the warblers they lodged.
Limbs lopped, reduction they may endure,
Root severance even, as long as the weathers contend,
A moon, though ghostly, glimmers,
A sun refutes her with waning but warmer beams.

Never, until the bulk of this willow grows wings
Blithely shall we line up
For a scheduled departure,
For a take-off in time
Towards the leafless, the birdless air.

RELICS

Four old ewes, past lambing,
No ram at their side, crop
A paddock once marsh, then meadow;
When shorn now, not for the wool
But coolness in dog-days, relief granted
By pensioners to the pensioned
For the tending alone
Of a fondness, a gratitude.

The near-solstice low sun
Of morning, evening mixes gold
Into the grey of their weathered full fleeces;
And the village that was,
Frugal in labouring love,
Subsists while they graze here still.

From *From a Diary of Non-Events* (2002)

DECEMBER

I

Sunshine on hoarfrost: one true winter day
After a whole year's cloudbursts, hurricane, drizzle,
Puddles on flowerbeds, the well-drained marsh a bog.

It's advertisers' Advent. GLOBAL WARNING
Where flood water creeps or sweeps, tall trees crashed down.

Outside this window residual birds are fed
Imported peanuts, packaged grain, assorted.
Rats have gnawed through
Another hardwood frame
To raid the apple store
As if no glut of fallen apples lay
On the rats' playground larger than room or house.
Or was it a squirrel so deregulated?
Those frames had lasted since the walls were built.

All's mending now, not making.
As beggared birds to gardens
Wildness draws in.
Their moors, their woods, their shores
Are less than the remembered.
From the near pasture plovers have vanished,
Snipe, red-legged partridge, skylark, thrush
Whose kinds were doubled in the wane of light,
Enriching it, left iciest winter true.

2

Lured by a virtual music,
Birdcalls clogged ears retain,
Abstract of what the seasons hid and held,
In mind alone I walk away from chores
Towards the sea, old matrix of all making
Depleted here of whales' meal, primal plankton,
Kelp jungle, mollusc, fish,
Capacious, though, as death, potential still.

Moonlight grows real again in these long nights,
Lets even land be real
For eyes that unreality estranged,
Promiscuous distraction dulled and dimmed.

I hear the barn-owl's wings, the never heard,
By them in starless darkness find my way.

from APRIL

I

Fools' Day has tricked the diagnostic view:
A visible sun has risen
At the pasture's far end from a scud
Not smoke but vapour released at last
From ground long sodden, puddled.
Out of that wispy whiteness contours emerge,
The whiter white and black
Of the Frisian cows grazing as ever,
Prodigious now as a Gipsy encampment surprised
In a German glade in April 1945,
A congregation of Jews untagged
In the centre of ruined Dresden.
Here too eugenics, the money-driven,
Doomed the defenceless breeds
To be slaughtered for purity by butchers mortal, impure.

In the foreground, survivors at one remove,
A family outing of pheasants runs
From no threat of gun or fox
Where once it was peewits that fed and nested,
A black and white, a greener lustre responded in feathers lit.

from JULY

I

A wane it is that rules this flowering,
High summer's, a descent,
Long light, brief petals with no power to cling,
Slowly evolved, prepared, but not to keep,
Even the packed, impenetrably deep
Of Gallica, Bourbon, Damask, Moss, Provence.

Look now, look hourly, so lavishly they're spent
Though never drenched or ruffled by one breeze;
Flimsier the cistus flowers – epiphanies
More instantaneous still:
Their mottled pattern splits, illegible.
Familiar foxglove, then, campanula,
The learnt by heart, plain brier – do they stay?
Hardly by repetition of the day
Gardeners labour, wait for, wearying:
Fulfilment sinks into sleep.

2

For my dead friend, searcher of silences
Through words that were not speech or song
Will it be wrong
To break a silence with words that would cohere?
Only by naming him I should intrude
As when, a stranger to him, my older friend
Who out of loneliness
Must flick quick darts that, probing, pricked, provoked,
Bantered 'Your trouble is, you've never suffered.'
And he, the reticent, austere, serene,
In rage rose from the table, tilting it,
The tea things toppled at a summer suit;
Then, hurt Achilles in his tent, sat brooding
Until sufficient silence hatched forgiveness.

Silence it was that in his words I read,
Rarely of selfhood suffered.
Small-talk at tables we have left as litter
In Texas, Mexico, 'my' Suffolk and 'his' Drôme.
Walking there, left met silences to roam,
Listening, looking for the never said.
His logic was elision, to let silence in,
A syntax of hiatus, false reason shredded.
This much I could know of him – and what we saw together,
Each then to work on in his own prevailing weather
Like the white-golden rose
Searched for in vain till for both gardens found:
Another silence shared on separate ground.

On what was 'his' in greater silence now it grows,
And, here, another too,
Come true from seed of one of his, mauve-red –
An archetype revealed, perfect regression? –
Denies he can be dead
While the same silence rounds that flowerhead.

From *Wild and Wounded* (2004)

WILD AND WOUNDED

I

Visit or visitation, when in frost
A heron descends to the garden pond
For any snack, late frog or goldfish fry,
Frustrated by the cover's netting stands
A monument to hunger, motionless?

So it has always been.
But on the snow-flecked lawn
As never yet in twenty-six winters here
A swan sat, whiter, hissed when we fed him bread,
For two days barely shifted, though he grazed
Within his lithe neck's radius,
Calmer than we were after another death –
Until he made to rise,
Dragging one leg, a wobbling majesty
Not come by choice, for refuge
From riveret pasture puddled now and iced,
Crash-landed, gashed while in flight or fight:
A casualty, a case,
Therefore to be removed, hospitalized.

2

Meddling is human, Adam said, and Cain,
Remembrance mortal too. The haunting ceases.
Get out your guest-book, then,
Your cenotaph of the fallen, who knows where,
No matter if incomplete:
For winter, jack-snipe, furrowing, red-legged partridge,
Fieldfare and redwing, song and missel thrush,
Three kinds of other rank sparrows, noted when they were gone,
The whole long field mottled with plovers daily,
Dusk marked by barn-owl's passing
And for top brass marsh harrier's whirl at prey.
Oh, and the swallows, martins more than missed
For their low muttering, wilderness brought home.

3

No loss to them, merged in their time unmeasured,
Nameless identity
That suffering, maimed, wants nothing but to be
Or perish, so humble their indifference.
Roused from complaisance, looking, walking, we
Clash with an empty cage
Which, wildering, we, for our not their defence
Blast in self-injuring rage
At absence, ours to feel, of trapped lives treasured:
End of an age, our age.

4

The tamed no less, the petted, the still tended,
Our cultivars driven wild:
Clenched rose in January, primrose and violet
Amid the aconites, growth without rhyme or season
By the mad weathers tricked, beguiled:
A warm breeze after hurricane, frost and rain
That seemed unending, flooded the kitchen floor,
Those weathers in our doings, in our minds.
When friends and strangers met for this New Year
The small-talk halted, ripped by small detonations –
Of course, the firework rockets in the street,
Defiant celebrations,
Larger explosions imminent, not here,
Too near the fission works long obsolete.

5

Dreaming, I see my father sixty-three years dead
Come to my work-room where engrossed, engaged
I ask the walking wounded
To wait a little in the sitting-room
Before I join him there.
But then it's travels, devious and drawn-out,
Uncertainties, delays.
At a forgotten house
I see my mother opening some back pantry door,
Her who died forty years later,
Remind her who I am. She seems preoccupied,
Almost fades out, the scene – a home? – suspended.
Perhaps, though, turning, less absorbed, she whispered:
'Come back when *you* have died.'

6

Frost has returned, rime to the swans' terrain
Beside the riveret
Where, whiter, distant, a family crops and wanders,
Even or odd, symmetrical, incomplete.
I'll count no heads now, lines or syllables
To fix this whiter whiteness quivering.

TRANSITION

On my own bed and she on hers beside it
From nightmare I woke into calm more uncanny,
Farther from me than my long departed her face.
A different light, not of the sun or moon
Suffused a space beyond recollection,
Inherent light, it seemed, yellowish overall.
If a green, blue, red dared mix in, it was merged
In shapes without shadows, mass without contour or kind,
So that wide awake as I was, I could not look
For the once nearest, most known –
All dissolved, my landmarks and ways,
The bounded ground of our tending,
Lifetime furniture put away into store.
Good riddance, blurred rockface gloated,
Here nobody, nothing, is mourned.
Only in this, a light so estranging, so still
Will you stir again to a meeting, mended by loss.

From *Circling the Square* (2007)

DOMESTIC

I

'Hardly a fantast, except in dreams,
All sorts of things you put into your poems,
Their auras, their mutations, vanishings –
But out of doors – by preference, evasion?
Now verse, while you can, the habitation too
Called yours for some three decades,
Not a herbarium, this time, nor a zoo.
For once pick an interior. Let us in.'

Into a medley of anachronisms?
Being not one but many succesive mixtures
Of styles, materials, fixtures,
Hotchpotch, some of it botched, of odds and ends,
Amalgam of five centuries or so
Dream-gathered for his father-in-law-to-be
By an eccentric poet-painter-architect
Adding a studio wing
To labourers' cottages durably plain?
And the full inventory that would bore
Anyone save an agent, auctioneer
Or TV archaeologist breathless in glib surprise
That there's a past, flashed into and out of eyes,
Into and out of ears already surfeited?

Reduction, blanks, restriction
Make readable both history and fiction:
Fragments are what we know –
Even of our own selves: they come and go.
Habits of beauty, skill and expectation?
Sudden and slow is perception's way.

Wandering sunbeam at play
On leaves indifferent yesterday,
This crest, these branches fed
By roots in darkness, never dug up till dead.

2

Well it's a listed building. Listed for what,
Often we've wondered. Could it be
That inconveniences so multifarious,
So cumulative make it a rarity?
Tudor garage, unheatable, and adjoining
Tudor bread oven, bricked over, defunct
In deference to an AGA cooker
Converted to oil, if later, for labour-saving,
Hot water piped to the lion-legged bathtub upstairs.

That garage, though, on a bend in the lane
Asks for collision by speed or stealth –
Experienced once, since when it serves
As an apple-store from autumn to spring . . .

If, curious, you search the middle cottage,
In a sitting-room closet you'll find
Proof that the Jacobeans, too, baked bread,
With that enrichment can load your head:
A second bread oven flue, dear to our cats;
Also, that leaded panes were made to last,
Like the wide hardwood floorboards,
Oak beams perennially wood-wormed, yet firm –
Unlike their deal replacements, brittle with rot . . .

An expert recently revealed
Signs of a late mediaeval pre-existence –
Intuited perhaps by the conflating architect
When in the 1920 studio he installed
A stone baronial mantelpiece of that period –
Genuine or replica the smoke-stains have concealed.

As for the after-life,
It's marked by a water-pump inscribed 1770 –
A date not indifferent to me, never mind why . . .
Or the various underground cisterns,
Why, when and where they were lined with care,
What need or luxury they supplied –
Rain water pumped into his lady's bath
By the late Colonel, our predecessor
Who to a gossipy Rector calling
Would say: 'I'll give you five minutes, Padre' . . .

3

Oh, this eccentric house –
A bit of everything, with gadgets that were modern
In 1920 or in 1930,
Now worn, senescent, dirty.
That studio was partitioned, central heating conducted
To part of the whole, still never warm in winter,
Source of the latest loss:
A leaking radiator, senile, that in our absence
Drenched the box files of irreplaceable papers
Left on the floor of the library it became.

So fondness has turned ironic,
Rhymes it comes up with limpingly Byronic
While we bear with them still, the drudgery, damage, bother,
Indulge them as one does a great-grandmother
In her third childhood . . . bustle on, though lame . . .
And could bleat on till silenced – but for shame.

4

Beyond the studio annexe, where the lane is straight
Stands that on which I'll concentrate:
A Nissen hut, crass utility plonked there
For a real war, the house requisitioned
As a rest-home for men commissioned
And more or less disabled –

Their attendants also to be housed or stabled –
Then, when the Colonel had bought the place,
He a handyman, contraption-maker,
A rusting memorial, transmogrified:
To him as good as listed,
Spacious enough, besides, for lumber and recollection . . .
Yes, and a car – or two, were a second required.

Inside, on what were shelves or dumped the length of the walls,
More relics, of detritus, disuse,
Timbers, slats half-decayed,
Weatherboards, doors, broken mowers,
Tools that might have been mended,
Bamboo canes from the marsh, stacked there so long
That they themselves would need propping,
Glass covers for the coldframe whose brick foundations
Long ago crumbled away . . .

Sixty years on, it's nature again, naturalizing,
That hides, redeems the intruding eye-sore,
Holds together – how? – the convenient structure,
Corrugated iron curved double sheets of the roof
Patched with plastic surrogates, rust-free, that crack,
Camouflaged now for a truce of sorts, sealed
By a cover of evergreen ivy,
Clouded in June with the clustered white
Of the most potent of rambler roses, tiniest multiflora.

True, no more swallows bravely whizzing
To their nests through a gap in the panes,
No more stove recalled from other rank service
That made such barrack room huts a home,
Floor palliasse our bedding –
Unless on groundsheets we slept out of doors,
Only canvas for shelter
And – neither stove nor dry ration carried –
With a bayonet filched a turnip,
Raw grub, from some farmer's field . . .

A hint, for you, of continuity
Which furniture, too, attests, and an archive salvaged
From wreck, disruption, deep forgetfulness –
But every salvaged thing threatened again by the sea . . .

5

Do I let you in?
So far, no farther, friend,
Halting, halted before the end of a story
That can no more end than begin . . .

Histories, mysteries, whether our own or another's
We took over, lived in, conserved where we could
And, if we can, shall pass on,
These tenants, too, gone.

The rest, much more, I must withhold,
If by interior you meant confession:
Vain words are poison worse than indiscretion,
From which a truth can spring, to one grown old,
The too much of a life untellable – if not already told
By intimation of what's intimate,
Mere moments, always, that could centre
Slow years, slow centuries of this eccentric house
Whose dubious core not you nor I can enter.

6

How did it come about, this tenancy?
Need you ask? – Absurdly, foolishly:
Random fancy first, then obdurate grimness,
Defiant, or loyalty as perverse
As blessing, sustenance capsuled in a curse.

It was a mulberry tree,
Centenarian at least, that seduced us buyers,
Made us the occupiers
Of what went with it, nobody sane would touch,

As the surveyor warned, dissuading us,
Listing the defects for clients deaf to such:
So mixed, these modesties are ruinous,
This minimality will prove too much . . .

An infamous hurricane laid our landmark flat,
Half the root ripped, the bulk and leafage sprawling
On flowerbed, lawn and path – a surgical case,
One upright branch only spared from sawing, lopping
In hope that the half-root, trunk's torso now prostrate
Might still sustain just that.

They did, made more of less,
New growth, new fruitfulness,
Out of near-death by amputation
Let a poor nucleus live.

And there's one positive
For you, within a wry narration,
Inaudible pulse within the real estate,
Unlisted throb, unlistable, unhoused.

AGING VII

On long vacation, year in, year out,
Residual guests in a once grand hotel,
We busy ourselves, planning the day's distractions
From vacuous repetition, seasonless:
Something a little different on our plates,
Exchange of words more and more strenuous,
For happening, real event
A voice from the past not silenced yet, gasping.

Or, wilder waters too far behind,
Goldfishes in a garden pond
That's plastic-lined
We linger on, contentedly confined,
Bred in a tank, need yearn for no beyond
But lurk, dart, wriggle while we can
Within a leaking inwardness, our dwindling span.

Else, conservationists
Of some patch small or larger we call home,
Servants of earth to the last,
With failing finger-joints, arthritic,
Legs that had lugged equipment for miles on forced marches,
Then released, for a lark slogged from London to Cornwall,
Worn out at the hip now, kneel as in prayer
To let through light for seedling, sapling planted,
Less than half-remembered, found under weeds by searching
That it may live, outlive our care –
Although it cannot, merged in the natural flux,
Razed by the murderous, bulldozing money's.

Further loss, worse, withheld, all must be well:
Defiance like acceptance leaves it so.
With given tongues only could we curse
Or, humbled, hold them, wiser.

Enough that in late June,
After such clotting cloud, ice winds that shrivelled
Apple leaves newly shaped
Our sky has cleared again – and is not ours.

3 *The Translator*

Johann Wolfgang von Goethe (1749–1832)

From *Goethe: Roman Elegies and Other Poems* (1996)

THE EARLIEST version of a Goethe poem I have found among my papers was done in 1939, at the age of fifteen. Intermittently I have been translating Goethe ever since, but it took the 150th anniversary of Goethe's death in 1832 to prod me into collecting these versions. The juvenile one is excluded, if only because I no longer like its original, 'Das Göttliche'; but I have now been able to add all the later translations excluded from the first edition of this book, because they were due to appear in an edition of Goethe's selected works in English then being prepared in America. If even the present gathering of all but my juvenile versions of poems by Goethe remains miscellaneous in character, one reason is that I have never been able to translate Goethe as persistently and consistently as I translated his younger contemporary Hölderlin; and all my repeated attempts suggest that much of Goethe's best poetry is hardly translatable into English. The evidence of two centuries of English Goethe renderings points to the same conclusion. Most of his lyrical poetry remains virtually unknown outside the schools and universities. *Faust* is translated again and again; but no single version has established itself as a standard text in the English-speaking world.

To reflect on the untranslatability and elusiveness of Goethe's poetic work as a whole is to go straight to the heart of his uniqueness, his staggering diversity and the extent to which many of his most original poems – especially the earlier lyrics – are inextricably rooted in their own linguistic humus. Though I hope that even the small selection that follows will at least intimate the range and scope of Goethe's shorter poems, the selection could not be a balanced one, because those songs and ballads in which Goethe came closest to folksong defied translation – and so did many of the poems of his middle and later years that go to the opposite extreme of intricately formal artifice.

The unity within the diversity of Goethe's work has been looked for mainly in his personality, which was documented with unprecedented diligence even in his lifetime – not without his connivance. Yet the 'open secret' of Goethe's unity seems to me to lie elsewhere: not in the ego so disliked by many of his readers and critics – the 'disagreeable, egotistical man and overrated writer' whom Patrick White's Waldo, of *The Solid*

Mandala, must have encountered in the *Conversations with Eckermann* or a biography rather than Goethe's own works – but in the degree to which Goethe's ego was always a vehicle for the 'it', whose discovery by Groddeck followed that psychologist's immersion in Goethe's works. 'There's something anonymous in it,' Goethe wrote in his old age about the identity we think we designate by people's names. The same is true of Goethe's poetry, even at its most confessional and seemingly most subjective. [. . .]

from the Introduction

From ROMAN ELEGIES (1788–90)

V

Happy now I can feel the classical climate inspire me,
    Past and present at last clearly, more vividly speak –
Here I take their advice, perusing the works of the ancients
    With industrious care, pleasure that grows every day –
But throughout the nights by Amor I'm differently busied,
    If only half improved, doubly delighted instead –
Also, am I not learning when at the shape of her bosom,
    Graceful lines, I can glance, guide a light hand down her hips?
Only thus I appreciate marble; reflecting, comparing,
    See with an eye that can feel, feel with a hand that can see.
True, the loved one besides may claim a few hours of the daytime,
    But in night hours as well makes full amends for the loss.
For not always we're kissing; often hold sensible converse.
    When she succumbs to sleep, pondering, long I lie still.
Often too in her arms I've lain composing a poem,
    Gently with fingering hand count the hexameter's beat
Out on her back; she breathes, so lovely and calm in her sleeping
    That the glow from her lips deeply transfuses my heart.
Amor meanwhile refuels the lamp and remembers the times when
    Likewise he'd served and obliged them, his triumvirs of verse.

XV

Caesar, I think, would never have dragged me to far-away Britons,
    Easily Florus instead into the taverns of Rome!
It's those dismal fogs of the North. Still I find them more loathsome
    Than a whole work-team of keen Mediterranean fleas.
And from today more devoutly than ever I'll celebrate wineshops,
    Osterie, as inns aptly by Romans are called;
For today one showed me my darling, her uncle beside her,
    He whom so often the dear hoodwinks to dally with me.
Here was our table, the usual circle of Germans around it,
    Next to her mother my love, seating herself over there,
Shifted the bench many times and cleverly managed to turn it
    So that one half of her face, all of her neck was in view.
Raising her voice rather more than do ladies in Rome, she took up the
    Bottle, looking at me, poured, when the glass was not there,
Spilling wine on the table, and then with her delicate fingers
    Over the table-top drew circles in liquid, and loops.
With her own she entwined my name; and attentively always
    Those small fingers I watched, she well aware that I did.
Lastly a Roman five she signalled resourcefully, nimbly,
    With an upright in front. Quickly, the signal received,
Circle through circle she wound to erase the letters and symbols,
    Yet that precious FOUR lingered, impressed on my eyes.
Silent I sat there meanwhile, biting my lips that were sore now,
    Partly from mischievous joy, partly from burning desire.
First, the few hours until nightfall; then four long hours of more
                       waiting!
    Sun up above, still you keep watch on your city of Rome!
Nothing greater you've seen and never will see a thing greater,
    Just as Horace your priest promised at one time, inspired.
But today, for once, do not stay, but avert your glances
    Soon from the Seven Hills, willing, for once, to depart!
For the sake of one poet curtail the magnificent daylight
    Which with eyes all aflame painters so relish and crave;
Glowing, take one more brief look at the palaces' lofty proportions,
    Cupolas, pillars and, last, up at the obelisks' tops;
Eagerly seek the sea and plunge in, all the sooner tomorrow
    Once again to behold age-old and godlike delight;

All these shores so moist, and so long overgrown with tall rushes,
　　All these heights for so long shaded with bushes and trees.
Few small hovels at first they revealed; then all of a sudden
　　Peopled you saw them, with crowds, fortunate brigands, they
　　　　　　　　　　　　　　　　　　　　　　　　teemed.
Every manner of thing then they hauled to these parts and assembled;
　　Hardly the rest of the globe now you found worthy of note.
Saw a world rise up here and then saw a world here in ruins,
　　Out of the ruins once more almost a greater world rise!
So that a long time yet by you I may see it illumined,
　　Let the Fate be slow, spinning that life-thread of mine.
All the quicker, however, the hour so invitingly signalled! –
　　Rapt, do I hear it now? No, but the third hour has struck.
So, dear Muses, once more you've beguiled the length of my waiting,
　　Tedious time-span that kept lover and lover apart.
Now farewell! As I hurry away, not afraid to offend you:
　　Proud you are, but to him, Amor, will always defer.

NATURE AND ART

Nature, it seems, must always clash with Art
And yet, before we know it, both are one;
I too have learned: Their enmity is none,
Since each compels me, and in equal part.

Hard, honest work counts most! And once we start
To measure out the hours and never shun
Art's daily labour till our task is done
Freely again may Nature move the heart.

So too all growth and ripening of the mind:
To the pure heights of ultimate consummation
In vain the unbound spirit seeks to flee.

Who seeks great gain leaves easy gain behind.
None proves a master but by limitation
And only law can give us liberty.

TO THOSE WHO THINK THEMSELVES ORIGINAL

I

Somebody says: 'Of no school I am part,
Never to living master lost my heart;
Nor any more can I be said
To have learned anything from the dead.'
That statement – subject to appeal –
Means: 'I'm a self-made imbecile.'

II

My build from Father I inherit,
His neat and serious ways;
Combined with Mother's cheerful spirit,
Her love of telling stories.
Great-grandfather courted the loveliest,
His ghost won't leave me alone;
Great-grandmother liked fine jewels best,
This twitch I've also known.
If, then, no mortal chemist can
Divide the components from the whole,
What in the entirety of that man
Could you call original?

Friedrich Hölderlin (1770–1843)

From *Friedrich Hölderlin: Poems and Fragments* (2004)

... SINCE I have never shared Hölderlin's religious allegiance to an idealized ancient Greece, or his grappling with its poetic forms, epic, lyrical and dramatic, inseparable as these were for him from a neo-Hellenism always in a state of tension with the culture of his time and place, what drew me to Hölderlin's work must have been something other than his themes and forms, something no more palpable, it may be, than his way of breathing in verse; and although I never know what has 'influenced' me, or how, I suspect that it was this, if anything, in Hölderlin, that entered into the writing of my longer poems and sequences. Once I had decided that I must retain his adaptation of classical forms in my versions, much more refractory though these forms have proved in English over the centuries than in German, my assimilation of his metres and rhythms also helped me to overcome the iambic compulsion dominant in most English verse later than the Anglo-Saxon, other than in verse measured by stress rather than syllable or 'foot' count or as free as some of Hölderlin's later poems became when 'free verse' was not a term in currency. This may be how dactyl and spondee came to mix freely in some of my later verse with the iambic beat.

. . . .

What meant more to me in my engagement with Hölderlin over the decades was his advocacy and practice of the 'modulation of tones' in longer poems, quite especially his inclusion of a 'naïve tone' among those to be modulated. Earlier on he had called this tone 'the language of the heart', as distinct from the sublime, idealistic, idyllic and heroic modes. My versions began only with the poems for which he had found this tone, self-critical enough as he was from his early youth onwards to have discarded the vapid rhetoric to which he had been moved by his theological and philosophical aspirations. This naïve tone must not be confused with dottiness. Hölderlin had once been the philosophical peer of his friends Hegel and Schelling, and remained anything but a simpleton in the critical prose I was too unphilosophical to translate, written in close proximity to his poetic concerns, up to the time of his Sophocles and Pindar versions and commentaries just before his self-alienation.

Having begun as so intellectual a poet – or 'sentimental' one, in terms of Schiller's distinction between 'naïve' and 'sentimental', that is, reflective poets – a deliberately placed 'naïve tone' became central to his practice and to his understanding of the nature of all poetry.

from Preface, 2003

TO THE FATES

One summer only grant me, you powerful Fates,
    And one more autumn only for mellow song,
        So that more willingly, replete with
            Music's late sweetness, my heart may die then.

The soul in life denied its god-given right
    Down there in Orcus also will find no peace;
        But when what's holy, dear to me, the
            Poem's accomplished, my art perfected,

Then welcome, silence, welcome cold world of shades!
    I'll be content, though here I must leave my lyre
        And songless travel down; for *once* I
            Lived like the gods, and no more is needed.

TO THE YOUNG POETS

Quite soon, dear brothers, perhaps our art,
   So long in youth-like ferment, will now mature
      To beauty's plenitude, to stillness;
         Only be pious, like Grecian poets!

Of mortal men think kindly, but love the gods!
   Loathe drunkenness like frost! Don't describe or teach!
      And if you fear your master's bluntness,
         Go to great Nature, let her advise you!

IN MY BOYHOOD DAYS ...

In my boyhood days
  Often a god would save me
    From the shouts and the rod of men;
      Safe and good then I played
        With the orchard flowers
          And the breezes of heaven
         Played with me.

And as you make glad
The hearts of the plants
When toward you they stretch
Their delicate arms,

So you made glad my heart,
Father Helios, and like Endymion
I was your darling,
Holy Luna.

O all you loyal,
Kindly gods!

Would that you knew how
My soul loved you then.

True, at that time I did not
Evoke you by name yet, and you
Never named me, as men use names,
As though they knew one another.

Yet I knew you better
Than ever I have known men,
I understood the silence of Aether,
But human words I've never understood.

I was reared by the euphony
Of the rustling copse
And learned to love
Amid the flowers.

I grew up in the arms of the gods.

EVENING FANTASY

At peace the ploughman sits in the shade outside
    His cottage; smoke curls up from his modest hearth.
        A traveller hears the bell for vespers
           Welcome him in to a quiet village.

Now too the boatmen make for the harbour pool,
    In distant towns the market's gay noise and throng
        Subside; a glittering meal awaits the
           Friends in the garden's most hidden arbour.

But where shall I go? Does not a mortal live
    By work and wages? Balancing toil with rest
        All makes him glad. Must I alone then
           Find no relief from the thorn that goads me?

A springtime buds high up in the evening sky,
    There countless roses bloom, and the golden world
        Seems calm, fulfilled; O there now take me,
           Crimson-edged clouds, and up there at last let

My love and sorrow melt into light and air! –
    As if that foolish plea had dispersed it, though,
        The spell breaks; darkness falls, and lonely
           Under the heavens I stand as always. –

Now you come, gentle sleep! For the heart demands
    Too much; but youth at last, you the dreamy, wild,
        Unquiet, will burn out, and leave me
           All my late years for serene contentment.

HEIDELBERG

Alcaic Version

Long I have loved you, and now for my own delight
    Would call you Mother, offer an artless song
        To you, of all the homeland cities
            Which I have seen the most lapped in beauty.

As over hilltops birds of the forest fly,
    Across the river gleaming past you the bridge
        Vaults over, sturdily and lightly,
            Loud with the traffic of feet and coachwheels.

As though divinely sent, an enchantment once
    Transfixed me on the bridge as I walked that way
        And right into the hills there came the
            Radiance and lure of far-distant places

And he, the youth, the river sought out the plains
    As sadly glad as hearts that, too full for ease,
        To perish out of love's abundance
            Hurl themselves down into time's quick torrents.

To him, the fleeting, well-springs you'd given, and
    Cool shade enough, and after him all the banks
        Now gazed, and from the rippled water
            Quivered their beautiful mirror image.

But heavy, hulking into the valley hung
    The fate-acquainted castle, the vast, all torn
        And battered down to its foundations;
            Nevertheless even there the sun now

Poured out renewing, youth-giving light upon
    That aging bastion's bulk, and around it bloomed
        The living ivy; kindly forests
            Breathed their soft murmur on brittle stonework.

Shrubs blossomed down to where in the valley's calm,
   Close to the hillside, leaning or fondly pressed
      Against the river-bank, your cheerful
         Streets are at rest beneath fragrant gardens.

NOTE: Hölderlin's poem is in the Asclepiadean metre, one that he rarely chose for his longer odes. Because, for all but epigrammatic effects, this metre is far more refractory in English than in German, I was unable to make my version flow across the caesuras in the first and second lines of each strophe. My original version, therefore, did not satisfy me, being neither truly metrical nor as free as I should have made it if I had not attempted to reproduce the metre. Since later attempts proved no more satisfactory, I transposed my version into Alcaics, a form that had become congenial to me in the course of translating Hölderlin, so that I could rely on my ear for it, rather than on 'scansion' and syllable counts.

    The whole vexed question of whether ancient quantitative metres can be imitated at all in English, or ought to be, must be left open here. I will mention only that the hexameters of A. H. Clough proved as flexible and natural a metre for him as the usual iambic pentameter for other English poets; and that some of Hölderlin's ode forms were successfully taken over by twentieth-century poets in English, Vernon Watkins and W. H. Auden among them.

THE TRAVELLER

Lonely I stood and looked out into African desert, unbroken
    Plains; and, standing there, saw fire from Olympus rain down,
Ravening fire scarcely more gentle than when in the same mountain
                                 ranges,
    Blasting their bulk with his rays, God made the heights and the
                                   depths.
Never on these, though, a forest with newly green leafage
    Into the resonant air, luscious and glorious, will rise.
All ungarlanded is the brow of this mountain, and eloquent torrents
    Hardly are known to it, brooks rarely complete their descent.
Noon by no murmuring well-spring goes by for the somnolent cattle,
    Not one hospitable roof amiably beckoned from trees.
Under dry bushes there sat a serious bird, never singing.
    But those migrants, the storks, hurriedly passed on their way.
Nature, not you did I ask for water there in the desert,
    But on the good camel's back only for drink could rely.
For the song of the groves, ah, and the gardens, my father's,
    Yes, I did ask – by the birds, migrants from homeland, recalled.
Then, though, you said to me: here also gods are, and they govern,
    Great is their measure, but men take as their measure the span.

And those words impelled me to look for other things also,
    Far off to the northern pole sailing I made my way.
Packed in its wrapping of snow a fettered life seemed to sleep there
    And for years iron sleep there had been waiting for day.
For not too long around Earth did Olympus wrap a fond arm here
    As Pygmalion's arm round his belovèd was wrapped.
Here with his sunny gaze he awakens no warmth in her bosom,
    Never with rain or with dew whispered those words that seduce;
And I marvelled at that, and I foolishly said to her: Mother
    Earth, will you always, then, waste, widowed, your time and your
                                   life?
When to give birth to nothing and nothing to lovingly care for,
    Never to see your own self imaged in children, is death.
Or in the heavenly beam after all still one day you'll be basking,
    Out of the dearth of your sleep raised by his breath after all;

And, like the living seed-grain, burst out of the husk that constricts
you,
    So that the world, unbound, tears itself loose and greets light,
All the strength so long gathered flares up in a springtime luxuriance,
    Roses glow and rich wine gushes in northerly dearth.

So I addressed her, and now I return to the Rhine, to my homeland,
    Feel, as I used to do, childhood's mild breeze on my face;
And my heart, the far-roaming, is soothed again by familiar
    Welcoming trees that before cradled the child in their arms
And the holy verdure betokening blissful and deeper
    Life in this world makes it new, changes the man to a youth.
Old in the meantime I've grown, and was blanched by the ice of
the Arctic,
    In the fire of the South lost many locks of my hair.
Yet if a man on his very last day as a mortal,
    Coming from far away, weary right down to his soul,
Were to revisit this country, once more to his cheeks must the colour
    Rise, and his eyes almost dimmed brightly would gleam once
again.
Blessèd valley, the Rhine's! Not one hill but is covered with vineyards,
    And with leaves of the grape garden and wall are adorned,
And on the rivers the ships are full of the drink that is holy,
    Cities and islands are all drunken with wines and with fruit.
Smiling and serious above them the ancient one, Taunus, reposes
    And his head crowned with oaks proudly the free one inclines.

And from the wood comes the stag now, from clouds comes the
daylight,
    Up in a sky that is clear now hangs the hawk and looks round.
But in the valley below where the flowers are nourished by well-springs,
    Look, the small village spreads out among meadows, relaxed.
Quiet it's here. Prom afar comes the noise of the mill-wheels revolving,
    But the day's decline church bells convey to my ear.
Pleasantly clangs the hammered scythe and the voice of the farmer
    Who, going home with his bull, likes to command and to curb,
Pleasant the mother's song as she sits in the grass with her infant;
    Sated with seeing he sleeps; clouds, though, are tinged now with
red,

And by the glistening lake where the orchard extends its full branches
    Over the open yard gate, window-panes glitter with gold,
There I'm received by the house and the garden's secretive half-light,
    Where together with plants fondly my father reared me;
Where as free as the winged ones I played in the boughs' airy
                                                    greenness
    Or from the orchard's crest gazed into spaces all blue.
Loyal you were, and loyal remain to the fugitive even,
    Kindly as ever you were, heaven of home, take me back.

Still do the peaches grow ripe for me, still at the blossom I marvel,
    Almost as tall as the trees gloriously rose-bushes flower.
Heavy meanwhile with fruit and dark has my cherry tree grown now,
    And to the gathering hand branches now proffer themselves.
Still to the woods by the path, as before, to the free-lying bower
    Out of the garden I'm drawn, down to the stream, where before
I would lie, with my mind cheered by the fame of those men, the
    Prescient mariners; and such was the power of your love
That to the oceans, the deserts, your valour compelled me to follow,
    Ah, while in vain they looked, father and mother, for me.
But where are they? You're silent? You hesitate, you, my home's
                                                    keeper?
    Hesitate? Well, so did I, counting my steps to the door,
As I drew near and, like pilgrims, awe-stricken slowed them, and
                                                    halted.
    Go inside, nonetheless, say: there's a stranger, your son,
So that they open their arms and receive me once more with their
                                                    blessing,
    So that they sanctify me, grant me the threshold once more.
Yet already I guess it: to holy remoteness they also
    Now have passed on and to me never again will return.

Father and mother? And if there are friends living still, they as well
                                                    have
    Found new pursuits, other gains, are not the friends who were
                                                    mine.
Though as before I come and address by love's names, by the old ones,
    All that I see, and adjure heart-beats that once would respond,

Utter silence will meet me. For so it is: much is bound by,
    Much is severed by time. I to them will seem dead, they to me;
And I'm left all alone. But with you, up there above clouds, my
    Fatherland's father, you, powerful Aether, and you
Earth and Light, unanimous three who love and who govern,
    Deathless gods, with you never my bonds I shall break.
Out of you originated, with you I have also travelled,
    You, the joyous ones, you, filled with more knowledge, bring back.
Therefore pass to me now the cup that is filled, overflowing
    With the wine from those grapes grown on warm hills of the Rhine,
That I may drink to the gods at first and then remember those others,
    Mariners, heroes, and then you, the still closer to me,
Parents and friends, and forget my whole load of afflictions and labours
    This and the next day, and soon be among those of my kind.

from BREAD AND WINE

TO HEINSE

I

Round us the town is at rest; the street, in pale lamplight, falls quiet
    And, their torches ablaze, coaches rush through and away.
People go home to rest, replete with the day and its pleasures,
    There to weigh up in their heads, pensive, the gain and the loss,
Finding the balance good; stripped bare now of grapes and of flowers,
    As of their handmade goods, quiet the market stalls lie.
But faint music of strings comes drifting from gardens; it could be
    Someone in love who plays there, could be a man all alone
Thinking of distant friends, the days of his youth; and the fountains,
    Ever welling and new, plash amid balm-breathing beds.
Church bells ring; every stroke hangs still in the quivering half-light
    And the watchman calls out, mindful, no less, of the hour.
Now a breeze rises too and ruffles the crests of the coppice,
    Look, and in secret our globe's shadowy image, the moon,
Slowly is rising too; and Night, the fantastical, comes now
    Full of stars and, I think, little concerned about us,
Night, the astonishing, there, the stranger to all that is human,
    Over the mountain-tops mournful and gleaming draws on.

NOTE: In this elegy Hölderlin develops his notion of alternating eras or cycles of Day and Night, epiphany and retraction. The conception, though new, owes something to the thought of Empedocles and his predecessors, and is pantheistic in its likening of history to natural processes. Hölderlin's purpose here is to 'justify the ways of God to Men', yet in a way consonant with his own tragic sense of life and his experience of God's absence in his own time. His notion of the 'searing beam', the unbearable brightness of God, on the other hand, is firmly rooted in Biblical, esoteric and poetic tradition. *Paradise Lost* presents parallels; and so does the poetry of William Blake, who wrote in 'The Little Black Boy':

    And we are put on earth a little space
    That we may learn to bear the beams of love.

6

Now in earnest he means to honour the gods who have blessed him,
    Now in truth and in deed all must re-echo their praise.
Nothing must see the light but what to those high ones is pleasing,
    Idle and bungled work never for Aether was fit.
So, to be worthy and stand unashamed in the heavenly presence,
    Nations rise up and soon, gloriously ordered, compete
One with the other in building beautiful temples and cities
    Noble and firm they tower high above river and sea –
Only, where are they? Where thrive those famed ones, the festival's
                                     garlands?
    Athens is withered, and Thebes; now do no weapons ring out
In Olympia, nor now those chariots, all golden, in games there,
    And no longer are wreaths hung on Corinthian ships?
Why are they silent too, the theatres, ancient and hallowed?
    Why not now does the dance celebrate, consecrate joy?
Why no more does a god imprint on the brow of a mortal
    Struck, as by lightning, the mark, brand him, as once he would do?
Else he would come himself, assuming a shape that was human,
    And, consoling the guests, crowned and concluded the feast.

7

But, my friend, we have come too late. Though the gods are living,
    Over our heads they live, up in a different world.
Endlessly there they act and, such is their kind wish to spare us,
    Little they seem to care whether we live or do not.
For not always a frail, a delicate vessel can hold them,
    Only at times can our kind bear the full impact of gods.

Ever after our life is dream about them. But frenzy,
    Wandering, helps, like sleep; Night and distress make us strong
Till in that cradle of steel heroes enough have been fostered,
    Hearts in strength can match heavenly strength as before.
Thundering then they come. But meanwhile too often I think it's
    Better to sleep than to be friendless as we are, alone,
Always waiting, and what to do or to say in the meantime
    I don't know, and who wants poets at all in lean years?

But they are, you say, like those holy ones, priests of the wine-god
　　Who in holy Night roamed from one place to the next.

8

For, when some time ago now – to us it seems ages –
　　Up rose all those by whom life had been brightened, made glad,
When the Father had turned his face from the sight of us mortals
　　And all over the earth, rightly, they started to mourn,
Lastly a Genius had come, dispensing heavenly comfort,
　　He who proclaimed the Day's end, then himself went away,
Then, as a token that once they had been down here and once more
　　　　　　　　　　　　　　　　　　　　　　　　would
　　Come, the heavenly choir left a few presents behind,
Gifts in which now as ever humanly men might take pleasure,
　　Since for spiritual joy great things had now grown too great
Here, among men, and even now there's a lack of those strong for
　　Joy's extremity, but silent some thanks do live on.
Bread is a fruit of Earth, yet touched by the blessing of sunlight,
　　From the thundering god issues the gladness of wine.
Therefore in tasting them we think of the Heavenly who once were
　　Here and shall come again, come when their advent is due;
Therefore also the poets in serious hymns to the wine-god,
　　Never idly devised, sound that most ancient one's praise.

9

Yes, and rightly they say he reconciles Day with our Night-time,
　　Leads the stars of the sky upward and down without end,
Always glad, like the living boughs of the evergreen pine tree
　　Which he loves, and the wreath wound out of ivy for choice
Since it lasts and conveys the trace of the gods now departed
　　Down to the godless below, into the midst of their gloom.
What of the children of God was foretold in the songs of the ancients,
　　Look, we are it, ourselves; fruit of Hesperia it is!
Strictly it has come true, fulfilled as in men by a marvel,
　　Let those who have seen it believe! Much, however, occurs,
Nothing succeeds, because we are heartless, mere shadows until our
　　Father Aether, made known, recognized, fathers us all.

Meanwhile, though, to us shadows comes the Son of the Highest,
  Comes the Syrian and down into our gloom bears his torch.
Blissful, the wise men see it; in souls that were captive there gleams a
  Smile, and their eyes shall yet thaw in response to the light.
Dreams more gentle and sleep in the arms of Earth lull the Titan,
  Even that envious one, Cerberus, drinks and lies down.

HALF OF LIFE

With yellow pears hangs down
And full of wild roses
The land into the lake,
You loving swans,
And drunk with kisses
You dip your heads
Into water, the holy–and–sober.

But oh, where shall I find
When winter comes, the flowers, and where
The sunshine
And shade of the earth?
The walls loom
Speechless and cold, in the wind
Weathercocks clatter.

MNEMOSYNE

Third Version

Ripe are, dipped in fire, cooked
The fruits and tried on the earth, and it is law,
Prophetic, that all must enter in
Like serpents, dreaming on
The mounds of heaven. And much
As on the shoulders a
Load of logs must be
Retained. But evil are
The paths, for crookedly
Like horses go the imprisoned
Elements and ancient laws
Of the earth. And always
There is a yearning that seeks the unbound. But much
Must be retained. And loyalty is needed.
Forward, however, and back we will
Not look. Be lulled and rocked as
On a swaying skiff of the sea.

But how, my dear one? On the ground
Sunshine we see and the dry dust
And, a native sight, the shadows of forests, and on roof-tops
There blossoms smoke, near ancient crests
Of the turrets, peaceable; for good indeed
When, contradicting, the soul
Has wounded one of the Heavenly, are the signs of day.
For snow, like lilies of the valley
By indicating where
The noble-minded is, shines brightly
On the green meadow
Of the Alps, half melted, where
Discoursing of the cross which once was placed
There on the wayside for the dead,
High up, in anger, distantly divining
A traveller walks
With the other, but what is this?

Beside the fig tree
My Achilles has died and is lost to me,
And Ajax lies
Beside the grottoes of the sea,
Beside brooks that neighbour Scamandros.
Of a rushing noise in his temples once,
According to the changeless custom of
Unmoved Salamis, in foreign parts
Great Ajax died,
Not so Patroclus, dead in the King's own armour.
And many others died. But by Cithaeron there stood
Eleutherae, Mnemosyne's town. From her also
When God laid down his festive cloak, soon after did
The powers of Evening sever a lock of hair. For the Heavenly, when
Someone has failed to collect his soul, to spare it,
Are angry, for still he must; like him
Here mourning is at fault.

NOTE: 'Mnemosyne' means 'memory', and she was the mother of the
Muses. Mourning for the past as the earlier hymns had already stated, is
not permitted to the poet, who must 'collect his soul' for a different task,
that of interpreting 'the signs of day', all that is present and actual. (Cf. the
conclusion of 'Patmos'.) Cooking in the opening line denotes the natural
process of ripening, as distinct from roasting or burning – a distinction
observed in ancient sacrificial rites. Paracelsus wrote: 'The ripening of
fruit is natural cookery: therefore what nature has in her, she cooks, and
when it is cooked, then nature is whole.' Serpents traditionally are
prophetic creatures. Since they slough their skins, they are also symbols of
renewal or (in oriental and Gnostic lore) of eternity. To 'sever a lock of
hair', in Greek mythology, is to mark a person out for death.

WHEN DOWN FROM HEAVEN...

When down from heaven there gushes a brighter bliss,
   A human joy approaches for human kind
      So that they feel amazed by much that's
         Visible, lofty and pleasing to them

How lovely, blended with it, sound holy hymns!
   How the heart laughs in canticles at the truth
      That to one image clings rejoicing!
    · Over the footbridge now sheep begin their

Long track that almost takes them to glimmering woods.
   The meadows, though, all covered with flawless green,
      Are like that heath which, in a fashion
         Usual enough, is not far away from

The gloomy wood. And there, in the meadows, too
   These sheep remain. The hilltops around those parts,
      Bare, arid heights they seem, are covered
         Sparsely with oaks and uncommon spruces.

There, where the river's frolicsome ripples are,
   So that a man who passes them on his way
      Is glad to see them, there the gentle
         Shape of the hills and the vineyard rises.

Although amid the grape-vines quite steeply steps
   Descend, where high the blossoming fruit tree looms
      And on wild hedges fragrance lingers,
         Hidden the violets grow and flower,

Yet waters trickle down, and though quiet, faint,
   A murmur there is audible all day long;
      The places in those parts, however,
         Rest after noon and for hours keep silence.

Hugo von Hofmannsthal (1874–1929)

From *Poems and Verse Plays* (1961)

HUGO VON HOFMANNSTHAL published his first poem in June 1890, when he was a schoolboy of just over sixteen, his first playlet or 'lyrical drama' in the following year. Though not unprecedented, this early emergence of a poet was extraordinary enough; and it was made more extraordinary by the emergence at the same time of the critic and man of letters – under the pseudonyms of Loris, Loris Melikow, Theophil Morren, or, in one case only, Archibald O'Hagan, B.A. From the autumn of 1890 onwards, this schoolboy poet and man of letters was also to be seen at the literary meeting-places of Vienna, such as the Café Griensteidl, at first in his father's company, later with older friends or alone. To say that he mixed on equal terms with established writers, is an understatement; for he was accepted at once not merely as a youthful prodigy and a writer of the greatest promise, but as a master of his art. 'Here at last,' Hermann Bahr wrote of this first impact in a book published in 1894, 'here at last was someone who contained the whole age, for all its thousand-fold contradictions and conflicts, within his mind.'

This first, predominantly lyrical, phase of Hofmannsthal's working life lasted for roughly ten years, the last decade of the century. Though he continued to write poems after this period, he himself considered his lyrical vein exhausted and thought only five of his later poems worth preserving in book form. Much has been made of this apparent break in Hofmannsthal's development and of the crisis to which it was due. The majority of those who admired the lyrical poet neither understood nor forgave the change; they felt about it much as Rimbaud's admirers might have felt if he had lived to become a member of the Académie Française. Hofmannsthal's fame declined; it was said about him that if he had died at twenty-five he would have been a great poet. This epigram, as wrong and foolish as it was cruel, is quoted only because it sums up a superficial view of Hofmannsthal which not only prevailed during the greater part of his later life but persisted long after his death, in 1929, and has only recently been corrected by the publication in Germany of a fifteen-volume edition of his works, supplemented by several volumes of correspondence. [. . .]

from the Introduction

AN EXPERIENCE

Silver-grey fragrance filled the vale of twilight
As when the moon's light trickles through the clouds.
And yet it was not night. In the dark valley's
Silver-grey fragrance my dim thoughts were merged,
And silently I drowned in the translucent,
Light-weaving ocean and left life behind me.
What marvellous flowers were there, with calyxes
Darkly glowing! A thicket of wild shrubs
Through which a radiance red and yellow as
Of topazes poured gleaming, in warm streams.
The whole was filled with a deep ebb and flow
Of melancholy music. This I knew,
Although I cannot grasp it, yet I knew it:
This must be death. Transmuted into music,
Intensely yearning, sweet and darkly glowing,
Akin to deepest sadness.
                          But how strange!
A nameless longing after life now wept
Within my spirit silently; it wept
As one would weep who on a massive ship
With yellow giant sails on dark-blue water
At evening time were sailing past his town,
His native town. There he would see the streets,
Would hear the fountains plashing, breathe the fragrance
Of lilac bushes and would see himself,
A child, stand on the shore with childish eyes
Timid and close to tears, and looking through
An open window see his room lit up –
But the vast oeean-going ship moves on,
Noiselessly gliding on the dark-blue water
With yellow, strangely fashioned giant sails.

INFINITE TIME

Are you truly too weak to remember the time that seemed blessèd?
Over the darkening vale slowly the stars climbed the sky –
Yet in the shadow we stood and were trembling. The towering
    elm-tree
Shuddered as in a dream, scattered a shower of drops
Pattering down on the grass: yet hardly an hour had gone by since
We heard that rain! And to me it seemed an infinite time.
For to the man who is living it, life seems to stretch: in the silence
Chasms of infinite dream open between two brief looks:
I had absorbed within me your twenty-year-old existence
While – so it seemed – still the tree held all its raindrops unshed.

BALLAD OF THE OUTER LIFE

And children grow with deeply wondering eyes
That know of nothing, grow a while and die,
And every one of us goes his own way.

And bitter fruit will sweeten by and by
And like dead birds come hurtling down at night
And for a few days fester where they lie.

And always the wind blows, and we recite
And hear again the phrases thin with wear
And in our limbs feel languor or delight.

And roads run through the grass, and here and there
Are places full of lights and pools and trees,
And some are threatening, some are cold and bare . . .

To what end were they built? With differences
No less innumerable than their names?
Why laughter now, now weeping or disease?

What does it profit us, and all these games,
Who, great and lonely, ever shall be so
And though we always wander seek no aims?

To see such things do travellers leave their homes?
Yet he says much who utters 'evening,'
A word from which grave thought and sadness flow

Like rich dark honey from the hollow combs.

THE OLD MAN'S LONGING FOR SUMMER

If only March would turn into July!

Nothing would keep me; resolute as before,
On horseback or by carriage or by train
I should go out to see the hills once more.

Great trees in groups quite close to me I'd find,
Old elm or oak, plane-tree or sycamore:
How long since last I saw one of that kind!

Then quickly I should dismount or else call out
Stop! to the coachman, and soon without a goal
Deep in the summer country stroll about.

And, resting, long beneath the trees I'd stay;
In their high crests it would be day and night
At once, and not as in this house where day

Too often is as desolate as night
And nights are black and louring as the days.
There all would be alive, glorious and bright.

And from the shade I step into the sphere
Of joy the late sun grants; a breath wafts by.
But nowhere 'All this is nothing' is whispered here.

The valley darkens; where there are cottages
Lone lights appear, the darkness breathes on me:
But not of dying speaks the nocturnal breeze.

I walk across the churchyard, and there I see
Nothing but flowers that sway in the last gleam,
And feel no other thing's proximity.

And between hazel shrubs already blear
Water flows by, and like a child I listen
And yet no whispered 'This is vain' I hear.

Then, quick, I strip and jump; when next I look,
Raising my head again, the moon is out,
And I am wrestling with the little brook.

Then from the icy ripples raise my hand,
Straighten my back and toss a smooth round pebble
And in the radiant moonlight tall I stand.

And on the moonlit summer country falls
A shadow far and wide: his, who so sadly
Nods here, propped up with cushions, caged in walls?

Who sad and dreary draws himself up in jerks
Long before dawn and glowers at the pale light,
Knowing that for us both an enemy lurks?

His, who this March is cheated of his rest
By evil winds, so that he sits all night,
Black hands clamped down upon his heart and breast?

Oh, where is that July and the summer country!

Rainer Maria Rilke (1875–1926)

From *An Unofficial Rilke: Poems 1912–1926* (1981)

'FAME, AFTER ALL, is only the quintessence of all the misunderstand-
ings that collect around a new name', Rilke wrote in his monograph on
Rodin. If Rilke's own fame bears out the truth of that observation, it is
no longer because a legend of his own making was substituted for
complex and uncomfortable realities. Both Rilke's work and his person
have received the most searching scrutiny and analysis. Few stones have
been left unturned either by his biographers or by the editors of his
works and letters, including works and letters highly adverse to the vari-
ous images of himself that Rilke wished to make public at successive
stages of his life.

Most of the poems chosen here are of that kind. They were left either
unpublished or uncollected by Rilke in his lifetime. Such a choice would
need justification in most other cases, since most authors must be allowed
to be the best judges of what constitutes their canon. Yet Rilke's case is a
special one, for several reasons. He himself made no provision for a clear
line to be drawn between his public and private work, his public and
private image; and there are good grounds for assuming that he was
indifferent to the rigorous impersonality upheld – even beyond their
deaths – by contemporaries like Stefan George or Hofmannsthal. Many
of his letters, for instance, can rightly be regarded as part of his literary
work, and may well have been written with a view to posthumous publi-
cation. For the greater part of his working life they served him not only
as his main line of communication with a large circle of friends and
readers, but as a complement to his poetry of a kind for which other
poets have adopted more public, more impersonal media like lectures or
critical essays. The many poems Rilke wrote for friends in his later years,
on the other hand, may have been primarily intended as presents to those
friends, but they were also a means of communication not wholly distinct
from either the letters or the books to which he attached them. Certainly
he himself made no rigid distinction between such dedicatory verses and
any others written at the same period but never collected by him for
publication in books; and even the *Duino Elegies* appeared with a dedica-
tion describing them as 'part of the property' of the lady to whom they
were dedicated.

That Rilke published no major collection of poems between the second volume of his *New Poems* in 1908 and the *Duino Elegies* in 1922 is another special circumstance, and an astonishing one if we consider how much uncollected verse he produced in those years, and how much of it now seems no more private, slight or occasional than a good deal of the work he did choose to collect both before and after the intermission. The relative neglect of the miscellaneous poems of this period, as against the *Duino Elegies* and the *Sonnets to Orpheus*, does point to a triumph of the legend over the reality. [. . .]

from the Introduction

THE DEATH OF MOSES

Not one who wanted glory and only fallen
angels; took weapons, deadly approached
the commanded man. But already
He clanked back again, upward,
roared out into the heavens: I cannot!

For calmly through his thickety eyebrows
Moses had seen Him and written on:
words of blessing and the infinite name.
And his eye was pure down to the bedrock of powers.

So the Lord, half the heavens swept up in the motion,
plunged and Himself made a couch of the mountain;
laid the old man down. From the house set in order
He called the soul; it was up and telling
many a tale of things shared, of measureless friendship.

But at last it had had enough. That it was enough
the made-perfect admitted. Then the ancient
God to the ancient man slowly inclined
His ancient face. In a kiss took him

into His age, the older. And with hands of creation
He closed the mountain. So that only the one,
one recreated, should lie under terrestrial mountains,
unknowable to mankind.

October 1915

THE HAND

LOOK AT the little titmouse,
astray in this room:
twenty heartbeats long
it lay within my hand.
Human hand. One resolved to protect.
Unpossessing protect.
But
now on the window-sill
free
in its fear it remains
estranged
from itself and what surrounds it,
the cosmos, unrecognizing.
Ah, so confusing a hand is
even when out to save.
In the most helpful of hands
there is death enough still
and there has been money

1921

... WHEN WILL, when will, when will they let it suffice,
the complaining, explaining? Have we not had masters to splice
human words, compose them? Why all this new endeavour?

Do not, do not, do not books for ever
hammer at people like perpetual bells?
When, between two books, silent sky appears: be glad ...,
or a patch of plain earth in the evening.

Louder than gale, louder than sea swell, men
have roared and yelled ... What preponderances of stillness
must reside in the cosmic spaces, when
the cricket is audible still to yelling mankind.
When stars, the silent, shine for us in the yelled-at heavens!

Oh, if they spoke to us, the remotest, ancient, most ancient
        forebears!
And we: listeners at last. The first human listeners.

1922

Paul Celan (1920–1970)

From *Poems of Paul Celan* (2007)

... EVEN BY 2002 my work as a translator and critic was very nearly at an end because in old age I found it necessary to cultivate my own garden and confine myself to the writing of my own verse. From the first my engagement with the work of Celan had been difficult and sporadic. Had it become a full-time occupation and specialization, it could have driven me into suicide, as it did his friend and interpreter Peter Szondi. Merely to correct the proof of the present edition was to revisit a battlefield, retrace my struggle over decades with texts that were a tug-of-war between life and death – though with extensions, developments and variations as wide-ranging as art and generous sympathies could make them.

.   .   .   .

Paul Celan spent his formative years in a Jewish community that had recently ceased to be within the frontiers of the Austrian Empire; and most of his productive years were spent in France. His poetic affinities were French, Romanian, Russian and English, as well as German and Austrian. Among his German-language contemporaries, those closest to him in sensibility and manner – though that is not saying much – were Johannes Bobrowski, a resident in East Berlin with distinctly Christian allegiances, and the West German poet Ernst Meister. Like them, Celan can be seen as continuing a line of development in German poetry that runs from Klopstock and Hölderlin in the eighteenth century to the later Rilke and Georg Trakl, at a time when the dominant trends in both Germanys were adverse to that line. [. . .]

One thing sets Paul Celan's work apart from that of most of his German coevals: he had hardly any use for realism of a kind that merely imitates and reproduces, for what Northrop Frye has called "the low mimetic". Direct social comment is not to be found in his work, though it became increasingly realistic in a different sense – the widening of its vocabulary to include twentieth-century phenomena and technologies. From *Die Niemandsrose* onwards, invective becomes prominent in Celan's poems, though the invective is as rich in cryptic allusions and intricate word-play as every other mode he employed. He was realistic, too, in doing full justice to the "foul rag-and-bone shop of the heart".

Yet he was never satisfied with mere reportage. As a very short late poem attests, he found Brecht's poetry of social and political comment too "explicit". One reason is that he wanted poetry to be open to the unexpected, the unpredictable, the unpredeterminable. His poems were "messages in a bottle", as he said, which might or might not be picked up. That element of risk was as necessary to them as the need to communicate. On the few occasions when he spoke about poetry in public he spoke of it as a process, a groping forward, a search. Paradoxically, once more, he spoke of its practice, and the practice of any art, as a driving of the practitioner into the "inmost recess of himself", his narrowest place, and as a "setting free". [. . .]

from the Preface to the Third Edition *and* Introduction

YOUR HAND full of hours, you came to me – and I said:
Your hair is not brown.
So you lifted it lightly on to the scales of grief; it weighed more
    than I . . .

On ships they come to you and make it their cargo, then put it on
    sale in the markets of lust –
You smile at me from the depth, I weep at you from the scale that
    stays light.
I weep: Your hair is not brown, they offer brine from the sea and you
    give them curls . . .
You whisper: They're filling the world with me now, in your heart
    I'm a hollow way still!
You say: Lay the leafage of years beside you – it's time you came
    closer and kissed me!

The leafage of years is brown, your hair is not brown.

Aspen tree, your leaves glance white into the dark.
My mother's hair was never white.

Dandelion, so green is the Ukraine.
My yellow-haired mother did not come home.

Rain cloud, above the well do you hover?
My quiet mother weeps for everyone.

Round star, you wind the golden loop.
My mother's heart was ripped by lead.

Oaken door, who lifted you off your hinges?
My gentle mother cannot return.

DEATH FUGUE

Black milk of daybreak we drink it at sundown
we drink it at noon in the morning we drink it at night
we drink and we drink it
we dig a grave in the breezes there one lies unconfined
A man lives in the house he plays with the serpents he writes
he writes when dusk falls to Germany your golden hair Margarete
he writes it and steps out of doors and the stars are flashing he
      whistles his pack out
he whistles his Jews out in earth has them dig for a grave
he commands us strike up for the dance

Black milk of daybreak we drink you at night
we drink in the morning at noon we drink you at sundown
we drink and we drink you
A man lives in the house he plays with the serpents he writes

he writes when dusk falls to Germany your golden hair Margarete
your ashen hair Shulamith we dig a grave in the breezes there one
    lies unconfined

He calls out jab deeper into the earth you lot you others sing now
    and play
he grabs at the iron in his belt he waves it his eyes are blue
jab deeper you lot with your spades you others play on for the dance

Black milk of daybreak we drink you at night
we drink you at noon in the morning we drink you at sundown
we drink and we drink you
a man lives in the house your golden hair Margarete
your ashen hair Shulamith he plays with the serpents

He calls out more sweetly play death death is a master from
    Germany
he calls out more darkly now stroke your strings then as smoke you
    will rise into air
then a grave you will have in the clouds there one lies unconfined

Black milk of daybreak we drink you at night
we drink you at noon death is a master from Germany
we drink you at sundown and in the morning we drink and we drink
    you
death is a master from Germany his eyes are blue
he strikes you with leaden bullets his aim is true
a man lives in the house your golden hair Margarete
he sets his pack onto us he grants us a grave in the air
plays with the serpents and daydreams death is a master from
    Germany

your golden hair Margarete
your ashen hair Shulamith

TENEBRAE

We are near, Lord,
near and at hand.

Handled already, Lord,
clawed and clawing as though
the body of each of us were
your body, Lord.

Pray, Lord,
pray to us,
we are near.

Askew we went there,
went there to bend
down to the trough, to the crater.

To be watered we went there, Lord.

It was blood, it was
what you shed, Lord.

It gleamed.

It cast your image into our eyes, Lord.
Our eyes and our mouths are so open and empty, Lord.
We have drunk, Lord.
The blood and the image that was in the blood, Lord.

Pray, Lord.
We are near.

ONCE
I heard him,
he was washing the world,
unseen, nightlong,
real.

One and Infinite,
annihilated,
ied.

Light was. Salvation.

I HEAR that the axe has flowered,
I hear that the place can't be named,

I hear that the bread which looks at him
heals the hanged man,
the bread baked for him by his wife,

I hear that they call life
our only refuge.

A LEAF, treeless
for Bertolt Brecht:

What times are these
when a conversation
is almost a crime
because it includes
so much made explicit?

From *German Poetry 1910–1975* (1977)

THIS ANTHOLOGY sprang out of two needs: to collect scattered translations done over the decades and to replace the earlier anthology *Modern German Poetry 1910–1960*, which has been both out of print and out of date for some years. The earlier anthology was compiled in collaboration with Christopher Middleton, who chose not to take on the work of co-editing this one. Since the additional texts – poems published in the last fifteen years, but also earlier poems omitted for one reason or another – called for a reappraisal and rebalancing of all the contents, it seemed best to begin again. In the editing of a bilingual anthology, selection and translation are so closely linked as to become very nearly inseparable. When it became clear that I should do the selecting on my own I decided to do all the translating also. [. . .]

from the Introduction

Gottfried Benn (1886–1956)

NIGHT CAFÉ

824: The Loves and Lives of Women.
The 'cello has a quick drink. The flute
belches three beats long: his tasty evening snack.
The drum reads on to the end of the thriller.

Green teeth, pimples on his face,
waves to conjunctivitis.

Grease in his hair
talks to open mouth with swollen tonsils,
faith hope and charity round his neck.

Young goitre is sweet on saddle-nose.
He stands her three half-pints.

Sycosis buys carnations
to mollify double chin.

B flat minor: Sonata op. 35.
A pair of eyes roars out:
Don't splash the blood of Chopin all over this place
for this lot to slouch about in!
Hey, Gigi! Stop!

The door dissolves: a woman.
Desert dried out. Canaanite brown.
Chaste. Full of caves. A scent comes with her. Hardly scent.
It's only a sweet leaning forward of the air
against my brain.

A paunched obesity waddles after her.

Georg Trakl (1887–1914)

DE PROFUNDIS

There is a stubble field on which a black rain fails.
There is a tree which, brown, stands lonely here.
There is a hissing wind which haunts deserted huts –
How sad this evening.

Past the village pond
The gentle orphan still gathers scanty ears of corn.
Golden and round her eyes are grazing in the dusk
And her lap awaits the heavenly bridegroom.

Returning home
Shepherds found the sweet body
Decayed in the bramble bush.

A shade I am remote from sombre hamlets.
The silence of God
I drank from the woodland well.

On my forehead cold metal forms.
Spiders look for my heart.
There is a light that fails in my mouth.

At night I found myself upon a heath,
Thick with garbage and the dust of stars.
In the hazel copse
Crystal angels have sounded once more.

GRODEK

At nightfall the autumn woods cry out
With deadly weapons and the golden plains,
The deep blue lakes, above which more darkly
Rolls the sun; the night embraces
Dying warriors, the wild lament
Of their broken mouths.
But quietly there in the pastureland
Red clouds in which an angry god resides,
The shed blood gathers, lunar coolness.
All the roads lead to blackest carrion.
Under golden twigs of the night and stars
The sister's shade now sways through the silent copse
To greet the ghosts of the heroes, the bleeding heads;
And softly the dark flutes of autumn sound in the reeds.
O prouder grief! You brazen altars,
Today a great pain feeds the hot flame of the spirit,
The grandsons yet unborn.

1914

Georg Heym (1887–1912)

AND THE HORNS OF SUMMER FELL SILENT...

And the horns of summer fell silent in the death of the meadows;
Into the darkness cloud upon cloud floated off.
But remotely the bordering forests were shrinking,
Muffled in morning like men that follow a hearse.

Loud sang the gale in the terror of fields that were fading;
It drove into poplars to shape a white tower between boughs.
And like the sweepings of wind there lay in the waste land
Below, a village, drab roofs in a huddle of grey.

But on and on, as far as the pallid horizon
The tents of autumn extended their fabric of corn,
The numberless cities, but empty, forgotten.
And no one was walking about in the streets.

And the shade of the night sang. Only the ravens still drifted
Here and there under leaden clouds in the rain,
Alone in the wind, as down in the dark of our foreheads
Black thoughts revolve and recede in disconsolate hours.

August 1911

Nelly Sachs (1891–1970)

THE SLEEPWALKER

The sleepwalker
circling upon his star
is awakened by
the white feather of morning –
the bloodstain on it reminds him –
startled, he drops
the moon –
the snowberry breaks
against the black agate of night
sullied with dream –

No pure white on this earth –

LINE LIKE

Line like
living hair
drawn
deathnightobscured
from you
to me.

Reined in
outside
I bend
thirstily
to kiss the end of all distances.

Evening
throws the springboard
of night over the redness
lengthens your promontory
and hesitant I place my foot
on the trembling string
of my death already begun.

But such is love –

Bertolt Brecht (1898–1956)

OF POOR B.B.

I, Bertolt Brecht, came out of the black forests.
My mother moved me into the cities while I lay
Inside her body. And the chill of the forests
Will be inside me till my dying day.

In the asphalt cities I'm at home. From the very start
Provided with every unction and sacrament:
With newspapers. And tobacco. And brandy.
To the end mistrustful, lazy, and content.

I'm polite and friendly to people. I put on
A stiff hat because that's what they do.
I say: they're animals with a quite peculiar smell,
And I say: Does it matter? I am too.

Sometimes in the morning on my empty rocking chair
I'll sit a woman or two, and with an untroubled eye
Look at them steadily and say to them:
Here you have someone on whom you can't rely.

Toward evening it's men I gather round me
And then we address one another as 'gentlemen'.
They're resting their feet on my table tops
And say: Things will get better for us. And I don't ask: When?

In the grey light before morning the pine trees piss
And their vermin, the birds, raise their twitter and cheep.
At that hour I drain my glass in town, then throw
The cigar butt away and worriedly go to sleep.

We have sat, an easy generation
In houses thought to be indestructible
(Thus we built those tall boxes on the island of Manhattan
And those thin antennae that amuse the Atlantic swell.)

Of those cities will remain: what passed through them, the wind!
The house makes glad the consumer: he clears it out.
We know that we're only tenants, provisional ones,
And after us there will come: nothing worth talking about.

In the earthquakes to come, I very much hope,
I shall keep my Virginia alight, embittered or no,
I, Bertolt Brecht, carried off to the asphalt cities
From the black forests inside my mother long ago.

1922

OF ALL WORKS

Of all works I prefer
Those used and worn.
Copper vessels with dents and with flattened rims
Knives and forks whose wooden handles
Many hands have grooved: such shapes
Seemed the noblest to me. So too the flagstones around
Old houses, trodden by many feet and ground down,
With clumps of grass in the cracks, these too
Are happy works.

Absorbed into the use of the many
Frequently changed, they improve their appearance, growing
    enjoyable
Because often enjoyed.
Even the remnants of broken sculptures
With lopped-off hands I love. They also
Lived with me. If they were dropped at least they must have been
    carried.
If men knocked them over they cannot have stood too high up.
Buildings half dilapidated
Revert to the look of buildings not yet completed
Generously designed: their fine proportions
Can already be guessed; yet they still make demands
On our understanding. At the same time
They have served already, indeed have been left behind. All this
Makes me glad.

1932

Marie Luise Kaschnitz (1901–1974)

RESURRECTION

Sometimes we get up
Get up as for a resurrection
In broad daylight
With our living hair
With our breathing skin.

Only the usual things are around us.
No mirage of palm trees
With grazing lions
And gentle wolves.

The alarm clocks don't cease to tick
Their phosphorescent hands are not extinguished.

And yet weightlessly
And yet invulnerably
Ordered into mysterious order
Admitted early into a house of light.

Johannes Bobrowski (1917–1965)

EAST

All my dreams
move across the plains, travel
windbright toward
untrodden forests, cold
lonely rivers, over which ring out
from afar the calls
of bearded boatmen –

There all songs are
without end, in the humblest
thing lies danger, ambiguous, –
not to be held with this or
that name: meadows,
moors, a ravine; like doom
it strikes down, strays, avoided, –
there, around the low hills
tracks run, fleeing.

Words do not count.
But a caress, greetings,
lightning flash under darkening eyelid
and in the breast that spasm;
stronger even than embraces.

Traders come from far places. Those
who live among us arc strangers.
Unsure they walk, asking,
roads that lead nowhere, always
linger at ferries and bridges
as though there lay certainty –

But we with ease know each other.
Our conversations all
rise from the same ground.

And in expectation forever
our hearts live.

1953

Wolfdietrich Schnurre (1920–1989)

DEAD SOLDIER

Now whistle to the woodlice under the stone,
so that they'll make their armour rattle
and in the tower of sand
the firebug marksman at his bren-gun post.
This war was started by the mouse,
its grey is only borrowed,
beneath it the mouse goes naked
and sinewy, blue and bare.
Its pelt was requisitioned,
the ears were not cut off:
Now grass keeps mum
and masked, wrapped up in silence
the fungus pushes a pale shoulder
at leafmould which, bubbly, bursts.
The bald oak officer has been discharged,
dust rises in the hollow family tree,
thickens to reddish clouds.
The moss, unnourished, bleeds to death.
Splinters were fixed to broken bones;
but what was healed decays,
and only what is legless, handless now
still dares to hope that it's alive:
the worm will win,
and the arm is losing.

Ingeborg Bachmann (1926–1973)

THE RESPITE

A harder time is coming.
The end of the respite allowed us
appears on the skyline.
Soon you must tie your shoelace
and drive back the dogs to the marshland farms.
For the fishes' entrails
have grown cold in the wind.
Poorly the light of the lupins burns.
Your gaze gropes in the fog:
the end of the respite allowed us
appears on the skyline.

Over there your loved one sinks in the sand,
it rises toward her blown hair,
it cuts short her speaking,
it commands her to be silent,
it finds that she is mortal
and willing to part
after every embrace.

Do not look round.
Tie your shoelace.
Drive back the dogs
Throw the fishes into the sea.
Put out the lupins!

A harder time is coming.

Jörg Steiner (1930–)

HIROSHIMA

At school the children hear a story,
they hear the story of Hiroshima,
Hiroshima is a village in England.

Hiroshima was settled by Celts,
at Hiroshima things are not too good,
the farmers at Hiroshima are dissatisfied.

Hiroshima needs industry,
the children read out in chorus,
the teacher writes a word on the blackboard.

Christoph Meckel (1935–)

THE PEACOCK

From Germany's ashes I saw no phoenix rise.
Stirring the ash with my foot
I uncovered glimmering fins, uncovered horns and pelts –
yet I saw a peacock, who whirling ashes
with one wing made of wood and one of iron,
growing gigantic whipped the flaky cinders
wherever fires were alight, and preened his plumage.

From Germany's ashes I saw old crows creep out
and bristly nightingales with throats grown hoarse
and cocks with swordfish beaks and combs grown bald
to whistle and to sing in praise of birds.
I saw them root in ashes of those fires
the wind swept through, and drove cold smoke
over wide spaces where little was gold that glittered.

From Germany's ashes I saw no phoenix rise;
yet saw a peacock in the shining season of his plumage,
and saw the radiance as he spread his tail
against a murk of ice-grey skies and northern lights,
and heard the jubilation of crows and sparrows, and saw
flocks of magpies fall on his golden feathers
lice grow darkly out of his plumage
man-sized ants devour his eyes.

From *East German Poetry* (1972)

THE POETS included here are those of interest to readers of poetry, as distinct from students of propaganda, outside the German Democratic Republic; and they are of interest to readers of poetry because their commitment is that of true poets anywhere, at any time, to the truth of their own perceptions, feelings, and convictions. Needless to say, their perceptions, feelings, and convictions may differ from those of poets living in other kinds of societies, under other kinds of government; but not so much as to be either incomprehensible or irrelevant on the other side of the Wall. The German texts of most of the poems have been published and read in West Germany. Some of them, like the poems of Peter Huchel and Wolf Biermann, have been published only in West Germany, because East German publication was prohibited.

Yet all these poets chose to live in East Germany, even if the politico-cultural bureaucrats have done their best to make them regret their choice, and all of them chose to stay there when, not so many years ago, they were still free to get out. All of them, beginning with Brecht, have been preoccupied with moral and social problems to a degree rare among non-communist poets; and that is another reason why their work is, or should be, of special interest to American and British readers with no direct experience of an almost totally collectivized society. [. . .]

That they are innovators, within the limits set by their social conscience, not within the limits prescribed by the dogmatists of 'social realism', is as much to their credit as their courageous insistence that no government made up of men and women has a moral right to treat other men and women as self-righteous Victorian parents treated their 'naughty children'; but this brings us back to the rigidities and hypocrisies of a régime that has carried out economic reforms to the exclusion of all other kinds, such as the psychological, and to the fear of psychological reforms inherent in the system itself. Poetry alone will not lead to a general change of heart; but as long as poets are true to their experience they cannot help upholding a number of basic freedoms, one of which is the freedom to change, to grow, to develop. In that way, if in no other, poetry remains a source of innovation, disturbing enough to those who fear it to be suppressed. [. . .]

from the Introduction

Bertolt Brecht (1898–1956)

A NEW HOUSE

Back in my country after fifteen years of exile
I have moved into a fine house.
Here I've hung my No masks and picture scroll
Representing the Doubter. As I drive through the ruins
Daily I am reminded of the privileges
That got me this house. I hope
It will not make me patient with the holes
In which so many thousands huddle. Even now
On top of the cupboard containing my manuscripts
My suitcase lies.

THE FRIENDS

The war separated
Me, the writer of plays, from my friend the stage designer.
The cities where we worked are no longer there.
When I walk through the cities that are still there
At times I say: that blue piece of washing there,
My friend would have placed it better.

From *Buckow Elegies*

THE SOLUTION

After the Uprising on June Seventeenth
The Secretary of the Authors' Union
Had leaflets distributed in the Stalinallee
Which said that the people
Had forfeited the Government's confidence
And could only win it back
By redoubled labour. Wouldn't it
Be simpler in that case if the Government
Dissolved the people and
Elected another?

EIGHT YEARS AGO

There was a time
When all was different here.
The butcher's wife knows it.
The postman walks with too straight a back.
And what was the electrician?

Reiner Kunze (1933–)

THE NEED FOR CENSORSHIP

Everything

can be retouched

except
the negative
inside us

PERSPECTIVE

No, don't
shift the furniture, dear

The man who
moves things around in his head
his desk must

stay put

Volker Braun (1939–)

PROVOCATION FOR ME

(when in the third quarter of the twentieth century poems became dispensable)

1

Comrades, persistent
We celebrate what is positive.
The postwoman's 'good morning' is no friendlier.
The girls love us and do not praise us.
Our friends praise us but do not love us.
They refuse us the honorarium of hearts.

2

Yet we write for those people:
Their hands celebrate what is positive, every finger
Celebrates it, their fingertips, their fists.
I have joined the postwoman's round, climbing stairs
I have besieged and searched the hearts of my friends
I have despatched expeditions across the foreheads of girls
I have lain awake in furrows ploughed by care.
I know: all these people celebrate what is positive.

3

But the postwoman doesn't deliver only cantatas of thanksgiving.
The girls don't love the man who desires nothing.
Our friends don't praise with our crazy recklessness.
They celebrate the plan by making changes.
But we only praise, don't improve anything, are dispensable.
We don't think ourselves quite responsible.
For the time being I call us negative poets.

Other Translations

Charles Baudelaire (1821–1867)

From *Twenty Prose Poems* (1968)

CONFITEOR OF THE ARTIST

How penetrating are the ends of days in autumn! Oh! penetrating to the point of grief! For there are certain delicious sensations whose vagueness does not exclude intensity; and no point is sharper than that of the Infinite.

Oh, the vast delight of gazing fixedly, drowning one's glance in the immensity of sky and sea! Solitude, silence, incomparable chastity of the azure! A little sailing-boat shuddering on the horizon, the paradigm, in its littleness and its isolation, of my irretrievable existence; monotonous melody of the surge; all these things reflect my thoughts, or I reflect theirs (for in the grandeur of reverie the ego is soon lost); they think, as I say, but musically and picturesquely, without quibbling, without syllogism, without deduction.

Nevertheless, these thoughts, whether formed within me or projected from things, soon grow too intense. The energy which pleasure does not absorb creates a kind of unrest and a positive pain. My nerves, now excessively tense, transmit only wailing and sorrowful vibrations.

And now the profundity of the sky perplexes me; the limpid light exasperates me. The insensitiveness of the sea, the immobility of the scene, revolt me. Oh, must we suffer eternally, or flee eternally from all that is beautiful? Nature, unpitying enchantress, ever-victorious rival, let me be! Leave off tempting my desires and my pride! The study of beauty is a duel in which the artist cries out in terror before being vanquished.

CROWDS

It is not given to everyone to take a bath in the multitude; to enjoy the crowd is an art; and only that man can gorge himself with vitality, at the expense the human race, whom, in his cradle, a fairy inspired with love of disguise and of the mask, with hatred of the home and a passion for voyaging.

Multitude, solitude: terms that, to the active and fruitful poet, are synonymous and interchangeable. A man who cannot people his solitude is no less incapable of being alone in a busy crowd.

The poet enjoys the incomparable privilege that he can, at will, be either himself or another. Like those wandering spirits that seek a body, he enters, when he likes, into the person of any man. For him alone all is vacant; and if certain places seem to be closed to him, it is that, to his eyes, they are not worth the trouble of being visited.

The solitary and pensive pedestrian derives a singular exhilaration from this universal communion. That man who can easily wed the crowd knows a feverish enjoyment which will be eternally denied to the egoist, shut up like a trunk, and to the lazy man, imprisoned like a mollusc. The poet adopts as his own all the professions, all the joys and all the miseries with which circumstance confronts him. What men call love is very meagre, very restricted and very feeble, compared to this ineffable orgy, to this holy prostitution of the soul that abandons itself entirely, poetry and charity included, to the unexpected arrival, to the passing stranger.

It is good occasionally to bring home to the happy people of this world, were it only in order to humiliate for a moment their inane pride, that there is a happiness superior to theirs, vaster and more refined. The founders of colonies, the pastors of peoples, missionary priests exiled to the ends of the earth, doubtless know something of this mysterious drunkenness; and, in the heart of the vast family which their genius has created for itself, they must laugh sometimes at those who pity them for their destiny that is so unquiet and for their life that is so chaste.

Peter Huchel (1903–1981)

From *The Garden of Theophrastus* (2004)

PSALM

That from the seed of men
No man
And from the seed of the olive tree
No olive tree
Shall grow,
This you must measure
With the yardstick of death.

Those who live
Under the earth
In a capsule of cement,
Their strength is like
A blade of grass
Lashed by snow in a blizzard.

The desert now will be history.
Termites with their pincers
Write it
On sand.

And no one will enquire
Into a species
Eagerly bent
On self-extinction.

WINTER BILLET

I sit by the shed,
Oiling my rifle.

A foraging hen
With her foot imprints
Lightly on snow
A script as old as the world,
A sign as old as the world,
Lightly on snow
The tree of life.

I know the butcher
And his way of killing.
I know the axe.
I know the chopping-block.

Across the shed
You will flutter,
Stump with no head,
Yet still a bird
That presses a twitching wing
Down on the split wood.

I know the butcher.
I sit by the shed,
Oiling my rifle.

Günter Eich (1907–1972)

From *Pigeons and Moles* (1991)

LATRINE

Over the stinking drain ditch,
paper all bloody, bepissed,
with glittering flies around it,
crouching, I strain and twist,

my gaze on riverbanks, wooded,
gardens, a boat pulled up.
Into the mire of corruption
petrified faeces plop.

Mad in my hearing echo
verses by Hölderlin.
In snowy pureness, mirrored,
clouds in the urine are seen.

'But go now with a greeting
to the beautiful Garonne –'
Under my tottering feet those
cloudlets have drifted, are gone.

MESSAGES OF THE RAIN

News intended for me,
drummed out from rain to rain,
from slate roof to tiled roof,
introduced like an illness,
contraband, delivered to him
who has no wish to receive it.

Beyond the wall my metal window-sill clamours,
pattering letters link up
and the rain speaks
in that language which once I believed
none but I could decipher –

Disconcerted now I hear
the messages of despair,
the messages of poverty
and the messages of reproach.
It hurts me to think they're addressed to me,
feeling guiltless of any offence.

And I say out loud
that I do not fear the rain or its accusations,
nor him who sent them to me;
and that all in good time
I will go out and give him my answer.

Franz Baermann Steiner (1909–1952)

From *Modern Poetry in Translation* (1992)

TACITURN IN THE SUN

Did not the voice call: where are you? where are you?
Oh, among human beings I linger.
There are many of them, and most have a house around them.
Songs I have often heard, words came and went,
I am on my way.

Did not the voice call: evening! evening!
Yes, it will be evening, as evenings are:
Over the reddening hills the shadows pour out,
And the flute of the shepherd
Repents the ripening of time.

Before noon I was at the cattle-market, heard the language of sheep,
Bargaining, men with knives ran about.
Near me someone counted his money. A strip
Of his headcloth, windblown, passed over my forehead
As I looked up.
Birds were circling up there.
Slowly, with sunshine, my face grew heavy and golden,
Someone counted his money.
One by one, with sunshine, the sheep fell silent.

Did not the voice call: evening! evening!
Did not the voice call: where are you? where are you?

Many gates has the holy city.
In the night it lies lonely
On silent, far-spreading mountains.

RUTHENIAN VILLAGE

The inn's lust-reddened eyes have been extinguished,
The flute of the lonely hill shepherd is silent,
    Wind and his lullaby's softness
    Gently have led him dreamward, flocks are asleep at his side.

The faces of the houses were locked by their thatches
From moon to the floor; and beneath every gable
    Girls' voices surge in their singing.
    Slowly each tree in turn entwines with clouds and the night.

The sows have been dismissed to their meal all in darkness
And wheezing they root up the daytime's remainders,
    Mightily roll in the ditches.
    Puddles all milky splash their bodies, the stones and the path.

Across the mossy centre the stars are in transit,
The walls and small gardens are merged in one blackness;
    Slavering mongrels are turning
    Spotted wry heads and, howling, mount their guard against night.

Franco Fortini (1917–1994)

From *Poems* (1978)

TRANSLATING BRECHT

All afternoon
a thunderstorm hung on the rooftops,
then broke, in lightning, in torrents.
I stared at lines of cement, lines of glass
with screams inside them, wounds mixed in and limbs,
mine also, who have survived. Carefully, looking
now at the bricks, embattled, now at the dry page,
I heard the word
of a poet expire, or change
to another voice, no longer for us. The oppressed
are oppressed and quiet, the quiet oppressors
talk on the telephone, hatred is courteous, and I too
begin to think I no longer know who's to blame.

Write, I say to myself, hate those
who gently lead into nothingness
the men and women who are your companions
and think they no longer know. Among the enemies' names
write your own too. The thunderstorm,
with its crashing, has passed. To copy
those battles nature's not strong enough. Poetry
changes nothing. Nothing is certain. But write.

Helmut Heissenbüttel (1921–1996)

From *Texts* (1977)

FRAGMENT III

All horizons are round.
On the plain's flat disc I am
The centre of remote church spires.

The voice on the radio says
FREEDOM IS AN IMPOSSIBLE THING.
After that
String Quartet No. 4 by Arnold Schoenberg.

FINAL SOLUTION

they just happened to think that up one day
who happened to think that up one day
that just happened to occur to them
to whom did that just happen to occur
to one of them that just happened to occur
one of them just happened to think that up one day
one of them just happened to just think that up one day
or perhaps more than one of them thought it up at the same time
perhaps that occurred to more than one of them together
and how did they carry out the thing that occurred to them

if one wants to get anything done one has to be for something and not
just something one happens to think up but something for which one
can be or at least something for which a lot of people would like to be
or at least something one imagines a lot of people would like to be for
and they just happened to think that up one day

they thought that up and then they hit on the idea when they wanted to start doing something but what they hit on was not something one can be for but something one can be against or better something one can bring most people round to being against for when one can bring most people round to being against something one needn't be so precise any more about the thing one can be for and the fact that one needn't be so precise about it any more has its advantages for if most people can just let themselves go they usually don't care what it is they are for

and so they hit on that idea when they'd started to just think up something of the kind

so they hit on the idea that what one is against must be something one can see touch revile humiliate spit at lock up strike down annihilate because what one can't see touch revile humiliate spit at lock up strike down annihilate one can only speak of and what one can only speak of can change and one never quite knows what it will turn into whatever one may say against it

and so they hit on that idea and did that

so they hit on that idea and did that and when they had done that they tried to bring most people round and when they had brought most people round to joining in they hit on the idea that what one is against so long as it's still there remains changeable and that only what's gone becomes unchangeable and so they forced those they had brought round to joining in to annihilate that which they had been brought round to being against to regard it like malaria mosquitoes or chickweed or wireworm that have to be exterminated and when they had managed that they called those they had brought round to doing that murderers and turned them too into malaria mosquitoes and chickweed and wireworm and kept them down as they had wanted to keep them down without being for anything but just to keep them down for ever

and that just happened to occur to them when they hit on the idea that one can do all those things

that just happened to occur to them when they wanted to do something and then they hit on the idea that all one needs is to bring some people round to being for something at first and to being against something and so on until they can't get out of it any more and run round in circles for all eternity or rather till there is no one left for that won't take them till all eternity but why did they think that up or didn't they think anything of it except that they wanted to do something perhaps because it was too boring for them as it was before that occurred to them and they hit on the idea

yes of course they carried it so far only so that in the end they themselves could plunge into it and put an end to themselves and to everything for people like that are always people who want to put an end to it but they don't want to go by themselves but everyone must go with them

so that's the kind of people to whom something like that just happens to occur

THE FUTURE OF SOCIALISM

no one owns anything
no one exploits
no one oppresses
no one is exploited
no one is oppressed
no one gains anything
no one loses anything
no one is a master
no one is a slave
no one is a superior
no one is a subordinate
no one owes anyone anything
no one does anything to anyone

no one owns nothing
no one exploits no one
no one oppresses no one
no one is exploited by no one
no one is oppressed by no one

no one gains nothing
no one loses nothing
no one is no one's master
no one is no one's slave
no one is no one's superior
no one is no one's subordinate
no one owes no one anything
no one does anything to no one

all own everything
all exploit all
all oppress all
all are exploited by all
all are oppressed by all
all gain everything
all lose everything
all are everyone's masters
all are everyone's slaves
all are everyone's superiors
all are everyone's subordinates
all owe everyone everything
all do anything to everyone

all own nothing
all exploit no one
all oppress no one
all are exploited by no one
all are oppressed by no one
all gain nothing
all lose nothing
all are no one's masters
all are no one's slaves
all are no one's superiors
all are no one's subordinates
all owe no one nothing
all do nothing to no one

Ernst Jandl (1925–2000)

From *Dingfest/Thingsure* (1997)

two kinds of signs

i cross myself
in front of every church
i plum myself
in front of every orchard

how i do the former
every catholic knows
how i do the latter
i alone

at the delicatessen shop

please give me a potted may meadow
a slightly higher altitude but not too steep
so that one can still sit on it.

all right, then, maybe a snowy slope, deep-frozen
but no skiers, please. a fir tree beautifully snowed on
can be thrown in.

you haven't? that leaves – i see you have hares hanging there.
two or three should be enough. and a huntsman of course.
where do you hang them? i don't see the huntsmen.

Günter Grass (1927–)

From *Selected Poems 1956–1993* (1999)

FAMILY MATTERS

In our museum – we always go there on Sundays –
they have opened a new department.
Our aborted children, pale, serious embryos,
sit there in plain glass jars
and worry about their parents' future.

MARRIAGE

We have children, that counts up to two.
We usually go to different films.
It's friends who talk of our drifting apart.
    But your interests and mine
    still touch, at the same points always.
    Not only the question about cufflinks.
    Little services too:
    just hold that mirror.
    Change the bulbs.
    Fetch something.
    Or discussions, till everything is discussed.
Two stations that at times
are both tuned in to receive.
Shall I turn myself off?
    Exhaustion simulates harmony.
    What do we owe each other? That.
    I don't like that – your hairs in the john.

But after eleven years the thing is still fun.
To be one flesh when prices fluctuate.
We think thriftily, in small coin.
In the dark you believe all I say.
Unpicking and knitting anew.
A stretched cautiousness.
Saying thank you.
    Pull yourself together.
    That lawn of yours in our garden.
    Now you're being ironic again.
    Why don't you laugh about it?
    Clear out, then, if you can.
    Our hatred is weatherproof.
But sometimes, distrait, we are tender.
The children's reports
have to be signed.
    We deduct each other from income tax.
    Not till the day after tomorrow will it be over.
    You. Yes, you. Don't smoke so much.

Hans Magnus Enzensberger (1929–)

From *Selected Poems* (1994)

THE END OF OWLS

I do not speak of what's yours,
I speak of the end of the owls.
I speak of turbot and whale
in their glimmering house,
in the sevenfold sea,
of the glaciers –
too soon they will calve –
raven and dove, the feathered witnesses,
of all that lives in the winds
and woods, and the lichen on rock,
of impassable tracts and the grey moors
and the empty mountain ranges:

Shining on radar screens
for the last time; recorded,
checked out on consoles, fingered
by aerials fatally, Florida's marshes
and the Siberian ice, animal,
reed and slate all strangled
by interlinked warnings, encircled
by the last manoeuvres, guileless
under hovering cones of fire,
while the time-fuses tick.

As for us, we're forgotten.
Don't give a thought to the orphans,
expunge from your minds
your gilt-edged security feelings
and fame and the stainless psalms.
I don't speak of you any more,
planners of vanishing actions,
nor of me, nor of anyone.

I speak of that without speech,
of the unspeaking witnesses,
of otters and seals,
of the ancient owls of the earth.

THE DIVORCE

At first it was only an imperceptible quivering of the skin –
'As you wish' – where the flesh is darkest.
'What's wrong with you?' – Nothing. Milky dreams
of embraces; next morning, though,
the other looks different, strangely bony.
Razor-sharp misunderstandings. 'That time, in Rome –'
I never said that. A pause. And furious palpitations,
a sort of hatred, strange. 'That's not the point.'
Repetitions. Radiantly clear, this certainty:
From now on all is wrong. Odourless and sharp,
like a passport photo, this unknown person
with a glass of tea at table, with staring eyes.
It's no good, no good, no good:
litany in the head, a slight nausea.
End of reproaches. Slowly the whole room
fills with guilt right up to the ceiling.
This complaining voice is strange, only not
the shoes that drop with a bang, not the shoes.
Next time, in an empty restaurant
slow motion, bread crumbs, money is discussed,
laughing. The dessert tastes of metal.
Two untouchables. Shrill reasonableness.
'Not so bad really.' But at night
the thoughts of vengeance, the silent fight, anonymous
like two bony barristers, two large crabs
in water. Then the exhaustion. Slowly
the scab peels off. A new tobacconist,

a new address. Pariahs, horribly relieved.
Shades growing paler. These are the documents.
This is the bunch of keys. This is the scar.

THE RICH

Wherever do they keep on coming from,
these luxurious hordes! After every collapse
they've crept out of the ruins,
unmoved; through every eye of a needle
they've slipped,
rich in number, good heels and blessings.

Those wretches. Nobody likes them.
Their burden bows them down.
They offend us,
are to blame for everything,
can't help it,
must be got rid of.

We've tried everything.
We've preached to them,
we've implored them,
and only when there was no other way
blackmailed, expropriated, plundered them.
We have left them to bleed
and put them against the wall.

But no sooner did we lower the rifle
and seated ourselves in their armchairs
than we knew, incredulous
at first, but then with a sigh of relief:
we too were irrepressible.
Yes, yes, one gets used to anything.
Till it happens again.

Marin Sorescu (1936–1996)

From *Selected Poems* (1983)

SYMMETRY

As I was walking along
suddenly two paths
opened up for me:
one to the left,
the other to the right,
and quite symmetrical.

I stopped,
blinked,
bit either lip in turn,
cleared my throat and
took the one to the right
(just the wrong one,
it turned out later).

So now I followed it.
Never mind the details.
And then suddenly
two chasms
opened up for me:
one to the left,
the other to the right.
Without thinking I dropped
headlong
into the one to the left, which, alas,
just wasn't the one padded with down!
On all fours I crawled on,
and as I crawled
suddenly
two open paths lay before me.
Just wait, I said to myself,
and this time took the one to the left.

Straight into misery.
The wrong choice, quite wrong; to the right
led the True, the Only, the Great one, *the*
Way, so it seemed.
Well, at the next fork
I put my trust,
body and soul, into the one on the right. Once more
it was the other which . . .
Now my pack is almost empty,
my gnarled stick, grown old,
no longer puts out leaves
that could give me shade
when despair takes hold of me.
My legs are worn down,
the stumps grumble and growl
that, no matter where I went,
it was one great mistake.

And suddenly now
two Heavens
open up for me:
one to the right,
the other to the left.

W. G. Sebald (1944–2001)

From *After Nature* (2002)

AS THE SNOW ON THE ALPS, VIII

With the painter on horseback,
sometimes, too, high up on the cart
sits a nine-year-old child,
his own, as he ponders in disbelief,
conceived in his marriage to Anna.
It is a most beautiful ride, this last
in September 1527, along the riverside
through the valleys. The air stirs the light
between the leafage of trees, and from the hillsides
they look down on the land extending around them.
At rest, leaning against a rock, Grünewald
feels inside himself his misfortune
and that of the water-artist in Halle.
Like starlings the wind drives us
into flight at the hour when
the shadows fall. What remains to the last
is the work undertaken. In the service of
the family Erbach at Erbach, Grünewald devotes
the remaining years to an altar-work.
Crucifixion again, and the lamentation,
the deformation of life slowly proceeds; and
always between the eye's glance
and the raising of his brush
Grünewald now covers a long journey,
much more often than he used to
interrupts the execution of his art,
for the apprenticing of his child
both in the workplace and outside in the green country.
What he himself learned from this is nowhere reported,
only that the child at the age of fourteen
for no known reason suddenly died
and that the painter did not outlive him

for any great length of time. Peer ahead sharply,
there you see in the greying of nightfall
the distant windmills turn.
The forest recedes, truly,
so far that one cannot tell
where it once lay, and the ice-house
opens, and rime on to the field traces
a colourless image of Earth.
So, when the optic nerve
tears, in the still space of the air
all turns as white as
the snow on the Alps.

DARK NIGHT SALLIES FORTH, VI

When morning sets in,
the coolness of night
moves out into the plumage
of fishes, when once more
the air's circumference
grows visible, then at times
I trust the quiet, resolve
to make a new start, an excursion
perhaps to a reserve of
camouflaged ornithologists.
Come, my daughter, come on,
give me your hand, we're leaving
the town, I'll show you the mill
set twice each day in motion
by the sea's current,
a groaning miraculous construct
of wheels and belts
that carries water power
right into stone, right
into the trickling dust and
into the bodies of spiders.

The miller is friendly,
has clean white paws,
tells us all kinds of lore
to do with the story of flour.
A century ago Edward FitzGerald,
the translator of Omar Khayyám,
vanished out there. At an advanced age
one day he boarded his boat,
sailed off, with his top hat
tied on, into the German Ocean
and was never seen again.
A great enigma, my child,
look, here are eleven barrows
for the dead and in the sixth
the impress of a ship with forty oars
long since gone, the grave of
Raedwald of Sutton Hoo.
Merovingian coins, Swedish
armour, Byzantine silver
the king took on his voyage,
and his warriors even now
on this sandy strip keep their weapons
hidden in grassy bunkers
behind earthworks, barbed wire
and pine plantations, one great
arsenal as far as the eye can see,
and nothing else but this sky,
the gorse scrub and, now and then,
an old people's home,
a prison or an asylum,
an institution for juvenile delinquents.
In orange jackets you see
the inmates labour
lined up across the moor.
Behind that the end
of the world, the five
cold houses of Shingle Street.
Inconsolable, a woman
stands at the window,

a children's swing
rusts in the wind, a lonely
spy sits in his Dormobile
in the dunes, his headphones
pulled over his ears.
No, here we can write
no postcards, can't even
get out of the car. Tell me, child,
is your heart as heavy as
mine is, year after year
a pebble bank raised
by the waves of the sea
all the way to the North,
every stone a dead soul
and this sky so grey?
So unremittingly grey
and so low, as no sky
I have seen before.
Along the horizon
freighters cross over
into another age
measured by the ticking
of Geigers in the power station
at Sizewell, where slowly
the core of the metal
is destroyed. Whispering
madness on the heathland
of Suffolk. Is this
the promis'd end? Oh,
you are men of stones.
What's dead is gone
forever. What did'st
thou say? What,
how, where, when?
Is this love
nothing now
or all?
Water? Fire? Good?
Evil? Life? Death?

4 *The Essayist and Critic*

From *Testimonies* (1989)
Shorter Prose Pieces 1950–1987

AN ESSAY ON THE ESSAY

EVEN THAT isn't quite right: an essay really ought not to be on anything, to deal with anything, to define anything. An essay is a walk, an excursion, not a business trip. So if the title says 'on', that can only mean that this essay passes over a certain field – but with no intention of surveying it. This field will not be ploughed or cultivated. It will remain a meadow, wild. One walker is interested in wildflowers, another in the view, a third collects insects. Hunting butterflies is permitted. Everything is permitted – everything except the intentions of surveyors, farmers, speculators. And each walker is allowed to report whatever he happens to have observed about the field – even if that was no more than the birds that flew over it, the clouds that have still less to do with it, or only the transmutations of birds or clouds in his own head. But the person who drove there, sat there inside his car and then says he was there, is no essayist. That's why the essay is an outmoded genre. ('Form' is what I almost wrote, but the essay is not a form, has no form; it is a game that creates its own rules.)

The essay is just as outmoded as the art of letter-writing, the art of conversation, the art of walking for pleasure. Ever since Montaigne the essay has been highly individualistic, but at the same time it presupposes a society that not only tolerates individualism but enjoys it – a society leisured and cultivated enough to do without information. The whole spirit of essay-writing is contained in the first sentence of the first great collection of English essays – Francis Bacon's of 1597: 'What is *Truth*; said jesting *Pilate*; And would not stay for an Answer.' A Jesting Pilate who asks questions but doesn't wait for answers is the archetypal personification of the essay, of essay-writing and essayists. The English essay flourished for three centuries, even when the earnestness of the Victorian age had begun to question its peculiar relation to truth. Only the totalitarian systems of this century turned walking without a purpose into a crime. Since the time of G. K. Chesterton and Virginia Woolf the essay has been a dead genre. Needless to say, people continued – and still continue – to write prose pieces which they call essays; but already George Orwell was too 'committed', too puritanical, too much aware of a crisis to take walks without a bad conscience.

The essay is not a form, but a style above all. Its individualism distinguishes it from pure, absolute or autonomous art. The point of an essay, like its justification and its style, always lies in the author's personality and always leads back to it. The essayist is as little concerned with pure, impersonal art as with his subject. Since the vast majority of so-called critical essays attaches primary importance to subjects, that is, to answers and judgements, the perpetuation of that genre does not prove that the essay has survived. Most critical essays are short treatises. With a genuine essay it makes no difference whether its title refers to a literary theme, whether to the origin of tragedy or the origin of roast pig.

But since the essay is not a form, the spirit of essay-writing can assert itself outside the genre. Where confidence in his readership was lacking, for instance, the essayist often changed into an aphorist. Lichtenberg, Friedrich Schlegel and Friedrich Nietzsche were laconic, partly repressed essayists. Essay-writing insinuated itself even into poetry: a pseudo-epic like Byron's *Don Juan* or Heine's *Atta Troll*, whose wit always points back to the personalities of their authors, whose plots are interrupted again and again by their narrators' peripatetic arbitrariness. Story-telling and essay-writing were inseparable in the prose pieces of Robert Walser, and it was no accident that one of them, an outstanding one, was called 'The Walk'. It was the spirit of essay-writing that drove Walser the story-teller into self-destructive parody: 'In Thuringia, at Eisenach if you like, there lived a so-called beetleologist, who once again had a niece. When shall I have done with nieces and the like? Perhaps never. In that case, woe is me! Grievously the girl in the house next door suffered under learned surveillance . . .'

Some of the digressions in Musil's *The Man without Qualities*, too, are genuinely essayistic, because Musil was a seeker, a man without designs who asked questions that he couldn't answer. So are the *Ficciones* of Jorge Luis Borges. So are many of the shorter writings of

Ernst Bloch, Walter Benjamin and Th. W. Adorno – however weighty their themes.

The spirit of essay-writing walks on irresistibly, even over the corpse of the essay, and is glimpsed now here, now there, in novels, stories, poems or articles, from time to time in the very parkland of philosophy, formidably walled and strictly guarded though it may seem, the parkland from which it escaped centuries ago to wander about in the wild meadow. But it is never glimpsed where that wild meadow has been banned from human consciousness even as a memory or possibility, where walls have become absolute and walking itself has become a round of compulsion and routine. It has come to terms with the overcrowded streets of large cities, but hardly with factories, barracks, offices, not at all with prison yards and extermination camps. Anyone who can never get these out of his mind cannot tolerate the aimlessness and evasiveness of essay-writing, but calls it shameless, egotistic and insolent. But somewhere or other the spirit of essay-writing is walking on; and no one knows where it will turn up. Perhaps in the essay again, one day?

A JUMBLE OF NOTES ON MYTH

I

MYTHS, roughly speaking, are fictions embodying beliefs or ideas common to a large number of people, or capable of becoming such common property. When twentieth-century writers assert that myths are no longer of use to literature, they may be confusing myth with mythology – i.e. knowledge of existing myths and systems of myths, of the kind that educated readers could once be assumed to share. Such a confusion between the thing itself and the science or knowledge of that thing, in any case, is characteristic of our age. People will talk of a person's 'psychology', when they don't even believe that he or she has a psyche. In the same way they will talk of Greek mythology when they mean Greek myths, in which they don't believe any more than they do in a psyche. If they do believe in those myths, it is likely to be on the grounds of a Jungian collective unconscious; and there another twentieth-century problem arises, namely, that we have too much of everything to have anything at all. Too many myths. Ours is the age of comparative religion, comparative philosophy, comparative mythology. With infinite learning the symbolism of countless myths is expounded in the countless works of authors whom collectively we shall call Hocus Pocus Polymyth. The no-nonsense writer may respond by wanting no truck with any myth whatever – much as the New Illiterates want no truck with any good literature whatever, because there is too much of it for them to cope with.

2

That very no-nonsense writer could produce a twentieth-century myth without knowing it. Within certain temporal and cultural limits, Philip Larkin's 'Mr Bleaney' could be accepted as a myth – simply by becoming the imaginative property of a sufficient number of no-nonsense readers who can identify with the fiction. If the poem does not transcend those limits, the reason is not to be sought in the absence of mythological trappings, but in the poem's entanglement in a specific scene or set of circumstances. Most naturalistic fiction, however good, fails to be mythical for that reason. Yet the true creators of twentieth-century myth, like Kafka, made as little use as possible of existing myths and systems of myths, of mythology. If Joyce's *Ulysses* contains a twentieth-century myth, it is not because Joyce hung his narrative on a mythological peg, the *Odyssey*, but almost in spite of it (though Joyce's need for that peg points to his concern with what is central). Samuel Beckett was quick to learn that lesson. Even within the conventions of naturalistic fiction, mythology is a snare that, more often than not, inhibits primary imagination, the mythopoeic faculty. Dostoevsky could write myths within the naturalistic convention. Thomas Mann wrote mythological novels that fall short of being myths. Did Homer know he was writing myths? I doubt it. Kafka certainly did not.

3

The difference became acute in the second half of the eighteenth century, when Schiller distinguished between 'naïve' and 'sentimentalist' (i.e. reflective) writers, as between what Homer's myths meant to Homer and what Homeric myths mean to a modern reader. Coleridge had similar preoccupations. Hölderlin, a poet obsessed with the truths embodied in classical and biblical myths, grew fierce in face of the mythological conventions still observed by elegant writers in his time:

> Cold hypocrites, of gods do not dare to speak!
>   You're rational! In Helios you don't believe,
>   Nor in the Thunderer or the Sea-God ; . . .

> Take comfort, gods! For yet you adorn their verse,
>   Though now the soul's gone out of your pilfered names,
>   And if some high-flown word is needed,
>   You, Mother Nature, they still remember.

Blake's fierceness sprang from the same source, and he was radical enough to make a clean break with the mythological convention by creating his own myths. At the time of his breakdown, Hölderlin was in the process of extending his myth-making to modern history, as in his fragmentary 'hymn' celebrating Columbus.

In the same period, myths other than the classical and biblical began to break through into the awareness of educated European readers – Teutonic, Celtic, Oriental. Comparative mythology was pursued by some of the German Romantics, and Goethe began to think in terms of *Weltliteratur*, drawing on Indian legends for poems and finally writing his *West-östlicher Divan*, his marriage of East and West. (Fitzgerald's *Rubáiyát* was a later, more public celebration of a similar marriage.) Goethe's *Faust* began as a mythical drama, but acquired a pan-mythological superstructure in the course of the decades spent over its composition. (If Schiller had lived to read *Faust*, Part II, or the *Divan*, he could not have seen Goethe as a 'naïve' writer.)

Neither of those late works by Goethe could become popular. (Mint copies of the first edition of the *Divan* were still to be found in German bookshops at the time of the First World War. *Faust*, on the other hand, was crammed down the throats of those who could make little of it, because it had come to be regarded as *the* monumental masterpiece of *the* monumental German writer in *the* monumental age of German national *Kultur*.) Hölderlin's recreations of myths could not become popular. Blake's most overtly and elaborately mythopoeic poems could not become popular, though some of his songs – like Goethe's – did.

4

Myth, then, may have to be re-defined for the twentieth century. Apart from the problem of pluralism, my dictionary says that a myth is a narrative. Yet, since *The Waste Land* at least, myth has found its way into poetry that is not narrative. However we define it, myth is not dead, though this or that system of interrelated myths may have lost its general accessibility and representativeness. David Jones wrote myths. Geoffrey Hill's *Mercian Hymns* are a myth. Ted Hughes's *Crow* is a myth – to name a few fairly recent works. Existing myths can be brought back to life by those who have experienced them not as mythology but as urgent truth; and new myths can be created without recourse to traditional systems. My dictionary also says that myths are narratives 'usually involving supernatural persons, actions, or events'; but modern mythical literature has a way of evoking supernatural presences without invoking them, or giving them names. Faith has dug itself in beneath comparative dogma, comparative theology. Myth has done likewise, underpassing the systems. It may be that such faith, such myth, does not amount to religion, that it cannot bind; but it does bear witness, in the only way it can, to the human condition.

MUSIC AND WORDS II: SCHUBERT

This talk was given at Snape Maltings, at the invitation of Peter Pears,
mainly to singers at the music school.

NOT BEING a singer or musician, I am acutely aware that anything I
can say here may be of little practical use to you, if not a positive
stumbling-block or provocation. As a poet and translator, I am not
competent to offer detailed analysis of particular texts set to music by
Schubert. My point of view will be quite different from a performer's
intent on achieving the best possible balance between music and
words in a song. All I can do is sketch in a little of the historical back-
ground of Schubert's literary culture, as revealed in his choice of
texts for the songs, and offer some tentative remarks on the relation-
ship of words to music in general and Schubert's songs more
specifically.

If we compare Schubert's entire output with that of his immedi-
ate predecessor, Beethoven, what is immediately striking is the
preponderance of songs in Schubert's work. One obvious reason, of
course, is that Schubert's most outstanding gift was for melodic
invention, that he was prolific of tunes, to a degree possibly
unmatched by any earlier composer. Yet the *zeitgeist* has something to
do with that. In the Renaissance, baroque and classical periods most
secular music had derived from dance measures, so that its basic
structures were rhythmic and social (because dances were social
conventions). The rise of individualism in the Romantic period was
conducive to the predominance of song, the immediate expression of
personal feeling. That is why it is characteristic of Schubert's age that
Mendelssohn should have called a collection of piano piece 'songs
without words'. Between Beethoven's and Schubert's generations
there had been a radical shift of taste and sensibility, as apparent in
the literature of the time as in the music. This shift was conducive to
the genre, the *Lied*, in which Schubert excelled – so much so that
even in his chamber and piano music he tended to take up themes that
had originated as songs. As far as music is concerned, this points to a
greater dependence on literary or poetic stimuli than was characteris-
tic of the classical composers, up to and including Beethoven; and if

we look at the poetry of Schubert's time, we find a predominance of modes especially close to song, almost crying out to be set to music. This has to do with the Romantic rediscovery of folk-song and a nostalgia for the kind of civilization that had produced it. In German literature this had proceeded in two stages – one of them much earlier than Schubert's time. Through his settings of poems by Goethe and a few other poets active in the eighteenth century, Schubert drew on both stages in the rediscovery and imitation of folk modes.

The earlier of the two is associated not with the Romantic movement but with what is called the *Sturm und Drang*, a movement of the 1770s and 1780s connected with Rousseau's radical revaluation of natural, as opposed to civilized, humanity, amounting to a reversal of views that had prevailed in the preceding centuries. In the arts this rehabilitation of natural or primitive humanity also led to an emphasis on feeling and sentiment, as opposed to reason and decorum. The turmoil which it generated was often seen as a precondition or cause of the French Revolution. In Germany the thinkers who prepared the way for the *Sturm und Drang* were Johann Georg Hamann and Johann Gottfried Herder; and in imaginative literature the most powerful breakthrough of the *Sturm und Drang* occurred in the early work of Goethe and Schiller, though both writers were to develop in directions that made them turn back to classical models and preferences. The connection with folk-song and ballads is apparent not only in Goethe's early poetry but in Herder's collection and translation of folk poetry of the most various nations, *Stimmen der Völker*, published as early as 1778 and 1779. With the help of Herder's ideas, Goethe had found his way to folk modes even earlier in the decade. Yet Goethe was to survive both Beethoven and Schubert. From Mozart, who set Goethe's early poem 'Das Veilchen' – a poem that could not have been written but for the emulation of folk modes – to Hugo Wolf, Goethe became one of the main literary sources of the German *Lied*. Since Schubert set Goethe texts of the most various kinds and phases in Goethe's development, let me outline that development very briefly before speaking of the second stage, the Romantic proper, in the rediscovery and imitation of folk modes.

Of Goethe's *Sturm und Drang* songs and ballads set by Schubert, 'Heidenröslein' (1771) is the most famous, and the one closest to folk-song sources, from which Goethe may have drawn the poem. Goethe's version of it became a folk-song once more – though in a setting other than Schubert's. 'Erlkönig', 'Der Fischer', 'Jägers Abendlied' and 'Willkommen und Abschied' belong to the same phase in Goethe's work, as do the songs from *Faust*, 'Meine Ruhe ist hin' and 'Der König in Thule'. Other Goethe lyrics set by Schubert, such as 'Meeresstille', 'Nähe des Geliebten', the two 'Wandrers Nachtlieder' and the lyrics from his novel *Wilhelm Meisters Lehrjahre* – the Mignon and Harpist songs – belong to Goethe's middle period when, together with Schiller, he was trying rather deliberately to create a German classicism; yet the poems of that phase chosen by Schubert are those closest to the folk mode. Even in his *Sturm und Drang* period, though, Goethe was also writing a kind of poem that derived from the Greek dithyramb and the Pindaric ode – poems in free verse, completely different in kind from those based on folk-songs and ballads. Schubert set some of these – 'Ganymed', 'Prometheus' and 'An Schwager Kronos' – in a manner not radically different from that of his other songs. In German one way of distinguishing this kind of poem from the other is to call it *Gesang* rather than *Lied*. It is characteristic of Schubert that his treatment of such poems was almost as lyrical and fluent as his treatment of texts conceived as songs, lyrics or ballads. Brahms, on the other hand, was to recognize the difference in kind when he set part of one of Goethe's dithyrambic poems, 'Harzreise im Winter', not as a *Lied* but as a rhapsody for voice and orchestra; and a related poem, Hölderlin's 'Hyperions Schicksalslied', also called for this more elaborate and solemn treatment in Brahms's setting. Schubert also set two poems of Goethe's old age, the two Suleika songs from the *West-östlicher Divan* (1819), a sequence inspired by one of Goethe's late loves and, at the same time, a fulfilment of his ideal of *Weltliteratur* – an ideal going back to Herder's example – since the whole sequence is based on oriental sources and motifs. In this late phase Goethe's beginnings were linked to his end, the confessional or rhapsodic mode of his youth reconciled with the classical austerity of some of his middle period work. Again, Schubert's settings of the Suleika poems are not as different in character as one might expect from his settings of early or middle period Goethe texts; and I shall return to this matter of Schubert's response to his literary sources.

The greater number by far of Schubert's texts for the songs was drawn from the second historical phase of the folk-song revival in the Romantic period, marked in Germany by a second collection of folk poetry, *Des Knaben Wunderhorn*, by the poets Arnim and Brentano, published in 1808. As far as I know, Schubert did not set any poems from this collection, as Mahler was to do; but much of the verse that he did set, including that of the cycles *Die Schöne Müllerin* and *Die Winterreise*, is folksy verse of the kind that established itself in the wake of this Romantic reversion to folk modes. Even many of the texts collected by Arnim and Brentano were not the authentic texts of true folk-songs. True folk lyrics are usually pithy, plain and gritty. The *Kunstlied* and *Kunstballade* written in imitation of folk modes right through the nineteenth century had a sentimentality, if not a mawkishness, foreign to true folk modes, because it sprang from a drawing-room culture at an immense remove from the sources of folk art – for all its longing for lost simplicities (which Yeats was to call 'the ceremony of innocence'). That is one reason why the Goethe texts set by Schubert are far superior as poetry to most of the other texts that he set, especially those by his coevals or near-coevals. (His late Heine settings are one exception; another outstanding one is Matthias Claudius's 'Der Tod und das Mädchen', but it belongs to the pre-Romantic, *Sturm und Drang* period, and Claudius himself was an anomaly among the poets.) In so far as the *Sturm und Drang* imitated folk modes, it did so out of a strong and genuine revolution-ary impulse – a revolt against the whole social *status quo* and its proprieties. In the nineteenth century, on the other hand, folk modes became a mere evasion of contemporary realities and experience; they also became an excuse for every sort of intellectual sloppiness, a pseudo-naïvety that was allowed to pass as a substitute for true origi-nality in the diction and structure of a poem. Hence the embarrassing triteness or absurdity of many of the lyrics that Schubert turned into incomparable songs – and not only when they are paraphrased in programme notes and the like for the benefit of those lucky enough not to understand the German.

Here I must freely acknowledge a certain bias against German Romanticism generally, and against the late Romantic period even more, since it was a period in which the cult of feeling declined either into a cult of sentimentality or into artistic megalomania, inflated grandeur. Schubert's contemporary and acquaintance, Franz Grillparzer, the Austrian dramatist, defined the progress of the nine-teenth century as one 'from humanity, through nationality' (meaning 'nationalism') 'to bestiality'; and it is symptomatic that whereas

Herder collected the folk poetry of all nations, Romantic anthologists confined themselves to texts in German. Some of the German Romantic writers turned into fanatical nationalists – one reason why they attacked Goethe, and why Goethe came to hate and condemn the Romantic movement. All this does not distract from Schubert's songs – or from all but a few of his songs that are marred as music by the taste and sensibility of his age; but it does apply to much of the verse that he chose to set to music.

(I have been studying the texts and music of John Dowland's books of airs, produced at another period when song was a predominant musical medium. Most of Dowland's texts are anonymous, and many of them may have been written by him, who did not claim to be a poet. Yet all of them are interesting in their own right, let alone as texts for music. This points to the difference between an age when literary culture was of a high order, so that even amateurs found it impossible to write a wholly bad poem, and an age like Schubert's, in which professional writers could win popularity with versified drivel.)

But enough of these polemical generalities! I have said that Schubert's gifts were melodic above all; and melody, the invention of tunes, is that part of music which has to do with feeling rather than with those almost abstract, almost mathematical, faculties that come into play in contrapuntal invention. Schubert, of course, was also capable of such invention, especially in some of his later works other than the songs; but his spontaneous response to the mood, as distinct from the intellectual substance, of a poem made him the prolific and outstanding song writer he was. Some later composers of *Lieder*, such as Schumann and Wolf or the French composers from Fauré onwards, may have been more sensitive than he to the nuances and subtleties of poems, superior to him as musical interpreters of textual detail; but Schubert's setting of the poetically unpromising text 'Die Krähe' is one instance of his ability to improve on his texts. The unexpected chromatic shifts in that song bring out the uncanny, macabre effects which the poet wished to convey, but failed to convey without Schubert's music, because the poem is utterly implausible and ridiculous. No composer excelled Schubert in his grasp of the gesture of a poem as a whole, his ability to translate that gesture into musical terms, to make it move and sing. Schubert struck his contemporaries as reserved and undemonstrative. So are most people with strong and deep feelings, especially if those strong and deep feelings are of a kind not easily merged in social conventions and concerns. Schubert's were reserved for his music and went into his music, with an extraordinary freedom and prodigality. The literary texts he used served him as catalysts.

That brings me to the relationship of words to music in any setting. If there is such a thing as a partnership between poetry and music, it is an unequal one. The reason is that music is a pure art, even lyrical poetry an impure one, because its material is words, and words are the medium of every sort of non-artistic communication. As an artistic medium, therefore, music is by far the stronger partner in any association between the two. If a composer wishes to give words the greater weight, he has to resort to something like Schönberg's 'Sprechstimme' in our time, or practise the kind of self-denial imposed by plainsong on composers of liturgical music, by Biblical texts on Bach for the recitatives in his Passions; and even Bach, being Bach, could not help writing beautiful music for those, and giving a new dimension to the plain sacred narrative. Poetry, of course, has its own music; and the better the poem, the more it may approximate to what Walter Pater called 'the condition of music', which is one of autonomy or self-sufficiency. I say 'approximate', because the essential impurity of the medium, words, does not permit more than an approximation. The words of a poem tend to have meanings that belong to an order other than that of poetry, whereas the material of music, tones, belongs to an order entirely its own.

In music, too, there are degrees of purity, since music has been used for all kinds of functions that have little or nothing to do with its essential nature; but the best composers have taken those functions in their stride and achieved purity in spite of them. That is why, in the end, it doesn't matter very much that Schubert set many texts which, as poetry, are inferior to his music. Even Bach did so, in the arias of the same Passions (which, to me, belong to a higher order of music than Schubert's songs). In certain cases it may even have been an advantage to Schubert to set poems that did not compete with the music, did not set up their own claims to autonomy as works of art.

The poor literary quality of most opera libretti is notorious. Very great problems and tensions arise when a text has qualities equal, or superior to, the quality of the music to which it will be set, as in the case of several opera libretti by Hofmannsthal set to music by Richard Strauss. The relationship between the two men was often stretched almost to breaking-point, not only because they were so different in temperament, but because Hofmannsthal's texts contained subtleties and profundities for which Strauss, both literally and idiomatically, had no use. Ultimately, even that tension may have profited the stronger partner, music, but at the other's expense. To do full justice to Hofmannsthal's texts we still have to read them on their own terms, without the music; and the same is true of any excellent poem set to music by Schubert or by any other composer. Only the inferior text is subsumed in any one setting, and need never be separated from the music that it served.

The relationship between poetry and music, then, is a highly complicated and problematic one; and it becomes more so if we add considerations of performance, on the one hand, translation on the other. I cannot enter into these complications here. But let me trace some of the progressions, which can also be seen as a series of translations or transpositions. Leaving aside texts, like libretti, written for a specific composer, what happens? Somebody writes a poem. In writing it, he or she transposes a state of mind and feeling into words, rhythms, images that correspond to it, or approximate to a correspondence. The better the poem, the closer it will come to what T. S. Eliot called the 'objective correlative' to a subjective state. This 'objective correlative' permits the communication of the subjective state to others. A composer then reads the poem, and responds to it; but the response, again, is necessarily subjective. So the composer dissolves the 'objective correlative' achieved by the poet in order to transpose, translate it into his or her medium, music, and a particular mode or kind of music at that, a mode or kind conditioned both by history – that is by the state of music at any one period – and by his or her personal idiosyncrasies and needs. To call this process an 'interpretation' of the poem is not very accurate. The medium of music cannot interpret either the realities that have been woven into the texture of a poem or its semantic substance, its potential meaning. In transposing the poem into the medium of music, a composer can render only its mood, possibly its modulations and shifts of mood, possibly – but not necessarily – something of its rhythm. If the composer so much as repeats a line or phrase or word in the poem, when no such repetition occurred in the poem, a drastic transposition has taken place. (If a poet repeats a line or phrase or word in his or her poem, that repetition has a function quite different from that of the repetition resorted to by most composers of songs, including Schubert, for reasons not semantic, but to do with the shape and balance of the musical composition.) The composer, therefore, has not interpreted the poem, but used it for purposes of his own, or of his music's, changing it utterly. If the setting is a good one, 'a terrible beauty is born' – terrible from the poet's point of view, because the new creation is something so different from the poem. (That may be one reason why Goethe was afraid of music, preferring to work with the tame musician Zelter, and had nothing to say of Beethoven's or Schubert's settings of his poems.)

Interpretation does take place at the next stage, that of performance; and at that stage the words become important again, not necessarily in their own right, but because a singer may need them to accomplish his or her own translation of notes in a score into sounds to be sung and heard. Here interpretation is the right word, because the singer's freedom is so much more restricted than the composer's was in relation to the text; and, for better or for worse, the words are part of what the singer has to render. Since the singer also has to respond emotionally and subjectively to the score, but is not free to indulge his or her subjectivity to the extent of violating the composer's intentions, in so far as these have been fixed by the score, the words may also help the singer to grasp the gist and gesture of a song. That is where a knowledge and understanding of the original language may become a prerequisite. The complications and transpositions introduced by the translated texts of songs are so painful that I would rather not speak of them, though I have some experience of them, not only as a translator.

As a mere listener to music, I have to confess that I tend to remember only the music of most songs, and forget the words – quite especially with many of Schubert's songs; and this in spite of being a poet and literary man. Or perhaps because of it – and because of everything I have said. Either I know the poems as poems, as something in their own right, separate from what Schubert has made of them; or else I don't want to know them at all, like the inanities of 'Alinde', or the third-hand folksiness, banality and mawkishness of most of Wilhelm Müller's verse. But here I speak as an *advocatus diaboli*, with a bias against the literary culture of Schubert's time, and out of personal preoccupations that have no relevance to the interpretation of songs in performance.

On the other hand I shall not attempt to praise the power and true originality – by which I mean that faculty which makes artistic works first-hand – of Schubert's music in the songs. Music speaks for itself, in its own terms so much more immediate than the medium of words. That is why Schubert could make perfect songs out of flawed or mediocre verse. The feelings these evoked in him were pure and strong; and, at an early age, he had the mastery needed to transform them into unprecedented and unsurpassed music as direct as the folk poems they imitated but were far from resembling. Most of the songs composed by Schubert's successors lack the directness, due to the primacy of the melodic line. By this I don't mean that his piano parts are a mere accompaniment to the voice. They are an integral part of the composition, full of delicate effects and modulations; but they strike me as less fussy and less elaborate than those of many later Romantic composers.

If I felt competent to act as a music critic here, I should now turn to specific songs, showing how the music parallels or complements or enhances the words, but for that I should need the technical knowledge of music that I lack. So I must end where a music critic would begin.

THE SURVIVAL OF POETRY

IF IN RECENT decades there have been fewer controversies about the 'death of poetry' than about the 'death of the novel', one obvious reason is that novels receive more attention in any case, because they can become best-sellers and can also be processed for the stage, radio, film, television or video-tapes. Another is that poetry was recognized to be an anachronism as early as the first Industrial Revolution in Britain. Its obsolescence was predicted in the early decades of the nineteenth century, when Thomas Carlyle, among others, declared that poetry could have no true function in what he called 'the Mechanical Age'. The prediction, of course, was not dialectical enough to allow for the Romantic movement, with its anti-mechanical, anti-realistic-impetus and its return not only to pre-industrial but pre-literary paradigms – folk-song, ballad and fairy tale. It was in the Victorian period up to the First World War that European poetry won an unprecedented readership, thanks to the spread of literacy, a mechanized publishing industry to supply it, a much larger leisured class, and the very need of that class for brief imaginative or sentimental respites from the economic realities of the 'Mechanical Age'. For centuries it had been illiteracy that restricted the readership for poetry, together with the decline of oral traditions in those countries and regions that had been industrialized, mechanized and/or educationally homogenized by a central bureaucracy.

Now, during the second, the electronic, Industrial Revolution, it is literacy, not illiteracy, that threatens the survival of poetry, though not the survival of literature as a medium of communication, however diminished that function may turn out to be in relation to the other, electronic, media. The reason is that literature still serves to convey information of many kinds regarded as useful – including information about poetry and the lives of poets! Literature is part of the information industry, as poetry, by its nature, never could and never will be. In the words of the Spanish poet Juan Ramón Jiménez, written in 1941, 'literature is a state of culture, poetry is a state of grace, before and after culture'.

Since man does not live by technology alone – though he is doing his best to die by it – once again the very developments that threaten the survival of poetry insure that it will be needed as long as the species survives. The electronic revolution is also in the process of creating a new leisured class, that of the millions made 'redundant' by the automation of industry and the destruction of whole crafts and professions. The more monstrously inhuman our civilization becomes, the more probable it is that at least a small proportion of the permanently unemployed will turn away from other media to a 'state of grace before and after culture', to the anachronism of poetry.

So far I have used 'anachronism' in the prevalent sense of 'at odds with the trends of the age', restricting myself to the civilization which I know, that of the so-called 'developed' nations. Like all the pure, as distinct from applied, arts, however, poetry is also anachronistic in another, more literal sense, that of timelessness. However unfashionable that word, an impulse towards timelessness remains part of the act of writing poems, regardless of the poet's subject matter, allegiances, manner, vocabulary, or the degree of modernity intended or attained by that poet. Without that impulsion, a verse writer can produce literature, but not poetry. Because the poet's medium, words, is more easily mistaken for a vehicle of information than the musician's or the visual artist's media – though images and sounds, increasingly, are also being used by the information and advertising industries – a great many readers, teachers and even writers of verse frequently fall into the error of confusing the functions that a poem can perform with the nature of poetry, which is to carry its temporal and occasional baggage into the dimension of timelessness.

Here I am not advocating any one kind of poetry – the hermetic, for instance – rather than another, and am very much aware that poetry has had, and continues to have, many different functions within different cultures and civilizations. Verse has served as a mnemonic – Mnemosyne was the mother of the Muses – as a means of telling stories, as a close associate of science and philosophy, ritual, celebration, prophecy and revelation, but also as play, entertainment, social reportage, social satire, social 'criticism and moral exhortation. I am not saying that any of these functions is inadmissible, though they are shared with other media, those of literature. What I am saying is that those functions do not and must not detract from the primacy of language in the art of poetry; and that this language, unlike the language of information, does not lose its power or relevance even when many of the data it has drawn upon have ceased to be the common property of any one historically conditioned audience or readership. This also accounts for the fascination of dictionaries – especially etymological ones – for many practising poets, as for the habit of poets so up-to-date in other regards as W. H. Auden or Bertolt Brecht of incorporating archaic words and idioms in their poetic vocabularies – words and idioms that they would avoid in prose texts that serve to inform or persuade. To a poet it can be more essential to know that the words 'real' and 'royal' or 'matter' and 'mother' have sprung from a common root than to be well informed about things that everyone is writing or talking about. To a poet, language is all it has ever been and is capable of becoming, all it has ever done or is capable of doing. In a sense, too, every poet who has ever written anywhere can be his or her contemporary in timelessness.

Just as poetry is anachronistic in the sense of being outside time, it is also utopian, both in the prevalent sense of the word and the more literal sense of being out of place, in no place; and this, once more, regardless of whether a poet wishes to be so, thinks of himself or herself as being so, considers himself or herself rooted in a particular environment or way of life. If they are to become poetry, such particularities, too, will be carried into a dimension that is nowhere and everywhere.

Outside their poetry, poets can be anything they are disposed or forced to be. They can be committed to causes, institutions and powers that no one would call 'utopian', or they can be the victims of those same causes, institutions and powers. They can be employed in any profession or trade that has a use for them, as a brief look at the lives of outstanding twentieth-century poets will show. What those professions or trades are, will depend largely on the public status accorded to poets in different countries, as well as on personal circumstances and qualifications. In a number of European and Latin American countries, for instance, the prestige of poets remains such that some have been considered fit for a diplomatic post. In other countries they are more likely to be found in universities and libraries. Where even universities and libraries are treated as potentially dangerous places, nations have become expert in giving poets economic security while keeping a tight rein on their liberties and keeping them out of any occupation in which their utopianism could 'prove subversive. Interesting though they are, these political and social differences have little to do with the survival of poetry, because poetry has survived in all circumstances, under all conditions, including those as adverse as can be to the survival of its makers.

What is relevant to the survival of poetry is the re-emergence even in highly technical, commercialized and pluralistic cultures of the most ancient, seemingly atavistic, functions of poets and poetry. Even the mythical archetype of Orpheus is among the recurrent figures. The vatic or bardic tradition had a great deal to do with the extraordinary appeal of Dylan Thomas to readers and audiences in the 1940s and early 1950s in Britain and the USA, though much of his work must have been obscure to the point of unintelligibility to most of his devotees. The resurgence of oral poetry, sometimes combined with music, that followed in the 1960s owed much to that precedent, as the choice of the name Dylan by one of its most famous practitioners attests, however different his practice and person. Other practitioners assumed other functions: that of the prophet, shaman or guru in North America, that of the clown, tumbler or folk entertainer in Britain, that of the satirist in Germany. (That Wolf Biermann, the satirist, lived in East Germany, making recordings for a West German public, is one of the many ironies of the decade.) Public readings won large audiences in Eastern Europe also, in response to needs much older than the political systems that permitted and censored them.

It is in economically 'backward' cultures that poets are most widely and spontaneously loved and revered as voices of the people; and that traditional relationship is not broken if the work of such poets makes intellectual demands that, elsewhere, would be thought quite incompatible with a mass appeal. In Latin America the work of Pablo Neruda is one of many instances. In Greece the funeral of Giorgos Seferis was a public event that honoured not only him but the threatened values he stood for; and as recently as 1984 a great crowd followed the body of Nodar Dumbadze, the Georgian poet, as it was carried in an open coffin from the Writers' Union in Tiflis to the cemetery. In all these cases, popularity has preserved its true meaning; it is a loyalty and affection not measured in sales or publicity. Under totalitarian régimes it can be manipulated and contained, but neither imposed nor eradicated, by the political system.

Although it has often been suggested that no major and consistent body of work can be produced by a poet without a sense of some such community, which is certainly more sustaining than any honour or recognition available to poets in societies that have ceased to be communities, ever since the late eighteenth century poets have learned to make do with a minimal response. Thanks to the anachronistic and utopian nature of their art, they could address themselves to anyone or no one among the living, or to Rilke's Orpheus or to the 'necessary angel of the earth' posited both by Rilke and Wallace Stevens. Long before them, Hölderlin's poetry had been sustained by a sense of community with the dead and unborn. More and more, too, the writing of excellent poetry has been felt to be a privilege so rare as to need no palpable recognition or response.

Deliberate attempts, like Brecht's, to make poetry useful again, above all to make it a socially and politically effective art, have come up against a formidable barrier. What Brecht proved was that poetry could be stripped again of all its Romantic and post-Romantic finery and speak in a language as unemotive as that of some of the Latin poets who were among his models. Hence his classical exemplariness, which was widely taken up in both East and West Germany. By revolutionizing himself, Brecht succeeded in producing the kind of poetry he thought suitable for his didactic purposes, but its usefulness and effectiveness were beyond his control. That is why his exemplariness, too, has begun to look utopian.

Like any other poet of the 'Mechanical Age', then, Brecht could only cast his bread upon the waters or – in the metaphor chosen by a poet as difficult as Brecht wished to be plain, Paul Celan – launch his message inside a bottle 'in the faith, not always supported by hope, that it could be washed up somewhere, at some time, on land, heartland perhaps.' The plain messages have fared no better and no worse than the cryptic, enciphered ones. This uncertainty is inseparable not only from the act of writing and publishing poems but from the special pleasure still to be derived from reading them. Because poets take that risk, can't be sure that they know what they are about or whether their bottles will be picked up at all, poetry satisfies a need that no other language can satisfy. The opposite of that language is not prose, since there is prose that takes the same risk. Nor is it silence, which remains the source and precondition of poetry, as of music. Rather it is the noise of literature, with its stock exchange of reputations and personalities, schools and trends and camps, ups and downs of acclaim or rejection. As critics and journalists, poets may contribute to that noise. If they are deafened by it, though, anything they write in verse will be literature at best; and their true readers, those who do not read out of vanity or curiosity, will be aware of it, because those readers are also in search of a language that takes risks, an immediate and urgent language that may not reveal where it's coming from or where it's going. As long as there are such readers and writers, poetry will survive.

THE UNITY OF T. S. ELIOT'S POETRY

NO ONE, I am sure, would now dispute that T. S. Eliot's poetry possesses one kind of unity to a most remarkable degree – a stylistic unity of diction, cadence and imagery. But in any discussion of his work one is likely to hear someone say that he likes the early poems and dislikes the later ones, or that he likes the later ones and dislikes the early ones. The dividing line, it then transpires, is roughly that fixed by Eliot himself when he issued his poems in two small volumes: his early poetry is taken to end with the publication of 'The Hollow Men' in 1925 and includes *The Waste Land*, published three years earlier. His later period begins with the Ariel poems, the first of which appeared in 1927, and includes 'Ash Wednesday' and the *Four Quartets*. It is well known that the dividing line corresponds to a crucial turning-point in Eliot's life, his entry into the Anglican Church. I certainly do not wish to deny the importance of what has been called Eliot's conversion, but I believe that the knowledge of this event has led to an over-emphasis on the difference between his early and later poetry.

Here I am not thinking only, or even primarily, of critics who have expressed an overt bias towards or against Eliot's religious orthodoxy; for very few of us – whether as private readers or as professional critics – are both perceptive and honest enough to make a clear distinction between our judgement of poetry as art and our judgement of poetry as an expression of ideas, attitudes and beliefs. It may be helpful, at this point, to quote from a criticism which does honestly state a bias against Eliot's religious orthodoxy. It is part of George Orwell's review of three of the *Four Quartets*, which he published in 1942: 'If one wants to deal in antitheses', Orwell wrote, 'one might say that the later poems express a melancholy faith, and the earlier ones a glowing despair. They were based on the dilemma of modern man, who despairs of life and does not want to be dead, and on top of this they expressed the horror of an over-civilized intellectual confronted with the ugliness and the spiritual emptiness of the machine age.' The later poems, on the other hand, Orwell accuses of expressing a negative attitude 'which turns its eyes to the past, accepts defeat, writes off earthly happiness as impossible, mumbles about prayer and repentance . . .' Orwell explains his own preference for the early poems by this 'deterioration in Mr Eliot's subject matter'.

The advantage of such a criticism is that we need not accept it we do not share the clearly formulated prejudices on which it is based. Orwell, it is true, also questions the artistic merit of Eliot's later poetry, but his reasons are so obviously personal that they do not amount to a serious indictment. All that we really learn from his criticism is that he, Orwell, prefers a 'glowing despair' to a 'melancholy faith'.

But those who, like myself, became acquainted with Eliot's later poetry either before reading the early poetry, or at about the same time, are not at all sure that Orwell's antithesis is a valid one. To speak for myself only, I found that the faith expressed in the *Four Quartets* is not always melancholy, and that much of the despair expressed in *The Waste Land* and 'The Hollow Men' is far from glowing; also that all the despair of the early poems is contained in the faith of the later ones, and that much of this faith was already implicit in the early poems, because of the peculiar quality of the despair which they express.

One of Orwell's objections is that in the later poems Eliot 'writes off earthly happiness as impossible'. If by 'earthly happiness' Orwell means a happiness attainable by purely earthly means – as other parts of his review would suggest – his observation is quite correct; but in this respect there is no difference between the early poems and the late. In the early poems, from 'The Love Song of J. Alfred Prufrock' onwards, Eliot inquires into the lives of those who do believe that 'earthly happiness is possible' – 'earthly happiness' in the sense in which I have defined it – and shows that their lives are empty and meaningless:

> For I have known them all already, known them all –
> Have known the evenings, mornings, afternoons,
> I have measured out my life with coffee spoons;
> I know the voices dying with a dying fall
> Beneath the music from a farther room.
>   So how should I presume?

Orwell could accept this kind of comment on life because it is non-committal and oblique; and because it could be interpreted as a comment only on a particular way of life, that of a certain class or social milieu. Such a comment would not conflict with Orwell's own belief that 'earthly happiness' could be brought about by changes in the material world, by social or economic reform. This, however, is a misinterpretation of Eliot's comment: the rest of the poem makes it quite clear that he is not merely satirizing one class or milieu, but every way of life that is based on the pursuit of 'earthly happiness'. Even the love between men and women is included in Eliot's questioning of the values by which the worldly live:

> And I have known the arms already, known them all –
> Arms that are braceleted and white and bare
> (But in the lamplight, downed with light brown hair!)
> Is it perfume from a dress
> That makes me so digress?
> Arms that lie along a table, or wrap about a shawl.

'The Love Song of Alfred J. Prufrock' is a very strange love song indeed; and one would need to be very biased or very perverse to call its ironic scepticism positive, and the answer to it – as provided by the later poems – negative.

It will not be possible here to trace Eliot's attitude to 'earthly happiness' through all his early poems and to show how every question asked in these early poems is answered in the later ones; a few examples will have to suffice. What I hope to show is that these questions, by their very nature, point to the kind of answer given in the later poems; not to a vindication of an 'earthly happiness' that can be attained through the fulfilment of worldly ambitions and desires.

Of the four satirical pieces with an obviously American setting, 'The Boston Evening Transcript', 'Aunt Helen', 'Cousin Nancy' and 'Mr Apollinax', it could once again be said that they question only a particular way of life, that of a wealthy, educated and leisured class in a certain place at a certain time; but their irony and their weariness go deeper than that. The ironic reference to 'Matthew and Waldo, guardians of the faith, the army of unalterable law' (in 'Cousin Nancy') is no mere accident; for Matthew Arnold and Ralph Waldo Emerson represent an eclectic humanism which is the prevalent substitute for religious faith} Eliot therefore makes a clear connection between the hollow lives led by all the characters in these poems and a philosophical outlook which is by no means confined to themselves.

In 'Mr Apollinax' Eliot introduces that method of contrast by allusion to myth and literature which he was to use with such powerful effect in *The Waste Land*; no comment on modern society could be more damning than the conclusion, with its return to the tea party with which the poem begins:

> 'He is a charming man' – 'But after all what did he mean?' –
> 'His pointed ears. . . . He must be unbalanced.' –
> 'There was something he said that I might have challenged.'
> Of dowager Mrs. Phlaccus, and Professor and Mrs. Cheetah
> I remember a slice of lemon, and a bitten macaroon.

A similar impression of lives completely meaningless is left by another poem from Eliot's first collection, 'Rhapsody on a Windy Night'. This poem, too, is set in America, but the scene could be any large city in any western country. After a walk through this city in the early hours of the morning, the person of the poem returns to his own lodgings:

> The lamp said,
> 'Four o'clock,
> Here is the number on the door.
> Memory!
> You have the key,
> The little lamp spreads a ring on the stair.
> Mount.
> The bed is open; the tooth-brush hangs on the wall,
> Put your shoes at the door, sleep, prepare for life.'
>
> The last twist of the knife.

In this poem all the imagery is sufficiently general, even universal, to preclude any suggestion that the poet has intended nothing more than a piece of social satire; the preparation for life – which is 'the last twist of the knife' – is the preparation for any life not sustained by a purpose which transcends that life; and the cruel finality of the last image conveys a despair so great that no material remedy could possibly prove effective.

Not all these early poems are cruel. 'Portrait of a Lady' ruthlessly exposes a life based on illusion, but it is also a poem full of pity – the same pity that Eliot expresses at the end of 'Preludes', before juxtaposing another image of cruel indifference.

I am moved by fancies that are curled
Around these images, and cling:
The notion of some infinitely gentle
Infinitely suffering thing.

Wipe your hand across your mouth, and laugh;
The worlds revolve like ancient women
Gathering fuel in vacant lots.

The pathos of 'Portrait of a Lady' derives from the poet's most deli-
cate treatment of a theme that had rarely been touched upon in
poetry at all: this theme is the impossibility of communication, and of
communion, between those whose lives are circumscribed by material
ends. Eliot conveys this terrible incompatibility between the elderly
lady and her young visitor by a characteristic juxtaposition of the
tragic with the trivial:

'Ah, my friend, you do not know, you do not know
What life is, you who hold it in your hands';
(Slowly twisting the lilac stalks)
'You let it flow from you, you let it flow,
And youth is cruel, and has no more remorse
And smiles at situations which it cannot see.'
I smile, of course,
And go on drinking tea.

That Eliot's own solution would be a religious one, and that it would
take the form of renunciation, is already intimated in the last poem
from his first collection, 'La Figlia che Piange'. We are not told who
the girl in this poem is; we are told nothing about her and it has even
been suggested that she is only the statue of a girl. But there can be
no doubt that she symbolizes a leave-taking, a renunciation, which
recurs throughout Eliot's later work – often in the form of images
closely related to the girl of this early poem:

Stand on the highest pavement of the stair –
Lean on a garden urn –
Weave, weave the sunlight in your hair –
Clasp your flowers to you with a pained surprise –
Fling them to the ground and turn
With a fugitive resentment in your eyes:
But weave, weave the sunlight in your hair.

So I would have had him leave,
So I would have had her stand and grieve,
So he would have left
As the soul leaves the body torn and bruised,
As the mind deserts the body it has used.
I should find
Some way incomparably light and deft,
Some way we both should understand,
Simple and faithless as a smile and shake of the hand. . . .

'La Figlia che Piange', too, is a poem of incompatibility, but of an incompatibility affirmed and transcended by renunciation. Much later, in 'Burnt Norton', Eliot identifies his recurrent image of the flower garden, in this case of the 'rose-garden', with 'our first world', that is to say with the garden of Eden. In 'Ash Wednesday', too, he writes of 'the garden where all loves end', meaning the Fall of Man and the origin of that sin which henceforth will attach to every human love. No such connection is made in 'La Figlia che Piange', but we can pursue the development of the garden, the girl and the flower images from this early poem to *The Waste Land*, 'Ash Wednesday', *The Family Reunion* and the *Four Quartets*. In this way the poem assumes a crucial significance and acts as a link between the early and later work.

'Gerontion', which opens Eliot's second collection, published in 1920, foreshadows both the mood and the message of the poetry which he wrote after his entry into the Church of England. Not only does it contain a quotation from an Anglican divine, Lancelot Andrewes, but it contrasts the 'thoughts of a dry brain in a dry season' of an unregenerate old man with 'the juvescence of the year' in which 'Came Christ the tiger'. 'Gerontion', too, is a poem of renunciation, renunciation of worldly ambitions and vanity:

After such knowledge, what forgiveness? Think now
History has many cunning passages, contrived corridors
And issues, deceives with whispering ambitions,
Guides us by vanities. . . .

And, as in 'La Figlia che Piange', there is the renunciation of love:

I that was near your heart was removed therefrom
To lose beauty in terror, terror in inquisition.
I have lost my passion: why should I need to keep it

Since what is kept must be adulterated?
I have lost my sight, smell, hearing, taste and touch:
How should I use them for your closer contact?

The satirical pieces in the same collection continue Eliot's inquiry into the lives of the worldly. As in 'Mr Apollinax', but with greater subtlety, he uses the technique of satire by contrast, by the juxtaposition of sordid contemporary scenes with allusions to the myth and literature of past ages; thus in 'Burbank with a Baedeker: Bleistein with a Cigar', a study of American tourists in Venice:

Burbank crossed a little bridge
    Descending at a small hotel;
Princess Volupine arrived,
    They were together, and he fell.

Defunctive music under sea
    Passed seaward with the passing bell
Slowly: the God Hercules
    Had left him, that had loved him well.

In the same way the London districts Kentish Town and Golders Green are contrasted with the splendour of past ages in 'A Cooking Egg': and once again the sordidness and triviality of modern life are concentrated into an image of unsatisfactory love between the sexes:

But where is the penny world I bought
    To eat with Pipit behind the screen?
The red-eyed scavengers are creeping
    From Kentish Town and Golder's Green;

Where are the eagles and the trumpets?

The waiter in Eliot's French poem of the same period, 'Dans le Restaurant', is identified with Phlebas the Phoenician, a character who also appears in *The Waste Land*, where he is not 'wholly distinct from Ferdinand Prince of Naples', from the one-eyed merchant and from Tiresias. This device of contracting several characters into one serves to bring out connections between one age, one civilization, one milieu and another, but, at the same time, to contrast them for the sake of satire. Another of these French poems, 'Lune de Miel', contrasts the boredom and petty annoyances of a modern honeymoon with one of the sights which the couple fail to visit. This is the basilica of St Apollinaire en Classe, which

> raide et ascétique,
> Vieille usine désaffectée de Dieu, tient encore
> Dans ses pierres écroulantes la forme précise de Byzance.

However cynical this reference to the basilica may seem, its asceticism and durability compare very favourably with the pleasures expected, but not experienced, by the young married couple of the poem: the implication is indirect but unmistakable.

It would be gross and presumptuous to include *The Waste Land* in a necessarily rapid survey of this kind. I can only touch on a few aspects of it that relate to my remarks on the shorter poems. The symbol of the waste land itself was already present in 'Gerontion', with its 'old man in a dry month . . . waiting for rain'; in the longer, more complex poem, this symbolism is both extended and clarified.

> . . . He who was living is now dead
> We who were living are now dying
> With a little patience.

> Here is no water but only rock
> Rock and no water and the sandy road
> The road winding above among the mountains
> Which are mountains of rock without water . . .

In this arid wilderness, inhabited by those who live only by secular values, every action and every aspiration is meaningless. An erotic encounter between a typist and a clerk exemplifies this lack of spiritual content:

> She turns and looks a moment in the glass,
> Hardly aware of her departed lover;
> Her brain allows one half-formed thought to pass:
> 'Well now that's done: and I'm glad it's over.'
> When lovely woman stoops to folly and
> Paces about her room again, alone,
> She smooths her hair with automatic hand,
> And puts a record on the gramophone.

In the fifth and last section of the poem, Eliot refers again to this episode as

> The awful daring of a moment's surrender
> Which an age of prudence can never retract
> By this, and this only, we have existed . . .

It is true that the words spoken by the thunder in *The Waste Land*, by the thunder which heralds rain and promises salvation from the wilderness, are taken not from a Christian text but from the Hindu Upanishads; but even in the Christian *Four Quartets* there are allusions to Hindu mysticism. Eliot, after all, is not a preacher but a poet; as such, he has always made use of whatever image or reference will best convey his own vision. I think I have said enough about the early work to show that this vision is a consistent one: that it is a vision which questions the lives of the worldly – typical people of our time – *sub specie aeternitatis*. Even the most despairing poem of all, 'The Hollow Men' of 1925, continues this questioning; and it not only takes up the image of the waste land – 'the dead land' or the 'cactus land' as it is called here – but by its fragmentary quotations from the litany and the Lord's Prayer suggests, even if it does not wholly embrace, the Christian solution. To the 'dead land' it opposes 'death's dream kingdom', thus confirming the paradox of a life beyond death that is more real than our lives on this earth; for in our present lives

> Between the idea
> And the reality
> Between the motion
> And the act
> Falls the Shadow

and

> Our dried voices when
> We whisper together
> Are quiet and meaningless
> As wind in dry grass
> Or rats' feet over broken glass
> In our dry cellar

Eliot's profession of Christian orthodoxy at this point was an event of the greatest importance; but, although it deeply affected his work as a critic, his experiments with drama and his attitude to society, its effect on his lyrical poetry has been exaggerated. Eliot himself has told us 'that the progress of an artist is a continual self-sacrifice, and continual extinction of personality... The more perfect the artist, the more completely separate in him will be the man who suffers and the mind which creates; the more perfectly will the mind digest and transmute the passions which are its material. Because Eliot is a consummate artist, he has always given us the 'objective correlative' of his own experiences, not those experiences themselves. With very few exceptions – such as the choruses from *The Rock*, which were written for a specific occasion and are more dramatic than lyrical – his later poetry is not a didactic exposition of Christian dogma. The style of his later poems, like that of the early ones, is highly individual; yet, to quote his own words once more, 'poetry is not a turning loose of emotion, but an escape from emotion; it is not the expression of personality, but an escape from personality. But, of course, only those who have personality and emotions know what it means to want to escape from these things.'

The essay from which I have been quoting, 'Tradition and the Individual Talent', was published in 1920, that is to say before Eliot's 'conversion'; but the view of the poet's function expounded in it is quite contrary to the views that were current at the time. Eliot's emphasis on the impersonal and super-personal nature of art at a time when all the stress was on individualism and personality points to the conclusion that he was a mystic before he was an orthodox Christian; and it is the mysticism of his later poems, not their orthodoxy, that makes them so difficult to understand. Eliot's mysticism, furthermore, is of a kind that is rare in modern poetry. It is not the mysticism of Rilke's *Duineser Elegien*, for that is a mysticism based on the poetic experience itself, on the poet's transformation of the visible world into poetry. Eliot's mysticism is a much more severe one: for it seeks a reality that is not manifested in the visible world at all and has no use for the sensuous experience by which Rilke apprehended the visible world before transforming it. Whereas Rilke's mysticism is aesthetic, Eliot's is ascetic.

This ascetic mysticism, as I have tried to show, preceded Eliot's profession of Christian orthodoxy; it is present in all the early poems, if only in the form of negation, the negation of worldly values, personal ambition and sexual love. The quotation from St John of the Cross which Eliot prefixed to his dramatic fragment of 1932, *Sweeney Agonistes*, sums up the character of his own mysticism: 'Hence the soul cannot be possessed of the divine union until it has divested itself of the love of created beings'. Rilke began with the love of created beings and, pantheistically, glorified the created world. Eliot began by questioning the reality of created beings and sought communion with the Creator not in, but beyond, the created world. Rilke, of course, was not a Christian poet at all; but even Christian poets like Gerard Manley Hopkins have chosen to praise the Creator by praising created things – an approach much more natural to poets than Eliot's asceticism.

The process of withdrawal, renunciation and depersonalization is carried further in the later poems; it is symbolized by the stairs of 'Ash Wednesday'. But the extreme difficulty of this divestment 'of the love of created things', and the temptation to backslide, is also evident from the same poem, and it is the girl and flower images that convey the soul's attachment to 'created beings':

> Blown hair is sweet, brown hair over the mouth blown,
> Lilac and brown hair;
> Distraction, music of the flute, stops and steps of the mind over
>   the third stair,
> Fading, fading; strength beyond hope and despair
> Climbing the third stair.

The *Four Quartets* are dominated by Eliot's mystical experience; so much so that the poet continually questions the ability of words to convey it. 'The poetry', he says in 'East Coker', 'does not matter'; that is to say, the poetry has become less important than the vision which it serves to embody. Yet the *Four Quartets* are not poems of escape from the temporal plane, for they accept and transcend it. The sordid and senseless world of the early poems is contained in them, as in the section of 'Burnt Norton' which recalls

> . . . . the strained time-ridden faces
> Distracted from distraction by distraction
> Filled with fancies and empty of meaning
> Tumid apathy with no concentration
> Men and bits of paper, whirled by the cold wind
> That blows before and after time . . .

'Not here / Not here the darkness, in this twittering world', the poet exorcizes these images and turns to the 'internal darkness' which is the 'darkness of God', the 'dark night of the soul'. Thus in 'East Coker':

I said to my soul, be still, and let the dark come upon you
Which shall be the darkness of God. As, in a theatre,
The lights are extinguished, for the scene to be changed
With a hollow rumble of wings, with a movement of darkness
    on darkness,
And we know that the hills and the trees, the distant panorama
And the bold imposing façade are all being rolled away –

  .   .   .   .

I said to my soul, be still, and wait without hope
For hope would be hope for the wrong thing; wait without love
For love would be love of the wrong thing; there is yet faith
But the faith and the love and the hope are all in the waiting.
Wait without thought, for you are not ready for thought:
So the darkness shall be the light, and the stillness the dancing.

At the same time, Eliot's vision has become wider and nature, too, has received a place in his vision; for having progressed so much further in his spiritual ascent, which is also a descent into the dark, the poet need no longer fear the rose-garden and 'the deception of the thrush'. This development explains the matrimonial dance in 'East Coker' and the affirmation of the 'dignified and commodious sacrament' of marriage – the 'necessary conjunction'; and it also explains the tribute to the 'strong brown god', a pantheistic river-god of 'The Dry Salvages', and Eliot's debt in these four poems to the pre-Socratic philosophers of Greece.

The emphasis now is not so much on the conflict and contrast between the timeless world and the temporal world as on their interaction and interrelation:

> The point of intersection of the timeless
> With time

The garden and flower images return and, although they symbolize experience in time, they also participate in the timeless world:

> The laughter in the garden, echoed ecstasy
> Not lost, but requiring, pointing to the agony
> Of death and birth.

Even human love is affirmed, though as a beginning, not an end in itself:

                    . . . not less of love but expanding
Of love beyond desire, and so liberation
From the future as well as the past.

It is the later poems, then – and especially the *Four Quartets* – in which Eliot suggests that 'earthly happiness' is possible, but possible only if we do not overrate its potentialities and scope. Eliot's own vision is still that of the mystic who has suffered the 'desolation of reality'; yet where the early poems harshly rejected the world, with all its aspirations, activities and pleasures, the later poems make a clear distinction between what is fitting for the mystic and the saint and what is fitting for those – the majority – who have no vocation of that kind. It is a distinction made by the Church also; and it could well be argued that Eliot's conversion has not restricted his vision, as Orwell claims, but helped to extend and enlarge it. Eliot's own experience of the world remains constant, or at least consistent, throughout his early and later work; but his real concern with those who do not and cannot share that experience has caused him to write with uncommon detachment, charity and wisdom about the world of time, which he himself learned long ago to transcend.

Nevertheless it is the asceticism of Eliot's vision that makes his poetry unique, an asceticism combined with worldly experience and sophistication as in none of the mystics to whom he is otherwise related. Even Milton, the so-called Puritan, is a sensualist and a pantheist by comparison; and no wonder, since sensualism and pantheism are not merely creeds congenial to poets, but states of mind hardly separable from the poetic process itself. In Eliot's own words, a poet's mind that is well equipped for its work 'is constantly amalgamating disparate experience: the ordinary man's experience is irregular, fragmentary, chaotic. The latter falls in love, or reads Spinoza, and these two experiences have nothing to do with each other, or with the noise of the typewriter or the smell of cooking; in the mind of the poet these experiences are always forming new wholes.' Well, I very much doubt that the ordinary man – whoever he may be – would fail to get Spinoza mixed up with the state of being in love; but Eliot's statement does bring out an important characteristic of the poetic process. What I have called the sensualism of the poet's state of mind is that same receptiveness to the smell of cooking; and its pantheism is its inherent tendency to discover connections everywhere, to posit a basically monistic universe and restore its wholeness by amalgamating 'disparate experiences'. T. S. Eliot differs from most modern poets in his ability to confine this magical function of the imagination to the poetic process itself, never allowing it to assume the status of a creed. He has achieved a rare discipline and a rare discrimination. Hence his opposition to the Romantics, despite those features of his poetry which strike his younger contemporaries as Romantic (in so far as Symbolism is a development of Romanticism), and his utter dissimilarity from Rilke or Wallace Stevens, whose whole 'philosophy' and religion are analogues of the poetic process. There will always be readers and writers of poetry who prefer that 'life-enhancement', that vindication and celebration of the earthly which the poetic imagination is so well and naturally equipped to provide; but Eliot's way, with its poignant ironies and renunciations, is the more difficult and the more extraordinary.

SAMUEL BECKETT AS A POET

Samuel Beckett, *Collected Poems in English and French*. New York, 1977; London, 1978.

BECKETT's work – other than his poems – has elicited an enormous, and still growing, body of exegesis. Yet to me he is an author who makes most critical comment look rather silly. Like Joyce before him he has chosen silence and exile, if not cunning. To speculate and elaborate on his vanishing act is a bit like gossiping about a man who, with great dignity, has just left the room.

Many of Beckett's poems have been in print for decades, but here his privacy has been respected. His poetry is not represented in any of the most officially 'representative' anthologies, from Yeats's to Larkin's *Oxford Book of Twentieth-Century English Verse*. One obvious reason is that so much of Beckett's poetry has gone into his prose. Most of his critics agree in regarding him as a poet, and he would be so regarded if he had never written or published lyrical verse. Besides, Beckett's poems have no place in what is still taken to be the English tradition. Neither, of course, has his other work, but it is in poetry that the purity of this tradition is most zealously guarded by spokesmen for the Club. Many of its members would have black-balled Beckett's entire work but for the success of *Waiting for Godot* and the Nobel Prize; some of them manage to do so still. As far as the poetry is concerned, they can always claim that it is a minor, if not negligible, adjunct to Beckett's prose fiction and plays.

If that sounds unduly polemical, see Dr Simon Curtis in *PN Review* I: 'Can Mr Munton claim that experiment hasn't had a fair crack of the whip? Is it not refreshing to hear someone intelligently call the achievement of Samuel Beckett (in comparison with Sean O'Casey, for example) or Henry Moore or Harold Pinter in question?' It would be refreshing, of course, to Club members who have had to make concessions to Beckett's fame; but an intelligent calling in question of Beckett's achievement would have to begin by using words in a responsible and meaningful way. To call Beckett an experimental writer, for instance, is meaningless (and becomes more patently so when Harold Pinter is assumed to be another). The only writers who can meaningfully be described as experimental are those primarily concerned not with expressing themselves or conveying their sense or experience of life, but with the quiddity, laws and possibilities of their medium. Only those writers are free to make words a material for experiment – as in 'Concrete' poetry or in related fields. Beckett never has been a writer of that kind, but one with ontological or existential obsessions, compelled by those obsessions to be more and more reductive. All his innovations have been in that direction – a discarding of many of the conventional resources of his media, because they had become superfluous and irrelevant. That applies to the poems also; and the progress of this reduction can be followed in this book from the relatively verbose *persona* poem 'Whoroscope' of 1930 to the two- or four-line variations on aphorisms by Chamfort of 1975–6. The only poem in the book that could meaningfully be described as experimental is the early anagrammatical homage to Joyce, 'Home Olga', because it is a language game.

The true difficulty over Beckett's poems lies elsewhere, and has to do with silence, exile, reduction, and bilingualism. (To be bilingual, for a writer, is not an accomplishment but an affliction, amounting to little less than a state of schizophrenia.) Compared to prose fiction or drama, lyrical poetry is necessarily reductive. Since Beckett has accomplished such reduction even in narrative prose and plays, his poems go farther in reduction than many readers, and especially British readers, can easily accept. Some of the earlier poems still convey a vivid sense of place and even of period – the Dublin of 'Enueg' or the London of 'Serena I' – but in later poems the expected correspondence between an inward gesture and its outward occasion tends to be diminished or withheld. The images are de-particularized, sometimes to a degree that may look like abstraction to those who expect a naturalistic sensuousness; the syntax loses its rhetorical and discursive functions, becoming minimal or skeletal. (*Echo's Bones* was the prophetic title of Beckett's early collection of 1933. That title, however, was eminently traditional, being taken from Ovid.)

Here the bilingualism comes in. Abstraction and hermeticism are the qualities that many British readers find it hard to take in much French poetry of this century; and Beckett became a French poet, as well as an Anglo-Irish one, in the 1930s. As a corrective, though, to any facile inferences from that circumstance we are given Beckett's translations from French poems in the same book; and his choice of texts shows a distinct preference for work solidly rooted in empirical experience, like that of Apollinaire and Éluard. (Rimbaud's 'Bâteau ivre', though imaginatively autonomous, is a pre-Mallarméan poem, drawing on a classical rhetoric. It is good to have Beckett's version of it at last – also in a separate, finely printed edition produced by the University of Reading.) We are also given Beckett's English adaptations of some of his French poems. A great deal is to be learnt from the changes that Beckett was moved to make in translating his own poems, and even from his reluctance or inability to translate some of them; such as

> musique de l'indifférence
> coeur temps air feu sable
> du silence éboulement d'amours
> couvre leurs voix et que
> je n'entende plus
> me taire

literally:

> music of indifference
> heart weather air fire sand
> of silence erosion of loves
> cover their voices and may
> I no longer hear
> myself be still

Apart from the lack of an active – and not too colloquial – English verb corresponding to 'se taire', and the ambiguity of both 'temps' (which could be either 'time' or 'weather') and of 'taire' itself (which could be either 'fall silent' or 'keep silent'), it is the starkness of this poem, the bareness, and generality of the string of phenomena in the second line, that makes it untranslatable in this literal way. Beckett's version would have been considerably freer. Or again:

> vive morte ma seule saison
> lis blancs chrysanthèmes
> nids vifs abandonnés
> boue des feuilles d'avril
> beaux jours gris de givre

literally:

live dead my only season
white lilies chrysanthemums
live nests abandoned
mud of April leaves
fine days grey with hoarfrost.

Here the reduction is syntactical. The images are more particular, but they are left to fend for themselves in a semantically neutral, wide-open space. It is the reader who has to connect and inter-relate them (as in Chinese poems). Again, one can only wonder what Beckett would have done to turn this into an English poem; but my guess is that the English version would have been longer, like Beckett's English version of his 1974 poem, 'Something There', with its twenty-six lines for the twelve lines of the French text.

Yet, apart from reduction, both poems are in a millennia-old tradition of lyrical verse, that in which an individual sensibility responds and relates itself to the world, whether that world be a cosmos or a socially conditioned *monde*. (It is those who insist that this world must be recognizably a social or moral one who substitute a convention for a tradition.) Those who find it paradoxical that Beckett's most recent poems are verse reductions of aphorisms by the last of the classical French moralists have forgotten the range of his work, or the nature of his need to condense, to pare down and strip his multiple material. Even some of those aphorisms are too long, too circumstantial for him. The prose of 'Quand on a été bien tourmenté, bien fatigué par sa propre sensibilité, on s'aperçoit qu'il faut vivre à jour de jour, oublier beaucoup, enfin éponger la vie à mesure qu'elle s'écoule' becomes: 'Live and clean forget from day to day,/mop up life as it dribbles away.' Experimental indeed! Classically spare and pithy, rather, and rhymed to boot. Austere, with a lifetime's experience and feeling packed into it.

Club members please note: though much of Beckett's work decidedly isn't cricket, he does know and like the game, and used to be quite a crack player himself. So might it not be refreshing to stop cold-shouldering him, at a time when the game badly needs outsiders to keep it going at all? Not that Beckett wants or needs to be admitted, having quite a following in foreign parts, and even among our own *media*. But mightn't it be refreshing to Club members themselves to learn from their betters for a change, instead of sneering at them for not being members? Just a tentative suggestion, of course.

ON TRANSLATION

THE TROUBLE with this subject, even if it is narrowed down to imaginative writing or poetry, is that there is no beginning, middle or end to it, because translation is not one thing but many things, a vast range of multiple and complex processes involving choices and adjustments of which the translator may or may not be aware. From time to time I am asked to write or talk about the 'problems of verse translation'. Again and again I find that those problems bore me, as the activity does not. If I comply with the request, sooner or later I am ringing the changes on Dryden's division of verse translation into three kinds – metaphrase, paraphrase and imitation – and affirming that, *mutatis mutandis*, it is as valid now as it was when he made it. At the same time I am nagged by the knowledge that beyond this useful distinction there are regions of speculation and analogy that could be metaphysical, anthropological or aesthetic; that in practice Dryden's three kinds tend to overlap; and that we now have modes of scientific, or quasi-scientific, analysis of language, meaning and interpretation, all of which suggest that translation is an impossibility. All this, however, doesn't prevent me from getting on with the job – doing the impossible thing. My 'problems', as a translator, are either solved in the act or never solved at all. So it is not my business to reflect on them. If I reflect on anything it is not on problems, which are the province of theorists, but on dilemmas, on specific failures either complete or partial. These can be explained, though no amount of explanation will help me to translate what, to me, is untranslatable.

A good many of the 'problems' usually raised in discussions of the subject are problems not of translation but of reading; and a good many more are problems not of translation but of writing. In 1775, for instance, Boswell was taken aback by a statement – as plain any statement can be – by Samuel Johnson: 'Patriotism is the last refuge of a scoundrel'. Boswell palliates the harshness of the dictum by referring to the context, a conversation about the hypocrisy of statesmen who 'in all ages and countries' have made 'pretended patriotism' a 'cloak for self-interest'. But Johnson, who was in the habit of saying what he meant, did not say 'a pretence of patriotism'. The word 'nationalism', like the phenomenon itself, as it developed in the course of the 19th and 20th centuries, was not yet current in 1775. Yet in his Dictionary Johnson gives 'bigoted to one's own country' as the second meaning of the word 'national'; and under 'patriot' he writes: 'It is sometimes used for a factious disturber of the government.' A twentieth-century translator of Johnson's plain apothegm, then, could well be tempted to substitute, and possibly be justified in substituting, the word 'nationalism' for 'patriotism' in his version; and he might be further tempted to interpret the 'scoundrel' as a person with an inferiority complex or with a chip on his shoulder, rather than as a hypocrite, because that, too, would be consonant with his own experience of the phenomenon. One twentieth-century reading of the apothegm, then, and one that could well convey more of Johnson's meaning than Boswell was capable of stomaching, would be: 'Nationalism is the last refuge of a person with a chip on his (or her) shoulder'; and even that version might still call for a rider about the ravages wrought by persons with chips on their shoulders in public and private life. Such a version could be rendering the sense and gist of Johnson's insight, while being true to the translator's interpretation of it, without the need for a psychological and historical gloss; yet it would be something other than a translation.

In the next century Franz Grillparzer noted in his diary that the 'course of culture in our time runs from humanity through nationality to bestiality' ('Der Weg der neueren Bildung geht von Humanität durch Nationalität zur Bestialität'). In translating his remark for an essay of my own I had to substitute the word 'nationalism' for his neutral 'Nationalität', because what Grillparzer evidently had in mind was the growing nationalism of his time in Europe generally and the Austrian Empire in particular. I should now be inclined to substitute a different word for 'bestiality', too, because I have come to regard the use of this word for certain varieties of human conduct as an unwarranted insult to animals. Yet the effect of Grillparzer's remark is due not only to its prophetic perspicacity but to its formal structure, which rests on the grammatical parity and parallelism of the three stages named, and the antithesis 'human/bestial', bridged by the seemingly disparate, but operative, middle part. One way out of the dilemma would be to change all the terms, to 'humanism', 'nationalism' and 'brutalism', though 'humanism' is weaker than 'humanity'. The grammatical parity would be preserved, and the slur on animals removed, since everyone knows that animals are not prone to 'isms'.

The structure of Johnson's apothegm would also be weakened by any psychologizing substitution for his blunt and undefined 'scoundrel', since its strength lies in the assertiveness of a simple equation. If either statement, then, were to be translated as a literary text its structure would have to be respected, and the translator's urge to interpret it would have to be suppressed or reserved for a commentary. So much for the plainest of statements in prose, and incongruences that are not even interlingual, but only historical.

One conclusion to be drawn from these examples – and it is borne out by my experience of translating prose of various kinds – is that poetry is not necessarily more untranslatable than any other sort of writing. A great many lyrical poems may be more difficult to 'understand'; but the more difficult the poem, the more complex and idiosyncratic its structure, the more likely it is that a good deal of its quiddity can be satisfactorily conveyed in translation. It is the plainest, most limpid, poem that may defy translation, because it leaves the least latitude for paraphrase and interpretation, and the plainness that may be a happy reduction in one language and literary convention can sound like an intolerable banality in another. The kind of translation I practise does require me to understand a poem, in so far as it can be understood, whereas a good many imitators prefer not to be constrained by that requirement, which would restrict their freedom.

That brings me back to the perennial debating point, related to Dryden's classification. What it boils down to is that verse translation can be seen primarily as a kind of writing, offering much the same satisfactions as any other to the writer, if not to the reader, or primarily as a form of interpretation. Linguistic, semantic and hermeneutical questions about the possibility of rendering in one language what has been written in another, tend to favour the freedom of imitation. If translation does not produce true equivalence, the argument runs, a verse translator may just as well give up the attempt to produce it. Far better for him to do his own thing, write a new poem in his own language, his own manner, using the original for his own 'creative' ends. I have no quarrel with that procedure, but believe that there is a point where it ceases to be translation and cannot be judged as such. Variations on a theme, in music, are judged as original works, no matter whether the theme is taken from another composer or not. Translation, as I understand it, is much closer to a transcription, re-arrangement or re-scoring of another composer's work, such as Bach's of works by Vivaldi. However free, such transcriptions remain interpretations of the work transcribed, and the liberties taken serve to carry it over into another convention, another age, not to break it up and appropriate some promising part.

The appropriation, of course, may be more fruitful aesthetically than anything that can be done in the way of translation; but that is a sacrifice a translator owes to the work translated. Any poet capable of reading translations of his own work is likely to prefer a careful, though imperfect, rendering of what he has written to an exercise in appropriation, if the result is going to be presented as a rendering of his text, not as a variation on it. That is not a plea for metaphrase, or pedantically literal translation. With texts of any literary distinction the mere crib or trot falls as short of translation as the free imitation overshoots it, because it ignores structure, rhythm, style. Faithfulness to the translated text may demand a considerable measure of freedom on the semantic level – just how much, will vary from author to author, from text to text, from language to language, from period to period. Every translation, as distinct from an appropriation, calls for an act of understanding that is also a weighing up of what constitutes the primary gesture of a poem and a judgement of how that gesture can be re-enacted in another medium.

Where that process does not occur, where no crystallization takes place, and I should have to resort to appropriation to make anything of the text in question, my choice is to give up. To explain why imitation does not attract me – though I have appropriated odd lines of translated texts in poems of my own – would take me into autobiography. Here it is enough to say that for me the alternative has never been one between freedom and accuracy, but one between service to a foreign text that might also be a service to the English language and its readers and writers, by the rendering of what is foreign to them, and the appropriation of material for my own writing. On the few occasions when I have incorporated lines by other poets in poems of my own, it was because those lines were part of the genesis of the new poem, a nucleus that fused with my own experience or imagination and prompted the writing. Those 'borrowings' or appropriations are my variations on a theme by Hölderlin or Celan, and if they are also tributes to those writers, they are tributes of a different order to those paid in the act of translation.

Versions of the kind I produce, of course, will be of limited validity, because they are not intended to replace the original texts, but to convey as much of their quiddity as I am able to convey, and to do so more effectively than could be done by description or analysis. To a greater or lesser extent the success of this carrying over depends not only on the translator's equipment – his power of penetration and empathy, his linguistic and literary skill – but on historical confluences and divergences beyond his control. The translators whose work has helped me most are those who combine capacity to read with a capacity to write; and this quality of responsiveness to sensibilities other than their own seems much more essential to me than their linguistic qualifications. If that is a 'negative capability', it also accords with Keats's description of the 'poetical character', the 'chameleon poet' who annihilates himself, so that other identities can 'press upon' him. Where a capacity to write is also to hand, a new identity may take shape.

From *Reason and Energy* (1970)
Studies in German Literature

From HÖLDERLIN

THE GNOMIC grandeur of Hölderlin's late poetry, his prophetic and visionary hymns, is of a kind that must strike an unprepared reader as not only strange and perplexing, but as anachronistic. These hymns have no parallel in any modern literature, either of Hölderlin's time or later. Yet, unique and esoteric as they are, the hymns become clearer in the light of Hölderlin's earlier work and even of general trends perceptible in the German literature of Hölderlin's time. Such background features, it goes without saying, can no more explain its unique qualities than the climate and soil of its setting explain the shape, colour, or scent of a plant; their only function here is to make Hölderlin's late poetry more accessible to readers who might other- wise be repelled by its oddity. It is well known that these hymns are the work of a poet who had suffered at least one serious mental break- down and was about to succumb to incurable madness; but the fact is irrelevant. The hymns show no slackening of intellectual control. What makes them difficult throughout, ambiguous and obscure in parts, is the heightened concentration of all the poet's faculties on a single task. They are incoherent only where they are fragmentary; and, unlike the poems of Hölderlin's madness proper, they are never inane.

Hölderlin's mature poetry was the product of so intense a devel- opment, compressed into a period of time so incredibly short, that one could easily be misled into treating it as a single poetic sequence, rather than a series of poetic sequences whose only unity is that of growth. The whole body of his mature work can be divided into three principal phases: the idealistic, the tragic, and the prophetic. These phases, as one would expect, are not wholly distinct; but they are sufficiently so to provide rough boundary lines that help one to find one's way. But since growth is a cyclic process, it is important to treat these phases as concentric circles; few poets have been as conscious as Hölderlin that the 'course of life' is circular, its end linked to its beginning. A few of the poems that Hölderlin wrote in his late adolescence, such as the powerful 'Die Bücher der Zeiten', are closer to his tragic and prophetic phases than to the idealistic phase that followed these early attempts.

Hölderlin's idealistic phase was coeval with the 'classical' phase of the German literary renaissance, which was instituted by Goethe and Schiller as a deliberate campaign against forces that they themselves had once invoked. It was the eruption of these forces, the chthonic powers, in the 1770s that made modern German literature different from any other. After releasing the chthonic powers in *Werther* and in his early dithyrambic verse, Goethe spent the rest of his life in the strenuous and multiple endeavour to put them back in their place. In the 1790s, after his own period of *Sturm und Drang*, Schiller applied his very different gifts to the same task; and Hölderlin, who began as Schiller's disciple and protégé, dedicated his early poetry to the same didactic, enlightening and educational function, that of a secular priest who expounds not scripture, but philosophy. Yet from the start, Hölderlin had grave doubts about this function. Schiller found it difficult enough to cope with the philosophy of Kant; but Hölderlin had to come to terms with the teaching of Kant's successors, especially with that of Fichte, whose lectures he attended in 1794 and 1795. Hölderlin's novel *Hyperion* shows how deeply and dangerously Fichte's ideas affected him.

Just because German classicism was so much of a hothouse growth, carefully and lovingly fostered in the shelter of little Weimar in defiance of the tempests raging outside, Goethe could not afford to be generous to younger writers, like Hölderlin and Kleist, whom he could not fit into his civilizing scheme. Just because his own balance was so precarious, Goethe grew intolerant of all that was morbid, one-sided or self-destructive. Hence his horror of the tragic in later life, the incongruous redemption of his Faust in Part II, his fear of music. (The 'spirit of music', which Nietzsche was to relate to tragedy, became a powerful influence on the Romantics; because Goethe was so susceptible to its vague incitements, but felt it to be an anti-classical force, he made a point of learning to use his eyes, of studying concrete phenomena and counting out hexameters on his mistress's back. Yet Goethe's all-embracing philosophy, his morphological view of nature, history, and art, resembled the thought of Hölderlin and Novalis in being syncretic; it could only attain the cohesion of a system by continually breaking down the barriers of orthodoxy, both theological and scientific, by resolving long-accepted antinomies and by applying an almost mystical vision to the most diverse empirical disciplines.) This achievement, made possible only by his genius and by that wisdom to which T. S. Eliot paid tribute, is unprecedented and inimitable; and so, in its different way, is Hölderlin's, though Hölderlin begged in vain to be admitted to the shelter of Weimar or Jena, struggled heroically with all the daemons of the age and transcended tragedy by approving his own destruction.

The transition from Hölderlin's idealistic phase to the tragic was gradual. Many of his early odes in classical meters – those written before 1799 – uphold the ideals of Hölderlin's youth against experiences and forces that threaten them. Thus in his ode 'Der Mensch', of 1798, his idealistic vision of man conflicts with a tragic one. Man is the most highly gifted and blessed of all living creatures. Like the rest of creation, he is the child of Earth, the material principle, and of Helios, the spiritual; but, unlike his fellow creatures, he has an irresistible urge to better himself, to explore, to advance, to idealize, 'to sacrifice a certain present for something uncertain, different, better and still better,' as Hölderlin explained in another context. The tension of the poem arises from Hölderlin's dual view of the human condition. Considered idealistically, Man's urge to improve himself accounts for human progress, in which Hölderlin the philosopher continued to believe long after Hölderlin the poet had begun to contradict him; considered tragically, it is the *hubris* that estranges men from Nature, offends the gods and involves the offender in endless conflict and suffering. Hölderlin does his best to reconcile the two views, by that progression through contraries so characteristic of his poetry; but 'Der Mensch' is one of the few poems of this period in which his tragic vision predominates.

Hölderlin's dualism – the dualism of a poet whose whole work, at the time, was directed toward pantheistic communion with 'all that lives', whose principal doctrine was the *hen kai pan*, One and All, of antiquity – would be difficult to understand but for his prose works of that period, *Hyperion*, the letters and the philosophical fragments. As we can see in *Hyperion*, with its cycles of exaltation and dejection,

Hölderlin's desire to be at one with the cosmos continually came up against his philosophical awareness of complete isolation from the rest of the created world. This awareness, confirmed by the solipsistic idealism of Fichte and its development by Hölderlin's own friends, Hegel and Schelling, accounts for those moments in *Hyperion* that shock the reader by their unexpected cynicism, by their nihilistic despair. *Hyperion*, in fact, is pervaded by the same dualism.

'Man is a god when he dreams, a beggar when he reflects' *Hyperion* writes. Dreaming here means the state of mind that permits communion with Nature; reflection, the self-consciousness that cuts off the individual from the rest of creation. It is the alternation of these states of mind, with infinite variations and a gradual progression toward synthesis, that gives *Hyperion* its peculiar structure, an almost musical structure that suggests sonata form. The two themes are elaborated in another Passage: 'There is an oblivion of all existence, a silencing of all individual being, in which it seems as if we had found all things.

'There is a silencing, an oblivion of all existence, in which it seems as if we had lost all things, a night of the soul, in which not the faintest gleam of a star, not even the Phosphorescence of rotten wood can reach us.'

The difference between these states of mind is that between being and existence. The positive state is that in which we forget ourselves because we feel at one with the world; the negative state is that in which we forget the world and are conscious only of ourselves. When *Hyperion* is plunged into this negative state of mind, what had been 'all' before suddenly turns into nothing; he becomes like one of those persons whom he pities for being 'in the grip of that Nothing which rules over us, who are thoroughly conscious that we are born for Nothing, that we love a Nothing, believe in a Nothing, work ourselves to the bone for Nothing, until we gradually dissolve into Nothing . . .'

It is clear enough from these extracts that Hölderlin's pantheistic faith had a reverse side of unmitigated pessimism. This dichotomy goes back to Rousseau's doctrine that what is natural is good, all evil is due to the corrupting influence of civilization. The German adaptation of this doctrine was to identify evil with consciousness itself, to deify Energy and discredit Reason. Schiller had contributed to this adaptation by his distinction between 'naïve' and 'sentimental' literature, for the 'naïve' embraced all that is natural and spontaneous, the 'sentimental' all that is the result of reflection Kleist was to make the antithesis even more extreme; and it has been developed by German writers ever since.

In a letter of 1797 Hölderlin characterized the evils of his time in terms of the following antinomies: 'Culture and crudity... Unreasoning cleverness, unclever reason. Mindless sensibility, insensitive mind . . . Energy without principles, principles without energy.' The remedy, he proposed in the same letter, was a marriage of the 'childlike heart' to the 'virile mind'.

Hölderlin's work entered its tragic phase when he could no longer accept any of the philosophical explanations of evil current in his time. Though he was reluctant to revert to any doctrine that reminded him of his theological studies, his view of the human condition – even in the comparatively early poem 'Der Mensch' – does presuppose something not unlike original sin. There is an obvious connection between the knowledge of good and evil in Genesis and the foreknowledge of death that distinguishes Hölderlin's Man from his fellow creatures. Hölderlin's pantheism, in essence, was the aspiration to return to the state that preceded the Fall of Man. Now this pantheism was gradually modified by Hölderlin's recognition that evil is inherent in Nature and in Man; and that there is a gulf between the human and the divine, a gulf that men ignore at their peril.

In his letters of this transitional period, Hölderlin still clung to the philosophic humanism of his youth. As late as 1799 he assured his half-brother of the 'salutary effect of philosophic and political literature on the education of our country.' Because the Germans, by nature, are 'glebae addicti and in one way or another, literally or metaphorically, most of them are bound to their little plots'; because they lack 'elasticity' and breadth, 'Kant is the Moses of our nation, who leads them out of their Egyptian inertia into the free and open desert of his speculations, and who brings down the rigorous law from the holy mountain.' Yet in the course of the same month Hölderlin confessed to his mother that all his philosophical studies – undertaken against his inclinations out of the fear that his poetry would be condemned as 'empty' – left him not only unsatisfied, but restless and unpleasantly excited: and that he always longed to return to his 'dear occupation', poetry, much as 'a conscripted Swiss shepherd longs for his valley and his flock.' The matter was not as simple as that. Hölderlin remained a truly philosophical poet; but the Philosophy to which he felt drawn as a poet was not that of contemporary Germany, but that of pre-Socratic Greece; a philosophy close to religious experience and to myth: a philosophy of nature unencumbered with modern subjectivity. It was not only because of his legendary suicide that Hölderlin made Empedocles the protagonist of an unfinished tragedy.

Hölderlin's last attempt to become a *praeceptor Germaniae* in the humanistic tradition of Goethe and Schiller was his plan to edit a journal, *Iduna*, in 1799. Its purpose, as he defined it in a letter to a publisher interested in the scheme, was as follows: 'The unification and reconciliation of the sciences with life, of art and good taste with genius, of the heart with the head, of the real with the ideal, of the civilized (in the widest sense of the word) with nature – this will be the general character, the spirit of the journal.' In a later letter to Schelling, whom he asked for a contribution, Hölderlin very aptly described it as a 'humanistic journal', but was careful to distinguish his own humanism from the so-called humanism of others.

The failure of this project, and Schiller's failure to find Hölderlin a congenial post as an alternative to the project, which he advised Hölderlin to abandon, was a decisive turning point. It meant that Hölderlin must give up hope, once and for all, of having any influence on the public of his time; and, since it deprived him of his last possibility of economic independence, it meant that he was faced once more with the drudgery and humiliation of being a private tutor, just when he was ready to write his greatest poetry and when his nerves could no longer bear the strain of petty frustrations and irritations. To read his subsequent letters is a harrowing experience. Even before his enforced separation from Susette Gontard he had felt that his fate would be a tragic one; but he had resisted this feeling. While he was at Homburg, where he would have remained if the journal had materialized, he was still able to communicate with Susette and to meet her, though only rarely and furtively. Now he was to lose his last support against the sense of personal tragedy. As he had foretold in 1798, all that remained was his art and the quite impersonal faith that sustained his art; he had come to the end of that respite for which he begged the Fates in 1798:

Nur Einen Sommer gönnt, ihr Gewaltigen!
  Und einen Herbst zu reifem Gesange mir,
    Dass williger mein Herz, vom süssen
      Spiele gesättiget, dann mir sterbe.

Die Seele, der im Leben ihr göttlich Recht
  Nicht ward, sie ruht auch drunten im Orkus nicht;
    Doch ist mir einst das Heil'ge, das am
      Herzen mir liegt, das Gedicht gelungen,

Willkommen dann, o Stille der Schattenwelt!
  Zufrieden bin ich, wenn auch mein Saitenspiel
    Mich nicht hinabgeleitet; Einmal
      Lebt' ich, wie Götter, und mehr bedarfs nicht.

                    .   .   .   .   .   .

One summer only grant me, you powerful Fates,
  And one more autumn only for mellow song,
    So that more willingly, replete with
      Music's late sweetness, my heart may die then.

The soul in life denied its god-given right
  Down there in Orcus also will find no peace;
    Yet when what's holy, dear to me, the
      Poem's accomplished, my art perfected,

Then welcome silence, welcome cold world of shades!
  I'll be content, though here I must leave my lyre
    And songless travel down; for *once* I
      Lived like the gods, and no more is needed.

What Hölderlin did not know when he wrote this poem is that long after his heart had indeed died, as he says, his 'mellow song' would continue; that the music of his strings *would* escort him down. And, whereas in 1798 he spoke of being denied the 'divine' rights that were due to him, later he was to regard the death of his heart as a just punishment. The question as to the immediate cause of his mental breakdown in 1802 seems almost pointless when one reads the terrible letters of the two preceding years. By 1800 Hölderlin had given himself up. In thanking his sister for writing to remind him of their family bond, he tells her that 'this sustains my heart, which in the end too often loses its voice in a loneliness all too complete and withdraws from our very selves.' If these words seem strange, so is the state of mind which they convey. Hölderlin's feelings were withdrawing from his own self and from all those who had once been Close to him. The poetry of his tragic and prophetic phases became more and more impersonal, till they were more like oracles than the utterances of a man; and he came to accept his own self-estrangement as a punishment for overreaching himself, for having lived once as the gods live. This is what he implies in one of his last intelligible letters, written after his return from Bordeaux, when he tells his friend that 'as one relates of heroes, I can well say that Apollo has struck me.' Hölderlin was probably thinking of the mythical poet Linos, who was killed by Apollo – or according to a different legend, brained with his own lyre by Hercules – for the sin of presumption, of *hubris*. The exact nature of the sin that Hölderlin imputed to himself is specified in his *Empedocles* fragments and in several of the late hymns.

· · · · · · · · · ·

THE TRANSITION from Hölderlin's tragic phase to the prophetic, again, is not one that can be neatly dated. 'Wie wenn am Feiertage . . .', the earliest of his hymns and the only one in which he attempted to reproduce the strict Pindaric structure, was written as early as 1799; but it remained unfinished, not so much, perhaps, because of the difficult form – Hölderlin had already mastered forms quite as refractory – as because Hölderlin was still overwhelmed by his personal affliction, and knew that Pindar's public ode form could not be adapted for the expression of a private grief. Where the public theme breaks off, Hölderlin's prose draft continues with an agonized confession of his own guilt. This passage not only clashes violently with the oracular character of the foregoing strophes, but seems to contradict what they say about the poet's religious function.

> Doch weh mir! wenn von
> [selbgeschlagener Wunde das Herz mir blutet, und tiefverloren
> der Frieden ist, u. freibescheidenes Genügen,
> Und die Unruh, und der Mangel mich treibt zum
> Überfluss des Göttertisches, wenn rings um mich]
>
> Weh mir!

[Und sag ich gleich, ich wär genaht, die Himmli(schen zu)
schauen, sie selbst sie werfen mich tief unter die Lebenden
alle, den falschen Priester hinab, dass ich, aus Nächten herauf,
das warnend ängstige Lied den Unerfabrenen singe.]

.   .   .   .   .

But woe is me! when from
[a self-inflicted wound my heart is bleeding, and deeply lost
are peace and the contentment of true modesty,
And when unrest and lack drive me towards
The superfluity of the gods' own table, when round about me]

Woe is me!

[And let me say at once: that I approached to look
upon the heavenly beings, they cast me down themselves,
far down beneath all the living
cast the false priest, so that now from the depth of nights
I should sing for the inexperienced my awed and warning song.]

This gruesome self-exposure – with its allusion to the Tantalus myth,
which identifies Hölderlin's sin with the *hubris* of Empedocles – is
certainly out of place in his oracular hymn; but it does not really
contradict what he has just said about the poet's function:

Doch uns gebührt es, unter Gottes Gewittern,
Ihr Dichter! mit entblösstem Haupte zu stehen,
Des Vaters Stral, ihn selbst, mit eigner Hand
Zu fassen und dem Volk ins Lied
Gehüllt die himmlische Gaabe zu reichen.
Denn sind nur reinen Herzens,
Wie Kinder, wir, sind schuldlos unsere Hände,
Des Vaters Stral, der reine versengt es nicht . . .

.   .   .   .   .

Yet, fellow poets, us it behooves to stand
Bare-headed beneath God's thunderstorms,
To grasp the Father's ray, no less, with our own two hands
And, wrapping in song the beautiful gift,
To offer it to the people.
For if only we are pure in heart,
Like children, and our hands are guiltless,
The Father's ray, the pure, will not sear our hearts . . .

What Hölderlin is making clear is the difference between the humility of the true priest and the arrogance of the false one; this is also the essential difference between his own idealistic phase and his prophetic one. In his idealistic phase he had been moved by the Titanic urge to violate the divine mysteries, instead of waiting patiently for the moment of revelation. God's lightning had seared his heart precisely because it was impure, filled with Titanic impatience.

This tragic impulse is not confined to heroes, poets, and seers; it can affect not only individuals, but whole peoples, as Hölderlin relates in his tragic ode of 1801, the second version of 'Stimme des Volkes' ('Voice of the People'):

> Du seiest Gottes Stimme, so glaubt' ich sonst
> In heil'ger Jugend; ja, und ich sag' es noch!
> Um unsre Weisheit unbekümmert
> Rauschen die Ströme doch auch, und dennoch,
>
> Wer liebt sie nicht? und immer bewegen sie
> Das Herz mir, hör' ich ferne die Schwindenden,
> Die Ahnungsvollen meine Bahn nicht
> Aber gewisser ins Meer hin eilen.
>
> Denn selbstvergessen, allzubereit den Wunsch
> Der Götter zu erfüllen, ergreift zu gem
> Was sterblich ist, wenn offnen Augs auf
> Eigenen Pfaden es einmal wandelt,
>
> Ins All zurük die kürzeste Bahn; so stürzt
> Der Strom hinab, er suchet die Ruh, es reisst,
> Es ziehet wider Willen ihn, von
> Klippe zu Klippe den Steuerlosen
>
> Das wunderbare Sehnen dem Abgrund zu;
> Das Ungebundene reizet, und Völker auch
> Ergreift die Todeslust und kühne
> Städte, nachdem sie versucht das Beste,
>
> Von Jahr zu Jahr forttreibend das Werk, sie hat
> Ein heilig Ende troffen; die Erde grünt
> Und stille vor den Sternen liegt, den
> Betenden gleich, in den Sand geworfen,

Freiwillig überwunden die lange Kunst
   Vor jenen Unnachahmbaren da; er selbst,
      Der Mensch, mit eigner Hand zembrach, die
         Hohen zu ehren, sein Werk der Künstler . . .

          . . . . .

The voice of God I called you and thought you once,
   In holy youth; and still I do not recant!
      No less indifferent to our wisdom
         Likewise the rivers rush on, but who does

Not love them? Always too my own heart is moved
   When far away I hear those foreknowing ones,
      The fleeting, by a route not mine but
         Surer than mine, and more swift, roar seaward,

For once they travel down their allotted paths
   With open eyes, self-oblivious, too ready to
      Comply with what the gods have wished them,
         Only too gladly will mortal beings

Speed back into the All by the shortest way;
   So rivers plunge – not movement but rest they seek –
      Drawn on, pulled down against their will from
         Boulder to boulder – abandoned, helmless –

By that mysterious yearning toward the chasm;
   Chaotic deeps attract, and whole peoples too
      May come to long for death, and valiant
         Towns that have striven to do the best thing,

Year in, year out pursuing their task – these too
   A holy end has stricken; the earth grows green,
      And there beneath the stars, like mortals
         Deep in their prayers, quite still, prostrated

On sand, outgrown, and willingly, lies long art
   Flung down before the Matchless; and he himself,
      The man, the artist with his own two
         Hands broke his work for their sake, in homage.

In the opening lines Hölderlin suggests that there is a difference between his youthful belief in the truth of *vox populi, vox dei* and his present, modified acceptance of it; but he does not say in what that difference consists. Coleridge's comment on the same dictum is illuminating: 'I never said that the *vox populi* was of course the *vox Dei*. It may be; but it may be, and with equal probability, *a priori, vox Diaboli*. That the voice of ten millions of men calling for the same thing, is a spirit, I believe; but whether that be a spirit of Heaven or Hell, I can only know by trying the thing called for by the prescript of reason and God's will.' Hölderlin, by 1801, was well aware of this ethical aspect of the tragic, self-destructive urge; and his awareness of it may well account for the reticent opening lines. If he never explicitly condemns the urge in this poem – except insofar as he disassociates himself from the river's impetuosity – but treats it under the aspect of sacrifice, it is mainly because the function of chronicler, which is Hölderlin's here, demands a perspective different from the prophet's and moralist's; but the tragic mystery remained present in his poetry throughout his prophetic phase. On the one hand, his understanding of tragic *hubris* brought him closer to a Christian view of good and evil; Lucifer is closely related to Prometheus and the Titans. On the other, it caused him to treat even the death of Christ as a tragic sacrifice, in a sense much more Greek than Christian.

Hölderlin's great elegies, written between 1799 and 1801, form a transition from the tragic to the prophetic mode. 'Menons Klagen um Diotima', written in 1800, still alternates between the tragic mode and the idealistic; although in the last section Hölderlin turns to the future, his prediction is not prophetic in the larger sense of the hymns. But 'Brod und Wein', begun later in the same year, 'Der Archipelagus' and 'Heimkunft' complete the transition.

The relation between the different modes is particularly striking in another ode of 1801, the second version of 'Ermunterung' ('Exhortation'), with its sudden modulation from personal lament to impersonal prophecy:

> Echo des Himmels! heiliges Herz! warum,
> > Warum verstummst du unter den Lebenden,
> > > Schläfst, freies! von den Götterlosen
> > > > Ewig hinab in die Nacht verwiesen?

Wacht denn, wie vormals, nimmer des Aethers Licht?
　　Und blüht die alte Mutter, die Erde nicht?
　　　　Und übt der Geist nicht da und dort, nicht
　　　　　　Lächelnd die Liebe das Recht noch immer?

Nur du nicht mehr! doch mahnen die Himmlischen,
　　Und stillebildend weht, wie ein kahl Gefild,
　　　　Der Othem der Natur dich an, der
　　　　　　Alleserheiternde, seelenvolle.

O Hoffnung! bald, bald singen die Haine nicht
　　Des Lebens Lob allein, denn es ist die Zeit,
　　　　Dass aus der Menschen Munde sie, die
　　　　　　Schönere Seele sich neuverkündet,

Dann liebender im Bunde mit Sterblichen
　　Das Element sich bildet, und dann erst reich,
　　　　Bei frommer Kinder Dank, der Erde
　　　　　　Brust, die unendliche, sich entfaltet

Und unsre Tage wieder, wie Blumen, sind,
　　Wo sie, des Himmels Sonne sich ausgetheilt
　　　　Im stillen Wechsel sieht und wieder
　　　　　　Froh in den Frohen das Licht sich findet,

Und er, der sprachlos waltet und unbekannt
　　Zukünftiges bereitet, der Gott, der Geist
　　　　Im Menschenwort am schönen Tage
　　　　　　Kommenden Jahren, wie einst, sich ausspricht.

　　　　　·　·　·　·　·　·

Echo of heaven, heart that are hallowed, why,
　　Why do you now fall silent, though living still,
　　　　And sleep, you free one, by the godless
　　　　　　Banished for ever to Night's deep dungeons?

Does not the light of Aether, as always, wake?
　　And Earth, our ancient mother, still thrive and flower?
　　　　And here and there does not the spirit
　　　　　　Love with a smile wield her laws as ever?

You only fail! Yet heavenly powers exhort,
 And silently at work like a stubble field,
  The breath of Nature blows upon you,
   She the all-brightening, soul-inspiring.

O hope! now soon, now soon not the groves alone
 Shall sing life's praise, for almost the time is come
  When through the mouths of mortals this, the
   Lovelier soul will make known her coming.

Allied with men more lovingly then once more
 The element will form and, not rich or full
  But when her pious children thank her
   Endless the breast of our Earth unfolds then,

And once again like blossoms our days will be
 Where heavenly Helios sees his own light shared out
  In quiet alternation, finding
   Joy in the joy of those mortal mirrors,

And He who silent rules and in secret plans
 Things yet to come, the Godhead, the Spirit housed
  In human words, once more, at noontide,
   Clearly will speak to the future ages.

The inception of this poem goes back to 1799; since Hölderlin blames his godless persecutors, rather than his own tragic offence, for the apathy of his heart, it may well have been written before the last version of *Empedocles*, during the crisis that characterized in retrospect as a loss of faith in 'eternal Love':

> I was now to fall into the terribly superstitious belief in that which is certainly a sign of the soul and of Love but, misunderstood in this way, is the death of both. Believe me, dearest brother, I had struggled to the point of deadly exhaustion to fix my faith and my vision upon that which is highest in life; indeed, I had struggled amidst sufferings which – to judge by all the evidence of which I know – were more overwhelming than anything that men are capable of enduring, though they exert their utmost strength. – I am not telling you this without good reason. – At last, when my heart was torn on more sides than one, and yet held fast, I must also be induced to embroil my thoughts in those evil doubts, that question so easily solved if only one's eyes are clear, namely: what is more important, the eternal source of all life or the temporal. Only

too complete a contempt for all that is necessary was capable of leading me into that greater error of gazing too intently, with a truly superstitious earnestness, at everything external, that is, at everything outside the realm of the heart, so as to make it my own. But I continued to struggle until I found out the truth . . . There is only one quarrel in this world: which is more important, the whole or the individual part. And that quarrel, in every instance and application, is proved invalid in action, because the man who acts truly out of a sense of the whole, for that very reason, is more dedicated to peace and more disposed to honour every individual person and thing, since his sense of humanity, just what is most individual to him, will sooner permit him to fall into egoism, or whatever you choose to call it, than into pure generality.

A Deo principium. Whoever understands this and acts accordingly . . . that man is free and strong and joyful . . .

This account of his Homburg crisis – and, more important still, of the renewed faith that followed the crisis – helps to explain why Hölderlin could now dispense with the progression through contraries of his earlier odes. Only the third strophe of 'Ermunterung' serves as a transition from the personal theme to the prophetic; and it makes the transition by implying that the poet's immediate state of mind, the apathy of his heart, does not have the absolute significance that he would once have attributed to it. The full frenzy of inspiration is withheld from him, but even that lack has its purpose in the divine order, just as winter has its place in the natural order of the year. Hölderlin can turn to prophecy because he has resolved the dilemma of his idealistic phase, with its tension between the particular and the general, between the ego conscious of its isolation and the holy cosmos with which it longs to unite. As the imagery of his early poetry shows, Hölderlin had once been apt to 'fall into pure generality'; for his idealism had hinged on the modern distinction between subjective and objective reality. Like his new faith, the poetry of his prophetic phase was to reconcile the timeless with the temporal, the whole with the part, the individual phenomenon with the Platonic Idea. The change, once again, is most apparent in his imagery: the visionary landscapes of the hymns are both concrete and symbolic, specific and general, just as the figures in those landscapes are both historical and mythical, individual and allegorical.

It is essential, therefore, to interpret Hölderlin's prophecies without too pedantic a concern with their temporal aspect. To complain that one of these prophecies has not yet come true is as foolish as to complain that Hölderlin's vision of ancient Greece does not accord with all the historical and archeological facts. The analogy is not irrelevant; for, in one respect at least, Hölderlin's visionary exploration of the past corresponds exactly to his visionary exploration of the future. The purpose of both journeys was to embody spiritual truths in a wholly poetic manner, that is, in a manner that bridges the gulf between the ideal and the actual without recourse to the language of philosophy. More than one of the hymns explores both the past and the future; and the present moment too receives its due, in the light that past and future shed on it to reveal both its temporal and its timeless significance.

· · · · · · · · · · ·

THE FORMAL and stylistic innovations of Hölderlin – of which I shall have more to say in a different context – are less puzzling to a modern reader than the peculiar vision that caused Hölderlin to make those innovations. The music of poetry – and music itself, for that matter – only seems self-sufficient, unrelated to anything outside itself, because we don't know how to interpret it in terms of another medium, the medium of expository prose; both poetry and music are symbolic media, governed by a logic different from that which governs prose argument – but a logic nonetheless. An infringement of that logic can offend us even if we know little about the art in question, less about what the artist wished to 'communicate'. The beauty of a work of art is inseparable from its peculiar logic; and the closer we get to understanding the difficult logic of a poem like 'Friedensfeier' – and by logic I don't mean its literal argument, but the law that rules its music as much as its sense – the closer we are to appreciating its beauty. It is easy to fall into the error of supposing that anything that a work of art communicates must be reducible to the logic of expository prose; and, where it obviously is not, that the work has no 'matter' at all or that such 'matter' is negligible.

That brings me to another possible stumbling block, the question of Hölderlin's beliefs. The 'suspension of disbelief' that we experience in reading great poetry is nothing other than our perception of its peculiar logic. Disbelief occurs only where the artist himself offends against the logic of his art, often because he is momentarily misled into a logic alien to it, which may well be closer to our own. A single momentary lapse of that kind can sever the thread that suspends our disbelief, so that it comes crashing down with a vengeance. To some extent, of course, the reader's response to a particular work of literature, however great, will depend on his own opinions and beliefs, and on the degree of balance or bias with which he holds them; yet the very fact that two persons of sound judgment, but entirely different opinions and beliefs, can agree about the merit of certain works of literature, shows that opinion and belief are not the decisive criteria. Such agreement has certainly been reached in the case of Hölderlin.

In *Goethe as the Sage* T. S. Eliot returned to this question of poetry and belief; and he qualified his earlier answer to it by making a valuable distinction 'between the *philosophy* of a poet and his *wisdom*'. The philosophy we can quarrel with; but the wisdom is 'the same for all men everywhere'. On those grounds, Eliot was able to make his peace with Goethe; and to recognize him as a 'great European poet'. Of Wordsworth and Hölderlin Eliot said in the same address: 'Wordsworth was surely a great poet, if the term has any meaning at all; at his best, his flight was much higher than that of Byron, and as high as that of Goethe. His influence was, moreover, decisive for English poetry at a certain moment: his name marks an epoch. Yet he will never mean to Europeans of other nationality, what he means to his compatriots; nor can he mean to his own compatriots what Goethe means to them. Similarly – but here I speak with becoming diffidence – it seems to me possible to maintain that Hölderlin was at moments more inspired than Goethe: yet he also, can never be to the same degree a European figure.'

Hölderlin lacked the universal range of Goethe's wisdom, a range as wide as it was deep; and he lacked Goethe's patient concern with the minutiae of nature – a concern that only the greatest poets can pursue without becoming trivial themselves. But Hölderlin's wisdom extended to heights and depths that few poets have had the strength to endure; and by wisdom here I mean neither knowledge nor experience, but the sense of 'measure' that is rarer than these. His influence, too, was as decisive for German poetry as Wordsworth's was for English poetry, though his moment did not come till long after his death: and it now seems that even his most difficult work has come to mean a great deal to Europeans – and even non-Europeans – of other nationality than his own.

From HEINRICH HEINE

'NO MAN thinks,' says the lizard in one of Heine's early travel books, 'only from time to time something occurs to people; these wholly unmerited flashes they call ideas, and the concatenation of these ideas they call thinking . . . No man thinks, no philosopher thinks, neither Hegel nor Schelling thinks; as for their philosophy, it's mere air and water, like the clouds in the sky.' A critic about to project his image of Heine has good reason to remember these words. Not only do they reveal the empiricism, the scepticism, and the flippancy which are authentic features of Heine's mind, but they contain a warning against too literal an approach. To take Heine literally is to run the risk of grossly misinterpreting his work, his character, and his function.

But how is one to take Heine? His underlying seriousness is of a kind that defies serious treatment. He is so elusive a writer that every statement about him immediately suggests its exact opposite. After vainly trying to produce a composite image of his work, and a composite image that makes sense, one is tempted to write three separate essays on authors whom one might call Harry, Heinrich, and Henri Heine, as Heine called himself at different stages of his life. Harry, then, would be the Romantic poet of the *Buch der Lieder*, which contains the verse of his first creative phase, the years between 1817 and 1826; Harry, one could assume, drowned himself in the North Sea, as Heine himself might well have done if he had taken his Romantic Weltschmerz just a little more seriously than he did. Heinrich would be the vitriolic publicist, deadly to his enemies and dangerous even to his friends, whose activities began in 1826 with the publication of his first travel book, the *Harzreise*, and continued intermittently until 1840, when he published his book on Ludwig Borne. Heinrich, for the sake of convenience, could be said to have been killed in his duel with Salomon Straus on September 7, 1841, as Heine himself could easily have been killed, instead of being only wounded, by the avenger of Börne's sullied reputation. Henri, a much more awkward proposition, would have to include the great prose writer and brilliant critic of the eighteen-forties and eighteen-fifties, the author of the *Romanzero* and last poems, and the *charmant esprit*, as Baudelaire called him, whose influence extended from Gautier, Gérard de Nerval, and Baudelaire himself to Matthew Arnold, Nietzsche, the early Rilke, and countless other writers in every European country; his works would certainly include the late book on France, *Lutezia*, the two ballet scenarios *Der Doktor Faust*, and *Die Götter im Exil*, the private notebooks and the autobiographical works. Yet even these three Heines would not only overlap, but could never be prevented from quarrelling with one another. Reluctantly, therefore, one returns to the composite image; but with little hope that it will do justice to every facet.

The difficulty is apparent from the image – projected by Heine himself – which was the subject of Matthew Arnold's essay of 1863:

> I know not if I deserve that a laurel-wreath should one day be placed on my coffin. Poetry, dearly as I have loved it, has always been to me but a divine plaything. I have never attached any great value to poetical fame, and I trouble myself very little whether people praise my verses or blame them. But lay on my coffin a sword; for I was a brave soldier in the war of liberation of humanity.

To begin with, 'brave' is a mistranslation of the German word 'bray', which means obedient, reliable, or good, in the sense in which we say that a child is good; and, contrary to Arnold's opinion, Heine was exceptionally brave, both morally and physically, but he was almost totally lacking in the humble virtues he imputed to himself in this passage. The second falsehood in the original is so blatant that Arnold's conscience compelled him to omit it from the translation; after 'divine plaything', Heine has 'or a consecrated means to heavenly ends'. The third falsehood, Heine's pretence of indifference to literary fame, did not take Arnold in any more than the second, but he let it pass because 'for his contemporaries, for us, for the Europe of the present century, he (Heine) is significant chiefly for the reasons which he himself in the words just quoted assigns.' Heine's significance for Arnold's generation was indeed what Arnold claimed; but even the general tenor of Heine's self-characterization conveys only a little fraction of the truth about his cultural rôle, as I shall attempt to show.

As for another notorious falsehood of a different order, Heine's statement that he was born on the first day of 1800, its primary purpose was not to make himself appear more than two years younger than he was – a kind of vanity inexcusable in a male poet – nor even to permit the witticism that he was '*un des premiers hommes du siècle*', but to conceal the fact that his parents were not legally married till after his birth. Heine himself does not seem to have been told exactly when he was born; and the social odds against him were so heavy as it was that one can hardly blame him for not offering this particular weapon to his enemies. Yet this factual falsehood has proved as misleading to Heine's biographers as his self-characterizations have proved to his critics and interpreters.

Heine's statements about himself are not always reliable; but the more one studies the works of nineteenth-century writers who had ideas but no philosophy, the more one is prepared to find that it is not their self-characterizations, their confessions, and professions, that reveal their vital preoccupations; not, at least, if taken literally and one by one. Rather, in an age of dialectics – of thesis, antithesis, and, one hopes, of synthesis – it is their self-contradictions. This formula, too, is not generally valid; but it does apply to Heine and to a great many other writers whose minds were melting pots for all the ill-assorted ideas thrown up by the age. In such cases one can be pretty sure that the issues that mattered most to them are those about which they were most apt to contradict themselves.

Heine made ample use of what Baudelaire called 'the right to contradict oneself'; but whereas Baudelaire worked hard for a synthesis, ideas in themselves mattered so little to Heine that he was content to let one idea cancel out another. He was prolific of ideas, but he did not respect his wealth. In the very worst sense of the word, he remained a 'subjective' writer; not because he made use of the first person singular in his poetry and prose, but because he was more interested in the uniqueness of his person than in its efficiency as a medium. He never learned that a great poet's 'I' is a functional, as distinct from a biographical, 'I'; that it is an instrument created by the poet for the sake of the poetry, an instrument that may have no value, often indeed no reality, apart from this function. There were times, such as the Middle Ages, when the poetic 'I' and the biographical 'I' might well happen to be identical; for individuals were no more than embodiments of impersonal virtues and vices, and they were judged by their capacity to perform an appointed rôle. When they spoke for themselves, they spoke for everyone. Modern poets have no such luck; unless they are very naïve or very mad, they have to create their poetic 'I', to abstract it from the irrelevances of circumstance. This Heine never succeeded in doing; his many *personae*, like the Quixotic knight-errant, the tragic jester, the romantic lover, and the analyst of love, did not coalesce. The 'I' of Heine's poetry – and of his prose, from which it hardly differs – shows all the inconsistencies that are forced upon individuals by changing circumstances, moods, and necessities, and by their changing conceptions of their own personalities. That is why writers on Heine are so apt to produce distorted, simplified, and contradictory images, and why one feels tempted to shirk the labour of a synthesis that Heine himself was too easy-going, too self-indulgent to provide. It is only by balancing one of his statements against another, and balancing every one of them against the facts of his life and works, that one can hope to arrive at anything like the complex truth.

The passage about the laurel wreath and the sword comes from an early prose work of Heine's, the *Journey from Munich to Genoa*; and Heine's early ideas on politics are inseparable from his biography. 'By the marching-route of my cradle,' as he put it later, he was committed to the political Left, just as he was divided from the start between German sentiment and French *esprit*. His native Rhineland was pervaded by French influences. It was a French writer, Rousseau, who had emancipated his mother from Jewish orthodoxy, and another Frenchman, Napoleon, who had emancipated the Jews of the Rhineland from the ghettoes and – what was more important to Heine – from their confinement to the mercantile trades that he hated and despised. The defeat of Napoleon brought back the old restrictions when Heine was about to enter professional life. Debarred from working as a lawyer or civil servant, he was faced with the choice between a business career under the aegis of his rich uncle Salomon – which he tried and gave up before escaping to the comparative freedom of the universities – and that certificate of baptism which he described as 'the ticket of admission to European culture'. Heine never really solved this dilemma; he became a Lutheran but made malicious remarks about other distinguished converts not necessarily less sincere than himself, remained partly dependent on his uncle, whom he both admired and hated, and never worked as a lawyer or civil servant. Although he was able to earn his living – or part of it –

by his pen, even the freedom of a writer was precarious in an age of strict censorship, frequent political upheavals, and conflicting literary factions.

It was personal, rather than political motives that drove Heine into polemical journalism: above all it was his sense of insecurity, economic pressure, an exuberant delight in controversy, and the spirit of the age itself, which he learned too late to resist. For the intricacies of politics he had no aptitude at all; and though he was vain, he was not ambitious for power. Yet even writers who had no personal grievance comparable to his, found themselves engaged in politics during those years. Gérard de Nerval, the author of a few poems as pure as the medium of words permits, began as the author of political odes; and as late as the Revolution of 1848, when Heine's attitude was one of indifference, even of hostility, Baudelaire acclaimed the event in the columns of *Le Salut Public*.

By conviction, by disposition and, one can almost say, by birth, Heine was a liberal. But liberalism did not exist in Germany; there were revolutionaries and reactionaries, and very little in between. Heine's very first allegiance, that to Napoleon, involved an obvious contradiction; and though he remained faithful to Napoleon's memory – even to the extent of supporting the régime of 'Napoleon le Petit' – his awareness of the contradiction forced him into the quibble that he was 'not an unqualified Bonapartist: my allegiance is due not to the actions of the man, but only to his genius.' A similar ambiguity attaches to Heine's later political associations with the 'Young Germans', with the Saint-Simonists and with Karl Marx; and though Heine had no aptitude for either abstract thought or practical politics, he had an almost infallible flair for the practical implications and potentialities of ideas.

Heine's allegiance to Napoleon also involved a conflict with the nationalistic factions, those 'Teutomaniacs' against whom he waged a particularly intense campaign. This issue again, was complicated by the connection between nationalism and the German Romantic Movement and by Heine's genuine, though unconventional, patriotism. To the Romantic School he owed his introduction to German literature, the personal encouragement of his teacher A. W. von Schlegel, his interest in medieval literature, history, folklore, and even his love of the *Volkslied*, on which he modelled his own verse: and in spite of his Francophilia, even because of it, he never ceased to feel a very special love for the unawakened, 'anonymous' Germany of his youth, a love made more poignant by absence in later years. When Bismarck chose to defend Heine against his anti-Semitic detractors, he did so on the grounds that 'Heine was a writer of *Lieder*, second to none but Goethe, and the *Lied*, of all poetic genres, is the one most specifically German.' This defence may seem more generous than just, now that Heine's lyrical poetry has been discredited for different reasons. Only a few staunch supporters still deny that his long courtship of the *Lied* was too inhibited by Voltairean *esprit* and Byronic self-consciousness ever to result in an altogether happy marriage; but, curiously enough, the general public seems to have relished this peculiar tension between poem and poet. The enormous popular success of the *Buch der Lieder* continued long after Bismarck's time. It was not until 1926 that a highly fastidious and learned man of letters, Rudolf Borchardt, sounded the alarm by explaining why he found it necessary to reduce Heine's poems to 'fragments' in order to include them in his anthology of the best German poetry. Like the Austrian satirist and moralist Karl Kraus, who had also condemned Heine's laxity and impurity of diction, going so far as to imply that Heine's poetry was no more than an imitation of specious Romantic modes, Rudolf Borchardt was of Jewish descent.

Heine's ambivalent attitude to the Romantic tradition in which he wrote his verse needs little explanation. An entry in his private note-books provides a gloss: 'Hatred of the Jews begins only with the Romantic School, with their delight in the Middle Ages (Catholicism, aristocracy), further increased by the Teutomaniacs.' And his treatise on the Romantic School, written in 1833 for a French periodical, deals fully with all his objections. But by 1833 he had left Germany for good, settled in Paris, and become involved with the politically active 'Young Germany' movement, a group of writers who hoped to launch an international Socialist revolution.

His Romantic – or semi-Romantic – period is the earlier one of his studies at Bonn and Göttingen, his unrequited love for his two Hamburg cousins, his travels in Germany, Poland, Heligoland, England, and Italy.

Even the political and social enthusiasms that are still associated with Heine's name belong to the same early period of his life. These enthusiasms reached their climax in the *Journey from Munich to*

Genoa, published in 1828; a second quotation from its rhetorical professions of faith will have to suffice. Heine is writing about the 'great task of our time', emancipation. 'Not only that of the Irish, Greeks, Frankfort Jews, West Indian negroes and similar oppressed peoples, but the emancipation of the whole world, especially of Europe, which has attained its majority and is now breaking loose from the iron leading-strings of the privileged, the aristocracy. Let a few philosophical renegades of freedom forge the most subtle chains of argument to prove to us that millions of human beings were created to serve as beasts of burden to some thousands of privileged knights; they will never convince us as long as they cannot show us that, in the words of Voltaire, the former were born with saddles on their backs, the latter with spurs on their feet.'

Three years after the appearance of this book Heine left Germany, attracted to Paris by the success of the 1830 Revolution. His connection with the 'Young Germany' movement and with the Saint-Simonists, formed at that time, seems paradoxical when one considers his writings of the early Paris years; for already in the Postscript of 1833 to his first *Salon* volume he began to recant his republicanism. In Paris he had the opportunity to study revolutionary politics in action, with the result that he wrote in 1833: 'It is my most sacred conviction that the Republican form would be unsuitable, unprofitable and uncomfortable for the peoples of Europe, and nothing less than impossible for the Germans.' But whereas the *Journey from Munich to Genoa* has circulated freely, and Heine himself had not been arrested, as he half expected to be at the time, his more moderate works of the eighteen-thirties were obstructed by a stiffening of policy. In 1835 a Romantic nationalist and former friend of Heine's, Wolfgang Menzel, attacked the Young Germans and caused their works – including Heine's prose works – to be banned in Prussia, Austria, and most parts of Germany. The same Menzel had previously attacked Goethe for his indifference to the pan-German aspirations of his juniors, his un-Christian morality, and his admiration for Napoleon. Heine, therefore, was in good company; but the Young Germans themselves were working for a united Germany; and most of its members had shared Menzel's disapproval of Goethe, the one prominent survivor from an age when writers were not necessarily committed to a political line. Meanwhile Heine's own position had moved closer to Goethe's than to that of his temporary allies, the

Young Germans; and it wasn't long before their leader, Karl Gutzkow, became one of Heine's most implacable enemies.

There were two principal causes for Heine's change of front. The first was his dislike of violent extremes, what I have called his liberalism. This he summed up very neatly in the same Postscript of 1833: 'The man who does not go as far as his heart demands and his reason permits is a coward; the man who goes farther than he wished to go is a slave.' Above all, Heine feared the effect of revolutionary doctrines on Germany, for reasons already implied in the Postscript and made very clear in a major prose work published soon after it, his *History of German Religion and Philosophy* of 1834. This formidable work, full of brilliant insights and inaccurate generalizations, contains Heine's famous warning to the French to refrain from rousing the Germans from their philosophical meditations, their notorious unworldliness. The Germans, he says, do not hate one another, as the French do, because of injured vanity, because of an epigram, say, or a visiting card not returned. 'No, what we hate in our enemies is what is deepest in them, what is essential to them, the idea itself . . . We Germans hate thoroughly, lastingly; since we are too honest, too clumsy also, to take our revenge by quick perfidy, we hate till our very last breath.' The actual prophecy of Germany's awakening takes a form characteristic of Heine's sensitiveness to the potentialities of ideas; for he conjures up a vision of 'Kantians who even in the world of phenomena will show no pity of any sort, but mercilessly, with sword and hatchet, will turn up the soil of European life to destroy the very last roots of the past.' Then there are 'armed Fichteans' who in their fanatical cult of the will, 'can be tamed neither by fear or self-interest, since they live on the plane of spirit and defy matter'; and lastly the philosophers of nature who 'will form an alliance with the chthonic powers of nature, know how to invoke the daemonic powers of ancient Germanic pantheism and revive that love of battle characteristic of the ancient Germans, which does not fight in order to destroy, nor in order to win, but only for the sake of fighting.'

Heine alludes to the second factor in his conversion when he says in the same work that, as a poet and scholar, he himself 'belongs to the sick old world'. All his later works, from 1833 to his death in 1856, show the unresolved conflict between two radically different views of life. These he called 'sensualism' and 'spiritualism'. On the one hand he continued to welcome every reform of existing institutions that promised more liberty to the individual; and he even wrote enthusiastically about material innovations like the railway. These were 'progress', and they belonged to the order of 'sensualism'. On the other hand, he doubted the value of such improvements and feared the implications of the philosophy that made them possible; for, as he wrote as early as 1833, 'the beginning and end of all things is in God.'

. . . .

WHEN HEINE died in Paris on February 17, 1856, his reputation was higher in France than in Germany, though parts of his early *Buch der Lieder* were familiar to a vast body of Germans, educated and uneducated alike, if only because they had been set to music popular to the point of anonymity; and, as lyrics to be sung, rather than read, Heine's early poems are surpassed only by the poems of Eichendorff, who had the advantage of genuine naïveté. During the following decades Heine's fame spread to every European country, to the United States and as far as Japan. By an exclusive emphasis on his 'modernity' – that is, on his liberalism, his materialism, and his irreverence – a vast nineteenth-century public, including scientists, politicians, and progressive intellectuals in every field, were able to turn Heine into one of the heroes of their time. As far as his poetry is concerned, Heine's modernity was only skin-deep; he never learned to do without conventional Romantic effects, nor does his imagery show a vital response to the large city in which he spent most of his mature life. It is probably wrong to expect the imagery of modern poetry to be urban, though much of it does reflect the poet's immediate environment; but much of Heine's imagery lacks the immediacy of active observation. With the single exception of the two *North Sea* cycles – whose free verse was by no means unprecedented in German literature, but attained a freedom of a different order – Heine contented himself with variety within an unusually narrow range of verse forms; too often, even in his last and most masterly poems, one feels that the trochaic meters are simply rattling on like some efficient but remorseless machine; and one wishes it would stop for a while, to give the poet a chance to look around.

Heine's prose, on the other hand, was not only modern, but unexcelled in his time. It can be said to have grappled with almost every important issue of the century – or, if not grappled with it, at least toyed with it most pleasantly. Much of his prose remains as stimulating now as it was to all the contemporaries and near-contemporaries who tried to imitate its verve, its wit, and its clarity; and the same qualities keep most of his poetry readable still – which is more than one can say for a great many talented poets writing at the same transitional period, the period when a moribund Romanticism was gradually giving way to Symbolism on the one hand, Naturalism on the other.

In order to overcome the limitations of that period and of his own position in it, Heine would have needed either genius or humility. Both genius and humility are destroyers of circumstance. His younger contemporary Eduard Mörike, a late successor to that 'provincial' Swabian school which Heine never tired of ridiculing, proved that even the older tradition of German lyrical verse was still capable of a new and genuine development; but Mörike's way was closed to Heine, for such local roots as Heine had were wrenched out in his youth. This uprootedness was one cause of the sentimentality concealed beneath his wit. To be cosmopolitan is not necessarily to be universal; but Heine's cosmopolitanism could have opened a way that he did not take, a way more vertical than horizontal that leads to universality, since all roots reach down toward the same centre. He could have grown deeper roots and become one of the 'transplanted' writers whom Remy de Gourmont distinguishes from the 'uprooted'. A still younger contemporary, Georg Büchner, proved what genius could do in the way of innovation; but Büchner had the ruthlessness of genius and of revolutionaries.

Heine feared nothing so much as to be possessed; this was his dilemma, the dilemma of liberalism in an age of extremes; and he faced it with insight, honesty, and the desperate courage that will not admit defeat. As Nietzsche said, 'it can be the sign of a noble mind to make fun of pathetic situations and to respond to them with undignified behaviour.' Nietzsche's remark is sound enough psychologically, even if its application to literature is more dubious. If it cannot justify Heine's lapses as a poet, it does help to explain them and to justify him as a man; and such a justification is not irrelevant in the case of a writer whose personality, for good or for ill, is present in all he wrote.

From GEORG BÜCHNER

GENIUS is an unfashionable word; and in attributing genius to Büchner, while denying it to Heine whose works exerted a world-wide influence when Büchner's were scarcely read even in his own country, I am aware that the word may call for qualification, if not for a re-definition that I am reluctant to attempt. As often as not, to speak of genius may be the last resort of a critic unequal to his subject, for genius is more easily discovered than analysed, more easily measured than located, being a sort of phlogiston whose existence in human minds and their products can be neither proved nor disproved by empirical means. The analogy, of course, is only partly apt, like every analogy between the methods of criticism and the methods of scientific research. No work of art can be analysed or assessed with a degree of accuracy comparable to that obtained in chemical experiments. One critical method may be more 'objective' or more rewarding than another, but none is infallible. Unlike the universal ciphers of mathematics, the terminology of literary criticism is capable of no precision other than that which results from an understanding between the critic and his reader.

What is meant by genius here can be best conveyed by stating that even after one has adduced evidence of Büchner's extraordinary talents and accomplishments, as a scientist, political thinker, and imaginative writer, as a moralist, psychologist, and visionary, there remains a residue of the inexplicable. His skill as a dramatist, to cite an example more verifiable than most, seems to have been acquired without the usual process of trial and error; and more generally one can say that Büchner's achievements demanded an incommensurable minimum of experience. Often, in his case, one looks in vain for the cause behind the effect; there is a difference between the mere aggregate of his talents and their totality. For this difference there is no single word but genius.

As German literature suggests all too frequently, genius can exist without the various talents that make it viable; but Büchner's capacity for sheer hard work was no less extraordinary than his genius. He had little of the arrogance of the very gifted, and none of their vanity.

Before the end of his short life he had attained a maturity rare enough in artists three times his age. When he died at the age of twenty-three, he was a Doctor of Philosophy and a lecturer in comparative anatomy at the University of Zürich; a former political revolutionary who had been formidable enough to be driven into exile from his native Hessen by the imminent danger of a prison sentence; and the author of those four literary works – three plays and a story – to which he owes his belated fame. The manuscript of a fourth play, *Pietro Aretino*, which his family regarded as his best, was lost or destroyed after his death. He had published a more than competent translation of two dramas by Victor Hugo and written a thesis in French on *le système nerveux du barbeau*; this thesis was followed by a paper on the cranial nerves, the subject of his trial lecture at Zürich. His notes for a projected course of lectures on the history of German philosophy after Descartes and Spinoza, prepared during the last months of his life, include some penetrating and original comments on the subject. It is no exaggeration to say that Büchner excelled at every activity to which he applied himself.

To Büchner's talents and outlook, but not to his genius, his family background is relevant. His father, paternal grandfather, and an uncle on his father's side were medical men; so was his favourite brother Ludwig, the first editor of Georg's posthumous works and himself the author of *Force and Matter*, *Man and His Place in Nature*, and *Mind in Animals*, important studies in evolution and animal psychology that were popularized in England by Annie Besant. Of Georg's other brothers and sisters, Wilhelm became a research chemist and Reichstag deputy, Alexander a professor of literature in France, Louise a writer in the feminist cause. Although Büchner's father disapproved of Georg's political activities, which were a grave embarrassment to a family enlightened and progressive rather than revolutionary, he was not unsympathetic to the convictions that gave rise to these activities and made his peace with Georg by letter a few months before Georg died in exile. It is also worth noting that the uncle to whom Georg turned when he was in trouble – Eduard Reuss, a brother of Georg's mother – was a Protestant theologian.

It was his meeting with another Protestant theologian, Pastor Weidig, that introduced Büchner to revolutionary politics. After attending school at Darmstadt, Georg Büchner studied the natural sciences – chiefly zoology and comparative anatomy – at Strasbourg, where he became secretly engaged to a pastor's daughter, Wilhelmine Jaegle, who had looked after him when he was ill in her father's house. In October, 1833, at the age of twenty, he moved to the University of Giessen, took up practical medicine at his father's request, but had to return home in the spring after a more serious illness, an attack of meningitis that left him subject to headaches and fevers for the rest of his life. Back in Giessen after his convalescence, he met Pastor Weidig, the leader of the Liberal movement in Hessen. Büchner joined the 'Society for the Rights of Man' and, in collaboration with Pastor Weidig, wrote and published an anonymous tract, 'Der Hessische Landbote', which called on the peasants to revolt. Büchner contributed facts about the exploitation of the peasants, Weidig the main body of the tract, evangelical exhortations based on quotations from the Bible. In April, 1834, Büchner returned to Strasbourg and announced his engagement to Minna Jaegle. During the Easter vacation he founded a branch of the Society at Darmstadt and, in July, attended a conference of delegates from the various branches; but he had already lost faith in mere Liberal reform, deciding that nothing less than a revolution would prove effective in Germany. On August 1, the stock of the 'Landbote' was seized by the government; one of Büchner's associates was arrested and Büchner himself interrogated. For the time being, he continued his studies at home, also giving public lectures on anatomy, but secretly prepared his escape. In order to raise money for his escape, he wrote his first drama, *Dantons Tod*, and undertook the translations from Hugo; Karl Gutzkow, the leader of the 'Young Germany' movement, saw to the publication of both books. Soon after getting away to Strasbourg in March, 1835, Büchner was denounced for his part in the authorship of the 'Landbote'; in June a warrant was issued for his arrest. *Dantons Tod* and Büchner's letters suggest that he had already grown tired of political action; at Strasbourg he wrote his French thesis, which won him admission to the *Société d'Histoire Naturelle*, his story *Lenz* and his comedy *Leonce und Lena* (which he wrote, but submitted too late, for a competition). In September, 1836, he was granted a Doctor of Philosophy degree by the University of Zürich and, after reading his paper on the cranial nerves, was appointed a lecturer there. Three months later, in February, 1837, he contracted typhus and died in Zürich on February 19.

Dantons Tod was first performed in 1902, *Leonce und Lena* in 1911, *Woyzeck* in 1913. Büchner, in fact, was too 'advanced' a dramatist to be acceptable even during the Naturalist 1880s and 1890s, when Ibsen, Hauptmann, and Sudermann dominated the German experimental theatres. Gerhart Hauptmann admired Büchner's works, editions of which had been published in 1850 and 1879; but it was not till after the experiments of Strindberg, Wedekind, and the first Expressionists that Büchner's plays established themselves on the stage. This very circumstance serves to confute the arguments of Georg Lukács and other critics of his school, who would like to persuade us that Büchner was an early practitioner of 'Social Realism', of an art primarily directed toward social or political ends. For a time, undoubtedly, Büchner's preoccupation with human suffering caused him to seek relief in political action, for tyranny and injustice were two obvious causes of human suffering in his time; but only a very prejudiced reader of his works, from *Dantons Tod* to *Woyzeck*, can fail to see that Büchner's realism goes far deeper than that of the Naturalists and their successors, the Social Realists of this century. Büchner's view of life was a tragic one; his intense pity for the poor, the oppressed and the exploited was never alleviated by the comfortable belief that human suffering is due to no other causes than poverty, oppression, and exploitation. If Büchner had wished to glorify the French Revolution or the ideology behind it, he would have made Robespierre the hero of his play, not the irresolute and dissolute Danton; but Büchner's dominant passion was the passion for truth, for the whole truth; and even if he had taken Robespierre as the hero of his play, it would have been Robespierre at the moment of his fall, the victim of the same inhuman system that had brought about Danton's death. Büchner, in short, was never a party man; he was never purblind, as every party man must be, because he hated ideologies that enslave the minds of men as much as he hated the economic and social orders that enslave men bodily. As a scientist, he knew that body and mind are interdependent; he therefore revolted against the 'idealistic' cant that denies or minimizes the extent to which material conditions affect us. Yet his true concern was with mental and spiritual suffering, Danton's vision of vanity and his fear of death, the religious torment of Lenz, the suicidal boredom of Leonce, the physical victimization of Woyzeck that leads to hallucination, paranoia, and murder. Büchner's realism was that of every great writer who seeks the truth about the human situation; a realism that is not incompatible with poetic vision.

I HAVE said elsewhere that, in the age of Hegelian dialectics, it was often the self-contradictions of a writer that revealed his vital preoccupations. Büchner, too, wrote out of a tragic tension between two conflicting views of life. What is so astonishing about his works is their consistency of purpose and achievement. One reason is that Büchner had no use at all for Hegel or for that idealistic German school from which Hegel derived; neither, in fact, had Heine, though he paid lip service to Hegel and concealed the stark pessimism of his last years behind the paraphernalia of a fancy-dress Romanticism. Büchner had no patience with half-measures; like Schopenhauer, whom he resembled in his pessimism and in his pity, he based his thinking not on metaphysical premises, but on the bare condition of man, on the reality of suffering, our participation in suffering not our own and our desire to relieve it. This basic existential preoccupation is at the root of all Büchner's works; but he was divided between a religious view of the human predicament and a cruelly deterministic view, brought home to him by his scientific studies and his reflections on history.

An early letter to his fiancée, written when he was twenty, contains a most poignant account of these conflicting views. The account is especially valuable because of its direct bearing on Büchner's first play, *Dantons Tod*. There can be no better introduction to it than Büchner's own reflections on the events with which it deals:

> I was studying the history of the French Revolution. I felt almost annihilated by the horrible fatalism of history. In human nature I discovered a terrifying sameness, in human institutions an incontrovertible power, granted to all and to none. The individual mere froth on the wave, greatness a mere accident, the sovereignty of genius a mere puppet play, a ludicrous struggle against an inalterable law; to recognize this law our supreme achievement, to control it impossible.

It was this experience of determinism that turned Büchner into a revolutionary of the most radical sort, as the same letter shows. It is the extremists of revolutionary politics, the Robespierres rather than the Dantons, who base their policies on the recognition of that 'unalterable law'. Yet the recognition ran counter to Büchner's nature and convictions, to his Christian sense of the value of the individual and his no less radical belief in free will. Hence the conflicting resolutions that follow:

Never again shall I feel obliged to bow to the parade horses and corner boys of History. I am accustoming my eyes to the sight of blood. But I am no guillotine blade. The word must is one of the curses pronounced at the baptism of men. The dictum: 'for it must needs be that offences come; but woe to that man by whom the offence cometh!" – is terrible. What is it in us that lies, murders, steals? I can't bear to pursue this thought any further. But oh! if I could lay this cold and tormented heart on your breast!

The relevance of this passage to *Dantons Tod* would be obvious even if Büchner had not put much of it into Danton's own mouth in Act II of the play. The conflict between Robespierre and St. Just on the one hand, Danton and his friends on the other, is a conflict between two different views of political and historical necessity. Their dramatic conflict would be less convincing if Büchner had not been able to do full justice to both arguments. At one time, there can be no doubt, he would have identified himself with the party of Robespierre and St. Just. Not only Danton expresses thoughts that we know to have been Büchner's; St. Just's great speech in Act II is an apology for the very determinism that Büchner had come close to accepting:

Nature calmly and irresistibly obeys her own laws; men are annihilated where they come into conflict with those laws. A change in the constitution of the air we breathe, a blazing up of the tellurian fire, a disturbance in the balance in a quantity of water, an epidemic, a volcanic eruption, a flood – each of these can cause the death of thousands. What is the result? An insignificant alteration of physical nature, hardly perceptible in the cosmos as a whole, that would have left no trace to speak of but for the dead bodies left in its wake.

Now I ask you: should mental nature show more consideration in its revolutions than physical nature? Should not an idea have as much right as a physical law to destroy whatever opposes it? Indeed, should not any event that will change the entire constitution of moral nature, that is, of humanity, be permitted to attain its end by bloodshed? The World Spirit makes use of our arms in the mental sphere as it makes use of volcanoes and floods in the physical. What difference does it make whether men die of an epidemic or of a revolution?

The appeal to Hegel's 'World Spirit' in this context may be an anachronism, but it is a significant one. Büchner was careful to grant both factions their fair share of religious, or pseudo-religious justification. Elsewhere Robespierre compares his mission to that of Christ:

He redeemed them with his blood, and I redeem them with their own. He made them sin, and I take this sin upon myself... And yet... Truly, the son of man is crucified in us all, we all sweat blood and writhe in the garden of Gethsemane, but no one redeems another with his wounds.

Dramatically, this passage serves to show that Robespierre too has scruples and affections, for he is moved to express these thoughts by Camille Desmoulins's desertion to Danton's party. Robespierre, who denies his scruples and affections in favour of impersonal ends, is no less deserving of pity than his victim, the individualist. But Büchner takes dramatic impartiality even further by throwing just a little shadow of doubt on the purity of Robespierre's motives, as indeed he suggests several possible explanations for the conduct of Danton himself. That is why *Dantons Tod* is a truly and profoundly tragic play; both Robespierre, who serves a certain ideal necessity, and Danton, who opposes it in the cause of individual freedom, are destroyed by the revolution, though Robespierre first destroys Danton for the Revolution's sake. The Revolution itself assumes a character akin to that of Fate in Greek tragedy; and the voice of the *people – vox populi, vox dei –* expresses a terrible indifference to the virtues and aspirations of both men. Yet amoral and brutish though they are, even the representatives of the people are not excluded from the pity that Büchner's play so powerfully evokes.

Danton's disillusionment, too, is Büchner's own. One can follow the process in the few letters and parts of letters by Büchner that have been preserved. In a letter to his family, written when he was nineteen, he defended the use of violence in the revolutionary cause, on the grounds that the so-called laws of the land are nothing more than 'a perpetual state of violence" imposed on the suffering people. A year later he could still express his hatred of the aristocracy, or rather of an attitude of mind which he called 'aristocratism', describing it 'as the most shameful contempt for the Holy Ghost in Man; against this I fight with its own weapons, repaying scorn with scorn, mockery with mockery.' The turning-point came when certain of the peasants, for whose sake Büchner was risking imprisonment by his part in the authorship of the 'Hessische Landbote', handed over their copies to the police. Büchner was no less critical than before of the bourgeois intellectual reformers, the Young Germans, who did not share his own conviction that 'the relation between rich and poor is the only revolutionary factor in the world,' as he put it to Karl Gutzkow in 1835; but he had come to fear that the servility of the German working class would frustrate every effort on their behalf. In a later letter to Gutzkow he added a second 'revolutionary factor'. 'With them (the working class), only two levers are effective: material misery and religious fanaticism. Any party that knows how to apply those levers will be victorious.' By 1836, Büchner had renounced every kind of political activity; but it must not be supposed that he had made his peace with the existing social order. His quarrel with 'the literary party of Gutzkow and Heine' was simply that they were wasting their time and energy in trying to bring about 'a total transformation of our religious and social ideas by polemical journalism'; and he was 'far from sharing their views on marriage and on the Christian religion.' Büchner remained a radical and an extremist; not because he clung to any rigid political doctrine, but because he believed that 'in social matters one must start out with an absolute principle of justice.' His own starting point was compassion with the poor; and that is why he stressed the economic basis of injustice in his time. A letter of 1836 to his family ends with a brief account of his visit to a Christmas fair, with its crowds of 'ragged, frozen children, who stood gazing with wide eyes and sad faces at all that magnificence, made out of flour and water, gilt paper and muck.'

As for our 'moribund modern society', he told Gutzkow in 1836 not to waste his talent on literary sallies against it, but to 'let it go to the devil' in its own time. 'Its whole life only consists in attempts to ward off the most horrible boredom. Let it die out, then, for that's the only new thing it's still capable of experiencing.' [...]

From *A Proliferation of Prophets* (1983)

Essays on German writers from Nietzsche to Brecht

From HUGO VON HOFMANNSTHAL

HUGO VON HOFMANNSTHAL published his first poem in June 1890, when he was a schoolboy of just over sixteen, his first playlet or 'lyrical drama' in the following year. Though not unprecedented, this early emergence of a poet was extraordinary enough; and it was made more extraordinary by the emergence at the same time of the critic and man of letters – under the pseudonyms of Loris, Loris Melikow, Theophil Morren, or, in one case only, Archibald O'Hagan BA. From the autumn of 1890 onwards this schoolboy poet and man of letters was also to be seen at the literary meeting-places of Vienna, such as the Café Griensteidl, at first in his father's company, later with older friends or alone. To say that he mixed on equal terms with established writers is an understatement; for he was accepted at once not merely as a youthful' prodigy and a writer of the greatest promise, but as a master of his art. 'Here at last,' Hermann Bahr wrote of this first impact in a book published in 1894, 'here at last was someone who contained the whole age, for all its thousandfold contradictions and conflicts, within his mind.'

This first, predominantly lyrical, phase of Hofmannsthal's working life lasted for roughly ten years, the last decade of the century. Though he continued to write poems after this period, he himself considered his lyrical vein exhausted and thought only five of his later poems worth preserving in book form. Much has been made of this apparent break in Hofmannsthal's development and of the crisis to which it was due. The majority of those who admired the lyrical poet neither understood nor forgave the change; they felt about it much as Rimbaud's admirers might have felt if he had lived to become a member of the Académie Française. Hofmannsthal's fame declined; it was said about him that if he had died at twenty-five he would have been a great poet. This epigram, as wrong and foolish as it was cruel, is quoted only because it sums up a superficial view of Hofmannsthal which not only prevailed during the greater part of his later life but persisted long after his death in 1929, and was only partly corrected by the publication in Germany of a fifteen-volume edition of his works, supplemented by many volumes of correspondence. A much larger critical edition, including previously unpublished works and fragments, has been in progress since 1975.

If one thing has become clear, it is that the whole of Hofmannsthal's work, from the first poems, playlets, and stories to the last librettos, essays, and plays, is linked by strong, though bewilderingly subtle, threads. Hofmannsthal himself traced such threads in notes on his own work, but there are many others which he was unable or unwilling to indicate. Every perceptive student of his works has been aware of them. To treat the poems and lyrical plays in isolation would be to perpetuate the legend of Loris, of the 'young prince', the 'marvellous boy' of the *fin de siècle*, of whom it was also said that he dipped his hand into a bowl of precious stones while he wrote his 'jewelled' verse. (The real Loris went to school, sailed, played tennis, and toured Italy on his bicycle; his parents were far from rich.) It will be necessary to stress not only the uniqueness of the early poems and plays – and Hofmannsthal's abandonment of his first media has a significance not confined to his personal development – but their relation to the whole of his work. Had this legendary Loris really existed, his writings would still maintain their prominent place in German literature beside the contemporary work of Stefan George and Rilke: but for historical reasons, rather than for their enduring power to move and to disturb us.

The truth is that the early admirers of Loris saw only those facets of his poetry and prose which answered the requirements of the age; above all, they saw him as the belated representative in Austrian and German literature of that aesthetic movement whose progress they had followed in France and England. Hofmannsthal's early essays on the Pre-Raphaelites, Swinburne, Pater, Wilde, on Viélé-Griffin and Bourget, his translations from Maeterlinck and D'Annunzio, and his association with Stefan George's *Blätter für die Kunst*, did point to a genuine affinity with an international movement opposed in various ways to mere Naturalism. What Hofmannsthal's contemporary readers and interpreters failed to see was that, however preoccupied with the reigning antinomy between art and life, even Loris, the real Loris, was as much intent on resolving the antinomy as the propagandists of a 'consistent' Naturalism; but in a very different way. Even the critical essays of Loris bridge the gulf between aestheticism and Naturalism. Ibsen's plays are treated not as social documents, but as self-confessions; Barrès, on the other hand, is censured for lacking a 'centre, style, form'. Swinburne is praised for his 'dionysian' fervour, but with this important reservation: 'These artists, as I said, do not come out of life: what they produce does not enter into life.' Throughout these early critical pieces Hofmannsthal shows only a half-hearted sympathy with the cult of decadence as such, much as he appreciates some of its artistic achievements. His marked preference for the English aesthetic movement from Ruskin to Pater was due to its habit of combining moral passion and social consciousness with the pursuit of beauty. Where these were lacking, Hofmannsthal disapproved, though he was still unsure of the grounds of his disapproval. A passing addiction to Nietzsche's vitalism is evident in several of the essays and reviews, then again a concern with the forms of social life, style in life, rather than in art, pointing to Hofmannsthal's later solution of the antinomy between art and life, introspection and activity, individualism and community, in comedies at once realistic and metaphysical, explorations of the symbolism and mythology of manners.

The paradox I am trying to indicate here is that it is the early lyrical plays of Hofmannsthal, the very works that were hailed as pure poetry in the sense defined by the French Symbolists and by Stefan George, which tended towards didacticism; and not even towards that didacticism into which the advocates of art for art's sake were apt to fall despite their creed – Villiers de l'Isle-Adam and George frequently did so – but towards one opposed to the creed itself. The richness and virtuosity of diction in these early plays, quite close at times to the freedom of Symbolist verse, make the contradiction not less, but more, acute. It is hardly surprising that Hofmannsthal could come to regard *Der Tor und der Tod* (1893) as the first in a series of morality plays continued much later by his *Jedermann* (1911) and *Das grosse Salzburger Welttheater* (1922). The paradox has something to do both with the 'impasse of aestheticism, – Hofmannsthal's own phrase in an early letter – and with the predicament of verse drama in his time. *Das kleine Welttheater* is the outstanding exception; for, having come to recognize the lyrical nature of his playlets, Hofmannsthal no longer aimed at dramatic effects in this work; it is, as he called it, a puppet play, a sequence of very loosely interrelated monologues with no obvious moral framework and no dramatic interplay of characters. W. B. Yeats, who was faced with similar problems throughout his active life, was to resort to a related form in many of his later plays; but his *Plays for Dancers* (1921), with their fusion of mime, music, mask, and the spoken word, offer a still more revealing parallel with Hofmannsthal's opera librettos and ballet scenarios of later years. Here it is important not to be misled by preconceptions about genres or by Hofmannsthal's greater readiness to effect an outward compromise with the requirements of the stage. In essence and conception, these works are as esoteric as those of Yeats, and both are late products of the Symbolist tradition. Hofmannsthal rightly emphasized the connection between his early lyrical plays and his librettos for *Die Frau ohne Schatten* (1913–14), *Ariadne auf Naxos* (1910 and 1916), and *Die ägyptische Helena* (1926).

To explain the transformation of the 'pure' poet into the 'mere' librettist of later years, the dramatist who did not disdain such 'humble' tasks as the adaptation of plays by Sophocles, Calderón, Molière, Otway, and Jules Renard, the writing of scenarios for Diaghilev and even for a film about the life and work of Daniel Defoe, I must turn back to the beginning. Hofmannsthal's precocity was a real one. In reading his letters of the early period one is struck by his astonishing capacity for receiving and absorbing disparate experience, so that his attitudes never remain fixed for long, but are perpetually modified, corrected, and strengthened by self-criticism. His openness to external influences of every order – including the aura of persons, things, and places, of institutions, ways of life, ways of thinking and feeling – was such as to amount to a danger. To take only the most obvious of relationships, the personal, he was always in danger of being fascinated, overwhelmed, and abused by those whose strength lay in their monomania, the one kind of strength opposed to his own. This danger was inseparable from his strength; and the magical inspiration of his early work was nothing other than the presentiment or intuition of a multiplicity and underlying unity which his later work could only embody in a corresponding multiplicity of media, themes, and forms. The difference, as he said, lay between 'pre-existence' and 'existence', between potentiality and realization, between the homunculus in his bottle – endowed with prophetic and magical faculties in Goethe's *Faust* – and the mature man's need to particularize, to separate, and to distinguish, a need inseparable from involvement in active life. Where Hofmannsthal's later works remain fragmentary or imperfectly realized, it is nearly always because the conception is too complex to be subordinated to the demands of the particular medium chosen, to be absorbed into the surface. So in the cases of his first prose comedy, *Silvia im Stern*, abandoned because too crowded with diverse characters and their intricate interactions, of the novel *Andreas*, the most tantalizingly enthralling of his many unfinished works, and, to a lesser extent, of his last tragedy, *Der Turm*.

All the hostility and misunderstandings to which Hofmannsthal's later work and person were subject arose from the prejudice that a writer so protean, so receptive, and so many-sided must be lacking in individuality and integrity. Yet even in the early poems and playlets Hofmannsthal's individuality had been nourished by his uncommon capacity for identification with what was not himself, whether experienced directly in his environment or indirectly in paintings, in the theatre, or in books. Unlike Yeats or Stefan George, he assumed no mask or anti-self, but relied on the social conventions to protect his privacy. 'Manners,' he noted, 'are walls, disguised with mirrors'; and 'manners are based on a profound conception of the necessity of isolation, while upholding – deliberately upholding – the illusion of contact.' In the same way, Hofmannsthal could at once project and conceal his individuality by borrowing the artistic conventions of past ages; his refusal to draw a categorical line between 'art' and 'life', past and present, not only absolved him from the false dichotomies of his time but gave him a scope and a freedom that far exceeded the resources of direct self-expression. Needless to say, it also exposed him to the charge that he was a mere imitator of obsolete conventions, a receiver and renovator of stolen goods. Only the most minute attention reveals how much of himself he put even into adaptations of other men's works. His so-called translation of Molière's little comedy *Les Fâcheux* is a good instance; it is nothing less than a preliminary sketch for Hofmannsthal's own comic masterpiece, *Der Schwierige*.

The escape of Loris from his legend and even the crisis recorded in the Chandos Letter (1902) were by no means the only turning-points in Hofmannsthal's development. His correspondence shows a marked change of style after the summer of 1892, when he left school to study law for a time, then Romance languages and literatures. If Loris ever existed, it was only till July 1892, when Hofmannsthal was eighteen years old. The affectation of *fin de siècle* languor – the French term occurs in several earlier letters, like other modish phrases – of sophistication, preciousness, and intellectual coquetry, hardly appears after this early period. The analogy with Rimbaud, in any case, is a far-fetched one. Hofmannsthal had never been a rebel or a bohemian; as the only child of parents who approved and fostered his interests, he had no cause to revolt. Though he was to find it necessary at times to remind his father that he was, after all, an artist – and an artist far more bizarre than even his father knew – neither at this time nor at any time of his life did Hofmannsthal wear his art on his sleeve. The more sober tone after this summer had several causes; one of them is too important to be omitted here.

In December 1892 Stefan George, who was staying in Vienna, was introduced to Hofmannsthal in a café. The meeting was followed by others, by a hectic exchange of notes, and by two poems written by Hofmannsthal, who was at once flattered and repelled by George's impetuous demands for friendship and loyalty. At one point George sent a bouquet of roses into Hofmannsthal's classroom at school! His other presents included not only an inscribed copy of his early *Hymnen* but a transcription in his own hand of Mallarmé's *L'Après-midi d'un faune*, made in Paris with Mallarmé's permission. If this was Hofmannsthal's introduction to the French poet's work, the gift proved more than a token of his initiation into the Symbolist fraternity. But George's behaviour was not priestlike; in one letter he addressed Hofmannsthal as 'my twin brother,' and begged him to save him 'from the road that leads to total nothingness'. Hofmannsthal's replies became more and more stilted and evasive; another meeting in a café was cut short by Hofmannsthal, apparently because George had kicked and sworn at a dog. Hofmannsthal refused further meetings and returned some of the books sent to him by George, who accused Hofmannsthal of insulting him and even mentioned a possible challenge to a duel. Hofmannsthal offered a formal apology, but, when George renewed his appeals, could no longer cope with the situation and had to ask his father to intervene. All this within a month. A second, seemingly calmer, phase followed in May, when George returned to Vienna and persuaded

Hofmannsthal to become a contributor to his periodical, *Blätter für die Kunst*. The two poets continued to correspond until 1906.

The shock of this early encounter with an artist diametrically opposed to him in temper and aims can be detected not only in Hofmannsthal's letters but in several of his later works, including his adaptation of Otway's *Venice Preserv'd* (1902–4), which he dedicated to George. Doubtless the shock was increased by the undercurrent of passionate courtship in George's first advances; but it was George's intellectual and moral demands – totally different from anything Hofmannsthal had known in his early friendships with Austrian writers like Arthur Schnitzler, Richard Beer-Hofmann, and Hermann Bahr – that left a deep imprint on his mind and work. Somehow George had succeeded in putting Hofmannsthal in the wrong; it was the younger man who appeared as the traitor, like Jaffier in *Venice Preserv'd*, enfeebled by that 'molluscoid impressionability and luke-warm susceptibility' of which George accused the Austrian artists of the time. 'It was my firm belief,' George complained in 1902, 'that we – you and I – could have exercised a most beneficial dictatorship in our literature for many years'. Hofmannsthal's failure to enter into this partnership – on condition, of course, of a complete acceptance of George's literary programme, which virtually excluded all contact with the *profanum vulgus* not dedicated to the aspirations of the Circle – was ascribed to Hofmannsthal's 'rootlessness'; and, accustomed as he was to social relations governed not by imperious demands for allegiance, but by tact and at least the appearance of mutual tolerance, Hofmannsthal was not always capable of the firmness and bluntness needed to make his own position quite clear. The extent of George's power over him, never as great at George wished or Hofmannsthal sometimes seemed to concede, is most apparent in his choice for a time of the title 'The Reflections, the Cut Stones, and the Speaking Masks' for the projected collection of his poems later published by George; this title, modelled on those of George's books, was reduced to the unpretentious *Selected Poems* before the collection appeared in 1903.

Another effect of the encounter with Stefan George, which assumed a kind of archetypal character for Hofmannsthal, as the first and extreme instance of several others that were to follow, was a gain in self-knowledge. Hofmannsthal began to understand his own need for an organic relationship with society, not for a dictatorship of the artist over his public, but a relationship essentially reciprocal. This need, he also recognized, was distinctly Austrian rather than German; and he became increasingly concerned with the distinction. 'Was George stronger than I?' he reflected in a letter of 1919: 'I don't know, there is too much that's artificial about him, *and he leaves out too much*. In any case, since my eighteenth year I have behaved quite consistently towards him, outwardly placing myself – not him – at a distance, for I had no use for the position of a *coadjutor sine jure succedendi* which he offered me pantomimically; all that was too German – fantastic for my taste – too bourgeois, ultimately and deep down.'

Hofmannsthal's humanism – quite different again from George's ideal of an artistic élite, with its hierarchy of fastidiously but arbitrarily selected exemplars – assumed the peculiarly Austrian form of a desperate attempt to reconcile all the component parts of a disintegrating culture, to re-integrate them rather than subordinate them, and to find that centre which alone could resist the tendency of things to 'fall apart'. To that centre, difficult to define but easy to sense in his writings, Hofmannsthal was committed with a fervour and a constancy that survived all his defeats; but everything was against him. In a centrifugal age the most fantastic and monstrous programme issued by any faction, sect, or party was more likely to attract adherents. The influence of George's exclusive circle radiated outwards, to the universities and the youth movements and into political life, though with consequences neither foreseen nor desired by its begetter. Hofmannsthal, one of the few writers of the time whose political views were determined less by personal prejudice than by a painstaking study of history, political theory, and current affairs, had to be content to be the representative of a 'society that does not exist'. At once liberal and mystical, because rooted in his early intuition of the unity within all diversity, his humanism lacked the appeal of those final solutions offered by the extremists of every colour. Yeats summed up the dilemma once and for all; but, though a gentleman according to Yeats's definition of the gentleman as 'a man whose principal ideas are not connected with his personal needs and his personal success', Hofmannsthal did not 'lack all conviction', only the 'passionate intensity' of monomania.

This dilemma became more acute, and incomparably more painful, in Hofmannsthal's later years, especially during the First

World War, when he undertook several missions of a semi-political kind, and in the post-war period; but his poetic crisis at the turn of the century had a social aspect touching on the dual function of language as self-expression and as a means of communication, and this linguistic crisis, too, was anticipated in many of Hofmannsthal's earlier works, both imaginative and critical. What he called his 'word-scepticism' and 'word-mysticism' are equally striking in an early book review, 'Eine Monographie' (1895): 'For people are tired of talk. They feel a deep disgust with words. For words have pushed themselves in front of things. Hearsay has swallowed the world. . . . This has awakened a deep love for all the arts that are executed in silence.' So much for the 'word-scepticism'; the 'word-mysticism' is its corollary: 'For usually it is not words that are in the power of men, but men who are in the power of words. . . . Whenever we open our mouths, ten thousand of the dead speak through us.' Though a peculiar ambiguity characterized Hofmannsthal's attitude to the social function of language – and indeed to society in general – it is this social aspect of his linguistic crisis that lends it a more than personal significance. The difficult transition from the Romantic-Symbolist premisses to a new classicism, or from individualism to a new impersonality, to put it differently, has confronted most of the major poet-dramatists of this century, from Claudel and Yeats to Eliot and Brecht; and the problem posed so succinctly and drastically in Hofmannsthal's Chandos Letter was an inescapable one.

It is characteristic of Hofmannsthal's works of every period, even the social comedies, that the most crucial thoughts and feelings of his personages cannot be rendered in words, only intimated by gesture, music, or silence; the conventions of speech are masks that conceal more than they convey, or ciphers that must be translated into a medium other than words. 'Form is mask, but without form neither giving nor taking from soul to soul,' Hofmannsthal wrote; and he meant not only form in works of art but the conventions that govern speech, manners, and appearances in life, the phenomenalizing principle.

Poetry, of course, had once had the power to combine both functions of language; but while lyrical poetry 'aspired to the condition of music', dramatic poetry – the public medium – had not evolved a satisfactory substitute for the rhetorical modes of past ages. After abandoning purely lyrical media, Hofmannsthal continued to experiment with adaptations of classical drama, both ancient and modern, before arriving at three distinct, or at least separable, solutions: the allegorical morality play, the fusion of words with music in opera, and the fusion of realistic dialogue with a concealed symbolism. Each of these solutions has its parallels in the practice of other poets – in Claudel's religious and Brecht's political drama, in Yeats's plays that draw on the Japanese Noh conventions, and in Eliot's comedies – and each is an attempt to arrive at a public medium as far removed from outmoded rhetoric as from the complacent trivialities of Naturalism.

'To introduce profundity into the mundane': thus an unpublished jotting defines the distinction at which Hofmannsthal aimed as a writer of comedies. His correspondence with Richard Strauss provides ample comment on the symbolism of his librettos. Hofmannsthal, in fact, was a penetrating critic and interpreter of his own works; and it may be that a writer so complex could not hope to be understood without his own help, which was largely withheld in his lifetime because he loathed self-advertisement and put his faith only in what was 'formed'. Certainly his part in the operas – that of a poet willing to sacrifice his immediate inspirations, though never his basic conceptions, to the requirements of a highly specialized and recalcitrant craft – was constantly belittled, if not despised as a concession to the vulgar; and his practice of 'concealing the depth in the surface', the mystical core of his plays in their social trappings, tended to perplex the mundane while antagonizing the professedly profound. Yet to bridge the gulf between private vision and social involvement, the language of ecstasy and the language of practical life, was no compromise on Hofmannsthal's part; it was his primal need, and the necessary fulfilment of his lyrical pre-existence, to be achieved at whatever cost to his happiness or his reputation. The Servant's speech in *Das kleine Welttheater* prefigures the later course:

> Mit dem ungeheueren Gemenge,
> Das er selbst im Innern trägt, beginnt er
> Nach dem ungeheureen Gemenge
> Äussern Daseins gleichnishaft zu haschen.
>
> .   .   .   .   .   .
>
> With the vast and multitudinous tumult
> That's within him, he begins to clutch at
> All the vast and multitudinous tumult
> Of the outward world, its correspondence. [. . .]

From AN UNOFFICIAL RILKE

... FROM 1910 to 1922 Rilke always insisted that he had lost not only
his way, but his very ability to write, as in a letter of 1915 to Princess
Marie: 'For five years now, ever since *Malte Laurids* closed behind
me, I've been standing around as a beginner, though as a beginner
who can't begin.' As late as 1920 he wrote to Leopold von Schlözer:
'As for work, I've done nothing. My heart had stopped like a clock,
the pendulum somewhere had collided with the hand of wretched-
ness and come to a halt.' Rilke cannot be blamed for his reluctance or
inability to see that there was something to be said for the collision –
a collision, amongst other things, with his own failure to be 'human'
and with facts of life he had used only as raw material to be processed
in his inward laboratory and transmuted into poetry or prose. Yet
where Rilke's earlier verse has become unpalatable for later readers –
and much of it has – it is almost always where Rilke's virtuosity of
feeling encountered too little resistance from the hard real quiddity of
things – and people, for that matter; where, as he confessed in
'Turning-Point', his inwardness had violated them. This was Rilke's
peculiar danger – a facility most conspicuous in his multiple rhyming,
alliteration, assonance – all of them linking devices that suggest
semantic, as well as sonic, affinities – and in the proliferation of simile
in his earlier verse.

Except for a brief period during the war, Rilke's workshop never
closed down for any length of time. His uncollected German poems
of the period after 1908 – and he wrote about half as many in French
– fill more than 500 closely printed pages in volumes II and VI of the
current edition of his collected works. These, admittedly, include
dedicatory verse, drafts, fragments and parts of sequences never
completed. Yet Rilke's failure to recognize or appreciate the excel-
lence of some of these poems is difficult to understand other than
subjectively, in terms of his own loss of faith, his own sense of
disjunction and disorientation. Even his criterion of completeness
and coherence for collections of poems is a somewhat questionable
one, at least in his own case. The *New Poems* are consistent only in
being imaginative penetrations of recognizable persons or things;

beyond that they function as separate poems, not necessarily 'grand' in the sense of nineteenth-century 'grand opera', 'grand piano sonatas', the Cathedral of Berlin or the gigantic statues of Bismarck erected there and in Hamburg; and such late nineteenth-century notions of grandeur, in any case, seem remote from Rilke's aesthetic, if not his social, sensibility at this point in his development. Some of the *New Poems*, like the admirable 'Orpheus. Eurydice. Hermes', also stand out from the collection as a whole because in form, theme and diction they anticipate the very developments associated with his crisis; and the completed *Elegies*, which are supposed to have resolved the crisis, are as much its product and expression as some of the short poems that Rilke virtually suppressed. It is the *Sonnets to Orpheus*, not the *Duino Elegies*, that are truly a post-crisis work; and they came to Rilke as a gift and a bonus, after all his anguish over the writing of the *Elegies*. Significantly, too, they revert to strict metre and rhyme, mastered with the almost complacent ease which the crisis years had called in question.

These crisis years of Rilke's coincided with unparalleled convulsions in the artistic life of Europe, and of Germany in particular, and there can be no doubt that Rilke was affected by them. Just as Rilke dated the onset of his crisis two years before he had conceived the writing of the *Elegies*, and four years before the outbreak of war, the eruption of new styles like Expressionism in Germany, and their counterparts elsewhere, preceded the political cataclysms. Rilke's concern with the work of three of the early Expressionist poets, Trakl, Heym and Werfel, is documented in his letters. All of them took an apocalyptic view of the state of European civilization. At the same period Rilke's attention was drawn to the work of Hölderlin by his acquaintance with Norbert von Hellingrath, who was editing texts by Hölderlin that had never appeared in their authentic form. The impact on Rilke of this discovery is attested not only in Rilke's letters and his poem on Hölderlin, but in the syntactic structure of several of his crisis poems and passages of the *Elegies* (whose dominantly dactylic rhythm may also derive from Hölderlin's elegiacs and hexameters).

Rilke's attitudes to revolutions in the arts, true, were as ambivalent and shifting as his attitudes, at the same period, to revolutions in politics. In 1915 he wrote to a friend: 'What else is our function but to present grounds for change, purely, greatly and freely, – have we performed it so badly, so half-heartedly, so little convinced and convincing?' But there was all the difference, for Rilke, between 'grounds' for change and the changes themselves, when they came to be carried out. His initial sympathy with the Bavarian revolution of 1918–19, which he experienced and watched in Munich, can be traced to its vanishing-point in his letters of those years, even though it was a revolution led by intellectuals whose intentions were undoubtedly 'pure, great and free'. One of the leaders, Gustav Landauer, was as vehemently opposed to Marxism as to capitalism, and a fellow admirer of Hölderlin. Rilke had nothing to say about the manner of his killing by the representatives of 'law and order' – the old order. By December 1918 Rilke, though still hopeful, voiced misgivings about the 'political dilettantism' of the revolutionaries – that was their distinction and their dignity – and wrote: 'By revolution, incidentally, I understand the overcoming of abuses in favour of the deepest tradition.' By this time he had also grown critical – and justifiably so – of the Expressionist movement as a whole: 'The Expressionist, that inward man turned explosive, who pours out the lava of his boiling emotions over everything, insisting that the fortuitous shape assumed by the crust is the new, the future, the valid contour of existence, is nothing but a desperate man.' The noisy, bombastic, expletive literature of later Expressionism, with its patent design on a reader's gut responses, is almost certainly the target of Rilke's poem '... When will, when will, when will they let it suffice' of 1922.

Throughout the war, whose outbreak he had hailed in poems celebrating 'the god of war' – not much in evidence in the trenches, as even Rilke must have realized to his acute embarrassment not long after their publication – Rilke had less to say about its carnage than about the loss of the personal belongings he had left behind in his Paris flat. 'The worst thing' about the war, for Rilke, was that 'a certain innocence of life, in which, after all, we grew up, will never again exist for any of us', as he wrote to Princess Marie in 1915. Another comment of the same year was that 'the world has fallen into the hands of men'. The 'god of war', evidently, had abdicated or failed.

Though interesting historically, a fuller account and analysis of Rilke's odd remarks on current affairs would shed little or no light on any of his poetry. By ceasing to earn his living at about the age of thirty – after his early work as a playwright, occasional lecturer, book reviewer, and his brief employment with Rodin – Rilke had virtually dropped out of economic realities, just as he had dropped out of the domestic realities of marriage and fatherhood, or out of the ties of fixed residence and nationality. (The fact of his Austrian nationality was brought home to him again during the war, with the threat of military service.) From 1912 to 1914 alone Rilke stayed in Paris, Venice, Spain, various parts of Germany, including Berlin, Duino on the Adriatic coast, Venice again, and Assisi. As soon as he could, after the war, he left for Switzerland, a country scarcely affected by the war. He felt as much, or as little, at home in Scandinavia, Russia, Spain, and even North Africa as in any German-speaking country or in France. During and immediately after the war his early prose poem on the love and death in action of an aristocratic ancestor, Cornet von Rilke, became a modest best-seller. When his publisher, who had generously subsidized Rilke for years – as did all the noble or wealthy ladies in whose houses Rilke had stayed for long stretches, the anonymous donor (Ludwig Wittgenstein) of a substantial money award to him, and the Swiss patron who provided him with his last home, Muzot – observed to Rilke in 1921 that if all the published 200,000 copies of *The Lay of the Love and Death of Cornet Christoph Rilke* were placed in a row, it would take a quarter of an hour to walk past them, Rilke's comment, in a letter, was: 'Practical as I am(!), I immediately thought: wouldn't that be a remedy for my cold feet?'

By this time money matters and commercial successes – which had meant a great deal to Rilke in his youth, as his letters to his early publisher Axel Juncker show – had become neither serious nor decent as far as he was concerned; and he also refused a decoration offered to him by the Austrian Government in 1918. In money he saw something like original sin, remarking in a letter of 1914 that it had 'become a thing of the mind or spirit ('geistig')'. Yet money seems to have been redeemed gardens or works of art, like the Picasso painting with which Rilke lived for months in a borrowed flat, transfiguring it into material for one of the *Elegies* – or when its owners had the 'innocence' of those who do not need to earn it.

When Rilke chose to focus his attention on public events and institutions, as he rarely did, he could be a penetrating critic; so in a letter of August 1915, already quoted here, weighing up the responsibility of the press for the lying propaganda that kept the war going.

Probably he had read the brilliant polemic against it by the theologian Theodor Haecker, published in the same annual issue of *Der Brenner* (1915) to which Rilke contributed a poem, and as devastatingly eloquent as any satire by Karl Kraus. The rubbing off on Rilke of Haecker's Kierkegaardian Christian radicalism in this piece would also explain Rilke's remark in his letter about the world's having 'fallen into the hands of men'. Yet, unlike Haecker's, all Rilke's attitudes and positions lead us back ultimately to his 'negative capability' as a poet, to an aesthetic specialization so intense as to subsume all his seemingly religious, ethical or social concerns.

* * *

RILKE's personal crisis – to do with a solitude and human unrelatedness taken on by him in the service of his art, and become not only unbearable, but subject to doubts about his own motives and so about the vocation itself – dominates the poems written from 1912 to 1915. These, in fact, were fruitful and crucial years, too, though Rilke could not admit it, intent as he was on a resolution of the crisis and on the completion of the *Elegies* he had begun at Duino in 1912. The *Elegies* were to have resolved the crisis poetically, if not practically, by balancing lament with the praise that Rilke considered the main function of poets and poetry, while conceding that lament, and even satire, might be the reverse, the dark side of the same celebration. 'Pearls roll away...' is the first of the stark laments that could not break through into celebration; indeed, it breaks off at the lowest point, where personal weakness, the fear of aging and being displaced (by children!) sets up a barrier of what Rilke must have felt to be almost abject pettiness.

More often though, in these crisis poems, as in the *Elegies* also, Rilke's personal confessions and his existential affirmations or negations are inseparable from questions about the function of poetry and poets. That is so in 'The Spanish Trilogy', 'The Spirit Ariel', 'Turning-Point' and most of the other poems of 1913–15. 'The Spanish Trilogy' enters into the very processes of poetry, as Rilke experienced them; complete with his wonderment at the way in which unrelatedness, strangeness, fortuitousness turn into the most intimate self-identification, and even with the awareness – characteristic of his crisis years – that most of his readers will find these processes unacceptable, if not ridiculous, because the poet's self-identification with the Spanish shepherd, or with the strange old men' in the hospice, can make no difference to them or to anyone or to anything, except by another empathetic transference – the act of reading. Rilke abjured his magic by letting readers into the mysteries, the secrets and the tricks; and that links 'The Spanish Trilogy' to 'The Spirit Ariel', also written at Ronda in Spain, Rilke's only real tribute to Shakespeare. (Rilke's bizarre aversion to English poetry and the English language, despite Kassner's prompting, was fully documented, investigated and assessed by Eudo C. Mason in *Rilke, Europe and the English-Speaking World*; as late as 1910 Rilke shocked Kassner by declaring that he had never read *Hamlet*!) Ariel, in Rilke's poem, stands for the inspiration that Rilke felt he had lost but Shakespeare appeared to have renounced graciously, if Shakespeare's self-identification with Prospero can be assumed to have been of the same order as Rilke's with Shakespeare and Prospero in this poem.

The Narcissus syndrome is as relevant to 'Turning-Point' as to the little poem called 'Narcissus' and to 'Waldteich' ('Woodland Pond'). The reciprocity of states of mind with what they reflect had been central to Rilke's work since the *Book of Images* and the *Book of Hours*. Multiple and complex interactions or mirrorings occurred in much other poetry of the period, as in that of Paul Valéry, whom Rilke translated. The operative and most uniquely Rilkean line in this brief interpretation of the Narcissus myth is

> Whatever left him he loved back again,

a formidably compact description of the kind of imaginative loving that Rilke could not abjure without giving up poetry; and 'Turning-Point' is the most radical of Rilke's attempts to face up to its cost to him and others on the level of human relationships.

The smooth rhymed iambics of 'Narcissus' enact the reciprocity, which becomes critical in this poem, being tantamount to self-destruction. 'Turning-Point' and 'Complaint', on the other hand, move with a rhythmic and syntactic freedom close to that of early Expressionist verse or to the 'organic form' evolved by Hölderlin for his late visionary poems. The same freedom, like Hölderlin's influence, distinguishes 'Christ's Descent into Hell'. Even without going into the theological implications of Rilke's rendering of the apocryphal Harrowing of Hell, readers of this poem can hardly avoid being struck by its lack of emphasis on judgement. What Rilke's poem stresses and reiterates are suffering and accomplishment – an expertise, a virtuosity in suffering that shames the torments of Hell.

'Complaint' (or 'Lament', as it could have been called) introduces the angels more familiar from the *Duino Elegies*, symbols of transcendence it is wisest to interpret not theologically but poetically, in terms only of Rilke's own system of infinite transmutation and metamorphosis. Much the same power to shatter and to transform is attributed to women in the poem 'A Man Has to Die . . .', as in many poems of Rilke's, because his world is one without hierarchic divisions between the natural and the supernatural. His resistance to such divisions has a bearing on his admiration in early years for what one might call the applied Christianity that impressed him in Russia and on his later sympathy with Islamic devotion. In a letter of 1915 he remarked to Princess Marie: 'For what is it I am seeking so desperately, if not the one point, the Old Testament point, at which the dreadful converges with the utmost greatness'; and he goes on to write: 'For one thing is certain, that the most divine consolation inheres in the human itself: we shouldn't know what to do with the consolation offered by a god; but our eye would have to grow just a little more seeing, our ear more receptive, the flavour of a fruit would have to come home to us more completely, we should be able to bear more smell, and have more presence of mind, be less forgetful, in touching and being touched – ; and at once we should derive consolations from our most immediate experiences, consolations more convincing, more preponderant, more true than all the suffering that can shake us.' Rilke's Old Testament poem 'The Death of Moses', written a few months after this letter, is also a search for the point where 'the dreadful converges with the utmost greatness', where the divine and the human meet in a relationship of intimate familiarity at once sensuous and spiritual. Hölderlin, in Rilke's poem to him, is praised for a similar capacity to reduce the distance between Heaven and Earth. Rudolf Kassner, in another essay, pointed out that Rilke never made the transition from the 'world of the Father' to the 'world of the Son', that he remained 'unconverted' in a special sense given to the word by Kassner – and incapable of grasping the full significance of sacrifice. The Kassner epigraph to 'Turning-Point' and the dedication to him of the Eighth Duino Elegy testify to Rilke's awareness of this crux, though his 'turning' never amounted to what Kassner meant by conversion. Such metanoia would have demanded the sacrifice of his poetry, or at least of the kind of poetry at which Rilke excelled. As Rilke's late 'Gong' poems show – he wrote another in French – he continued to explore the borders of sensuous perception, to a point of such refinement that the sensuous seems to fuse with the spiritual.

The ironic, bitter poem 'Death' represents the negative side of Rilke's celebrations, like the related passage about the 'modiste, Madame Lamort' in the Fifth Duino Elegy. The poem is negative about the negation and trivialization of death – which to Rilke meant a corresponding negation and trivialization of life – in the contemporary world. Here death becomes the very reverse of the great event rendered in 'The Death of Moses'.

By 1922, and the fragment beginning 'As long as self-thrown things', Rilke was emerging from the crisis, though that poem is as thorough in its exposure of his poetic weakness – his dangerous facility, rooted in narcissism – as the crisis poems had been of his human ones. In its rhythmic structure too, and in its self-propelling, self-propagating metaphors, it comes close to reading like a parody of Rilke's own earlier manner. Rilke was never afraid of exposing himself to ridicule, and quite capable of laughing at himself. Even his absurdities and mannerisms were wholly his own, never adopted to impress others or for the sake of being 'different'. Like most major artists, Rilke incorporated several minor ones: his whimsical and mischievous wit, for instance, may be less conspicuous in the official canon than in poems like the one about his mother or in 'Will-o'-the-Wisps', though even the *Elegies* are not as consistently solemn as they have been made out to be. He was capable of an extraordinary formal range and adventurousness, confronting energies or realities, whether outward or inward, that endangered his mastery. The poems of the early twenties have a new delicacy, lightness of touch and self-detachment, even a new playfulness in the self-portraiture of 'My shy moon-shadow . . .'.

The next crisis was Rilke's last, that of his slow death by leukaemia. A last legend, too, was put into circulation, to accord with Rilke's epitaph for himself and his conviction that one should have a death of one's own, just as one has a life of one's own: the legend that his illness was due to being stung by the thorn of a rose. In his last poem, though, the legend plays no part. Rilke's religion of aesthetic contemplation and metamorphosis is put to its ultimate test not in images of the self-sufficient rose but in images of burning, of being consumed by pain; and Rilke rises even to this event, by celebrating it not as his end but as one more transmutation. Touchingly and bravely, he includes notes for a recasting or continuation that will differentiate this last experience from early ones, childhood illnesses that did not disrupt the continuity of selfhood, memory and consciousness.

[Verzicht. Das ist nicht so wie Krankheit war
einst in der Kindheit. Aufschub. Vorwand um
grösser zu werden. Alles rief und raunte.
Misch nicht in dieses was dich früh erstaunte]

．　．　．　．　．

[Renunciation. Not what illness was
in childhood once. Postponement. Pretext for
a growing-up. When all things called, urged on.
That early wonderment, keep it out of this]

Unlike the epitaph, this parenthetical codicil is not exquisite, finished, or metaphysically suggestive; but it proves beyond doubt that Rilke's existential dedication to art was total and wholehearted even in the face of death, down to a last scruple and discrimination. That was truthfulness, too, and heroism of a kind.

From GEORG TRAKL

OF ALL the early Expressionists, Trakl was the least rhetorical and the least dogmatic; and he was an Expressionist poet only in that he was a modernist poet who wrote in German. Expressionism happened to be the name attached to modernist poetry written in German; but Trakl would not have written differently if there had been no movement of that name. Nor did he have any contact with the initiators of the movement, all of whom were active in Berlin; whatever he had in common with Hoddis, Lichtenstein, Heym, and Benn, he owed to the *Zeitgeist*, not to any programme or theory. If Trakl had written in English – but, of course, it is inconceivable that he should have done – he would have been called an Imagist, though it is most unlikely that he ever heard or read this word. Neither label is very useful, but Imagist would at least have the virtue of indicating the most distinctive characteristic of Trakl's art; all poets express themselves, but Trakl expressed himself in images. To treat Trakl's poems as self-expression, that is to say, as fragments of an autobiography, is to misunderstand them; for Trakl's dominant aspiration was to lose himself.

Trakl has also been called an Existentialist; and I have already alluded to the intimate, though obscure, connection between an existential mode of thought and imagist practices. Just as Existentialists tend to leap straight from the bare condition of existence to the absolute – God, if they believe in Him, Nothing if they do not – so imagist poets deal with bare phenomena in the form of images, not as an ornament added to what they have to say, or as a means of illustrating a metaphysical statement, but as an end in itself. The mere existence of phenomena is their justification; and to understand their Being is to understand their significance. The poetic image, then, becomes autonomous and autotelic' or as nearly so as the medium of words permits. It follows that the pure imagist technique is likely to break down as soon as a poet wishes to convey truths of a different order from the ontological; and that is one reason why nearly all the poets who once practised a purely imagist technique either modified or abandoned their practice. Poetic statements bearing on religious dogma, on ethics, history, and social institutions require such a modification, since the pure image is unrelated to all these spheres.

Every interpretation of Trakl's works hinges on the difficulty of deciding to what extent his images should be treated as symbols – to what extent they may be related to the spheres named above. This, of course, raises the question of his beliefs, for belief comes into play as soon as we attempt to 'interpret' an image at all; a purely existential image has no meaning other than itself. Since Trakl undoubtedly lent a symbolic significance to his images – or to some of them at least – these two basic questions are bound to be raised. Trakl's poetry is so essentially ambiguous – so 'laconic', as one of his interpreters has observed – that many different interpretations of its symbolism are possible. The most one can hope to do is to avoid too heavy a personal bias toward one symbolism or another; and to allow each reader to make his own choice.

Georg Trakl was born at Salzburg on 3 February 1887. His mother, née Halik, was the second wife of Tobias Trakl, a prosperous ironmonger who belonged to a Protestant family long established in this Roman Catholic city. Both the Trakl and Halik families were of Slav descent; the Trakls had originally come from Hungary, the Haliks – much more recently – from Bohemia. The family house at Salzburg, with its old furniture, paintings and statuary, as well as the family garden in a different part of the city, contributed images to many of Trakl's poems, especially to the sequence 'Sebastian in Traum'. The whole of Salzburg – or Trakl's vision of it – is present in much of his work; it is the 'beautiful city' of his earlier poems, a city in decay because its present does not live up to its past.

It is difficult to say whether Trakl's childhood was as melancholy and as lonely as his retrospective poems suggest. From accounts of him by his school friends it appears that he showed no signs of extreme introversion until his late adolescence; and the first part of 'Sebastian in Traum' is a vision of childhood that can no more be reduced to factual narrative than any other poem of Trakl's, for all its references to identifiable objects:

> Mutter trug das Kindlein im weissen Mond,
> Im Schatten des Nussbaums, uralten Holunders,
> Trunken vom Safte des Mohns, der Klage der Drossel;
> Und stille
> Neigte in Mitleid sich über jene ein bärtiges Antlitz,

Leise im Dunkel des Fensters; und altes Hausgerät
Der Väter
Lag im Verfall; Liebe und herbstliche Träumerei.

Also dunkel der Tag des Jahrs, traurige Kindheit,
Da der Knabe leise zu kühlen Wassern, silbernen Fischen
    hinabstieg,

Ruh und Antlitz;
Da er steinern sich vor rasende Rappen warf,
In grauer Nacht sein Stern über ihn kam;

Oder wenn er an der frierenden Hand der Mutter
Abends über Sankt Peters herbstlichen Friedhof ging,
Ein zarter Leichnam stille im Dunkel der Kammer lag
Und jener die kalten Lider über ihn aufhob.
Er aber war ein kleiner Vogel im kahlen Geäst,
Die Glocke lang im Abendnovember,
Des Vaters Stille, da er im Schlafe die dämmernde Wendeltreppe
    hinabstieg.

                    .   .   .   .   .   .

Mother bore this infant in the white moon,
In the nut-tree's shade, in the ancient elder's,
Drunk with the poppy's juice, the thrush's lament;
And mute
With compassion a bearded face bowed down to that woman,

Quiet in the window's darkness; and ancestral heirlooms,
Old household utensils
Lay rotting there; love and autumnal reverie.

So dark was the day of the year, desolate childhood,
When softly the boy to cool waters, to silvery fishes walked down,

Calm and countenance;
When stony he cast himself down where black horses raced,
In the grey of the night his star possessed him.

Or holding his mother's icy hand
He walked at nightfall across St Peter's autumnal churchyard
While a delicate corpse lay still in the bedroom's gloom
And he raised cold eyelids towards it.

But he was a little bird in leafless boughs,
The church bell long in dusking November,
His father's stillness, when asleep he descended the dark of
    the winding stair.

On the evidence of these lines it has been suggested that Trakl's mother must have been a drug addict, like her son! But narcotics and intoxicants, in Trakl's poetry, are associated with original sin. Drunkenness, traditionally, began after the Flood, when men were so far removed from their first state that life became unbearable without this means of escape. For the same reason it is with compassion that the father's bearded face looks down at the mother of this poem.

Trakl seems to have been fond of both his parents and at least one of his five brothers and sisters, Margarete, who became a concert pianist and settled in Berlin. Much has been made of Trakl's attachment to this sister, for critics of the literal persuasion insist on identifying her with the sister who appears in his poems; but neither the references to incest in Trakl's early work nor the personage of the sister in his later poems permit any biographical deductions. Incest is one of many forms of evil that occur in Trakl's work; and the personage of the sister is a kind of spiritual alter ego, an anima figure, so that in certain poems a brother-sister relationship symbolizes an integration of the self. Trakl used many other legendary or archetypal personages in his poetry; not to write his autobiography, but to compose visionary poems of an unprecedented kind.

As a boy, Trakl shared Margarete's love of music and played the piano with some skill. At school, on the other hand, he proved less than mediocre. When he failed his examinations in the seventh form, he was unwilling to sit for them again and decided that he was unfit for the professional or academic career originally planned for him. For a time he received private tuition at home. An Alsatian governess taught him French; and he took this opportunity to read the French poets, especially Baudelaire, Verlaine, and Rimbaud. Other influences on his poetry are those of Hölderlin, Mörike, and Lenau; and his thought was decisively influenced by Kierkegaard, Dostoievsky, and Nietzsche. When, toward the end of his life, he decided to do without books, it was the works of Dostoievsky with which he found it hardest to part. Already at school Trakl belonged to a literary club. Toward the end of his school years he grew taciturn, moody, and unsociable; he began to speak of suicide, drank immoderately, and drugged himself with chloroform. The career he now chose, that of a dispensing chemist, gave him easy access to more effective drugs for the rest of his life.

From 1905 to 1908 Trakl was trained for this career in his native town. During this time, two of his juvenile plays were publicly performed; *Totentag*, acted in 1906, was something of a *succès de scandale*; *Fata Morgana*, a one-act play put on later that year, was an unqualified failure. In the same year Trakl began to contribute short dramatic sketches and book reviews to a local paper. He left Salzburg in October 1908, to complete his training at the University of Vienna, where he took a two-year course in pharmacy. His hatred of large cities dates from this period. At this time he worked at a tragedy, *Don Juan*, of which only a fragment remains, and at an extant puppet play on the Bluebeard theme. After his second year in Vienna, during which his father died, Trakl entered on one year's military service as a dispensing chemist attached to the Medical Corps; he was posted to Innsbruck, then back to Vienna, but took the earliest opportunity of being transferred to the Reserve.

In 1912 he considered emigrating to Borneo; but in the same year he began to write his best work and met his patron, Ludwig von Ficker, in whose periodical *Der Brenner* most of Trakl's later poems first appeared. It was mainly owing to Ficker's friendship and support that Trakl was able to devote the remaining years of his life to the writing of poetry. In January 1913 he accepted a clerical post in Vienna, but returned to Innsbruck after three days' work. Except for a number of other journeys – to Venice, Lake Garda, various parts of Austria, and Berlin, where he visited his sister Margarete and met the poet Else Lasker-Schüler – and three more abortive attempts to work for his living in Vienna, Trakl moved between Innsbruck and Salzburg till the outbreak of war. In 1913 Trakl's first book, a selection of his poems made by Franz Werfel, was published by Kurt Wolff; a second collection appeared in the following year.

By 1913 Trakl had become a confirmed drug addict. In December of that year he nearly died of an overdose of veronal; but in spite of this and his alcoholic excesses, his physical strength remained prodigious, as various anecdotes testify. A prose poem, 'Winternacht', derives from one of Trakl's own experiences: after drinking wine near Innsbruck, he collapsed on his way home and spent the remainder of the night asleep in the snow – without suffering any ill effects. In July

1914, Ludwig von Ficker received a considerable sum of money – 100,000 Austrian crowns – with the request to distribute it as he thought fit among contributors to *Der Brenner*. Trakl and Rilke were the first beneficiaries; but when Herr von Ficker took Trakl to the bank to draw part of the grant, Trakl's good fortune so nauseated him that he had to leave the bank before the formalities had been completed. Long after the event Ficker revealed the identity of Trakl's and Rilke's patron; he was the philosopher Ludwig Wittgenstein, who gave away most of his inheritance at this time. Later, Wittgenstein wrote to Ficker about Trakl's poetry: 'I don't understand it; but its *tone* delights me. It is the *tone* of true genius.'

Late in August 1914, Trakl left Innsbruck for Galicia as a lieutenant attached to the Medical Corps of the Austrian army. After the battle of Grodek Trakl was put in charge of ninety serious casualties whom – as a mere dispensing chemist hampered by the shortage of medical supplies – he could do almost nothing to help. One of the wounded shot himself through the head in Trakl's presence. Outside the barn where these casualties were housed a number of deserters had been hanged on trees. It was more than Trakl could bear. He either threatened or attempted suicide, with the result that he was removed to Cracow for observation as a mental case. His last poems, 'Klage' and 'Grodek', were written at this time.

Trakl now feared that he, too, would be executed as a deserter. According to the medical authorities at Cracow he was under treatment for *dementia praecox* (schizophrenia); but his treatment consisted in being locked up in a cell together with another officer suffering from delirium tremens. During this confinement Ludwig von Ficker visited Trakl and asked Wittgenstein, who was also serving in Poland, to look after Trakl; but Wittgenstein arrived too late. After a few weeks of anguish, Trakl took an overdose of cocaine, of which he died on 3rd or 4th November 1914. It has been suggested that he may have misjudged the dose in his state of acute distress; this was the opinion of his batman, the last person to whom Trakl spoke.

APART from his juvenilia – poems, plays, and book reviews – Trakl's work consists of some hundred poems and prose poems written between 1912 and 1914, the year of his death at the age of twenty-seven. The horizontal range of these poems is not wide; it is limited by Trakl's extreme introversion and by his peculiar habit of using the same operative words and images throughout his later work. But Trakl's introversion must not be mistaken for egocentricity. 'Believe me,' he wrote to a friend, 'it isn't always easy for me, and never will be easy for me, to subordinate myself unconditionally to that which my poems render; and I shall have to correct myself again and again, so as to give to truth those things that belong to truth.' Trakl's inner experience is objectified in images and in the symbolic extension of those images; his concern, as he says, was with general truths and with the rendering of general truths in a purely poetic manner. For that reason, the melancholy that pervades his work was only a premiss, not the substance, of what he wished to convey; it is as important, but no more important, than the key of a musical composition. It was certainly a limitation of Trakl's that he could compose only in minor keys; but the same could be said of Leopardi and of other lyrical poets whose poetry conveys a distinct mood. Nor should Trakl be assessed in terms of optimism and pessimism, categories that are largely irrelevant to his vision. As Rilke was one of the first to point out, Trakl's work is essentially affirmative; but what it affirms is a spiritual order that may not be immediately perceptible in his poems, filled as they are with images pertaining to the temporal order that he negated.

'Trakl's poetry,' Rilke wrote, 'is to me an object of sublime existence ... it occurs to me that this whole work has a parallel in the aspiration of a Li-Tai-Pe: in both, falling is the pretext for the most continuous ascension. In the history of the poem Trakl's books are important contributions to the liberation of the poetic image. They seem to me to have mapped out a new dimension of the spirit and to have disproved that prejudice which judges all poetry only in terms of feeling and content, as if in the direction of lament there were only lament – but here too there is world again.' This tribute is especially important for two reasons; because of Trakl's influence on Rilke's own work, and because Rilke interpreted Trakl's poetry existentially when other critics, less close to Trakl's way of thought, read it as a record of Trakl's morbid states of mind. As late as 1923, in a letter to Ludwig von Ficker, Rilke reaffirmed his admiration for Trakl's poetry. What Rilke meant by 'world' in the letter cited is what professional Existentialists would call 'being' and he believed that it is the poet's business to affirm whatever aspect of being is manifested to him, whether it be bright or dark. The mood is incidental; what matters is the intensity of the poet's response to the world and his ability to render his perceptions in words and images. Rilke always insisted that praise and lament are not mutually exclusive, but complementary functions; for lament, too, is a kind of affirmation, a way of praising what is lost or unattainable, a way of accepting the limitations of human life or even – in a sense different from that intended by Blake – of 'catching a joy as it flies'. That is why dirges and laments are a traditional form of poetry, though poetry, by the same tradition, is always affirmative. Within the bounds of a Christian orthodoxy that has very little in common with Rilke's private existential creed – but rather more with Trakl's beliefs – the poet's dual function in an imperfect world emerges from George Herbert's lines in 'Bitter-sweet':

> I will complain, yet praise,
> I will bewail, approve;
> And all my sowre-sweet dayes
> I will lament, and love.

It was Rilke's insight, then, which directed the attention of Trakl's readers away from the categories of optimism and pessimism and toward that 'truth' which Trakl himself thought more important than his own predicament. As the work of so many of Trakl's contemporaries shows, optimism can be just as morbid a symptom as pessimism, because there is a kind of optimism that is a hysterical perversion of the truth; its premisses give it the lie. Trakl, on the other hand, wrote of what he knew; he was true to his premisses, and these premisses were positive enough.

The temporal order that Trakl's poems negate was that of materialism in decay. That is the significance of the decaying household utensils in the first part of 'Sebastian im Traum'. To this order, Trakl opposed an existential Christian faith akin to Kierkegaard's and an unreserved compassion akin to that of certain characters in Dostoievsky. All this is implicit in Trakl's poetry, since he rarely stated or defined his beliefs, but translated them into images. Yet all the external evidence supports this interpretation of his beliefs; and, shortly before his death, Trakl handed the following short note to Ludwig von Ficker: '(Your) feeling at moments of deathlike existence: all human beings are worthy of love. Awakening, you feel the bitterness of the world: in that you know all your unabsolved guilt;

your poems an imperfect penance.' Because poetry is an imperfect penance, Trakl castigated himself to the point of self-destruction.

What Trakl lamented was not the fact or the condition of death, but the difficulty of living in an age of cultural decline and spiritual corruption. The immediate background of Salzburg, an ancient and beautiful city unable to live up to its past, was one element in his melancholy, though it does not account for his own obsession with guilt and death. 'No,' he wrote as early as 1909, 'my own affairs no longer interest me'; and in 1914 – after his breakdown on active service – 'already I feel very nearly beyond this world'. The dead who people his poems – the mythical Elis, for instance – are more vivid, more full of life, than the living. In the poem 'An einen Früh-verstorbenen' ('To One who Died Young'), the surviving friend is haunted by the other who

> ... ging die steinernen Stufen des Mönchbergs hinab,
> Ein blaues Lächeln im Antlitz und seltsam verpuppt
> In seine stillere Kindheit und starb;
> Und im Garten blieb das silberne Antlitz des Freundes zurück
> Lauschend im Laub oder im alten Gestein.
>
> Seele sang den Tod, die grüne Verwesung des Fleisches ...
>
> .   .   .   .   .   .
>
> ... walked down the stone steps of the Monchsberg,
> A blue smile on his face and strangely cocooned
> In his quieter childhood, and died;
> And the silvery face of this friend remained in the garden,
> Listening in leaves or in ancient stone.
>
> Soul sang of death, the green putrefaction of flesh ...

It is the dying friend who smiles, the survivor who becomes obsessed with death and decay. The reason, it appears from other poems, is that those who die young preserve 'the image of man' intact; wherever they appear in Trakl's poems they are associated with righteousness and with images of the good life; and this, in turn, is associated with an earlier stage of civilization, opposed to modern life in the large cities. One thinks of Rilke's cult of those who died young; but Trakl's dead are symbolic of a state of innocence that cannot be identified with youth or childhood, or even with a rustic and pastoral stage of civilization. It is an innocence that precedes original sin. That is why, in his poem on the Kaspar Hauser legend, Trakl describes the murdered boy as 'unborn'. Kaspar Hauser is murdered as soon as he reaches the city, after living in the woods in a wild state. The whole poem is an allegory of the relation between innocence and death, not, as one might easily think, a glorification of a 'noble savage' murdered by the corrupt inhabitants of the city.

Trakl, of course, can be criticized for his inability to bear the guilt of being alive. Shortly before his death he said of himself that as yet he was 'only half born'; and he did not want his birth to be completed. . . .

THE DIFFICULTY of summing up Trakl's work as a whole, and the much greater difficulty of interpreting it as a whole, are two reasons why his work stands out from the German poetry of his time. Trakl's plagiarisms – and especially his self-plagiarisms – lend a deceptive consistency to his work – deceptive, because his poems are essentially ambiguous. His ambiguities derive from the tension between image and symbol, the phenomenon and the Idea. Sometimes this tension remains unresolved, so that one cannot tell whether an image is to be taken descriptively or symbolically, an epithet synaesthetically or qualitatively. It is true that each of Trakl's poems offers some kind of clue to the next; but it is a clue that can be very misleading.

Trakl's ambiguities are not deliberate or cerebral; he was an imaginative poet, not a fanciful one. That is why his plagiarisms are never disturbing or offensive. His debt to Hölderlin alone was such that, by all the usual criteria, his work should be very nearly worthless. He appropriated Hölderlin's imagery, rhythms, and syntax; yet Trakl's originality is beyond doubt. Any group of three lines detached from one of his later poems is immediately recognizable as his own. Trakl carried plagiarism farther by continually quoting himself, repeating, varying, and adding to his earlier poems. But there is no reason why a poet should not steal his own property in order to rearrange it; and this very habit points to the harmlessness of Trakl's borrowings from other poets. The laws of property do apply to literature, insofar as no writer can deliberately steal what he lacks himself and get away with the swag; but they do not apply to the imagination. The imagination can only borrow, never steal; and, by its very nature, it can only borrow those things to which it has a right.

Trakl's debt to Hölderlin is a curiosity of literature; it does not mean that his symbolism can be interpreted in terms of Hölderlin's or that his vision begins where Hölderlin's left off. Heidegger not only presupposes such a tradition of vision and prophecy, but reads his own philosophy into Hölderlin and applies this reading to Trakl. The result is a fascinating, but ruthless, gesture, which sweeps away all evidence of Trakl's own thought in order to turn him into the prophet of an Occident regenerated by the philosophy of pure being. It is true that existential creeds tend to look alike, especially if they have been expressed in poetry alone; and Trakl's Christian faith was an existential one. But this faith is essential to his poetry, as most of his critics agree. Heidegger's exegesis would not have been possible at all but for Trakl's imagist practice; because of the non-committal character of imagism, it would also be possible to argue that Trakl was an alchemist (as his astrological metaphors confirm!) or a Marxist (because of his vision of capitalism in decay!).

In an age of conflicting creeds and sects, such openness is an advantage. Horizontally, Trakl's range is that of a minor poet, but his vertical range is out of all proportion to it. By 'vertical' here I mean neither profundity nor sublimity, but a dimension related to harmony in music. Trakl's poetry is a series of microcosmic variations, poor in melodic invention, rich in harmonic correspondences. Another way of putting it is to say that his work is valid on many 'levels' of meaning. It depends as little as possible on the poet's person, opinions, and circumstances. One reason is that Trakl was conscious neither of himself nor of his reader; all his poems had his undivided attention. Of T. S. Eliot's 'three voices of poetry', Trakl had only the first; but because it never even occurred to him to cultivate the others, his monologue was strangely quiet and pure.

From GOTTFRIED BENN

... BENN'S REVIVAL of the doctrine of Art for Art's sake – which he
called '*Artistik*' – is simply another aspect of his denial of 'reality', of
moral and political institutions, of the importance of history, of all
that men achieve by conscious endeavour. 'Works of art,' he has writ-
ten, 'are phenomena, historically ineffective, without practical conse-
quences. That is their greatness', and '*Artistik* is the attempt of Art to
experience itself as a meaning within the general decay of all mean-
ing, and to form a new style out of this experience; it is the attempt of
Art to oppose the general nihilism of values with a new kind of tran-
scendence, the transcendence of creative pleasure. Seen in this way,
the concept embraces all the problems of Expressionism, of abstract
art, of anti-humanism, atheism, anti-historicism, of cyclicism, of the
'hollow man' – in short, all the problems of the world of expression.'
    The doctrine itself is not new; it goes back to Nietzsche and, with-
out its conscious connection with nihilism, to the German Romantics
and the French Parnassians, Symbolists and Naturalists. Mallarmé
and Villiers de l'Isle-Adam went as far as Benn in their disparagement
of 'reality'. In his Oxford lecture on music and literature, Mallarmé
said: 'Oui, que la Littérature existe, et, si l'on veut, seule, l'exclusion
de tout.' Benn has not done better than that; but Mallarmé was a
devout Platonist and only denied reality in favour of the Idea. Art,
therefore, was truly transcendental, not 'autotelic', like a kitten chas-
ing its tail. Mallarmé's disparagement of 'reality' was a gesture of
sublime scorn that makes Benn's pronouncement sound like the
crudest of simplifications; the difference is in the diction. Mallarmé's
words, too, occur in a lecture, but that was no reason for making them
any clearer or any more direct; to do so, would have been a shameful
concession to the very 'reality' that they scorn: 'Un grand dommage
a été causé à l'association terrestre séculairement, de lui indiquer le
mirage brutal, la cité, ses gouvernements, le code, autrement que
comme emblèmes ou, quant à notre état, ce que des nécropoles sont
au paradis qu'elles évaporent: un terreplein, presque pas vil.' One
may disagree with that statement, one may even smile at it, but one
must respect it in spite of oneself; other men may dismiss human

institutions as a brutal mirage, but no one, ever again, will have the courage and the composure to pronounce the 'presque pas vil' that qualifies the condemnation.

It always the qualifications that one misses in Benn's pronouncements. Paul Valéry, too, believed that the outstanding characteristics of true works of art are their uselessness and their arbitrariness; he speaks of the artist's 'useless sensations' and 'arbitrary acts'. But he continues: 'The invention of Art has consisted in trying to confer on the former a kind of usefulness; on the latter, a kind of necessity.' Because it lacks the necessary qualifications, Benn's statement about the nature of works of art invites contradiction. It is simply untrue to say that works of art are historically ineffective; they have proved to be most effective in modern times, and nowhere more so than in Germany. If Benn meant to say that they ought to be historically ineffective, his statement would be provocative, but valid as a definition of their nature, as opposed to their function; and the same qualification applies to his statement that they have no practical consequences. As for his definition of *Artistik*, it is the definition of a vicious circle; for the 'general nihilism of values' which he wants Art to transcend has been largely brought about by those who – like himself – are out for the destruction of these values. It is only Benn's wholly specious determinism that allows him to regard nihilism as a biological, historical or otherwise general predicament. Nor was Benn true to his own premises; for he persistently advocated nihilism as an attitude to life, in terms no less didactic than those of any preacher or humanist. The very word transcendence in that context is meaningless. All that Benn's definition conveys is the fact that human nature abhors a vacuum; for, after denying the seriousness of every human pursuit, he insists that the game which is his own substitute for these pursuits is not only serious, but 'transcendent'. *Artistik* is a pathetic attempt on Benn's part to climb out of the nihilistic pit that he has dug for others. But reality is indivisible. Art may be a fungus that thrives on the decay of other values, as Benn would have it, but even decay presupposes growth; and Benn would have his fungus grow in the dry dust of organisms which, according to him, were dead even before he began to write.

Perhaps one ought not to take Benn's theories and critical pronouncements too seriously; but though he believed in 'absolute prose' and 'the absolute poem, the poem without faith, the poem without hope, the poem addressed to no one, the poem made of words which you assemble in a fascinating way', he was also what Valéry called a *poète de la connaissance*, a poet who deals in ideas as much as in words and images.' And Valéry also said that 'every true poet must necessarily be a critic of the first order'. If Benn's 'absolute poem' were possible in practice, one could leave his theories alone and confine one's attention to the way he assembles words. But words have a habit of conveying meaning; and when these words are made public, they also have the 'practical consequence' of being a means of communication, as well as their essential function of merely existing as 'Significant Form' (and even form is *significant*, even where we prefer not to say of what). If Benn had not wished to communicate anything, he would have kept his work to himself; and he would certainly not have troubled to explain the creative process to others, or to defend his own premisses with such stubborn persistence. It is therefore necessary to point out a few of the basic inconsistencies that result from Benn's false premisses and his egocentric habits of thought.

What Benn means by 'absolute prose' is a kind of prose whose primary function is expressive, rather than logical. For that reason, his critical essays may suddenly modulate from sober exposition to prose poetry, or even to verse thinly disguised as prose. The following is a passage of this type from an early essay:

> Vier Jahrtausende Menschheit sind gewesen, und Glück und Unglück war immer gleich: Wende dich ab von deinem Nächsten, wird die Lehre sein, wenn jetzt die Memnonsäule klingt.
>
> .   .   .   .   .
>
> Four thousand years of human kind have passed, their fortune and misfortune still the same: to turn your back upon your neighbour, will be the doctrine now, when next old Memnon's statue sounds.

This is a new departure in prose, and an admirable one; it relieves the tedium of prose rhythms and the stale vocabulary of criticism. But even if this passage is addressed to no one, or to Benn himself, it is undoubtedly didactic: it proclaims a philosophy of cyclic recurrence – borrowed from Nietzsche – that is 'anti-historical' and 'anti-humanistic'; and it specifically invites the (nonexistent?) addressee to turn his back upon his neighbour – in explicitly anti-Christian terms.

Benn has done his best to dissociate himself from the commandment, by attributing it to Memnon's oracular statue; but he would need a more subtle device to be able to disclaim responsibility for the doctrine.

Another passage of 'absolute prose' from his essay 'Das moderne Ich' of 1920, renders the isolation and introversion of the modern poet:

> Erloschenes Auge, Pupille steht nach hinten, nirgends mehr Personen, sondern immer nur das ich; Ohren verwachsen, lauschend in die Schnecke, doch kein Geschehnis, immer nur das Sein.
>
> .   .   .   .   .   .
>
> Extinguished eye, the pupil turned about, no persons anywhere, but always only the Ego; ears closed to sound, listening into the helix, but no event, always only being.

It is with amazement, therefore, that one reads Benn's dictum of 1928 that 'poets are the tears of the nation', words quite incomprehensible in the context of Benn's work; but they occur in a tribute to a dead writer and friend, on one of the few occasions where Benn leaves the prison of his own ego not in order to sneer, but to praise. One has to make similar allowances for many of Benn's critical utterances, first ascertaining whether they refer to himself or to others. When he says that 'God is a bad stylistic principle', he is criticizing others; when he says that 'God is form', he is justifying himself, on the same grounds on which he has asserted that 'style is superior to truth'. Style, however, is not superior to truth, but inseparable from it; that is why Benn is capable of stylistic lapses no less offensive than his half-truths.

On page 53 of his *Ausdruckswelt* (1949), Benn argues that the State has no right to complain of the damage done by artists as long as it wages wars that kill off three million men in the space of three years; on page 107 he writes: 'In my opinion, the West is not being destroyed by the totalitarian systems or the crimes of the S.S., nor by its material impoverishment or its Gottwalds and Molotovs, but by the dog-like grovelling of its intellectuals before the political concepts.' The blatant contradiction between these two statements can only be understood by allowing for Benn's extraordinary dialectic: in the first instance Benn is referring to intellectuals like himself under a régime hostile to them, in the second to intellectuals hostile to him under a different régime. The real question, of course, is whether or not writers are responsible for what they write; but this is not a question that Benn cares to answer in either context, since he wants one law for himself, another for those whom he dislikes.

Benn's 'anti-historicism' is another case in point. His whole view of life and art is based on the assumption that nihilism is a *fait accompli* and that the destructive trends in contemporary Europe are a biological phenomenon. Such a view cannot possibly be called 'anti-historical', though it substitutes a biological determinism for both the religious and the humanistic conceptions of history. His 'anti-historicism' is really an aesthetic doctrine and, more particularly, an excuse for his own addiction to exotic fantasies. This becomes clear from a remark in his 'Roman des Phänotyp': 'Remote things are much nearer to one than things that are near; indeed, the things that are present are strangeness itself.' What Benn is against is not the historical view, but the encroachment of the present on his consciousness. It suited Benn to see himself as a link in that process of 'progressive cerebralization' which he associated with the 'odour of annihilation and burnt flesh pervading the century' and, ultimately, with the end of the 'cycle' known as Western civilization. He made it clear enough that he found this odour stimulating artistically; and that his 'transcendental' pleasure in art was none other than the pleasure of fiddling while Rome burns. Benn himself described his method of composition as a 'prismatic infantilism. It probably reminds everyone of children's games: we ran about with small pocket mirrors and caught the sun, to cast its reflection on shopkeepers on the other side of the road, arousing anger and ill feeling, but we ourselves kept in the shade.'

As a method of composition, this game is beyond criticism; it has led to delightful colour effects in prose and verse. One only wishes that Benn had really 'kept in the shade'; but he continually drew attention to himself, now to show off his naughtiness, now to protest his innocence. This is the disadvantage of a childish attitude to society: however resourceful and inventive, a child's naughtiness remains dependent on adult standards, and on the adults' capacity to be annoyed. Benn's lapses of style and taste are due to a childish egocentricity, a childish lack of tact. His attitude to society remained unchanged since the 1920s, when he wrote in 'Zwischenreich':

    ... die Massenglücke
    sind schon tränennah,
    bald ist die Lücke
    für die Trance da.

        .   .   .   .   .

    ... mass pleasures, mass joy
    are closer to tears,
    already a gap clears
    for trance to break through.

Trance certainly did break through about a decade later; but when
Benn discovered that this general trance was not conducive to his
private one, it never seems to have occurred to him that his attitude
called for revision. Writing of Berlin in 1947, he describes the ruined
city, its starving population, and the luxuries imported by the occu-
pation forces; and continues: 'The population looks on greedily
through the windows: culture is advancing again, little murder, more
song and rhythm. Inwardly too the defeated are well provided for: a
transatlantic bishop arrives and murmurs: my brethren; – a humanist
appears and chants: the West; – a tenor wheedles: O lovely Art, – the
reconstruction of Europe is in progress.'

The bad taste of that observation is especially offensive because 'O
lovely Art' is also a summary of Benn's own creed; and since he
regarded art as a drug, he had no grounds at all for thinking his own
variety superior to any other. The value of a drug is measured by its
effectiveness. The same moral obtuseness permitted him to enumer-
ate the misfortunes of his own family in the Preface to his
Ausdruckswelt, a work in which he elaborates his anti-humanism and
criticizes the Nazi régime on no other grounds than its lack of 'style'
and its lack of understanding for the independent artist. If the reader
accepts Benn's standards, he must reject this account of Benn's
family as irrelevant; if he sympathizes with Benn or with Benn's
family, he must reject Benn's standards. This question of sympathy
arises frequently over Benn's prose works, strange mixture of fact and
fantasy, statistics and self-confession that they are. It is peculiarly
irritating to be asked for sympathy on one page, only to have it
violently rejected on the next, when the pervading mood of cynical or
stoical toughness takes over from a passing mawkish one.

Benn is Baudelaire's 'dandy' up to date, *au fait* with all the
sciences and even with the newspapers; Benn too 'ne sort jamais de

soi-même'. But the dandy was only one of Baudelaire's *personae*; Baudelaire was also the 'homme des foules', who could lose himself in others and complete himself. Like every great poet, he contained a moralist. Benn's chief limitation as a poet and critic was that nearly all his thinking was determined by a reaction against one thing or another – against literary or ideological fashions, against a bourgeoisie already hard pressed from other directions, or against his own better nature; but reaction is only a different sort of dependence. Always to be sneering at the vulgar is a sort of vulgarity.

With very few exceptions – the essay 'Goethe und die Natur-wissenschaften' is an outstanding one – Benn's prose writings are not an exploration of other minds, but comments on his own practice and justifications of his own attitude. He even found it necessary to assure his readers that he was human by writing an account of his 'double life' (*Doppelleben*), here the difficulty of reconciling his two selves – the conscientious doctor and the amoral artist – proved insuperable and involved him in arguments too silly and too casuistic to bear repetition. The sharp self-awareness that results from self-division enabled him to write brilliantly about the creative process, as experienced by himself; particularly in 'Probleme der Lyrik'. His belief in 'absolute' prose and poetry – that is, in prose and poetry written for their own sake, without a primarily didactic purpose – had the very salutary effect of opposing the tendency, still very widespread in Germany at the time, to think that poetry is only a matter of expressing sublime sentiments in regular stanzas. He made up for the early Expressionists' indifference to questions of form and diction; but he did so with an exclusive emphasis on art as self-expression – or rather as self-indulgence – which may well have repelled readers more squeamish than he.

Benn's writings are highly exhilarating and abysmally depressing in turn, as befits an intoxicant. They can induce a euphoria of infinite possibilities, which results from the total release of energy from the bonds of reason; and a corresponding hangover, when Benn returns to himself and reminds us that despair is the mother of all his inventions. Self-pity is the chink in Benn's armour, as in Nietzsche's, who also dramatized his solitude, though with more justification than Benn; for in spite of his claim to the contrary, Benn's solitude was less extreme than Nietzsche's, if only because Nietzsche had already charted the place. Benn himself has summed up his dilemma; but for 'we' read 'I': 'We lived something different from what we were, we wrote something different from what we thought, we thought something different from what we expected; and what remains is something different from what we intended.'

It is probably too early to say what will remain of Benn's work; generally, one is inclined to agree with him, that which was farthest from his intentions, farthest from the tedious dialectic of nihilism. In view of his professed aestheticism, one might expect his poetry to have the consistent quality of – say – Valéry's, Stefan George's or, of his own generation, Trakl's; but even Benn's aesthetic standards are curiously unreliable. Almost every one of his collections contain pieces that are not only grossly inferior to his best work, but simply unformed – cerebral jottings in loose free verse or mechanical rhyme that all too clearly communicate something – Benn's concern with his own ego or with ideas not realized poetically. Again it is Benn who has indicated the reason, in one of the few passages of a late work that qualify his earlier views: 'Nihilism as the negation of history, actuality, affirmation of life, is a great quality; but as the negation of reality itself, it means a diminution of the ego.'

But, as his last collections show, Benn continued to diminish his ego by perpetuating the quarrel between subject and object which – however fruitful a field for metaphysicians – is full of dangers for modern poetry. I have already said that all poetry, whatever its theme, affirms life; it does so because form itself is the progeny of the marriage of mind and matter. Only the unformed poem, the bad poem, can be negative. That is why Benn's 'subjectivity' is depressing; subjectivity did not become odious until the first ego asserted its independence from the external world; Pascal's *moi haïssable* was the direct consequence of the *cogito ergo sum* of Descartes. The ego has been growing more and more odious since, because more and more interested in its own reflection in the mirror. Benn's nihilism and Winckler's 'affliction of thinking' are the recoil of consciousness from a mirror that has lost its mercury and become a blank prison wall.

Very little of Benn's work breaks down this prison wall; but what little of it does so derives a special importance from the point where this breach is made. *Ex nihilo nihil fit*; if Benn's best poems seem to contradict this maxim, it is because they affirm life despite their author's intention. (And of course it is nonsense to affirm 'reality' without affirming life, as Benn claims to have done, unless by life he means only some particular mode or manifestation of life, an environment he dislikes.) The poems of Benn's best period, the early nineteen-twenties, are almost consistently remarkable; but only two or three of them are faultless. The difference has to do with truth as much as with style; for the fault is always due to the intrusion of irrelevant ideas and inessential phenomena into a poem that ought to have been purely imaginative; and these ideas and phenomena always appertain to Benn's immediate environment. The most blatant of these faults is the introduction of abstract neologisms and scientific terms – witty, and therefore self-conscious – where they have no business to occur. I refer to such new compound words as *Bewusstseinsträger* (consciousness-bearer), *Satzbordell* (sentence brothel) and *Tierschutzmäzene* (Maecenases of the RSPCA) and of scientific terms like *Selbsterreger* (auto-exciter), used in the manner of clever journalism. These words – and many more of the same kind – appear in Benn's most outstanding collection of poems, his *Spaltung* of 1925. Of the twenty-eight poems in this book, only one is wholly free from such satirical irrelevances; and one or two more are successful in spite of them, because the tension between myth and modernity is essential to them.

These poems, unfortunately, are the least translatable, precisely because they are the nearest possible approximation to Benn's ideal of 'absolute poetry'. As an example of the fruitful tension between myth and modernity – and of a single line that is 'absolute' in the sense of being pure music – I shall quote the opening stanza of 'Die Dänin':

> Charon oder die Hermen
> oder der Daimlerflug
> was aus den Weltenschwärmen
> tief dich im Atem trug,
> war deine Mutter im Haine
> südlich, Thalassa, o lau –
> trug deine Mutter alleine
> dich, den nördlichen Tau –

Benn has never written with greater mastery than at this time and in this medium – poems in trochaic or sprung rhythms, in short lines with alternating feminine and masculine rhymes. The poem quoted, as it happens, is one positive even in theme, a poem in praise of a Danish girl, which affirms the present as well as the mythical past,

Greece and Scandinavia; because of this affirmation, there is no incongruity in the 'Daimlerflug' of the second line. The line of 'absolute poetry' to which I alluded – 'südlich, Thalassa, o lau' – is an elliptical rendering of the whole Mediterranean and tropical complex so rich in associations for Benn; he is particularly addicted to the 'au' sound and therefore evokes a vision of blue skies and seas. And indeed the colour itself presents itself without fail in the next stanza:

> meerisch lagernde Stunde,
> Bläue, mythischer Flor . . .

In the later stanzas, unfortunately, the tension between past and present is heightened almost to breaking point, again out of a self-conscious ingenuity, a virtuosity bordering on the specious:

> Philosophia perennis
> Hegels schauender Akt: –
> Biologie und Tennis
> über Verrat geflaggt.

Benn's tendency to be distracted into the merely topical or into abstract slogans would not matter so much if it were confined to separate poems like the jazzy, polyglot, and obscene 'Banane-', though even this poem detracts from the others by parodying them. Benn summed up his purpose at the time in the phrase *trunken cerebral* (drunkenly cerebral); his poems break down where they become cerebral without being drunken.

This is always due to his basic self-division, which assumes the guise of a conflict between inward and outward reality. When this conflict becomes too acute, the mind cries out for its own dissolution or for the destruction of the world. Most of his poems of this period dwell on the second possibility; but where they do so with sufficient intensity, the conflict itself is reconciled and Benn's very nihilism becomes an affirmation of life. So in 'Namenlos', 'Spuk', and – most flawlessly of all – in 'Palau'. True, what 'Palau' affirms is a biological life force, 'bestial' and indestructible; but its philosophical implications are suspended, because it never lapses into cerebral abstractions:

> 'Rot ist der Abend auf der Insel von Palau
> und die Schatten sinken –'
> singe, auch aus den Kelchen der Frau
> lässt es sich trinken,

Totenvögel schrein
und die Totenuhren
pochen, bald wird es sein
Nacht und Lemuren.

Heisse Riffe. Aus Eukalypten geht
Tropik und Palmung,
was sich noch hält und steht,
will auch Zermalmung
bis in das Gliederlos,
bis in die Leere,
tief in den Schöpfungsschoss
dämmernder Meere.

Rot is der Abend auf der Insel von Palau
und im Schattenschimmer
hebt sich steigend aus Dämmer und Tau:
'niemals und immer'
alle Tode der Welt
sind Fähren und Furten,
und von Fremdem umstellt
auch deine Geburten –

einmal mit Opferfett
auf dem Piniengerüste
trägt sich dein Flammenbett
wie Wein zur Küste,
Megalithen zuhauf
und die Gräber und Hallen,
Hammer des Thor im Lauf
zu den Asen zerfallen –

wie die Götter vergehn
und die grossen Cäsaren,
von der Wange des Zeus
emporgefahren –
singe, wandert die Welt
schon in fremdestem Schwunge
schmeckt uns das Charonsgeld
längst unter der Zunge –

Paarung. Dein Meer belebt
Sepien, Korallen,
was sich noch hält und schwebt,
will auch zerfallen,
rot ist der Abend auf der Insel von Palau,
Eukalyptenschimmer
hebt in Runen aus Dämmer und Tau:
niemals und immer.

       .   .   .   .   .

'Evening is red on the island of Palau
and the shadows sink –'
sing, from woman's chalices too
it is good to drink,
deathly the little owls cry
and the death-watch ticks out
very soon it will be
lemures and night.

Hot these reefs. From eucalypti there flows
a tropical palm concoction,
all that still holds and stays
also longs for destruction
down to the limbless stage,
down to the vacuum,
back to the primal age,
dark ocean's womb.

Evening is red on the island of Palau
in the gleam of these shadows
there issues rising from twilight and dew:
never and always';
all the deaths of the earth
are fords and ferries,
what to you owes its birth
surrounded with strangeness –

once with sacrificial
fat on the pine-wood floor
your bed of flames would travel
like wine to the shore,
megaliths heaped around

434 · *Gottfried Benn*

and the graves and the halls,
hammer of Thor that's bound
for the Aesir, crumbled, falls –

as the gods surcease,
the great Caesars decline,
from the cheek of Zeus
once raised up to reign –
sing, already the world
to the strangest rhythm is swung,
Charon's coin if not curled
long tasted under the tongue –

Coupling. Sepias your seas
and coral animate,
all that still holds and sways
also longs to disintegrate,
evening is red on the island of Palau,
eucalyptus glaze
raises in runes from twilight and dew:
never and always.

'Palau' transcends nihilism not because it is 'absolute' in any sense invented by Benn, but rather because in it Benn has found the precise 'objective correlative' for his state of mind. The poem, therefore, is positive, even if the state of mind is not; it is a poem of tragic affirmation and, as such, requires no reference to the author's intentions or beliefs. Benn's best poems succeed in spite of his theories, because he could not keep reality out of them. He could be indifferent to the meaning of his poetry and to its effect on others; he could disclaim responsibility for it on the grounds that he had no other purpose than to express or please himself; but he could not prevent the isolated fact and the autonomous fantasy from returning to the indivisible reality of which they are parts. He could banish his mind to an island, but he could not make that island disappear from the universe.

Gottfried Benn is one of the very few Expressionist poets who did their best work during Phase II, the inter-war years. It was not till his incantatory poems of the nineteen-twenties that he learned to avail himself of the new freedoms and to combine them with a discipline peculiar to his work. 'Palau' makes good use of the dynamic syntax of Expressionism, but its form is much closer to that of the choric poems in Goethe's *Faust* than to any verse form cultivated by the other Expressionists.

With Benn's later work – that of the period which he called Phase II and I have called Phase III of Expressionism – I can deal only very briefly here. Already his *Statische Gedichte*, a collection of poems written mainly between 1937 and 1947, contains poems in at least three distinct styles: the incantatory style of 'Palau', a more sober neoclassical style – sometimes clearly derivative from Goethe's later lyrics, as in the poem 'Ach, der Erhabene' – and a self-consciously 'modern' style mainly confined to poems in loose free verse. These three styles recur in Benn's last collections.

But for his prose works of the same period, which remained as provocative as his earlier ones, it would be clear to everyone that what Benn calls 'Phase II' is no more than an 'aprèslude' to Expressionism. Indeed, even his late prose works are not quite as belligerent as the earlier, though one has to read between the lines – or skip a good many – to arrive at the truth about a development that Benn did his best to resist. His *Drei Alte Männer*, published in 1949, belongs to a genre especially dear to Benn, being a peculiar mixture of fact and fantasy, prose lyricism and polemical journalism. The three old men of the title meet at the house of one of them to reflect on their experiences of the past, discuss their attitude to the present, and prove their superiority to the future – in the shape of a young man whose main function is to prompt the main speakers. These speakers are not sufficiently differentiated to qualify as distinct characters; their dialectic is that of Benn's own mind; and their preoccupations those which we know to be his own. Many of their utterances are mere reiterations of the nihilistic or aesthetic commonplaces familiar enough from the earlier works. 'God is a drug', for instance; 'the only thing that really belongs to us is what we drink'; or 'we only live when we forget'. But there is also a new note, a mood of melancholy resignation and hopeless courage. 'We were a great generation,' one of them says: 'sorrow and light, verses and weapons, sorrow and light, and when night comes, we shall endure it.' The nihilism is unchanged, but it has lost its dynamism, its ecstasy, and its aggressiveness. These old men too speak of the 'occidental finale: to believe that something exists', but instead of mocking this belief – as Benn did a decade earlier, in his *Weinhaus Wolf* – they attribute the greatness of Western man to its recurrence after every possible kind of breakdown. The main trend of *Drei Alte Männer* is toward a stoical acceptance of the worst: 'To err, and yet to be compelled to renew his belief in his own inner motives, that is man; and beyond both victory and defeat his fame begins.'

Die Stimme hinter dem Vorhang ('The Voice Behind the Curtain'), a later work by three years, is also a conversation piece. The voice is that of the Father; and 'the programme is: what does the progenitor say to his sons and daughters – nowadays.' A number of 'examples' – presumably meant to be representative of these sons and daughters – give accounts of themselves. There is a man of sixty whose chief aim in life is to commit adultery with young women; an old-age pensioner who is content to let the government provide for him and hopes that 'the others will die' before his turn comes; a woman who keeps a brothel that caters for all tastes; and a landlord who is obsessed with different ways of exploiting and cheating his tenants without infringing the law. When they first appear, these characters profess the belief that 'what is holy is manifested in all things'. In the second part, various sons and daughters confront the Father with a Sunday paper, which provides them with opportunities to poke fun at such institutions as modern democracy, psychoanalysis, and the PEN Club. Their taunts and complaints culminate in more serious accusations, but mainly that of cruelty and indifference to their well-being. To every charge the Father replies: 'Well, what do you expect,' but finally loses patience and roars out a string of coarse insults that put an end to the discussion. The third conversation takes place two months later, when the 'examples' reappear with a Chorus; they accept the fact that 'the Old Man too has left us in the lurch' and decide to make do without him. Once again, resignation is their last resort: 'To live in the dark, in the dark to do what we can.'

In *Monologische Kunst –?* (1953) – an exchange of letters between Gottfried Benn and the Austrian poet Alexander Lernet-Holenia – Benn answers his correspondent's objections to this unorthodox morality play. He argues that faith is a gift which has not been granted to him; that he does not deny the existence of a Creator, but that a 'distant' relationship to Him is preferable to one that 'exploits God' by too immediate a dependence. 'To gape at Him continually with eyes and lips, in my view, is a great offence, for it presupposes that we mean something to Him, while my veneration assumes that He only passes through us with some force, with very limited force, and that it then passes on to something other than ourselves.' Lernet-Holenia also tells Benn that 'it is time you began to speak to the Nation', proposing the example of Hofmannsthal and warning Benn that it was solitude that brought about Nietzsche's ruin. Benn defends both Nietzsche's solitude and his own; but after rightly distinguishing between Nietzsche's solitary habits and his mental isolation from the community, he proceeds to confuse the issue by a discussion of his own personal habits. Benn affirms that he will not try to emulate the cultural rôle of Hofmannsthal, a rôle for which he was wholly unfitted; but he does qualify his earlier insistence on the totally isolated ego. He admits a certain invisible link between one ego and another, as he must after professing belief in the Creator. 'Express your I,' he concludes, 'and you will be passing on your life to the Thou, passing on your loneliness to the community and the distance.'

Both in *Monologische Kunst –?* and another late prose work, *Altern als Problem für Kunstler* (1954), Benn still insisted on the antinomy between truth and style. The last fifty years, he claimed in the essay on Nietzsche appended to the former work, were marked by strange movements, 'above all, by those that have done away with truth and laid the foundations of style'. In the later work, an interesting investigation of the effect of old age on artistic production, he repeated that 'art, of course, isn't concerned with truth at all, only with expression'. But 'style,' one of his old men says, 'is exaggeration; expression is arrogance and suppression: by such foul methods the mind proceeds'. Literature, to Gottfried Benn, remained a form of self-indulgence, the most effective of the drugs that make life bearable. It is therefore of the same order as any other stimulant or narcotic, such as crime, which one of his characters recommends for similar reasons: 'And indeed only crime gets us any farther.'

There is something admirable as well as pathetic about these attempts of Benn's to cheer himself up and startle his readers with squibs kept in storage for thirty years or more; but the poem knows better than the poet, and much of Benn's later poetry contradicts this obstinate clinging to his function of *enfant terrible* and *fort esprit*. Of Benn's three styles in his collections of the nineteen-fifties the neoclassical was a neutral, impersonal style almost free from the more drastically expressive syntax of his modernist phase. Many of the best poems in *Fragmente*, *Destillationen*, and *Aprèslude* are of this kind, regardless of theories that Benn continued to expound. 'Blaue Stunde', for instance, is a love poem, clearly addressed to someone and someone other than Benn himself. All of them communicate something that would be valid even if translated into prose. The lessons of recent history are implicit everywhere behind the stoical despair – tinged with remorse in 'Die Gitter' or even with compassion in 'Denk der Vergeblichen'.

The informal free-verse poems, on the other hand, may look like a reversion to Benn's earliest mode, to the manner of *Morgue*, *Söhne* and *Fleisch*. Yet Benn's unacknowledged change of heart is even more striking in these informal pieces than in the best of the neoclassical poems, such as 'Der Dunkle', 'Jener' and 'Eingeengt'. The informal, less general and less abstract diction of the free-verse poems admits not only direct personal experience but the historical consciousness that Benn had done his best to oppose and exclude in the inter-war years. Indeed, the deliberate prosiness of his late free verse is at the opposite pole to 'absolute poetry', as defined by Benn or by his French predecessors. It is close to the practice of Brecht and to that of younger poets writing after World War II. Part of the poem 'Spät' (in *Destillationen*) corresponds word for word with a passage in the prose dialogue *Die Stimme hinter dem Vorhang*. Whereas in the earlier phase Benn's prose had tended to erupt into lyricism, in the later phase quite a number of his poems tended toward the rhythms, diction, and syntax of prose. So in 'Ideelles Weiterleben?' ('Ideal Survival?'):

> Bald
> ein abgesägter, überholter
> früh oder auch spät verstorbener Mann,
> von dem man spricht wie von einer Sängerin
> mit ausgesungenem Sopran
> oder vom kleinen Hölty mit seinen paar Versen –
> noch weniger: Durchschnitt,
> nie geflogen,
> keinen Borgward gefahren –
> Zehnpfennigstücke für die Tram,
> im Höchstfall Umsteiger.

Dabei ging täglich soviel bei dir durch
introvertiert, extrovertiert,
Nahrungssorgen, Ehewidrigkeit, Steuermoral –
mit allem musstest du dich befassen,
ein gerüttelt Mass von Leben in mancherlei Gestalt.

Auf einer Karte aus Antibes,
die ich heute erhielt,
ragt eine Burg in die Méditerranée,
eine fanatische Sache:
südlich, meerisch, schneeig, am Rande hochgebirgig –
Jahrhunderte, dramatisiert,
ragen, ruhen, glänzen, firnen, strotzen
sich in die Aufnahme –
Nichts von alledem bei dir,
keine Ingredienzien zu einer Ansichtskarte –
Zehnpfennigstücke für die Tram,
Umsteiger,
und schnell die obenerwähnte Wortprägung:
überholt.

        .   .   .   .   .

Soon
a sawn–off, out–of–date
man who died early or may–be late,
of whom one speaks as of a singer
whose soprano is worn out
or of poor little Todhunter and his handful of verses –
even less: average,
never flew in a plane,
never drove a Borgward –
pennies paid out on the tram
a return fare at the most.

Yet daily so much passed through you
introverted, extroverted,
money troubles, marriage vexations, tax morality –
with all these you had to concern yourself,
a full measure of life in many a shape.

On a postcard from Antibes
which I received today

a castle looms over la Méditerranée,
a fanatical object, that:
southerly, snowy, marine, alpine at the edges –
centuries, dramatized,
loom, rest, gleam, glaze, swell
into the photograph –
Nothing of all this about you,
no ingredients at all for a picture postcard –
pennies paid out on the tram
return fares,
and quickly then the above-named caption:
out of date.

The person, as well as the subject, of that poem is the man whom
Benn had once relegated to a life separate and distinct from that of
the 'absolute' poet. Although Benn retained his habit of addressing
himself in the second person, the autobiographical character of the
poem is as unmistakable as its concern with an order of reality, the
empirical and worldly, which Benn's ecstatic poem of the nineteen-
twenties had negated or dissolved in an inward flux. The relaxation
of this poem's gesture is carried to the point of slackness, as in the
placing of the word 'man' (line 4) so close to the 'Mann' of line 3 in
stanza one.

Another reversal of Benn's premisses and assumptions occurs in
the late poem 'Menschen Getroffen' ('People Met'), which not only
admits but celebrates the 'neighbour' so consistently banished from
his earlier works. But for those premisses and assumptions Benn's
belated recognition here that other people exist might seem so naïve
or perverse as to make the reader wonder not at those people but at
the poet's wonderment:

Ich habe Menschen getroffen, die,
Wenn man sie nach ihrem Namen fragte,
Schüchtern – als ob sie garnicht beanspruchen könnten,
Auch noch eine Benennung zu haben –
'Fräulein Christian' antworteten und dann:
'Wie der Vorname,' sie wollten einem die Erfassung erleichtern,
Kein schwieriger Name wie 'Popiol' oder 'Babendererde' –
'Wie der Vorname' – bitte, belasten Sie Ihr Erinnerungsvermögen
    nicht!

Ich habe Menschen getroffen, die
Mit Eltern und vier Geschwistern in einer Stube
Aufwuchsen, nachts, die Finger in den Ohren,
Am Küchenherde lernten,
Hochkamen, äusserlich schön und ladylike wie Gräfinnen –
Und innerlich sanft und fleissig wie Nausikaa,
Die reine Stirn der Engel trugen.

Ich habe mich oft gefragt und keine Antwort gefunden,
Woher das Sanfte und das Gute kommt,
Weiss es auch heute nicht und muss nun gehn.

.   .   .   .   .

I have met people who, when asked what their names were,
Apologetically, as if they had no right to claim one's attention
Even with an appellation, would answer,
'Miss Vivian,' then add, 'Just like the Christian name';
They wanted to make things easier, no complicated names
Like Popkiss or Umpleby-Dunball –
'Just like the Christian name' – so please do not burden your
     memory!

I have met people who grew up in a single room together with
Parents and four brothers and sisters; they studied by night,
Their fingers in their ears, beside the kitchen range;
They became eminent,
Outwardly beautiful, veritable *grandes dames*, and
Inwardly gentle and active as Nausicaa,
With brows clear as angels' brows.

Often I have asked myself, but found no answer,
Where gentleness and goodness can possibly come from;
Even today I can't tell, and it's time to be gone.

What matters is that Benn continued to develop as a poet until his death at the age of seventy – even while denying the change of heart which made that development possible. Benn's 'Phase III' of Expressionism may strike us as a reluctant retreat from a position that history had made untenable, but the retreat did carry his poetry over into the post-war, post-Expressionist and post-modernist era, as well as enabling others to bridge the same gap; and as Benn wrote in his 'Epilogue' (1949) to his early and late work:

Leben ist Brückenschlagen
über Ströme die vergehn.

   .   .   .   .   .

Life is the building of bridges
over rivers that seep away.

In a different and more crucial sense, it is Benn's earlier, exclu-sively and frenziedly expressive work that is regressive, because its intensity was attained at the cost of reason and consciousness, the emotional drive channelled as narrowly as possible to produce the more energy. Unlike the singing voice of Benn's more ecstatic poems – those written in the nineteen-twenties – the speaking voice of the late free-verse poems is that of a civilized man, aware of history, of society, of the little realities that make up our outward lives. Whether he acknowledged it or not, Benn had seen or sensed the connection between absolute art and absolute politics, alike in their total rejection and elimination of all that is not grist to their mill, and the poet had learned the lesson, even if the essayist and public speaker had not. Seen as a whole, Benn's poetry has the full range and tension of those perennial contraries Reason and Energy, realism and imagination, phenomenon and idea; and he produced rather more than the 'six or eight consummate poems', which he claimed to be all that a poet of his time could achieve. [. . .]

EXPLORERS: MUSIL, KAFKA

From *Explorers: Musil, Robert Walser, Kafka*

... WHEN ROBERT MUSIL died in 1942 he was almost forgotten both in his native Austria and in Germany, where he had spent the most active years of his adult life. Difficult though it is to be sure about the effect of exile on the progress of his long novel, his letters and journals suggest that it was considerable. Whereas the earlier letters and journals communicate the literary and philosophical interests which one would expect them to communicate, those of Musil's Swiss exile are little more than variations, now brave, now disconsolate, on the need for money. Added to these material worries and the humiliation of a great writer reduced to dependence on charity, there was the condition of exile itself.

'Imagine a buffalo,' Musil wrote in the last year of his life, 'whose mighty horns have been replaced by a different skin formation, in fact by two ludicrously sensitive corns. This creature of the mighty brow, which once bore weapons and now bears corns, is the man in exile. If he was a king, he talks of the crown he once possessed and feels that people doubt that it was so much as a hat; indeed in the end he himself doubts whether he still has so much as a head on his shoulders. It is a wretched, but just as much a ridiculous, and therefore a doubly wretched, situation.' The various associations of anti-Nazi writers abroad did little to remedy this cruel and unjust neglect of his works, despite the efforts of Thomas Mann himself. As Musil knew well, his work, by its very nature, could be appreciated only by a readership that did not yet exist; he himself called a collection of his later short prose pieces 'literary remains in my lifetime'.

It is Musil's earlier works, from his first short novel *Die Verwirrungen des Zöglings Törless* (1906) to the stories and the plays, that are unmistakably experimental – so much so that Musil was often included among the Expressionists. His unfinished *magnum opus*, *Der Mann ohne Eigenschaften*, seemed more objective, more realistic and more analytical than the early works, as though Musil – in typically Austrian fashion – had made his peace with tradition, or even with convention. In her brief foreword to the third volume of the English edition, Eithne Wilkins pointed out that English readers 'have shown a tendency to regard *The Man Without Qualities* as primarily, if not wholly a satirical work, and largely to ignore certain aspects of it'. Since the satirical aspects were most conspicuous in the earlier parts of the novel, these were more immediately acceptable to readers and critics accustomed to the social preoccupations of English novelists. Wilkins rightly felt that the third volume would confront such readers and critics with unexpected difficulties.

As for Musil's metaphysical and psychological interests – apparent enough, but not too obtrusive in the earlier volumes – the invocation of names like Proust or Thomas Mann served to palliate their disturbing novelty. In certain respects, the Musil of these two volumes seemed a more conventional novelist than either Proust or Mann; his narrative did not show the modern obsession with past time or with the stream of consciousness, his diction was sober and factual beside the self-conscious rhetoric or the post-Joycean exercises of Mann. Even his scepticism and his little speculative digressions had their counterparts in Aldous Huxley's early novels, his satirical acerbity in those of Evelyn Waugh.

Yet all these analogies are deceptive. The essentially complex structure even of the early volumes is evident as soon as we ask ourselves what Musil thought about any general phenomenon treated in his book; about love, for instance, or more precisely about the relationship of the sexes. In spite of the little treatises so liberally interpolated in his narrative, we shall be quite unable to pin Musil down to a simple answer. Instead, we find a whole scale of possible kinds of love, from Ulrich's simple desire for Leontine to his more complex feelings for Bonadea, thence through subtle gradations that can be traced in his dealings with Diotima and Gerda, to the intense Platonism of his relationship with Agathe. It is not that Musil's answers were ambivalent as Mann's were; the crucial difference is that Musil wrote novels in order to discover what he thought and felt about human life, not to expound a thesis. Even the little digressions are essays in the sense that they are tentative; as such they partake of the essentially experimental, exploratory nature of Musil's writing.

The relations between other characters are similarly graded, from that between Soliman and Rachel to that between Diotima and Tuzzi, Diotima and Arnheim, Clarisse and Meingast, thence to the terrible correspondence between the perversions of Moosbrugger and the perversions of Clarisse, between the highest and lowest planes. No conceivable gradation is missing, except for a certain gap in the middle register; this could only have been filled by a marriage relationship less extraordinary than that between Walter and Clarisse, more complete than that between Tuzzi and Diotima. Another way of putting it would be to say that Musil never presents us with a final synthesis; but to do so would have offended against the very principle of openness that was Musil's distinction and risk. Even if Musil had lived to complete his masterpiece, it would have been left to the reader to draw the final conclusions. In spite of its wealth of ideas – indeed because of this wealth of ideas, their multiplicity, complexity and subtlety – *The Man Without Qualities* should never be read as a *roman à thèse*. Like a human life, it moves on many levels towards a destination that can be guessed at, but never foretold with certainty – even by the author. Its characters develop according to their own laws, not according to a superimposed scheme. Nor did Musil have Proust's advantage of a circular frame, for his novel is directed towards the future as much as towards the past.

The early volumes do not even raise the question of ultimate direction. We can respond to the various entanglements as we respond to those in our own lives, without troubling too much about where they will lead; and Musil's lightness of touch – that irony utterly different from Mann's, which he himself was sorry to miss in the later parts – maintains the illusion of comedy as few of us are capable of maintaining it in our own lives. The Collateral Campaign proceeds from absurdity to absurdity; Ulrich becomes lightly involved with Gerda, the Fischel family and Gerda's circle of 'Christiano-Germanic' youths. They, in turn, introduce us to a whole complex of 'super-rational and sub-rational' impulses which, two decades later, will crystallize into a national creed. Moosbrugger emerges into greater prominence, as do Clarisse and, eventually, the 'prophet' Meingast, whose activities on the super-rational plane correspond to Moosbrugger's on the sub-rational. Mann's *Dr Faustus* presents obvious thematic parallels: but Musil does not need to resort to the far-fetched framework of a poetic myth, nor to the *alter ego* of a bourgeois and philistine narrator, to ensure that the 'demonic' will be acceptable.

Musil has no public commitments. We may laugh at all his characters, or at none. Where other writers use irony as a means of cunningly manipulating the reader's sympathy, while pretending to be impartial, Musil's irony is open, generous and uncalculating, a proof of real greatness and subtlety of mind.

It is the third volume of the English edition that permits no escape from the recognition that Musil was an experimental novelist in a very special sense; not merely an innovator in diction, chronological sequence or presentation of character – Musil had been all these in his earlier works – but as a writer whose very conception of reality was an experimental one. His hero was a 'man without qualities' precisely because his qualities had to be acquired in the course of the novel's development. In this respect the work is close to the German type of the *Bildungsroman*; but what distinguishes it from any earlier example is that the hero does not proceed from a given way of life to a different one, either chosen or imposed, but begins with the complete rejection of every existing system and code, and moves on to no predictable solution. Ulrich is an experimental hero in this special sense; and the novel could almost be described as utopian in its search for a reality so new as to involve the risk of eluding both its hero and its creator. Musil's intellectual daring was scarcely matched among the novelists of his time. Even his social satire, the monstrous unfolding of the Collateral Campaign, makes little sense until we relate it to this central concern with a reality and a way of life yet to be discovered.

The point of view implicit in satire is usually that of common sense, or else of a definite ideological commitment; but Musil's scepticism – akin only to that of his compatriot Wittgenstein among contemporary thinkers – was so free from either that it could turn at any moment into its opposite, the mysticism which so many readers find it hard to reconcile with the satirist's mundane poise. The subtitle of the third volume, 'Into the Millennium', is significant in its ambiguity; for it applies equally to the increasingly futile exertions of the Collateral Campaign, that is, to Musil's satirical intentions, and to Ulrich's increasingly daring experiments in the perfecting of love. Ulrich's absorption in his newly discovered sister Agathe seems to conflict with his involvement in the campaign; but there are subtle parallels between the political developments on the one hand, Ulrich's personal life and intimate thoughts on the other.

Detached and individualistic though he seemed, Musil never lost the Austrian – as distinct from the German – writer's sense of being rooted in a community. 'On this frontier between what goes on inside us and what goes on outside,' Ulrich observes to Agathe, 'there's some communicating link missing nowadays, and the two spheres only transform into each other with enormous losses in the process.' The search for this missing link is one of the unifying themes of the novel. (And *Vereinigungen* had been the title of the two long stories that Musil published in 1911.) Ulrich makes this remark when Agathe has threatened to commit an *acte gratuit* which is also a criminal act – one of the significant parallels between the planes of individual and corporative behaviour in the book, for the Collateral Campaign has also reached the stage of resolving to act for the sake of action.

His penetrating insight into the psychology of politics was one of Musil's foremost distinctions; when he says of Walter's 'over-stimu-lated surrender to faith' in the specious prophet Meingast that it was 'one of the elementary needs for passion that life nowadays breaks up into little fragments, and jumbles up until they are unrecognizable', he is also commenting on the later political mania that drove Musil himself out of Austria. Something of this desperate need for faith and commitment attaches even to Ulrich's experiments in mystical love and mystical religion; even here the satirist and social critic in Musil are inseparable from the seeker after new experiences and a new truth. Though his scepticism is never suspended in these later sections of the book, Musil too was trying to overcome what he called 'the modern superstition that one must not take anything too seri-ously'. Needless to say, there is all the difference in the world between the Millennium proclaimed by political fanatics and Ulrich's Millennium of 'the sort of love that has no goal, that isn't like a flowing stream, but like the sea – a state of existence'. Yet Musil never forgets the common predicament from which the two very different possibilities arise. The essential difference, he seems to suggest, is that the highest faith must spring from the highest degree of doubt; and this doubt is not discarded for the sake of the faith, but merged in it. 'We shall cast off all egoism,' Ulrich goes on to say of his Millennium, 'we shall not accumulate possessions or knowledge or lovers or friends or principles, not even ourselves'; but even this programme is no more than an experiment, and Ulrich wonders whether 'he was blaspheming or being fanciful'.

That Musil did not live to finish his novel is not the only reason why it remains tantalizingly inconclusive. There was something in the nature of his experiment itself that prevented him from arriving at a conclusion; and he had no circular scheme, like Proust's, that would have linked the end to the beginning. Musil's novel is like a living organism that gropes its way into an uncertain future; neither his sharp and supple intelligence nor his immense artistic skill could prevent this organism from going its own way. Yet its very inconclusiveness makes it inexhaustible. It would be difficult to reduce Musil's book to the kind of dialectical skeleton to which Thomas Mann's fiction is so frequently, and usefully, reduced. The situations and actions of Musil's characters are not subordinated to the author's ideas; more often than not even Musil's reflections on them have the spontaneity of genuine astonishment.

*　　*　　*

IT IS a measure of Musil's durability that the Kaisers' English translation could be reissued not long before the centenary of Musil's birth. That reissue of the three translated volumes of *The Man Without Qualities* deserved to be an event, all the more so because the time was as unpropitious as possible. To judge by present trends in reading habits, a novel unlike any other, in three or four volumes – the fourth volume contains the controversial posthumous fragments of the work – and incomplete at that, and translated from the German, is not exactly the kind of thing many English or American readers are looking for. Yet the reception of Musil's novel has always been as extraordinary as the novel itself. Though largely ignored by reviewers and academic critics in his lifetime, Musil could even then count on a readership of about 8,000; and it was an article in the *Times Literary Supplement* that led to Musil's rediscovery and reinstatement in Germany after the last war. Ever since, he has been appreciated in Britain, America, France and Italy no less than in the German-speaking countries.

If British readers have tended to go for the social comedy and satire in Musil's novel, rather than the comedy of ideas that was his speciality or for his 'deeper' concerns, there is no harm in that. Musil was an Austrian, not a German. His fellow Austrian, Hofmannsthal, who responded to his work, wrote that 'depth should be concealed – in the surface'. As his English translators, who were also prominent as critics, scholars and editors of his work, once pointed out, the Austrians, unlike the Germans, have a word for 'muddling through'.

On all sorts of levels Musil's novel is the account of a vast muddling-through. There is also the old Austrian joke about a situation that is 'desperate but not serious'. That, too, could ring a good many bells in England now. Musil himself, in any case, was unable to say how he wanted his novel to be read or understood. Much as his protagonist, Ulrich, is described as a 'man without qualities' (who does not even have a surname at any point in the story), Musil could describe his novel only by negatives, by saying what it is not – and with typical irony that cocks a snook at logic:

> It is not the immemoriably long-awaited great Austrian novel, although . . .
> It is not a depiction of the age, in which Mr . . . recognizes himself, warts and all . . .
> Nor is it a depiction of society.
> It does not contain the problems that beset us, but . . .
> It is not a satire, but a positive construction.
> It is not a confession, but a satire.
> It is not the book of a psychologist.
> It is not the book of a thinker . . .
> It is not the book of a singer, who . . .
> It is not the book of an author who is successful, who is not successful.
> It is not an easy or a difficult book, for that depends on the reader.
> Without more elaboration, then, I think I can say that anyone who wants to know what this book is will be well advised to read it himself (not rely on my or other people's judgement but read it himself).

That was Musil's draft for a 'self-advertisement', and it goes to the heart of the matter. If Musil could not describe or classify his novel, after working on it for decades, the reason is that *The Man Without Qualities* is none of those things only because it is all those things, and more. As Musil mentioned in another note, it is also an historical novel – or had become so while still in progress, because it is set in 1913–14, the year that was the end of an era. It is also an autobiographical novel, like Proust's, but distanced from the self by much more than third-person narrative, and in search not of time past as much as of the future, a new kind of individual and a new kind of society. As such it is also an utopian novel, but the utopia towards which it gropes has to hold up against the utmost scepticism – that of an author trained in the exact sciences, as a mathematician, engineer, logician, experimental psychologist, artillery officer, staff officer and civil servant in the Foreign and War Offices, as Musil was at different periods of his life, without wishing to make a career of any of these occupations, just as he made no use of the title of nobility he had inherited from his father. His novel is also one of the funniest ever written, and one of the most serious. That is why it is easy reading for anyone who can rid his mind of the prejudice that seriousness must be solemn, or that any novel which includes what people think as well as what they do and feel must be 'highbrow' or turgid. Those are two of many prejudices Musil could not even stop to consider, when his most serious purpose was to set out on an adventure that would take him to an unprecedented and unpredictable destination, beyond all the divisive prejudices and categorizations of his time and ours – the 'two cultures', for instance, technology and humanism, mindless action and encapsulated intellect and, less explicitly, male and female specializations.

Musil himself ascribed his failure to finish the book to the loss of his private income in the inflation of the twenties and the loss of his literary income after his emigration to Switzerland, and he was still working on it the day he died suddenly, in 1942, with a look of surprise on his face, while doing his daily physical exercises. Yet he could certainly have finished it if its conclusion had been predictable, or if the synthesis towards which it was moving had not turned out to be a mystical one, because only mysticism could resolve the antinomies he had tackled on the way.

It is the daring and adventurousness of this enterprise that makes his novel as topical, relevant and shocking now as it was at any stage of its history. Although it did deal with the problems that beset Austria and a whole civilization in 1913, from a perspective enlarged by foresight as much as by hindsight, Musil saw those problems not as narrowly political or ideological, but primarily as a yawning gulf between the technical capacities and the emotional needs both of individuals and nations. The doomed Austrian Empire, which he called Kakania (from its bureaucratic use of the initials K. K. or K. & K., imperial and royal, to mark its uniqueness), may have been an especially suitable laboratory for his social satire, but social satire was not his dominant concern, and what matters is not the laboratory but the experiment. (The 'great Austrian novel' it was not his ambition to write was undertaken much more deliberately, on a more securely realistic level, after Musil's death, by Heimito von Doderer.) Musil's satire, true, was devastating but constructively' so, since he loved his country, and love was the potentiality he was after. In the same way his psychology was devastating, but constructively, even in face of the 'sex' murderer, Moosbrugger, or the false prophets, including those of Nazi racism, whose pseudo-mystical panaceas were based on lies. Musil did not think it his business as a novelist to judge societies or individuals. He exposed their absurdities, with the precision, coolness and wit peculiar to him, in the hope that this could prove more reme-dial than heavy didacticism. What looks like non-narrative interpolat-ions in his novel is an intrinsic part of the action. The political plot hinges on the fantastic Collateral Campaign, launched to celebrate the Austrian Emperor's forthcoming jubilee in 1918 in a manner that will distinguish it from the German Emperor's jubilee due in the same year. The German word for this is *Parallelaktion*, and the struc-ture of the whole novel, too, is based on such parallel actions, in which ideas are no less and no more important than the individuals they motivate and mislead. Even Moosbrugger, a scarcely articulate working man, resorts to ideas to justify his seemingly sexual, but really anti-sexual, violence against a prostitute. Parallel actions link both the violence and the ideas to everything else that goes on in the novel, on every social and intellectual plane.

In one sense *The Man Without Qualities* is not even a long novel. Unlike Proust's, it has no *longueurs* – no drawn-out descriptions or analytical passages, though Musil had been a pioneer of the 'stream of consciousness' in his early fiction. Musil was profoundly sceptical of words, and sparing of them. In that, and in the tension between extreme scepticism and mysticism, he resembles his compatriot Wittgenstein.

Wittgenstein was a thinker, and Musil claimed not to be one, but was, amongst other things. The same goes for the 'singer' or poet Musil claimed not to be. His tribute to Rilke, another compatriot, is only one pointer to Musil's poetic sensibility, and the importance to him of those sudden 'epiphanies' or revelations out of which poetry is made. Most of Musil's shorter narrative works – some of which remain to be translated, like his essays, lectures, notebooks, letters and aphorisms – revolve around moments of heightened conscious-ness, and in his late novel, too, it is such moments that make for progression.

Musil's draft for an author's note on the novel asks the reader to read the novel twice: once for the parts, once for the whole. Though he apologized for the request, it was a modest one compared to Joyce's demands on readers of *Finnegans Wake*, and helpful again in going to the heart of the novel's distinction. Every tree is as clearly presented as anyone could wish, yet the wood remains mysterious, not only because we shall never know where its limits were to have been drawn. [. . .]

. . . .

. . . IF KAFKA'S life and person continue to arouse curiosity, one reason is that his works continue to defy every attempt to arrive at a definitive interpretation, or only a definite approach. Because Western man hates nothing so much as to be left in doubt, any potential clue to the 'meaning' of Kafka's works is eagerly pounced upon; and since one thing is now certain about Kafka, that he was a psychopathological case, what could be more reasonable than to approach the writer through the casebook to which the man contributed with a readiness itself pathological? If the validity of the psychological approach is challenged, its practitioners can always appeal to the authority of Edmund Wilson whose theory of the wound and the bow has been applied so profitably to other writers. Even Klaus Wagenbach, in his excellent book on Kafka's youth, justified his scholarly, painstaking and wholly untheoretical researches on the grounds that Kafka's 'infantilism' lends a special importance to his formative years.'

Wagenbach's study is a real contribution to this baffling writer's biography and a most valuable complement both to Max Brod's more comprehensive work and to Kafka's own diaries and letters; it sheds new light on a great variety of issues, not only biographical, but literary, linguistic and textual, such as the controversial question of Brod's editing of the works. Yet if Wagenbach proves anything – and he did not set out to do so – it is that neither the categories of psychology nor Wilson's ingenious theory are adequate in this particular instance. Wilson's theory does not apply for the simple reason that Kafka had no use for his bow, almost wholly engrossed as he was in probing and deepening his wound, in the 'systematic destruction of myself' recorded in his diaries; and even his imaginative writings were a means to that end, not an alternative or a 'compensation'. There is no lack of writers who have accommodated themselves to their personal deficiencies, even to neuroses no less acute than Kafka's, by condemning the world. It was Kafka's originality and greatness to reverse this somewhat vulgar process, to make his peace with the world by condemning himself with a rigour and intensity which may be pathological, but which places him beyond the reach of all rubrics and categories.

This is not to deny that Kafka was a case of infantilism; that he was physically 'juvenile' is confirmed by a medical examination which he underwent in 1906 in order to be admitted to the staff of the Assicurazioni Generali. He himself said in 1911: 'Till my fortieth year I shall look like a boy, and than I shall suddenly turn into a shrivelled old man.' But far from solving the Kafka problem once for all, such rubrics as infantilism or masochism can never begin to account for this rare phenomenon – psychotherapy by self-destruction.

True, this very peculiarity has been held against Kafka by Günther Anders. His short book on Kafka, originally published in 1951 under the title *Franz Kafka: Pro et Contra* had an explosive force all the greater for being touched off at the time of the general vogue that followed Kafka's belated rediscovery in Germany. It was, and is, a brilliant book, but, like all the works of this distinguished author, it confronts the translator with problems partly insuperable. In this, as his later and more ambitious works *Die Antiquiertheit des Menschen* and *Der Mann auf der Brücke* – investigations, respectively, of the effects of technology and of the atom bombs dropped on Hiroshima and Nagasaki – Anders found it necessary to coin a new terminology to render the horrors and aberrations of our century. It must be said at once that *Franz Kafka* is not so much a work of literary criticism as a tract against the times; it is as such that it should be read, and as such that it remains valid in the very different literary climate of later decades, long after the decline of the Kafka vogue in Germany, much longer after its decline in England. Clearly and intelligently argued though it is, the book has serious weaknesses as an indictment of Kafka's works, let alone as a piece of unbiased criticism; but it has lost none of its force or intensity as a defence of humanism in an inhuman age.

Kafka, according to Anders, was not a myth-maker, but a 'realistic fable-writer', whose 'imagination puts the Muse of realism to shame'. The author's charge against Kafka is that he was too much of a realist, that he represented his time too well, and anticipated the totalitarian systems that were established after his death; and the main ground for this charge is that Kafka's work contains 'a plea for de-individualization and servility'. Kafka was a 'prophetic realist', and it is this that makes his work 'philosophically and morally suspect'; for he was not only the realist of the dehumanized world, but its exalter'. Kafka is treated as an agnostic and atheist, but one who 'makes of atheism a theology', a 'Christianizing theologian of the Jewish world'. The reason why he ordered his work to be destroyed, Anders concludes, is that, in the last analysis, 'it contained only artistic perfection'. Kafka the man is absolved from the indictment; and even his work 'will be of use to us if it becomes imprinted on our minds as a warning'.

Part of this argument is already familiar to readers of Erich Heller's *The Disinherited Mind*, but Heller's essay also added an important corrective: 'Only a mind keeping alive in at least one of its recesses the memory of a place where the soul is truly at home is able to contemplate with such creative vigour the struggles of a soul lost in a hostile land; and only an immensity of goodness can be so helplessly overcome by the vision of the worst of all possible worlds.' This reservation made by Heller could be taken to apply only to Kafka the man, like the similar reservation in Anders's book; but if we are going to make Kafka responsible for attitudes which he never explicitly advocated in his works or out of them, but only recorded either imaginatively or as part of his auto-therapy by self-criticism, we must also allow for his personal neurosis, his clear recognition of its power over him, and his unceasing endeavours to overcome it. Anders's criticism, then, becomes a criticism only of those readers simple-minded enough to assume that Kafka did, in fact, write a kind of inverted *Pilgrim's Progress*, and that he intended it as a moral example to others – Anders rightly shows that neither was the case. If Kafka's works conveyed nothing more than a warning, their value would be polemical, like that of Anders's book; but what they offer is catharsis, and the more purely imaginative a work, the greater is the risk of moral ambiguity. We cannot have one without the other.

If Kafka's early interpreters had fully appreciated the novelty of his experiment we should not still be confronted with the diverse and incompatible Kafkas offered to us by the theological, psychological and sociological schools of criticism; nor would it have been necessary for Max Brod to defend Kafka once more against the charge of nihilism and despair. Brod was right, of course, and right to protest against the reiteration of this foolish charge; but Wagenbach's documentary evidence will carry a good deal more weight than the selected quotations which Brod opposes again and again to the increasingly subtle stratagems of Kafka's detractors. Moreover, Professor Wilhelm Emrich's exhaustive study of the structure and symbolism of Kafka's works, which resolves their seeming contradictions and paradoxes to reveal a basic unity of conception, has confuted the charge on strictly textual grounds; and Professor Walter H. Sokel's study has added an equally minute analysis of the development in Kafka's work, while casting a different light on its unity. It requires faith to undertake the systematic destruction of oneself, faith in the norm against which this self offends, the faith that there is something greater than self beyond the act. If this faith is not always obvious in Kafka's works – though it is implicit everywhere – the infinite complexities of the process must be taken into account. Most of Kafka's imaginative works are not allegories, predetermined by any intention whatever, but the closest approximation to dreams that has ever been achieved in fiction; and though responsibility may begin in dreams, they are hardly the prototype of didactic art. As for Kafka's comments on the progress of the experiment, these too were part of it. To have declared his faith in the outcome would have been to ruin the experiment in advance, to commit what Kafka considered the greatest, if not the only, sin, impatience. 'Whoever has faith cannot define it,' Kafka remarked to Gustav Janouch, 'and whoever has none can only give a definition which lies under the shadow of grace withheld. The man of faith cannot speak and the man of no faith ought not to speak.'

It was Novalis who observed that *Selbsttötung* (destruction of the self) is 'the true philosophical act, the real beginning of all philosophy'. In Kafka's case the justification was less general. He was aware that there are individuals so warped by their personal experience as to be incapable of seeing anything in perspective; his unspoken faith was that even these are not damned if they have the strength to expose themselves utterly. 'Not everyone can see the truth,' he noted, 'but everyone can be the truth.' His self-therapy was the heroic attempt to bear witness to the truth which his own afflictions prevented him from seeing. The source and nature of these afflictions are well known, but Wagenbach's account of Kafka's social and family background, his school and university years and his activities generally up to 1912 adds many revealing details.

Hermann Kafka, the writer's physically and mentally overbearing father, and the source of his greatest affliction, grows more palpable than ever before. Brought up in a small Czech village in extreme poverty and physical hardship, linguistically and culturally a member of the Czech proletariat, not of the German-speaking ruling and middle classes, Hermann Kafka was impelled by the obsessive urge to 'make good', to prove his worth in the only way open to him. The ruthlessness, narrowness and intolerance of mind of which Franz accused him were the reverse side of the single-mindedness to which he owed his success. That Hermann Kafka also belonged to the Jewish minority was of sociological and psychological, rather than religious, significance, since he was not a devout man; undoubtedly it exacerbated those dominant characteristics and the sense of insecurity, or 'shame', from which they sprang.

In so far as the religious heritage of Judaism affected Franz directly in his youth – and for a long time he rebelled against the outward observances to which it had been reduced in his immediate family – it was through his mother's side; whether as rabbis or as professional men, Kafka's relatives and forbears on this side maintained the spiritual and intellectual tradition of their faith. Had Kafka's father not been utterly estranged from it by the values of a secularized society, he would have shown more sympathy for his unambitious and introverted son. As it was, his example could only serve as a warning to Franz to beware of compensation'.

Franz Kafka, of course, became highly efficient at both his professions; but merely out of conscientiousness, not out of ambition. In his self-destructive way he remarked in an early letter that his lack of professional ambition was not due to 'striving after ideal usefulness', but indifference to practical usefulness'. How scrupulous and conscientious an employee he nevertheless became – especially when his duties put him in personal touch with the workers whose insurance policies he administered – is confirmed by the information provided by Wagenbach, who includes Kafka's own writings on the legal technicalities of insurance written at the request of his employers and published in journals and company reports. Kafka's lack of literary ambition needs no further documentation.

Wagenbach is equally illuminating about the peculiarities of Kafka's narrative style, traces of which, incidentally, appear even in his writings on insurance, including the occasional flash of Kafkaesque humour. His interesting investigations show that imaginative, as distinct from descriptive and didactic, writing had no place in Kafka's school curriculum, and was frowned upon by the bureaucratically-minded staff; Kafka's 'dead-pan', minute and 'objective' treatment of his fantastic subjects can be partly ascribed to this early discipline. Later Kafka also reacted against the bookish and inflated German characteristic of other Prague-born writers, whose linguistic oddities were those of a literary enclave out of touch with the vernacular; this is particularly relevant to the important contribution of the Jewish minority, who had 'moved from a religious into a sociological ghetto' (Pavel Eisner), though it also applies to non-Jewish Prague-born writers like Rilke. The spoken language of these writers was poor in vocabulary, besides being influenced by Czech usage; to make up for this deficiency, they tended to resort to rhetoric, archaism and stereo-typed poeticisms or – as in the case of Rilke – to mannerism and neologism. Kafka observed in a letter to Milena that he had never lived among German people and 'though German is my mother tongue and therefore natural to me, Czech has a much more cordial ring'.

Very much earlier, at the age of seventeen, he expressed his mistrust of words; and in 1902 he wrote to his friend Oskar Pollak: 'When we talk to each other the words are hard, one walks over them as over a badly cobbled street.' But here the linguistic aspect is insep-arable from the semantic, from a deeper mistrust extending to every kind of usage. If Kafka finally succeeded in writing 'the clearest German' of his time, as Wagenbach affirms, it was because he used words with the same conscientiousness that distinguished all he did; because he took infinite pains over actions which others perform unthinkingly and, in his 'naïve wonder at the strangeness of things', discovered the world for himself.

Kafka's self-absorption, too, has been exaggerated. Wagenbach not only considers the great variety of literary, philosophical and artistic influences to which Kafka was subject in his youth – from his early Darwinism and atheism, the Nietzschean periodical *Kunstwart*, which even affected his style for a time, and Spinoza, to Flaubert, Kleist, Hofmannsthal, Robert Walser, Chinese poetry and art, the philosophy of Franz Brentano and, mainly after 1918, Kierkegaard – but traces his active interest in politics. Kafka became a socialist as early as 1898, read Masaryk's newspaper *Čas* and, from 1909 to 1914 regularly attended the meetings of an Anarchist group. Wagenbach included a speech delivered by Jaroslav Hasek, not yet the author of *The Good Soldier Schweik*, which made even Kafka laugh; and no wonder, for it must be one of the funniest electioneering speeches ever put on record. When several members of the Anarchist group were arrested, Kafka went to Police Headquarters and offered to pay bail for his friend Mares, at considerable risk to his own freedom. At this period Kafka seems to have identified himself with the Czech cause, and the cause of the working-class in particular. His concern with Yiddish drama and literature did not begin till 1910, and he remained decidedly anti-Zionist until 1914.

Even science played a part in Kafka's education; in 1901 he interrupted his legal studies to take up not only German literature and the history of art but chemistry. At the Fanta home he met both philosophers and scientists, including Einstein. At the same time he remained susceptible to movements like vegetarianism or Rudolf Steiner's anthroposophy, though his acutely critical intelligence was never in abeyance for long; he was ready to give anyone the benefit of the doubt – anyone but himself, that is – but soon after his meeting with Rudolf Steiner he remarked that 'theosophy is only a surrogate for literature'.

Wagenbach sums up this period when he says that Kafka vacillated between the two poles of 'uncertainty' and 'the search for truthfulness'. No one who has read his book should ever again mistake this uncertainty for nihilism or despair. If Kafka ever despaired it was only of his own capacity for truthfulness, never of truth itself; and even his uncertainty vanished as soon as he applied himself to other people's problems, as he was always ready to do in later life with a whole-hearted sympathy and a depth of understanding which say much for his experiment. Brod mentions his letters of advice to Minze E., and points to an important aspect of *The Trial*, Kafka's condemnation of himself at one stage of his development as a man incapable of love; and he quotes Martin Buber's profound analysis of the theological implications of Kafka's writings in relation both to Christianity and Judaism.

Apart from the chronology of two of Kafka's early stories, which he establishes almost beyond doubt, Wagenbach vindicated Brod's editing of Kafka's works, even in the controversial matter of

Professor Uyttersprot's suggestion that the chapters of *The Trial* have been placed in the wrong order. A new critical edition of Kafka's works was certainly called for; but even this edition is indebted to Kafka's first editor, biographer and untiring advocate, but for whose early recognition of Kafka's excellence, most of his works would have been neither published nor preserved. Wagenbach's biography also stresses Kafka's personal debt to the encouragement and devotion of his closest friend. Max Brod's early writings are prominent in the list of books known to have been in Kafka's possession, which forms another valuable appendix to Wagenbach's study. Kafka's fondness for autobiographies, diaries and memoirs of every period brings out the existential, rather than literary, nature of his preoccupations.

It is not the least of Kafka's distinctions that there is no end to the meanings which we can read into or out of his works, because he wrote 'as though into a tunnel, into the dark', without knowing how the characters will develop; because of the dreamlike daring and autonomy of his inventions. The reason why most interpretations of his work are so unsatisfactory is that he combined this uncommon freedom with the highest degree of consciousness – so that it is impossible to treat them as mere specimens of automatic writing or as surrealist fantasies – and that the categories of criticism have proved too crude to contain this seeming paradox. The truth is that all the principal criteria – theological, sociological, psychological and aesthetic – are relevant to his work, if only we were capable of applying them together, instead of making an ideology of one to the exclusion of all the others. What is needed is an interpretation at once as undeliberate and as meaningful as the works themselves; and it would have to begin with the knowledge that human reality is complex, multiple and indivisible. This demand may be excessive; but in that case Kafka criticism as a whole will continue to be a distraction rather than an aid, an indication of fragmented values not in Kafka, but in his interpreters.

Kafka himself remained both subtle and naïve, minutely analytical and full of wonder; the very opposite of a theorist. A judgement on the outcome of his experiment would be as impertinent as a judgement on life itself. His refusal to insulate himself from the horrors and the strangeness of life was a form of commitment more absolute than any that can be deduced from his attitudes and beliefs; it was this exposure that made Milena say of him that he was 'like a naked man among people who are clothed'. All we know is that there is nothing infantile about his conversations with Gustav Janouch, those of a man who 'has said yes to everything' and learnt that even death is 'only an ingredient in the sweetness of life.' If this is spiritual masochism, so are most of the ultimate recognitions of the wisest men. This wisdom differs from cleverness in not being a weapon of the combatant self. When Janouch remarked on the stupidity of a common acquaintance, Kafka replied: 'To be stupid is human. Many clever people are not wise and therefore in the last resort not even clever. They are merely inhuman out of fear of their own meaningless vulgarity.' If it had produced no more than this knowledge, Kafka's experiment in self-destruction would be worth our attention.

From *After the Second Flood* (1986)

Essays on Post-War German Literature

From TOWARDS CLASSICISM:
BRECHT AND HIS SUCCESSORS

... FOR TWO HUNDRED years or so the progress of European and American poetry was one towards autonomy. The more 'advanced' the poet, the more his or her language differed from the language of discourse, exposition and plain talk. Not only metre, rhyme and metaphor – still regarded as 'ornament' by Dryden – served to remove poetry from those prosaic media of communication; more significantly still, the very syntax of poetry evolved in such a way that ambiguity or multiplicity of meaning came to be regarded as a distinguishing and essential feature of poetic utterance. The language of poetry, its practitioners and exegetes assumed, is unlike any other language. Far from being only a fine or memorable vehicle for thoughts, feelings or assertions that could be conveyed by other media, true poetry is at once the vehicle and substance of its utterances; not a different way of putting things, but the only way of putting things that could not be said at all in any language but the language of poetry.

Non-specialists continued to complain of the peculiar difficulty or obscurity of modern poetry. Specialists continued to relish it, accepting Archibald MacLeish's dictum that 'a poem should not mean but be', while devoting long books and articles to the analysis of difficult poems and their dubious or multiple meanings. Among sophisticated poets with a middle-class background and education, Brecht was virtually alone in writing a large and varied body of poetry that was clearly intended to convey a single meaning in a language as plain and unfigurative as the best prose. (That Brecht could also write quite differently, if he chose, is evident in early poems like his 'Psalms'.) Quite deliberately, Brecht set himself the aim of reversing the two-century-old development in question. Since believers in the aesthetic self-sufficiency of poetry – beyond the autonomy of all art he himself insisted on in the teeth of agit-prop and crude notions of 'socialist realism' – found it impossible to deny that Brecht was both a modern and a good poet, though his theory and practice alike contradicted their basic tenets, most of them found it prudent to ignore Brecht's poetry.

Whether we see it as a revolution or as a counter-revolution, Brecht's achievement in poetry was not only remarkable in itself but inseparable from the survival of poetry after the Second World War, at least in those parts of the world in which the very foundations of aesthetically self-sufficient poetry had been demolished by moral, social and political upheavals. If Brecht's later poetry is a kind of anti-poetry or minimal poetry by Romantic-Symbolist standards, no other kind of poetry could withstand the anti-poetic fury of those who had seen European civilization reduced to a heap of rubble. It was Brecht's anticipation of this crisis that prompted him to 'wash' the language of poetry, as he put it, long before the crisis occurred; and what he washed out of poetry was nothing less than the sediment of the whole Romantic-Symbolist era, with its aesthetic of self-sufficiency.

Needless to say, Brecht's poetic development was bound up with his political and social concerns, which led him to identify the Romantic-Symbolist aesthetic with an order dominated by the bourgeoisie and by bourgeois individualism. Yet even among Marxist poets Brecht was very nearly alone in the radicalism with which he applied historical or sociological insights to the practice of poetry. His contemporary Johannes R. Becher, who became Minister of Culture in the German Democratic Republic, reacted against Expressionist obscurity as Brecht did, but achieved no more by his language-washing than an old-fashioned banality of diction and a slackness of sentiment indistinguishable from that of the worst nineteenth-century versifiers. For a poet, ideology is not enough. To become effective in diction, stance and tone, the ideological commitment must enter his or her bloodstream like a food or a drug, pervading his or her entrails, his or her dreams. Having done so, it becomes something other than mere ideology. That is why Brecht's later poems, for all their didacticism, can be appreciated and assimilated by non-Marxists, as Becher's later poems cannot.

Another way of putting it is that the Romantic-Symbolist in Brecht – and throughout the 1920s and early 1930s he produced

remarkable poems of a visionary, imaginatively individualistic kind –
was not suppressed or silenced by an ideological decree, but remained
a dialectical presence beneath the hard, dry and spare surface of the
later poems. The process of reduction was gradual, organic and total,
involving the whole man. It began with the projection of an image,
that of the tough, hard-bitten, urban poet dramatized in the early
Villonesque self-portrait 'Vom armen B. B.':

> . . . In der Asphaltstadt bin ich daheim. Von allem Anfang
> Versehen mit jedem Sterbsakrament:
> Mit Zeitungen. Und Tabak. Und Branntwein.
> Misstrauisch und faul und zufrieden am End.
>
> Ich bin zu den Leuten freundlich. Ich setze
> Einen steifen Hut auf nach ihrem Brauch.
> Ich sage: es sind ganz besonders riechende Tiere,
> Und ich sage: es macht nichts, ich bin es auch.
>
> In meine leeren Schaukelstühle vormittags
> Setze ich mitunter ein paar Frauen
> Und ich betrachte sie sorglos und sage ihnen:
> In mir habt ihr einen, auf den könnt ihr nicht bauen. . . .
>
> .   .   .   .   .
>
> . . . In the asphalt city I'm at home. From the very start
> Provided with every unction and sacrament:
> With newspapers. And tobacco. And brandy.
> To the end mistrustful, lazy and content.
>
> I'm polite and friendly to the people. I put on
> A stiff hat because that's what they do.
> I say: they're animals with a quite peculiar smell,
> And I say: Does it matter? I am too.
>
> Sometimes in the mornings on my empty rocking-chairs
> I'll sit a woman or two, and with an untroubled eye
> Look at them steadily and say to them:
> Here you have someone on whom you can't rely. . . .

The later self-portraits, of which there are many, right up to
Brecht's last illness and the little poem in which he confronts his
imminent death, can do without the brashness and self-conscious

posturing of those lines, which were written as a provocation to the bourgeoisie and their expectation that poems ought to convey elevated sentiments. In the later poems the toughness has become more than a gesture, so that Brecht can also admit tenderness and gentleness, just as he could admit that love of nature about which he tended to feel uneasy, suspecting that it might be a residue of bourgeois self-indulgence, escapism and idyllicism. (In the self-portrait of the 1920s, pine-trees are said to 'piss' in the early morning, and the birds in them become their 'vermin'.) Above all, in the later poems he has ceased to care about his image, or about himself at all as an individual. Though he draws freely on his own experience, even on his dreams, and has no qualms about using the first person singular, he can do so just because he is not writing autobiography, but availing himself of useful material for reflections on the complexities of human motives and behaviour. Here is one such poem, written in the 1930s.

Fahrend in einem bequemen Wagen

Fahrend in einem bequemen Wagen
Auf einer regnerischen Landstrasse
Sahen wir einen zerlumpten Menschen bei Nachtanbruch
Der uns winkte, ihn mitzunehmen, sich tief verbeugend.
Wir hatten ein Dach und wir hatten Platz und wir fuhren vorüber
Und wir hörten mich sagen, mit einer grämlichen Stimme: Nein
Wir können niemand mitnehmen.
Wir waren schon weit voraus, einen Tagesmarsch vielleicht
Als ich plötzlich erschrak über diese meine Stimme
Dies mein Verhalten und diese
Ganze Welt.

.   .   .   .   .

Travelling in a comfortable car

Travelling in a comfortable car
Down a rainy road in the country
We saw a ragged fellow at nightfall
Signal to us for a ride, with a low bow.
We had a roof and we had room and we drove on
And we heard me say, in a morose tone of voice: No
We can't take anyone with us.

We had gone on a long way, perhaps a day's march
When suddenly I was shocked by this voice of mine
This behaviour of mine and this
Whole world.

This poem projects no image of Brecht as a poet or as a man that could distract us from his real concern, that with a general truth. The 'I' of the poem is confined to a strict function, which is impersonal. We are not asked to condemn Brecht's callousness or to grow mawkish over his remorse. We are asked to participate in the delayed shock at an action which could be and is anyone's. The poem has political, as well as psychological, implications, but the moral is neither rubbed in nor even explained in ideological terms. It is enacted in terms of a simple occurrence simply told, yet without the simplification that would make it undialectical. The impersonality of Brecht's concern is brought out by the strange phrase 'we heard me say' and by the concluding reference to 'this whole world'. One dialectical implication of the poem, that it is not enough to be a Marxist, as the reader knows Brecht to be, would not have come across so forcefully if the first person had been squeamishly avoided.

I say 'forcefully', though the little poem dispenses with all the devices that serve to heighten the language of poetry for the sake of eloquence, euphony or evocativeness. It dispenses with rhyme and regular metre – though Brecht had been a master of both in his earlier verse – with alliteration and assonance, with metaphor and simile, with inversion and dislocation of syntax. Brecht's art has come to lie in the concealment of art, as Horace wrote that it should; in a manner as seemingly casual, throw-away, undemonstrative as possible. What distinguishes such poems from prose is a rhythmic organization inconspicuous precisely because it is right, perfectly accordant with what the poem says and does; and an economy of means, a tautness and conciseness that are rarely attained in a prose narrative. (The tautness begins with the very first word; the present participle construction unusual in German, but adopted by Brecht before English had become his second language. Latin is his more likely model here.) By renouncing emotive effects and that vagueness which Baudelaire considered an essential element in Romantic art, Brecht was able to create a didactic poetry that seems innocent of any design on the reader, but all the more persuasive and convincing for that. Brecht's language here is anyone's language, if anyone were capable of putting the right word in the right place, of saying neither more nor less than what he wants to say. Brecht's ability to do so consistently, in hundreds of poems written in this later manner, amounted to the establishment of an art at once modern and classical. To read Brecht's later verse is an experience akin to the reading of Horace – whom Brecht repeatedly read in his later years – the Catullus of the social epigrams, or any Latin poet at home not only in his art but in his world.

This does not mean that Brecht accepted his world uncritically, any more than the Latin poets accepted theirs uncritically, either before or after his residence in a Communist country. It means that in Brecht's later poems personal and public concerns are inseparable. The sequence of short poems which he called *Buckower Elegien* – though by modern criteria they are much closer to epigram than to elegy – was written after Brecht's return from Germany, yet its dominant tone is one of satirical or self-questioning unease, as in the opening poem, 'Der Radwechsel':

> Ich sitze am Strassenrand
> Der Fahrer wechselt das Rad.
> Ich bin nicht gern, wo ich herkomme.
> Ich bin nicht gern, wo ich hinfahre.
> Warum sehe ich den Radwechsel
> Mit Ungeduld?

.   .   .   .   .   .

> *Changing the Wheel*
>
> I sit on the roadside verge
> The driver changes the wheel.
> I do not like the place I have come from.
> I do not like the place I am going to.
> Why with impatience do I
> Watch him changing the wheel?

I have written that Brecht's later manner dispenses with metaphor and simile, and so it does, except in so far as idiomatic usage is intrinsically figurative. Yet the very reduction of means in this short poem – more Chinese or Japanese than Latin, one would suppose – its extreme spareness and plainness of diction, invite us to read more into the poem than it says, to read it as an allegory. Since self-projection and self-expression are not what we look for in Brecht's later poems, the extension of meaning we are likely to provide in this instance is of a political or historical order; and, however we interpret them, the implications of the poem are very far from the optimism encouraged, if not positively enforced, under Communist régimes. Several other poems in the sequence quite unambiguously disparage or censure this official optimism. The impatience in 'Changing the Wheel' has little to do with it, though it could be related to Ernst Bloch's 'principle of hope' that can and must assert itself in facing up to the worst. (Bloch, an early dissident, chose to spend his last years in the other Germany.)

It could well be that this poem has no direct bearing on anything political at all. This possibility occurred to me when I came across this anonymous poem, probably medieval in origin, but transmitted in various dialect versions over the centuries. I quote the version closest to Brecht's poem, though others substitute living and dying for the travelling imagery:

> Ich komme, ich weiss nicht woher,
> Ich fahre, ich weiss nicht wohin,
> Weiss nicht, warum ich so fröhlich bin.
>
> . . . . .
>
> I've come, I don't know from where,
> I'm going, I don't know where,
> Don't know how it is that I feel such cheer.

This is the (modernized) version of the poem quoted and praised by Gustav Landauer in a letter to his daughter Gudula in 1918. Brecht is more likely to have known it from his youth, and I have found no evidence of his ever having read Landauer, an anti-Marxist, anti-materialist socialist familiar enough to Brecht's friend Walter Benjamin. A four-line version of the poem was painted on to a house as late as 1791 at Illerbeuren, quite close to Brecht's home town, Augsburg. In any case the traditional verses must have served Brecht as a source for 'Changing the Wheel', either consciously or unconsciously; and any attempt to relate Brecht's poem to his immediate situation in the GDR must take account of the traditional, Christian, source.

If the dialect of 'Der Radwechsel' hides some of its implications between the lines, leaving room for speculation and extensions of meaning, other poems in the sequence could not be more explicit in their insistence on truthfulness: truthfulness in the dealings between government and subjects in 'Die Lösung' (The Solution), truthfulness about moral complexities, including the poet's own, in 'Böser Morgen' (A Bad Morning). Brecht's utopianism in clinging to the principle of hope through such truthfulness is the theme of another elegy, 'Die Wahrheit einigt' (Truth unites us).

The accusing fingers of working men, in 'Böser Morgen', and the poet's guilty conscience deflected into a counter-accusation of ignorance, their ignorance, point forward to Brecht's successors in the German Democratic Republic no less than does his insistence on truthfulness, on intellectual and moral rigour, and on a manner austere to the point of self-denial – though Brecht's later manner was as distinctive and unmistakable as that of any poet writing in his time. Compared to poets who grew up under the régime which granted Brecht a privileged position, he had little reason to doubt that the freedom of literature was compatible with corporative needs on the one hand, government directives on the other. Towards the end of his life he could write another poem that illuminates his Horatian classicism:

Ich benötige keinen Grabstein

Ich benötige keinen Grabstein, aber
Wenn ihr einen für mich benötigt
Wünschte ich, es stünde darauf:
Er hat Vorschläge gemacht. Wir
Haben sie angenommen.
Durch eine solche Inschrift wären
Wir alle geehrt.

. . . . . .

I need no gravestone

I need no gravestone, but
If you need one for me
I wish the inscription would read:
He made suggestions. We
Have acted on them.
Such an epitaph would
Honour us all.

Writing from later experience of the relations between intellectuals and government in the GDR, the eminent critic Hans Mayer remarked on the arrogance of Brecht's assumptions in that poem. (Hans Mayer had been a Professor of Literature at Leipzig, where Uwe Johnson was among his students, and, like Johnson, had been forced to leave for West Germany. Mayer's volumes of autobiography document that history.) Whether or not they are arrogant, Brecht's assumptions here are certainly different from those of his younger successors, who would not dare to suppose for one moment that the rulers of their country might feel honoured to take their advice. To Brecht, though, the question of his personal arrogance or humility was an irrelevance. What mattered to him was not the statement about himself in this poem, but what the poem implied about a proper relationship in a Communist State between independent, critical thinking and government policies. Brecht's confidence in that regard – a confidence essential to what I have called his classicism, though both the classicism and the confidence may now look utopian – goes back to an earlier phase of revolutionary enterprise, when it did seem that independent thought and vision would be allowed to make a real contribution to the shaping of a new, socialist order. After Brecht's death that confidence, or that arrogance, became the prerogative of those who were not his successors, of the unthinking, unintelligent and uncritical purveyors of authorized party pap to the people. It is the language that marks the difference, palpably and immediately: the language of Brecht's successors is hard, spare, precise like his own, cryptic only by omission and reduction. The language of the conformists is vague, abstract, inflated, turgid with all the poeticisms that Brecht had washed and scrubbed out of the texture of verse.

*   *   *

BRECHT'S awareness that his stance had become utopian – when realism and truthfulness were what determined that stance – can be seen in these lines, written shortly before his death in 1956:

Und ich dachte immer

Und ich dachte immer: die allereinfachsten Worte
Müssen genügen. Wenn ich sage, was ist
Muss jedem das Herz zerfleischt sein.

Dass du untergehst, wenn du dich nicht wehrst
Das wirst du doch einsehn.

.   .   .   .   .

And I always thought

And I always thought: the very simplest words
Must be enough. When I say what things are like
Everyone's heart must be torn to shreds.
That you'll go down if you don't stand up for yourself –
Surely you see that.

Even these laconic and sad lines require an effort of imagination and intelligence on the reader's part. They, too, are plain bread, not the cream puffs offered by the propagandists and – so the poem suggests – preferred by the consumers. It is the reader who has to fill the gaps in their dialectic, beginning with the gap bridged by the casual, abrupt 'and' with which the poem begins. One thing the gaps tell us, but the words do not, is that Brecht must have had cause to question the effectiveness of his simple words – most probably because too many of his readers in the GDR had been too thoroughly brainwashed to respond to his language-washing. Most of his later poems became available in West Germany before they were published in his own country, and some of the more uncomfortable ones were deliberately withheld in the GDR. The person to whom these lines are addressed is not identified; that makes the person anyone or everyone who has failed to stand up for himself or herself in the Republic Brecht had once hoped he could help to shape.

In Brecht's last poems dryness, matter-of-factness and seeming casualness become cryptic again – at times more cryptic than many poems by other authors who cultivated word magic, unreason or ecstasy. Here is another instance:

Schwierige Zeiten

Stehend an meinem Schreibpult
Sehe ich durchs Fenster im Garten den Holderstrauch
Und erkenne darin etwas Rotes und etwas Schwarzes
Und erinnere mich plötzlich des Holders
Meiner Kindheit in Augsburg.
Mehrere Minuten erwäge ich
Ganz ernsthaft, ob ich zum Tisch gehen soll

Meine Brille holen, um wieder
Die schwarzen Beeren an den roten Zweiglein zu sehen.

    ·   ·   ·   ·   ·

Difficult Times

Standing at my desk
Through the window I see the elder tree in the garden
And recognize something red in it, something black
And all at once recall the elder
Of my childhood in Augsburg.
For several minutes I debate
Quite seriously whether to go to the table
And pick up my spectacles, in order to see
Those black berries again on their tiny red stalks.

How is one to read this poem? As confessional, a poem of
personal experience? Or still as a didactic poem, of the kind expected
of Brecht? Or perhaps as a 'nature poem', with special reference to
other tree, plant and garden questions posed in earlier poems by
Brecht, and m view of his famous assertion that 'conversations about
trees' could be a crime at times that were always difficult? And of
what kind were the difficulties named in the title? Were they personal
difficulties of Brecht's? Or general, political and social ones?

Such distinctions – whose validity I question in any case – give us
no access to Brecht's last poems, because in the course of the decades
Brecht had politicized his thinking and feeling to such a degree that
he was now free again to write poems in the first person that could not
be merely confessional, merely personal, when for him anything
personal had come to include its opposite, society, and every individ-
ual's part in society. For the same reason, all such poems must remain
didactic poems – precisely by virtue of an implicit understanding that
this was how his poems were to be read. Brecht had learned to use the
observation of his own inclinations and hesitations for his didactic
ends. Since to him, who had made it his business to determine the
bounds of individuality, self-knowledge was something other than
self-reflection, he could now assume that confessions in poems must
be something other than self-confessions. His very choice of the first
person singular for so many of his later poems had a political
significance, for it served to correct the abuse of the 'collective', the
'people', as a stick for beating those individuals of whom the people is

made up. (His poem 'The Solution' had pointedly satirized this abuse by inviting the Government to 'dissolve' the people and elect another.) The 'I' of Brecht's later and last poems is a subject that has been objectivized to a certain degree; but not to the degree of becoming an abstraction.

This does not mean – as late Marxist polemicists, especially in non-Communist countries, sometimes like to think – that everything private or subjective in poems can be dismissed as 'bourgeois', as though the 'working class' were a new variant of the human species entirely contained within its economic function and with no needs or emotions beyond it. (If that were true of anyone, it would apply to a different social class, to the administrators, functionaries and technocrats, and their fellow travellers among intellectuals.) What Brecht wanted was a balance, not a suppression or repression of individuality.

As for 'nature poetry', though we may associate it with the romanticism that Brecht opposed, Brecht was sufficiently well versed in classical literature to know that nature was celebrated in antiquity, by Greek and Latin poets for instance, as a refuge, a liberation from social ties and obligations, amongst other things. With all his scepticism towards modern nature cults and his awareness – as in his poem 'Der Bauer kümmert sich um seinen Acker' (The farmer's concern is with his field) – that workers on the land have little time for a romanticized nature, Brecht also wanted conditions in which 'conversations about trees' would not be a crime. Besides, in this poem there is no nature of which one could make a cult, in which one could lose oneself. There is an elder tree, with its black berries hanging from red stalks.

As in many late poems by Brecht, such general considerations do not enter his text, but are left between the lines, in front of them and behind them. Brecht's classical aesthetic rests on a kind of solidarity with his readers, on the expectation that every reader will be able to retrace a dialectic that is scarcely intimated – much as earlier classical writers could assume that every reader would catch even the most subtle of allusions to mythical or historical figures. What Brecht relies on, though, is not the learning, but the intelligence and sensitivity of his readers – and this to an extent astonishing in a poet who had wished to be a popular poet, like Kipling.

What makes this poem mysterious has to do with its withheld didacticism, its withheld dialectic, and its withheld conclusion; also with the deliberate, provocative triviality of the events it relates. A reader incapable of complementing the things left unsaid in this poem, or one brought up to believe, as many Germans were, that poems have to be about great resolutions, great gestures and great issues affecting 'humanity' or 'the people', could well be perplexed by this poem. He or she would ask why Brecht found it necessary to record and fix this moment of hesitation – which was not a moment, though, since it lasted several minutes – or this (sentimental?) re-emergence of a childhood memory; and Brecht, of all people, known to be so unsentimental, so hard-bitten, so cold! This very perplexity and puzzlement would induce such a reader to look for a meaning beyond the event – if he or she could be bothered at all with such work; perhaps, too, to wonder about what is great, what is small. It was to the Far East that Brecht owed many models for the smallness of his later poems, small forms and small gestures, as well as much of the mentality that prefers the small to the great (and which Robert Walser, too, called 'Chinese').

It is Brecht's scepticism, rightly, that is always emphasized; but, as every poet knows, for the fixing of such small events in poems one needs a great confidence, a trust not only in an existing or potential readership, but in the capacity of the written text to signify more than its occasion. (True, it can also happen out of a very naïve self-impor-tance or a monomania that lends every personal experience a value it does not have for others. That Brecht was not prone to such self-effusion should need no proving.)

Nor is 'Difficult Times' about a sentimental recollection of child-hood. (What sentimental nature-worshipper, at the moment of being moved by an image emerging from his remote childhood, would think of putting on his spectacles?) It is about the hesitation, about being in two minds, and also about the clear recognition of a specific phenom-enon that would be a recognition, inasmuch as one never wholly forgets a natural phenomenon that has impressed itself in childhood, but also a new cognition, from the altered viewpoint of a man preoc-cupied with other things, other experiences, and a man who might have to overcome a certain indifference and lassitude to give in to this urge for knowledge or confirmation, and who is standing at his writing desk, presumably in order to work. It goes without saying that a certain tenderness for the elder tree, a certain wonderment at the continuity of a human life and the constancy of natural phenomena –

perhaps, too, at his own susceptibility – are part of the complex; and a change in Brecht's attitude to the things of nature, still more explicit in a poem about his own death.

Certainly there were still other considerations and circumstances that entered into his hesitation – personal *and* political ones to which the title alludes, but of more interest to biographers or historians than other readers. One supposes that the spectacles were not fetched, the black berries and red stalks not looked at closely; but this too is neither certain nor important. A poem has a right to its mysteries. That is why I have not interpreted this one, only pointed to some of the background from which this so simply and casually related small event draws its significance.

Brecht's poem about his death, one of his very last, does not differ in tone or manner from hundreds of earlier ones; and once again it can be read either as a poem of experience or a didactic poem, if we are foolish enough to distinguish between those kinds in Brecht's case:

Als ich in weissem Krankenzimmer der Charité

Als ich in weissem Zimmer der Charité
Aufwachte gegen Morgen zu
Und die Amsel hörte, wusste ich
Es besser. Schon seit geraumer Zeit
Hatte ich ja keine Todesfurcht mehr. Da ja nichts
Mir je fehlen kann, vorausgesetzt
Ich selber fehle. Jetzt
Gelang es mir, mich zu freuen
Alles Amselgesangs nach mir auch.

. . . . . .

When in a White Ward of the Charité

When in a white ward of the Charité
I awoke around dawn
And heard the blackbird, I knew
Better. For quite some time
I had not feared death. Since there is nothing
I can lack, provided
I myself am lacking. Now
I succeeded in being glad
Of every blackbird's song after me too.

Even that in the end it was a blackbird's song that concerned Brecht, will astonish only those who had not noticed how hard it had always been for Brecht not to be a 'nature poet', that is, not to conduct 'conversations about trees' when more urgent matters claimed his attention. In the face of his own death, though, he could leave those more urgent matters to others. To have treated this death as a public, collective event, would have been truly arrogant in any case. If Brecht could be arrogant and presumptuous, it was mainly over questions of freedom and authority in public affairs, as in the poem about his gravestone. That was part of his commitment, not of his self-importance.

This poem is about pleasures, so important to Brecht in earlier poems, and the inevitable loss of pleasures; hence the very Brechtian words, 'succeeded in being glad'. It is also a poem, once more, about the relation of the individual to the species; and, since Brecht could not resort to 'another life', a life after death, for a continuity beyond death, he found it in what Ernst Bloch called 'natural time', as distinct from 'historical time'. At the end, then, Brecht confronts the loss of his pleasures and accepts it by puffing himself in his place, as an individual not essentially different from others, to whom he leaves the particular pleasure of hearing the blackbird's song. Here the 'historical time' to which Brecht had devoted so much of his energy would not have served his purpose, since historical time is the arena of conflict and change.

Blackbirds, besides, are as much a part even of city life as the white ward of a hospital, and neither is more real than the other. If the poem pursues an implicit dialectic – and it does, of course – it is not a dialectic of nature as opposed to civilization, but of the selfishness of our pleasure-seeking and the bounds of individuality – one of Brecht's recurrent concerns. In a manner as matter-of-fact as ever, and as cool, Brecht strips himself of the residual selfishness that would prevent him from being glad in the face of his death; but the transcendence he celebrates goes back on nothing he had professed or practised, when to be glad of the pleasure that others will take in the blackbird's song remains a pleasure. To the last, then, Brecht remained true to himself and his unemphatically didactic art. To the last, he used himself to 'show other people what they are like'; in this case, by drawing a fine distinction between an egotism to be avoided and an individualism to be affirmed.

*   *   *

MOST of Brecht's successors in the German Democratic Republic had to take over his function of truth-telling without so much as a glimmer of hope that this function would be honoured by official approval, let alone by such reciprocal usefulness as Brecht claimed for writers in 'I need no gravestone'. Many of them were tormented by serious and recurrent doubts as to the propriety of writing poems at all under a system that denied all value to the individual conscience, the individual voice. After a 'language-washing' mainly directed at purging poetic diction of the accretions left by a long process of individuation to the point of solipsism, Brecht had been able to strike a classical balance between private and public concerns, as his liberal use of the first person singular attests. (The index to his *Collected Poems* of 1967 – two supplementary volumes were to be added in 1982 – lists nearly eighty poems that begin with the word 'I'. That quite a number of these poems are written in persons other than his own, confirms the importance he attributed to personal experience as the only reliable means of enacting general truths.) In the work of Brecht's immediate successors that balance was upset once more, because the relationship between private and corporative needs had become dubious, critical and precarious.

A New Year stocktaking poem by Peter Gosse (born 1938) contains these lines:

> ... Drei Jahre, zwei Pfund Lyrik,
> während mein Staat schuftet und schwitzt.
> Schluss mit der Kindheit.
> Ich werde exportreife Radars mitbaun,
> werde Mehrprodukt machen,
> Werde mitmischen.
>
> .   .   .   .   .
>
> ... Three years, two pounds of verse,
> while my State drudges and sweats.
> Stop being a child!
> I shall help to make radars for export,
> shall help to increase productivity,
> I shall muck in.

The colloquial diction of this poem, 'Inventur Sylvester 64', is close enough to Brecht's – as distinct from the old-fashioned rhetoric of the propagandist poets – to bring us up with a shock against the loss of nerve exemplified in the literal weighing up of the poet's output over the years; and against the coarseness of a colloquialism taken over indiscriminatingly from the language of slogans and directives. This materialism has ceased to be dialectical, even if we give the poet credit for a certain irony that his diction and stance fail to enact. Yet, ironic or not, the bad conscience in the poem was real and pervasive among Brecht's immediate successors. The accusing finger that pointed at Brecht in a nightmare had become a familiar and inescapable presence in waking life.

For all its plainness and reductive simplicity, Brecht's poetic idiom was a distillation made from a great variety of components, literary and historical, as well as the current vernacular. Gosse's diction, at least in the passage quoted, is crudely mimetic. It is the contrast between his practice here and in other poems, which are verbally idiosyncratic to the point of mannerism, that leads one to suspect an ironic or satirical sub-stratum which he may not have intended.

There is no suspicion of irony in a short poem by Kurt Bartsch (born 1937) that also relates the writing of poems to the national economy, in terms less extreme and more Brechtian than Gosse's:

poesie

die männer im elektrizitätswerk
zünden sich die morgenzigarette an.
sie haben, während ich nachtsüber schrieb,
schwitzend meine arbeitslampe gefüttert.
sie schippten Kohle für ein mondgedicht.

poetry

the men at the power station
light their morning cigarettes.
while I was writing at night
sweating they fed my work lamp.
they shovelled coal for a moon poem.

Brecht's direct lineage is as evident in this poem's diction as in its structure. Its compressed dialectic is rendered in terms of factual observation, not of abstract generalities. Inferences are left open, so that the poem can be read as the discovery of a happy interdependence of poetic and manual labour, or as a condemnation of poetry for being parasitical on the exertions of working men. If the scales are weighted towards the latter reading, it is only by the single word 'moon' in the last line; and since Bartsch did not write 'moon poems', but poems of social awareness, when he worked in the GDR, the word was chosen because it heightens the dialectic and the poem's unemphatic play on contrasting sources of light. Moon poems, the undialectic materialistic would object – and the West German poet Peter Rühmkorf quite specifically placed moon poems under an interdict, at a time when it was usual for German poets to prescribe what kind of poems were, and were not, to be written at a particular historical moment – are useless to those useful men; but so are the cigarettes which they light all the same. The questions left open by those five brief lines could be debated at indefinite and boring length. One reason why Brecht's short later poems proved such a fruitful precedent for younger poets is that, even in the GDR, such poems could not be expected to debate or answer all the questions they raised; and that was a distinct advantage under an ideological censorship that was to drive Bartsch into emigration, like so many of his outstanding fellow poets.

Brecht's contractions and reductions, in fact, were carried farther by several of his successors, as by Günter Kunert (born 1929), whose early poems are like a continuation of Brecht's in their moral searchingness and their epigrammatic sharpness. It is the reader who has to fill in the background of this little poem, 'Unterschiede', and any reader with first-hand experience of totalitarian systems will know how to fill it in:

> Betrübt höre ich einen Namen aufrufen:
> Nicht den meinigen.
>
> Aufatmend
> Höre ich einen Namen aufrufen:
> Nicht den meinigen.
>
> .   .   .   .   .

Differences

Distressed, I hear a name called out:
Not mine.

Relieved,
I hear a name called out:
Not mine.

Apart from making a point about vanity and fear, what this poem enacts by its sparseness of diction and gesture is that sparseness has become the precondition of survival – the survival of truthful poets and truthful poems. The 'I' of this poem is incomparably more depersonalized than Brecht's, because it has been stripped not only of idiosyncrasy but of circumstance. The 'I' of this poem is only what is left of it in the eyes of bureaucracy – if bureaucracy had eyes for anything but its function. This bureaucracy decides whether an individual is to be allowed to function or not; and it is to this alternative that the vanity and fear respond.

Where Kunert's concern was the survival not of the individual but of the species, as in his poem 'Laika', he could be a little more circumstantial, since such general concerns were not proscribed. Yet 'Laika' has the same terse structure, based on parallelism, as in the other poem, and packed into a single sentence:

In einer Kugel aus Metall,
Dem besten, das wir besitzen,
Fliegt Tag für Tag ein toter Hund
Um unsre Erde
Als Warnung,
Dass so einmal kreisen könnte
Jahr für Jahr um die Sonne,
Beladen mit einer toten Menschheit,
Der Planet Erde,
Der beste, den wir besitzen.

.   .   .   .   .   .

Laika

In a capsule of metal,
The best that we have,
Day after day around our Earth

A dead dog rotates
As a warning
That so in the end
With a cargo of human corpses
Year after year around the sun
This planet Earth could rotate,
The best that we have.

Since Laika was the dog sent into space by the USSR in an early pioneering experiment, even this warning could easily have been taken amiss; but at the time Kunert enjoyed privileges not unlike those granted to Brecht and published his work in both republics. In other poems he resorted to allegory or fable for relief from the dual pressure of outer and inner censorship; for the self-effacing austerity of the kind of poems I have quoted was due to the poet's conscience as much as to the repression of independent judgement.

This can be seen most clearly in the work of Reiner Kunze (born 1933), a subtle, witty and fearless critic of bureaucracy and repression in the GDR. (Both Kunert and Kunze now live in West Germany.) The loss of Brecht's balance between personal and collective needs was the subject of this fable:

Der hochwald erzieht seine Bäume

Sie des lichtes entwöhnend, zwingt er sie,
all ihr grün in die kronen zu schicken
Die fähigkeit,
mit allen zweigen zu atmen,
das talent,
äste zu haben nur so aus freude,
verkümmern

Den regen siebt er, vorbeugend
der leidenschaft des durstes

Er lässt die bäume grösser werden
wipfel an wipfel:
Keiner sieht mehr als der andere,
dem wind sagen alle das gleiche

Holz

    · · · · ·

The timber forest educates its trees

By weaning them from light compels them
to send all their green into their tops
The ability
to breathe with every bough,
the talent
of having branches for the sheer joy of it
are stunted

The forest filters rain, as a precaution
against the passion of thirst

Lets the trees grow taller
crest to crest:
None sees more than another,
to the wind all tell the same thing

Wood

The fable here does not liberate the poet from his self-imposed austerity, since it serves only to convey something he would not be allowed to say without it; and since this something is the utter drabness of conformity, a conformity imposed and enforced, the language, too, must not depart from drabness. Kunze had no illusions about the transparency of the disguise. Another of his poems of the period was called 'Das Ende der Fabeln'. In fairy-tale guise it shows why fables – and fairy-tales with a moral such as this one – had become too dangerous to escape censorship:

Es war einmal ein fuchs . . .
beginnt der hahn
eine fabel zu dichten

Da merkt er
so geht's nicht
denn hört der fuchs die fabel
wird er ihn holen

. . . . .

Once upon a time there was a fox . . .
the cock begins
to make up a fable

But realizes
it can't be done like that
for if the fox hears the fable
he'll come and get him

So much for outer censorship, which Kunze continued to oppose and satirize in full consciousness of the risks involved. Inner censorship could be even more constricting, since it nagged the poet with constant reminders that even his defiance would change nothing. Reiner Kunze also wrote a poem that positively dissolves itself into silence and blankness, making all the crucial connections between minimal poetry, minimal language, and the shrinking space occupied by the individual where the 'collective' is worshipped as an omnipotent deity:

Entschuldigung

Ding ist ding
sich selbst genug

Überflüssig
das zeichen

überflüssig
das wort

(Überflüssig
ich)

.   .   .   .   .

Apology

A thing's a thing
sufficient to itself

superfluous
the sign

superfluous
the word

(superfluous
I)

The elliptic syntax of that poem – as compared with the regular and logical syntax of Brecht – serves to avoid the presumption of statement of assertion. This was poetry with its back to the wall, uttering the barest of dispensable words to bear witness still to the truth, even if that truth was its own dispensability.

Kunze wrote another fable called 'Das Ende der Kunst' (The End of Art), but the dialectic and paradox of poetry demand that even silence be articulated, even defeat and exasperation recorded. The danger of being silenced by force – as Wolf Biermann was within the GDR, and Kunze, who defended him, also came to be before being allowed to leave the country – did not deter him. He wrote a poem about that, too, in a poem without a fable and closely akin to Kunert's 'Differences':

Zimmerlautstärke

Dann die
zwölf jahre
durfte ich nicht publizieren sagt
der mann im radio

Ich denke an X
und beginne zu zählen

.   .   .   .   .

Low Volume

Then for
twelve years
I was forbidden to publish says
the man on the radio

I think of X
and start counting

The implied analogy with a writer silenced under the twelve years of National Socialist rule made this the most daring and provocative of all Kunze's poems in defence of freedom, for it was a most sensitive point in a state that claimed to have made a clean sweep of Nazism, unlike the other Germany, in which both Kunze and Biermann were ultimately compelled to settle.

Only Kunze's minimal language preserved him from the blatant and outraged defiance of the 'collective' in Biermann's poem 'Rucksichtslose Schimpferei' (All-in Tirade), with its opening assertion 'Ich ich ich'. Not only this emphatic assertion of the personal principle, but his preference elsewhere for ballads and pop-song lyrics (which were recorded in the GDR for export to the Federal Republic, while Wolf Biermann was forbidden to perform or publish them in his own country), brought Biermann closer to the position of the early, pre-Marxist Brecht than any of his East German contemporaries. Even this defiant and exasperated poem contains an admission of personal fallibility, and Biermann, too, has his place in the later Brecht's succession. With a charm and a lightness of touch peculiar to him, he employed minimal diction and epigrammatic trenchancy in this short poem:

Ach freund, geht es nicht auch dir so?

ich kann nur lieben
   was ich die Freiheit habe
     auch zu verlassen:

dieses Land
diese Stadt
diese Frau
dieses Leben

Eben darum lieben ja
wenige ein Land
manche eine Stadt
viele eine Frau
aber alle das Leben

     .   .   .   .   .

Oh friend, don't you find it's the same with you?

I can only love
   what I am also free
     to leave:

> this country
> this city
> this woman
> this life
>
> And that's the reason why
> so few love a country
> some love a city
> many love a woman
> but all love life.

A great many more poets and poems could be cited in this context; and Brecht's successors included West German poets, as well as East European poets writing in languages other than German. Brevity in itself did not necessarily arise from the needs and intentions with which I have been concerned. In America, for instance, oriental forms like the *haiku* – which also influenced Brecht – were cultivated for purposes and reasons quite different from those of Brecht or his East German successors, giving prominence to the very autonomous image that Brecht virtually banished from his later verse. Nor was Brecht's the only line of succession in the GDR. From Peter Huchel and Stephan Hermlin, Erich Arendt and Johannes Bobrowski to Volker Braun and Karl Mickel, right down to the youngest generation represented in the anthology *Berührung ist nur eine Randerscheinung* of 1985, good poetry has been written in the GDR quite independently of Brecht's lineage, and it is now as diverse as that of any pluralist society.

Historically, the whole phenomenon of minimal language in poetry, whether in East or West Germany, was never a purely literary one. Poetry has always tended towards compression, so much so that Ezra Pound wanted the German word 'dichten' – to make poetry – to be derived from the adjective 'dicht' (dense), though etymologically it is not. Brecht's language, though, was not particularly dense or condensed. Except where he was cryptic, deliberately so, for good and cunning reasons, his plain language was logical and relaxed, minimal only in its avoidance of ornament, emotive devices, and the subjective associations cultivated by Romantics and Symbolists. What Brecht wanted, and would have achieved if political developments had allowed it, was a social poetry of dialogue about matters of interest to everyone. This eminently classical relationship between writer and reader had long been made impossible by the individualism of writers and readers alike, and nowhere more so than in serious and 'advanced' poetry, with its need to escape from vulgar norms of communication in every conceivable direction. It was to put poetry and poets back where he thought they belonged, in society and in history, that Brecht undertook his drastic and rigorous revision of the functions and practice of the art.

Brecht's successors, Marxists like himself when they began, accepted his premises and wished to work along the same lines; but the freedom granted to Brecht as a special cultural asset was not granted to most of them. Far from welcoming the advice and criticism of poets whose social and moral awareness did not turn them into conformists, the Party executives grudgingly tolerated them at best – with fluctuations not always of their choice, when the GDR itself was under pressure from the Soviet Union – publicly disgraced or silenced them at the worst, so forcing them to emigrate, if not actually expelling them. The more repressive those authorities who claimed to represent the will of the masses, the more the poets questioned the reality of such a collective will. The very medium which Brecht had evolved for plain speaking in poetry became the last remaining receptacle for frantic messages so abbreviated as to be almost more cryptic than the hermetic poetry it had replaced. To carry that development any farther would have amounted to self-imposed silence, and thus to defeat. It followed that poetry had to put on flesh again, as it did in the work of Volker Braun, Karl Mickel, and Sarah Kirsch – a poet far less austere from the start, who also left for West Germany. These, and others, also began to draw much more freely on immediate personal experience, not only of the socially exemplary kind.

Even in its extreme reduction – dispensable words set down by dispensable poets – minimal poetry should remain of interest as an instance of the extraordinary resilience of poetry, its power to survive and function when it was little more than a skeleton, stripped of all the sensuous appeal traditionally associated with it. Though by omission, ellipsis, disguise, it managed to tell the truth about itself and society, when no other medium could do so. When outer and inner pressures forbade the free play of imagination, feeling and perception, its very austerity and reticence served to uphold that freedom, if only by reminding readers of its loss. Unlike some of the protest poetry written elsewhere, in other circumstances, it cannot be dismissed as a form of self-indulgence, since it admitted no personal idiosyncrasy, no expansive gesture, no intoxicating or intoxicated eloquence; and it was written by men who had no illusions about the effectiveness of protest in poetry. Yet, by a self-effacement that was also political self-exposure, they protested none the less. If, by another dialectical twist, that desperate defiance points back to the fundamental autonomy of poetic language, Brecht himself granted that 'art is an autonomous realm', though as a Marxist he distinguished this necessary autonomy from what he called 'autarchy'. Not till after the great exodus of good poets from the GDR in the late 1970s – precipitated by the expulsion of Wolf Biermann – did there seem to be a general recognition that norms cannot be enforced in imaginative literature, simply because 'the spirit bloweth where it listeth'. Yet even the 1985 anthology I have mentioned, containing work by little-known poets who have little in common but independence, was published in the Federal Republic, though it was edited in the GDR.

From DIVIDED COMMITMENTS

[Heinrich Böll]

... OF ALL the writers associated with the *Gruppe 47*, the one most generally accessible to a large reading public, and in both Republics at that, was Heinrich Böll, whose standing as a post-war *praeceptor Germaniae* was confirmed by the award to him of the Nobel Prize for Literature and many other honours. (Nelly Sachs received the prize not as a German author – she never settled in Germany after the war – but as a survivor of the 'Holocaust', sharing it with another Jewish writer S.J. Agnon. Nor was Elias Canetti ever a German author other than in language, though in his later years his work was as much part of German literature as that of Nelly Sachs or that of Paul Celan, who never lived in Germany at any period of his life. Nelly Sachs had been a German author before she became a Jewish one.) Much as Johannes Bobrowski – born in the same year as Böll, 1917 – was seen as a representative of the Lutheran Church and of what had been Eastern Germany before the war, Heinrich Böll was seen as a representative of the Roman Catholic Rhineland that had become the centre of the Federal Republic after the loss of Berlin as a capital. He was also one of the first younger post-war writers to learn the lessons of the war both as an ex-soldier, and as a writer open to the example of American and British writers of fiction, especially of the short story, avoiding the German temptation to construct no less than whole sociologies or cosmologies in novel form. Together with Wolfgang Borchert, a writer much more strident than Böll, and one who did not live long enough to get over his obsession with his wartime experiences, Böll won that representative standing with his early stories about returning soldiers, followed almost at once by stories and short novels that confronted the problems of civilian life in a newly constituted West Germany still very unsure of itself. More than Alfred Andersch, who spent his later life in Switzerland, Böll never ceased to grapple with whatever issues seemed most urgent and topical in a manner straightforward enough in most of his major novels to make those issues look like anyone's concerns, yet with a seriousness and integrity that made no concessions to a specious popularity. If his work as a whole can be read as a kind of history of post-war West Germany and its tensions, this was less because he deliberately set out to be representative than because he was more identified by nature and background than most German writers with a certain way of life, in which a great many other people could recognize their own. In other words, Böll did not need to 'socialize' himself. He was social from the start – a genuine and very rare distinction where a sense of belonging could not be taken for granted among intellectuals and writers. Realistic fiction was congenial to him for that reason, though he also excelled at fantasy and satire. His radical Christian commitment, which was also a humanistic commitment, gave him the humility and compassion that made 'ordinary' people interesting enough for sustained character studies, drawn with a realism he rightly called 'sacramental'. That same realism, much less rare in other twentieth-century literatures than it is in German writing in either Republic, despite demands for 'socialist realism' in the GDR at one time, also contributed to his international accessibility.

The same commitment, however, made Böll a critic of the society of which he felt part, and a critic of the Church to which he belonged; and that function, too, went back to his beginnings, as he recorded in one of his last books, his autobiographical sketch *Was Soll aus dem Jungen bloss Werden* (1981; What's to Become of the Boy). This account of his last four school years, under the shadow of Nazification and re-militarization, is also a piece of history, a memoir of that period rather than an autobiography, since he was less concerned with the unique sensibility of the adolescent who was to turn into the most representative of post-war West German novelists than with experiences and attitudes not peculiar to himself. For that very reason, the memoir is not only consistent with his works of fiction but a key to them. Though the story breaks off at his matriculation, before his brief apprenticeship as a bookseller, followed by labour service, university studies, military conscription and marriage, Böll's readers knew what became of the boy. What they did not know, until he told them, is that it was the adolescence that shaped the writer we know, a writer who managed to be at once representative and a highly controversial figure. He was repeatedly smeared and attacked as subversive in the West German media, especially after the publication of his long story *Die Verlorene Ehre der Katharina Blum* (1974; The Lost Honour of Katharina Blum), which was misread as a defence of terrorists.

From his adolescence onwards, Böll consistently avoided the introversion and introspection which, according to Thomas Mann, had long been the moral and political alibi of other German writers in the face of unacceptable institutions and régimes. Böll's memoir begins on 30 January 1933, when Hindenburg handed over the Chancellorship to Hitler, and Böll happened to be fifteen years and six weeks old – not with any psychological pre-history or trauma that might have made his subject interesting in any but a representative way. Characteristically, too, Böll was wary of the tricks that memory plays on autobiographers more intent on fine writing than on a truthfulness that could be drab, admitting almost at once that 'I am no longer sure of how some of my personal experiences synchronize with historical events', and exposing two of his memory's tricks. I have said that autobiography is a form of fiction. Böll's little book is not an autobiography, but a memoir, because he resisted the imaginative processes that would have made it fiction. Since literal truthfulness was his purpose, he also refused to pretend that he suffered acutely under the German school system even when it came under pressure from Nazism, merely stating that he was allergic to that creed, and clarifying the allergy in these words:

> My unconquerable (and still unconquered) aversion to the Nazis was not revolt: *they* revolted *me*, repelled me on every level of my being: conscious *and* instinctive, aesthetic *and* political. To this day I have been unable to find any entertaining, let alone aesthetic, dimension to the Nazis and their era, a fact that makes me shudder when I see certain film and stage productions. I simply *could not* join the Hitler Youth, I did not join it, and that was that.

Böll's refusal to say more, or to apologize for the measure of outward compromise forced on his family for survival, makes his account much more convincing than the self-questioning and moral condemnation in which he might have indulged.

Although there are very few wholly evil or wicked characters in Böll's fiction – his realism and his compassion forbade such demonization – this early revulsion stayed with him as a distrust of officialdom and its blinkered servants, his hatred of the surveillance that was to be practised in the Federal Republic also, and his opposition to the Cold War propaganda disseminated by the powerful Springer Press. It is recognizable in the clash of principles, in

Ansichten eines Clowns (1963), denoted by 'the sacrament of the Lamb' and 'the sacrament of the Buffalo' – where English readers must know that the German word 'Buffel' has the colloquial sense of 'lout' or 'thug'.

In the memoir, one way in which the adolescent minimized those sufferings at school which Böll calls 'mandatory for German authors' was by playing truant as often as possible, walking the streets instead; and he links that expedient to his immediate background by observing elsewhere that 'a dedicated feeling for legality does not form part of the Cologne attitude to life'. Though he tells us no more about the characters and inner lives of his parents, brothers and sisters than about his own, what the memoir conveys most vividly is the degree to which he regarded himself as the product of a particular conditioning by his family, social class, religion and region. As a self-employed cabinet maker, his father belonged to an economically imperilled and insecure class – that artisan class which would include writers also if, like Böll, they could rid themselves of the pretence that they are 'unacknowledged legislators' – whose mentality Böll described as 'that explosive mixture of lower middle class vestiges, Bohemian traits, and proletarian pride, not truly belonging to any class, yet arrogant rather than humble, in other words, almost class-conscious again.' The 'arrogance' here is independence and cussedness; and the 'class-consciousness' is only the refusal to acknowledge class superiorities, rather than spiritual and moral ones. The family's Roman Catholicism, too, was deep-rooted, yet anything but conformist. 'The elements of those three classes', Böll wrote, 'to none of which we truly belonged, had made what might be called "bourgeois" Christianity absolutely insufferable to us.' At the time of the Concordat between the Vatican and the newly established Third Reich, Böll's family considered leaving the Church, but 'Catholic was what we wanted to be and remain, in spite of all our derisive laughter and abuse.' This seemingly contradictory stance placed the family in a limbo under Nazism; and it was to lead the writer into a public controversy with an Archbishop in his opposition to what he called 'the capitulation of German Catholicism to post-war opportunism'.

As for the boy's education, though much of it was acquired in 'the school of the streets' or at home, where he read Jack London but also Greek and Latin texts, Böll's Roman Catholic secondary or grammar school was so far from being thoroughly Nazified that it was closed down before the end of the war. It was the school of the streets that shocked Böll into the awareness essential to the story writer he became, for, relatively civilized though it remained, the other school 'prepared us not for life but for death'. The shocks that stand out in Böll's account are the Concordat, the summary decapitation, at Goering's orders, of seven young Communists, and the occupation by German troops of the previously demilitarized Rhineland. Again they are consistent with the imaginative writer's lifelong concern with the victimized and rejected – more often women than men – in his best novels, like *Gruppenbild mit Dame* (1971; Group Portrait with Lady), but not always. In the early novel *Und sagte kein einziges Wort* (1953; Acquainted with the Night) the narrative is divided impartially between the male and female protagonists. In *Ansichten eines Clowns* it is the 'clown', Schnier, who is sacrificed to the 'post-war opportunism' implicating the Church, when it is suggested that his cohabitation with Marie, who deserts him to marry a Catholic functionary, was the true sacrament – Böll's 'sacrament of the Lamb'.

That Böll came close to studying theology, rather than Classics and German, after school, and at least considered taking holy orders, will scarcely astonish careful readers of this subversive and representative writer. British readers may find it harder to understand how his economically insecure parents could afford to give all their children a university education, and without creating the kind of social and cultural estrangement the British class structure would have made inescapable at the time, and almost inescapable even now. That is why the 'class-consciousness' of which Böll wrote in the book should not be taken too literally, when in fact it was a consciousness of being classless, and liking it. Böll was never an advocate of any kind of class war, though he was a socialist; and his sympathies as a story-teller cut across the classes, as his radical Christianity demanded that it must.

Another difference between the two countries comes out when Böll refers to 'elderly and successful politicians, church dignitaries, writers, etc.' – but I have said enough about the German anomaly that placed eminent writers in that league. Not the least of Böll's distinctions was that he performed the public function expected of him in that capacity, but never succumbed to the self-importance and pomposity it so often induced in German writers similarly honoured; and that he performed it bravely and generously, paying the full price for it by provoking outrage, malice and vituperation. The memoir, too, is an utterly unpretentious work. Because he remained true to his beginnings, his family, region and convictions, the elderly and successful writer Böll became had no need to patronize, romanticize or apologize for the easy-going boy he had been. The representative standing he was able to maintain for almost four decades, as a writer who could be attacked and disparaged but never dismissed, because he stood for the values which others merely professed when that was expedient, is unlikely to be assumed by any other West German writer. The centre that held for Böll until his death in 1985 – only just, in his last years – holds for few others now; and no writer can represent a society not held together by a centre of that kind. [...]

From DISPLACED PERSONS

[Ingeborg Bachmann]

... THE WORK OF Ingeborg Bachmann, whose early death in Rome was felt to be as great a loss as the suicide of Paul Celan in Paris at the age of forty-nine – the same age at which Uwe Johnson died in England – shows an extraordinary tension between her regional Austrian roots and a self-exile maintained from 1950 until her death in 1973, at the age of forty-seven. The poems to which she owed her early fame combined a modern and individual sensibility with a prosody and diction that seemed traditional, compared with the work of most of her coevals of whatever lineage, that of Benn, Brecht or the linguistically experimental that has flourished in Austria since the 1950s. The uninhibited eloquence of poems like 'An die Sonne' (To the Sun) from her second collection *Anrufung des grossen Bären* of 1956, was attributed to a peculiarly Austrian traditionalism – also striking in the work of Christine Lavant, another Carinthian even more idiosyncratic within her traditional forms, or of Christine Busta, as firmly rooted within her native Vienna. Yet already in Ingeborg Bachmann's first collection of 1953, *Die Gestundete Zeit*, there were poems much more halting and uneasy, in theme as much as in rhythm; and the lyrical flow that had reassured readers still attuned to the euphonies of an earlier era could not be carried over into her later work at all. No third collection of poems followed those early books; and her few later poems enact a loss of spontaneity that has to do with displacement.

Ingeborg Bachmann had also been a prose writer from her youth, contributing short stories to periodicals when she was in her early twenties. These were apprentice work; but two unpublished stories written before those in her book *Das dreissigste Jahr* (1961) and included in her posthumous *Werke* are remarkable. They are 'Anna Maria', a study in the conflicting views of a woman's character and conflicting rumours about her actions, that reduces realism to speculations like Uwe Johnson's about his Jakob, and 'Der Schweisser'. The welder of the story finds a book by Nietzsche in a café, reads it, and begins to live by it, losing his job, neglecting his consumptive wife and the children, and finally killing himself. The 'blinding light' in welding is linked symbolically to the 'blinding light of knowledge'. A doctor in the story tries in vain to make that connection for Reiter, the welder, but he is as fatuous as the Doctor in Büchner's *Woyzeck*, and the two orders cannot be bridged. Alienations of this kind were to preoccupy Ingeborg Bachmann as a writer of fiction. The most pervasive of these alienations has to do with an ambivalent relationship to Austria found in many Austrian writers. For Bachmann, this relationship was complicated by the clash between the values she associated with the Carinthia to which her fiction continued to return and those of Vienna, where she lived for a time. This, too, is an old antagonism for Austrian writers. The love-hate relationship to Vienna comes out most strongly in the title story of her collection *Das dreissigste Jahr*, in which Vienna becomes that 'bonfire city in which the most splendid works of music were thrown on the pyre, in which they reviled and spat on that which came from the righteous heretics, the impatient suicides, the daring explorers and inventors, and everything that was straightest in spirit'. This is part of a long rhetorical tirade more biblical, but no less damning, than some of those in the books of Thomas Bernhard, and it resembles Bernhard's, too, in suddenly veering into praise, the celebration of a Joycean 'epiphany'. Another of Ingeborg Bachmann's recurrent themes – she had studied both Heidegger and Wittgenstein, and Vienna was still haunted by the shade of Karl Kraus, the castigator of linguistic corruption as the root of all evils – is also announced in the same story: 'No new world without a new language'. Personal confession and story-telling do not quite cohere in 'Das dreissigste Jahr'. The male protagonist of the story remains a *persona*, and his antagonist, Moll, never puts on much flesh and blood, any more than the girls who appear and vanish. Reality of that kind is what eluded Ingeborg Bachmann in the city, as in later places of exile. In the collection of stories it is 'Jugend in einer österreichischen Stadt' – set in Bachmann's home town, Klagenfurt – that merges her own person in a community.

In the story 'Alles', the linguistic theme becomes part of the plot, since the experiment conducted by the parents hinges on their denying the baby they call 'Fipps' access to the old language that stands in the way of a 'new world'. Predictably, instead of finding his own language and hence his own mode of awareness, precondition of the new world, Fipps backslides into the old Adam and dies, after trying to knife another boy at school. It is the father and narrator of the story who, briefly, experiences a rebirth, before the boy's death and the father's estrangement from his wife, Hanna. Ingeborg Bachmann's quest for the new language, new awareness, and new world was also to be thwarted, whether in Vienna, Zurich, Berlin or Rome. On the political level – and, like most of her coevals, she wanted a change of heart that would transform society – one reason for that is suggested by the story 'Unter Mördern und Irren', about a reunion of war veterans in a Vienna inn and its intrusion on another gathering there of professional men, who also reminisce about the war from contrasted points of view. One thing they have in common is that they leave their wives at home, and these wives wish that their husbands would die. This feminist concern was to become more and more acute in Ingeborg Bachmann's work. In the story it is not a woman, but a stranger who appears at the inn to tell how he could not bring himself to shoot in the war, and was punished for that by imprisonment and psychiatric treatment, who speaks for the alternative order. When he moves from the gathering of professional men to the war veteran group and provokes them, he is killed by them.

The exclusion of men by an erotic transformation is weighed up in the story 'Ein Schritt nach Gomorrah'. A young girl, Mara, stays behind after a party given by Charlotte, a married woman whose husband is away on a business trip, and refuses to leave. Charlotte tries to escape Mara's demands on her by consenting to go out to a night club, though she is tired, and her husband is expected back in the morning. They return to Charlotte's flat, where Charlotte begins to consider the possibility of a liberation through a lesbian relationship. Mara becomes more and more desperate and begins to break things in the flat. The conflict in Charlotte is not resolved. The feminist concern is even more drastic in Bachmann's re-telling of the 'Undine' legend, in which every man whom Undine meets is the same 'Hans' or Jack to her, good at making and using machines, even capable at times of healing or helping, but unable to immerse in the feminine element, water.

Another aspect of the new language and the new world is at the centre of the story 'Ein Wildermuth', about a judge who has to try a namesake, a young man who killed his father and who is incapable of speaking anything but the truth. The judge, who had also loved truthfulness in his youth, suffers a breakdown in court, exasperated by factual evidence that turns on a button expert's quibbling about a button. The judge gives up his profession. His marriage, too, is unsatisfactory, because his wife, Gerda, is a woman who invents the truths by which she lives. Here Bachmann's recurrent, but many-sided, utopia founders against 'a truth of which no one dreams, which no one wants'. Evocative and provocative as they are, the stories in this book are prose complements to Ingeborg Bachmann's poems, prose correlatives never quite 'objective' enough to fuse her concerns with characters and situations that would engage us in their own right.

The later collection of stories, *Simultan* (1972), adds a more secure grasp of the externals of the alien, cosmopolitan Europe of smart sets and intellectuals that still brought Ingeborg Bachmann no closer to a 'new world'. Though the title story is set in Calabria, the man and woman who have met on their travels for a brief, unsatisfactory affair are both from Vienna. It is the character study of the man, a United Nations executive, that marks Ingeborg Bachmann's progress as a writer of the prose fictions on which she concentrated in later life. Psychological penetration, as well as a new lightness of touch, also distinguishes the story 'Probleme, Probleme', her study of a somewhat narcissistic young woman, Beatrix, who finds everything but sleeping a 'horrible imposition', not excluding her friendship with a married man, Erich, much older than herself. Apart from sleeping, only her hairdresser and her make-up are of interest to her. Sexual and personal relations have become a marginal business, with the implication that men and their world can be endured, just, as long as one does not have to take them seriously.

Fictional autonomy is also achieved in the story 'Ihr glücklichen Augen', even though the act of seeing had been celebrated in earlier poems by Ingeborg Bachmann, and diminished sight may have been a personal concern. Miranda, in the story, uses her bad sight both as a means of seeing only what she wishes to see, or can bear to see, and as a way of ensuring her husband Josef's protectiveness. When Josef becomes involved with Miranda's friend Stasi, who is about to be divorced from her husband, Miranda pretends that she, too, has a lover, so as to make the separation easier for herself and for Josef. After a meeting with Josef and Stasi she receives a blow from a revolving door, due to her near-blindness that is both organic and willed. Bachmann's new lightness of touch gives the story a fine balance between comedy and tragedy.

The two last stories in *Simultan* set up tensions between youth and old age, between the urban world of professional people and an older rural order, between new sophistication and old certainties. In 'Das Gebell', it is the attempt by the third or fourth wife of an eminent and rich psychologist to do something for his eighty-five-year-old mother living in poverty and neglect in a city that must be Vienna. The old woman is haunted by a recurrent barking associated with the dog she got rid of when it had attacked her son on one of his rare visits. Franziska, the daughter-in-law, pays with her own money for gifts to alleviate the old woman's extreme poverty, pretending that the money comes from her famous husband, whose complex relationship with his mother is rendered with subtle and mischievous wit. Franziska, though, cannot keep up her own relationship with the man. She returns to her native Carinthia and dies there. Leo Jordan, the psychologist, marries yet again. Franziska's brother receives the bill for the taxi service that had been one of Franziska's presents to the old woman. Such confrontation is even more direct in 'Drei Wege zum See', the concluding story, set in Ingeborg Bachmann's home province, Carinthia, where Elisabeth, a photographer and journalist, is on a visit to her old father. On her mountain walks and in conversation with her father she ponders her life in the cities and her love affairs. Trotta, the man she had come closest to loving wholeheartedly, had died after their separation. Once more, love between women and men is found wanting:

> There was nothing more to be made of it, and it would be best for men and women to keep a distance, have nothing to do with one another, till both have found a way out of a confusion and the distraction, the discordance of all relationships. Then one day something else could evolve, but only then, and it would be strong and mysterious and possess true grandeur, it would be something to which everyone could submit.

She is in the process of separating from her current lover, Philippe, in Paris. At an airport she has a strange encounter with Trotta's Yugoslav cousin, who has something of the aura of Mandryka in Hofmannsthal's comedy *Arabella*. The same vanished Austria of Imperial times is embodied and represented for her in her father, who clings to his old ways in rural solitude, with a dignity and self-sufficiency lost to younger generations. Elisabeth, of course, will have to resume her way of life, take up her career and entanglements. Ingeborg Bachmann was to grapple with hers in ambitious novels only partly completed before her death.

It is her later poems, though, that most poignantly enact the displacement she had chosen and could not undo. 'Exil' was published in 1957 in the international review *Botteghe Oscure*.

> Ein Toter bin ich der wandelt
> gemeldet nirgends mehr
> unbekannt im Reich der Präfekten
> überzählig in den goldenen Städten
> und im grünenden Land
>
> abgetan lange schon
> und mit nichts bedacht
>
> Nur mit Wind mit Zeit und mit Klang
>
> der ich unter Menschen nicht leben kann
>
> Ich mit der deutschen Sprache
> dieser Wolke um mich
> die ich halte als Haus
> treibe durch alle Sprachen
>
> O wie sie sich verfinstert
> die dunklen die Regentöne
> nur die wenigen fallen
>
> In hellere Zonen trägt dann sie den Toten hinauf
>
> .   .   .   .   .   .
>
> A dead man I am who travels
> not registered anywhere
> unknown in the realm of the prefects
> redundant in the golden cities
> and in the countryside's green
>
> written off long ago
> and provided with nothing
>
> Only with wind and with time and with sound

who cannot live among human beings

I with the German language
this cloud around me
that I keep as a house
drive through all languages

Oh, how it darkens
those muted those rain tones
only few of them fall

Up into brighter zones it will carry the dead man

That it should be language, the exile's home, that is endangered by
the very displacement which has made it his only home, is clarified by
the stories. There language is not only the poet's own, but the vehicle
of that change in consciousness, conscience and society that Ingeborg
Bachmann had left her regional home to find and help bring about.
Her later poem 'Ihr Worte', dedicated to Nelly Sachs and contributed
in 1961 to a volume in her honour, was followed by only six more
poems written between 1964 and 1967. 'Ihr Worte' tells us why
Ingeborg Bachmann had come up against a barrier which Nelly Sachs
and Paul Celan could cross only by making it the starting-point and
precondition of their work.

Ihr Worte, auf, mir nach!,
und sind wir auch schon weiter,
zu weit gegangen, geht's noch einmal
weiter, zu keinem Ende geht's.

Es hellt nicht auf.

Das Wort
wird doch nur
andre Worte nach sich ziehn,
Satz den Satz.
So möchte Welt,
endgültig,
sich aufdrängen,
schon gesagt sein.
Sagt sie nicht.

Worte, mir nach,
dass nicht endgültig wird
– nicht diese Wortbegier
und Spruch auf Widerspruch!

Lasst eine Weile jetzt
keins der Gefühle sprechen,
den Muskel Herz
sich anders üben.

Lasst, sag ich, lasst,

ins höchste Ohr nicht,
nichts, sag ich, geflüstert,
zum Tod fall dir nichts ein,
lass, und mir nach, nicht mild
noch bitterlich,
nicht trostreich,
ohne Trost
bezeichnend nicht,
so auch nicht zeichenlos –

Und nur nicht dies: das Bild
im Staubgespinst, leeres Geroll
von Silben, Sterbenswörter.

Kein Sterbenswort,
Ihr Worte!

     . . . . .

Up, you words, follow me!
and if we have gone farther,
too far already, once more
farther let's go, to no end.

It casts no light.

The word
will only drag
other words behind it,
one sentence another.
So world

with finality
would impose itself,
be already said.
Do not say it.

Follow me, words,
so that it will not be final –
not this lust for words
and saying, gainsaying.

For a while now let
none of the feelings speak,
the muscle heart
differently exercise.

Let, I say, let

into the highest ear
nothing, I say, be whispered,
nothing occur to you about death,
let, and follow me, not gently
not bitterly,
not consolingly,
with no consolation
signifying not,
and so not signless either –

And least of all this: the image
in dust floss, empty rolling
of syllables, dying words breathed.

Don't breathe one dying word,
you words!

It would be impertinent to explain or 'interpret' that poem, which is almost untranslatable too, beginning with the German plural 'Worte', which means 'utterances' or 'statements', as distinct from the other plural form, 'Wörter' (vocables). Those two senses of the word are in conflict throughout the poem; and 'Sterbenswort' has an idiomatic sense. 'Kein Sterbenswort', idiomatically, means 'Don't breathe a word!'. Yet poetry has a habit of taking idioms literally, and the 'dying' is very much part of the sense, in a poem on the brink of silence – where even 'on' becomes ambiguous! The trilogy of novels on which Ingeborg Bachmann was working in her last years was to have the overall title *Todesarten* (Ways of Death). They are what remained of Ingeborg Bachmann's utopia, of the 'new world' and the 'new language' for which she had left her home. [...]

From THE NON-REPRESENTATIONAL ALTERNATIVE

[Ernst Jandl]

... ALTHOUGH he has written concrete poetry of the purest kind, Ernst Jandl began as a writer of 'representational' verse and has continued to go not his own way, but his own ways, wherever they might lead him. His first book of poems, *Andere Augen* (1956), appeared five years after the opening of the Vienna 'art club' and the formation of the Vienna Group, but neither the contents nor the design of this book, published in a series devoted to Austrian writers predominantly traditional, would have given its readers any reason to associate him with either. Yet his next publication was a preface to a book edited by H. C. Artmann, who was at the centre of the club and the Group. If that seems an inconsistency or a contradiction, it was a fruitful one, for it was out of the tension between all the possibilities open to writers in his time that Jandl drew the energy for his prolific and various work of the next three decades. His next books of poems were published in Stuttgart and at Frauenfeld, the two headquarters of experimental and concrete writing in German, his fourth, with the characteristically Anglo-German title *mai hart lieb zapfen eibe hold* (1965), in London. When Jandl published his substantial collection *Laut und Luise* in 1966, with an epilogue by Helmut Heissenbüttel, he was prominent mainly as a performer of his sound poems, which could communicate their energy, if not their meaning, even to the English audiences who heard them at the Albert Hall and elsewhere. His immediately popular poems were sound poems like 'schmerz durch reibung' (pain through friction) made out of the sounds in the single word 'Frau'; or 'schtzngrmm' made out of the consonants in the German word 'Schützengraben' (trench). Poems of this kind needed to be heard rather than read, since the letters on the page are a mere notation more difficult to take in through the eye than a musical score; and because no one but the poet himself can vocalize them exactly as they are meant to be vocalized, a gramophone record was issued as a complement to the text. The last line of 'schtzngrmm', for instance, 't-tt', looks like an onomatopoeic enactment of rifle or machine-gun fire on the page, whereas in the poet's reading it also conveys a dying fall and the German word 'tot'. Jandl had lived in England as a German teacher in the early 1950s, and worked as an English teacher in Vienna before becoming a full-time writer. It was to those occupations that we owe his English poems and his bilingual poems like 'calypso', which begins:

> ich was not yet
> in brasilien
> nach brasilien
> wulld ich laik du go

(where the 'du' in the last line reflects the Austrian and South German difficulty in distinguishing between 'd' and 't', but also adds a delightful illogicality by introducing an irrelevant 'you').

Though sound poems preponderated in that collection, these sound poems could be witty or serious, mimetic or fantastic, satirical or expressive; and there were also prose poems – like the sequence about England, 'prosa aus der flüstergalerie' (prose from the whispering gallery) – more akin to some of the experimental texts of Heissenbüttel, and other sequences whose main appeal is to the eye or to the intellect. Jandl's sound permutations draw on a great variety of idioms, particularly on Viennese dialect – in which Artmann had written a brilliant sequence of poems, 'med ana schwoazzn dintn' (1958) – and those Austrian responses to the sounds of the English language. Elsewhere his sources could be literary, like the line by Wordsworth that provided the title for his London book, or when phrases from Goethe and Hölderlin are taken up in the sequence 'zehn abend-gedichte' and in the longer variations 'klare gerührt'.

Jandl's practice has always borne out Heissenbüttel's claim that experiment and tradition are neither incompatible nor irreconcilable, and that Jandl's poems are not absolutely different from any others written in the past. Quite apart from the 'tradition of the new', many of Jandl's texts in verse and prose can be seen as developments of recognized and time-honoured forms. The sequence 'epigrams' in *Laut und Luise* is only one of many instances. Nor could Jandl ever be accused of narrowing down the resources and effects of lyrical poetry. Observation, reflection, feeling and pure invention have their place in his work, even where the material has been reduced to the components of a single word. Even the dramatic potentialities of his media, which were to be fulfilled in his stage play *Aus der Fremde* in 1980, were already latent not only in his earliest sound poems but in the little play made out of the names of three cities, London, Paris and Rome, included in *Laut und Luise*.

It is not often that a poet responds adequately when asked to talk about his own work, for reasons that are woven into the argument of Jandl's lectures *Die schöne Kunst des Schreibens* (1976; enlarged edition, 1983). Jandl's performance was not only adequate, but exemplary, because he decided that if he was going to respond at all to such an occasion he might as well make the most of it, for his audience and for himself, producing texts that not only illuminate his own practice but enter searchingly and truthfully into the whole question of what a poet can usefully say about his own craft. His conviction that, basically, a poem is one thing, whatever is said about it – by the author or anyone else – quite another, underlies all his observations; but it does not prevent him from revealing what he does know about the genesis and quiddity of his poems, and revealing it with such sustained attentiveness both to the matter itself and to the needs of his listeners that he could not fail to do more than the occasion demanded. He begins with examples of the four kinds of poems he has written: the poem that uses everyday language and normal grammar; the poem for reading aloud ('Sprechgedicht'); the pure sound poem ('Lautgedicht'), whose structure approximates to music but, in Jandl's case, does not necessarily exclude a message of sorts; and the 'silent' visual poem. (Examples of the last were projected on to a screen, and his remarks on them are not included in the first edition of the printed text, perhaps because they were extemporized.) In the process he not only analyses the examples, but explains why he found it necessary to write those different kinds of poems and why, for him, there are essential links between them. He also discusses language norms, necessary deviations from them in poetry, and the degree of serious, or not so serious, word-play that each kind of poem demands for its functioning.

> i love concrete
> i love pottery
> but i'm not
> a concrete pot

is one of his less serious explanations of why he has been able to excel in all those four kinds, including the 'straight' poem that renders an experience or insight without splitting words or syntax. Although little biographical information is relevant to Jandl's concerns in these lectures, he does comment on his formative years in England; and perceptive readers of the book will not need Jandl's acknowledgement of how much this wholly unacademic poet owes to his profession of English teacher – not least, the courtesy, patience and directness with which he communicates radical and complex discoveries.

These have to do not only with language, but with the relationship between theory and practice in literature, his distinction between three kinds of literary theory, the normative, the deductive and the prescriptively programmatic, and the reasons why it is easy for practising writers to fall into error when trying to make theoretical deductions from their own practice. Another outstanding passage deals with the relationship between a writer's person and his work. Here Jandl quietly and humorously demolishes the cult of personality – or, more precisely, of names and signatures – in the arts, showing just how little the name attached to it has to do with the essentially autonomous work, while admitting that his very opportunity to say so would not have arisen but for curiosity about his person and name. Characteristically, again, he does not sneer at this curiosity, but defines it with delicate precision and a total lack of vanity. Throughout the lectures Jandl takes nothing for granted. Just as in his poems he attains a stringent and questioning simplicity, so in his manner of elucidating them he uses plain words in sentences that may be anything but simple, because they register his awareness of countless contradictions and paradoxes.

As he mentioned in an earlier lecture of 1969, concrete poetry, to Jandl, fulfilled a desire for the 'absolute poem' that goes back to Mallarmé, for a kind of poem that 'is an object, not a statement about an object'; but that desire or aspiration comes up against the fact that 'whoever operates with words, operates with meanings'. Art, for Jandl, is 'the perpetual implementation of a freedom', a freedom he has maintained for himself by access to the whole field of tensions between the different kinds of writing he has practised. Far from making concessions to 'the demon of progress in the arts' (Wyndham Lewis), though, Jandl did not even claim a personal 'development' for himself. Not only did he state that 'merely by writing poems' the experimental poet 'continues a tradition', although that tradition consists of many traditions, but he wrote: 'By the time I was 9 years old I had written my first poem. I still stand in the same place.'

This astonishing remark becomes clearer in the light of Jandl's later work. When – astonishingly once more – he managed to produce a second workshop report without repeating himself, his Frankfurt lectures on poetics *Das Öffnen und Schliessen des Mundes* of 1985, he had added several sub-divisions to the four kinds of poem listed in the earlier report. One of these, a variant of the 'straight' or conventional poem, was what he called 'verkindlichte Sprache', a diction made child-like; and it had been misread as a kind of 'pidgin' German akin to that spoken by some of the foreign 'guest workers' before they had mastered the new language. On the level of personal 'development', this new departure was a regression. Linguistically and poetically, it gave Jandl a whole new range of possibilities, since both childhood and inarticulateness are human realities, as valid and worthy of being enacted in poems as any other. In his books of poems *der gelbe hund* (1980) and *Selbstporträt des schachspielers als trinkende uhr* (1983), as well as in his stage play or 'opera for speaking voices', *Aus der Fremde* of 1980, Jandl was as unreservedly honest as ever about the personal crisis that had pushed him into this regressive mode. What was more important to him was to make the best of that crisis as a craftsman and artificer, persist in his struggle with language even when he had no other matter for verse than what came out of that struggle. The act of writing itself had always been of interest to Jandl. That is why his reports on it are exemplary, in their truthfulness, precision and detachment. In his very first book of poems there had been one about the act of writing, 'Stilleben' (Still Life):

> Ich habe meinen Kugelschreiber, der rot-blau schreibt,
> auf die Zündholzschachtel gelegt.
> Das ist aufregend wie die Feuerwehr,
> verglichen mit dem Schreibpapier daneben.
>
> Das gelang mir nach dem Versuch,
> einen grossartigen Gedanken zu haben.
> (Ein Blatt Papier starb dabei an einem Ausschlag
> von hässlichen blauen Buchstaben.)
>
> .   .   .   .   .
>
> I have laid my ball-pen which writes
> red or blue on the matchbox.
> That is thrilling as the fire engine,
> compared with the sheet of paper beside it.

I succeeded in that after trying
to have a magnificent thought.
(In the process a sheet of paper
died of a rash of ugly blue letters.)

Even this early poem is characterized by self-detachment, humour and frankness, but also by a childlike wonderment at things and processes so ordinary that for most grown-up people, let alone most poets, they would not be worth writing about, but dismissed and put away as childish things.

    der gelbe hund contains no sound or visual poem. The poems in this book are a factual, almost day-to-day, record of a profound depression and, at the same time, an attempt to overcome it by the act of writing, as this one, 'der nagel', enacts in its regressive, primitive diction:

festnageln ich will
diesen da tag, jeden da
jeden da tag da fest
nageln ich will dass nicht
mir er entkomme mir dass nicht
mir er entkomme mehr dass nicht
einer entkomme mir mehr nicht ein
einziger mehr mir entkomme wie
vorher als so viele ich nicht
festgenagelt habe mit gedicht

   . . . . .

the nail

nail down I will
this here day, every here
every here day here nail
down I will so that
it shall not slip away again
not slip away from me so that
not one shall slip away not one
single day slip away from me as
before when so many I did not
nail down with poem one jot

This would have been a risky or impossible undertaking for any poet less skilled than Jandl in the art of letting language have its own way.

As it is, these poems – carefully dated to preserve their chronological sequence – rarely fail to be engaging, instructive and witty, though they make no bones about the desperation from which they sprang. Jandl's trust in the power of words to create meaning, when everything else had grown meaningless for him, proved well-founded. An extreme honesty and an extreme indifference to the self-exposure involved in the exercise – carried even farther in *Aus der Fremde*, a play about himself, writing the play, and his long-standing association with the writer Friederike Mayröcker – were its precondition. All the data of the experiment are set down:

nichts und etwas

nichts im kopf
setze ich mich
an die maschine
spanne ein blatt ein
mit nichts darauf

mit etwas darauf
ziehe das blatt ich
aus der maschine
und lese als text
etwas aus meinem kopf

.   .   .   .   .

nothing and something

nothing in my head
I sit down
at the typewriter
insert a sheet
with nothing on it

with something on it
I extract the sheet
from the typewriter
and read as a text
something out of my head

This is minimal poetry with a vengeance, not even distanced here by sub-literary diction, rhyme, or by the reported speech subjunctive maintained throughout in *Aus der Fremde* and in some of the poems in this and Jandl's next collections. Yet this little poem celebrates a miracle and mystery of sorts. Something has really come out of nothing, thanks to the reductive simplicity and starkness of the act that is its own description and interpretation, with no evasion by way of metaphor, 'heightened' diction or emotive appeal. Other poems in the book are more intricate, such as the self-analysis 'a man of achievement' – the title is in English – which does resort to the distancing device of reported speech, like the dialogue in *Aus der Fremde*.

In both the play and the poems extremes meet once more, in that linguistic experiment fuses with its opposite, the most drastic realism in the rendering of psychological, biographical and social truths. For by his clinical self-detachment in dealing with his own crisis, Jandl makes it more than a personal matter, just as the verbal play in his early sound poems had not prevented them from engaging most effectively with the moral and political issues that preoccupied the 'mainstream' realists. At least one poem in *Selbstporträt des schachspielers als trinkende uhr* takes him well beyond the accurate transcription of the data and results of his desperate experiment in the defiance of blankness and silence:

das schöne bild

    spar aus dem schönen bild den menschen aus
    damit die tränen du, die jeder mensch verlangt
    aussparen kannst; spar jede spur von menschen aus:
    kein weg erinnere an festen gang, kein feld an brot
    kein wald an haus und schrank, kein stein an wand
    kein quell an trank, kein teich kein see kein meer
    an schwimmer, boote, ruder, segel, seefahrt
    kein fels an kletternde, kein wölkchen
    an gegen wetter kämpfende, kein himmelstück
    an aufblick, flugzeug, raumschiff – nichts
    erinnere an etwas; ausser weiss an weiss
    schwarz an schwarz, rot an rot, gerade an gerade
    rund an rund;
    so wird meine seele gesund.

    · · · · ·

the beautiful picture

withhold the human from your beautiful picture
so that you can withhold the tears for which
all human beings call; withhold the very trace:
let no path mark firm passage, no field recall bread
no forest house or wardrobe, no stone a wall
no spring their drinking, no pond no lake no sea
a swimmer, boat, oar, sail or navigation
no rock a climber, not one little cloud
those who resist the weather, no patch of sky
an upward glance or aircraft space-ship – let
nothing recall anything, but white recall white
black, black, red, red, straight recall straight
round recall round;
then shall my soul be healed, again be sound.

This poem does not shun rhetoric or pathos, and places itself most firmly in an older poetic tradition. (I, for instance, can hear an echo in it of Gonzalo's utopian speech in *The Tempest*; and this echo adds to the negative utopia of Jandl's poem, his exclusion of everything human from the picture that celebrates it by the very negation and exclusion – as though the utopia, now, can be reached only on the other side of extinction. Every negation in the poem posits its opposite; and this very appeal for an abstract picture becomes the least abstract poem in the book.) As for the personal crisis, this poem transcends it by facing up to its more than personal implications; it becomes a breakthrough, and a breakout from the language laboratory and its isolation. Jandl's experiment in that laboratory had proved that the very act of writing could wrest minimal meaning from meaninglessness. This poem is like a reward for the persistence and sheer industry the experiment had demanded. By regression in time and manner that also admits an old richness of import and allusion, it gathers up the various threads in Jandl's art and liberates all his faculties, as *homo faber*, *homo ludens* and *homo sapiens* combined. The antiquated thing once called inspiration, too, may well have contributed to this generally human poem about the exclusion of everything human. [. . .]

From A PRODIGIOUS EQUIPOISE

[Günter Grass]

IF THERE IS one West German post-war writer who has confounded all the critical categories and classifications, it is Günter Grass; not so much because of his range of media, from lyrical poetry to drama and prose fiction, from essays and dialogues to political speeches, as because within those media he has maintained a balance peculiar to himself between otherwise divisive antinomies. That Grass has also been a boy soldier, wounded in action before the end of the war, a miner, stone-mason and sculptor, or that he remains a graphic artist of distinction and an accomplished cook might be mere biographical accidents or circumstances if Grass's diverse activities had been kept separate, if it were not his way to bring each of them to bear on the other. Günter Grass, in fact, could have been approached in the context of any of the foregoing chapters of this book, but not one of those contexts could have encompassed his significance or his scope.

In the first chapter, for instance, I wrote about the polarization of the conflicting principles and practices of Gottfried Benn on the one hand, Bertolt Brecht on the other, between Benn's 'absolute poetry' – 'words assembled in a fascinating way' and not subject to moral, social or historical criteria – and Brecht's insistence on the uses and usefulness of literature. We have only to ask ourselves to which of these sides or trends Günter Grass belonged as a poet, at the time of his emergence in the early 1950s, to come up against one instance of his capacity to embrace and balance extreme opposites. Shortly after the publication of his first book, *Die Vorzüge der Windhühner* (1956), Grass wrote three short prose pieces that appeared in the periodical *Akzente* under the title 'Der Inhalt als Widerstand' (Content as Resistance), in which imagination and verisimilitude, fantasy and realism, are treated not as alternatives but as generators of a necessary tension. The middle piece, a brief dialogue between two poets, Pempelfort and Krudewil, on a walk together, presents the extreme alternatives. Pempelfort is in the habit of stuffing himself with indigestible food before going to bed, to induce nightmares and the (then fashionable) genitive metaphors he can jot down between fits of sleep;

the quoted specimens of his poems place him in the line of development that includes German Expressionism and the Surrealism that was being rediscovered by young German poets at the time. Krudewil, for his part, wants to 'knit a new Muse' who is 'grey, mistrustful and totally dreamless, a meticulous housewife'. This homely and practical Muse points to the school of Brecht, who drew on dreams not for metaphors but moralities. Grass's treatment of these two characters is good-humouredly and comically impartial. Grass's own early poems, with their free associations and their synaesthesia, their polymorphic playfulness, might have biased him towards Pempelfort. In later years, when ideology reigned, his moderation – and moderation as such – was to be attacked as indifference or weakness or equivocation. In fact the dialogue was an early instance of a strength rare among German intellectuals, the strength of those who don't lose their heads in a crisis. Grass would not have bothered to write the dialogue at all if he had not been deeply involved in a conflict that was to turn German literature into a battlefield in the course of the next decade. It was by quarrelling with himself that he prepared for the battles to come.

Nearly ten years later, when Grass had become a celebrated writer and a controversial public figure, he published another prose piece in the same periodical. It was the lecture 'Vom mangelnden Selbstvertrauen der schreibenden Hofnarren unter Berücksichtigung nicht vorhandener Höfe' (On the Lack of Self-Confidence among Writing Court Fools in View of Non-existent Courts). The very title, with its baroque and ironic identification of writer with court fools, was an affront to the solemn self-righteousness of the dominant radicals, who disapproved not only of Grass's incorrigible addiction to clowning in his verse and prose fiction, but also of his commitment to a political party, the Social Democrats, more evolutionary than revolutionary, and so guilty of moderation and compromise in their view. What is more, Grass came out in favour of a position half-way between what the radicals understood by commitment – the subordination of art to political and social programmes – and the demand of art itself for the free play of imagination, the freedom that Grass, with historical wisdom, traced to the old privilege of court fools or jesters to tell the truth, however subversive that truth might be of the order that had power over them. Unlike most of his radical opponents, Grass had taken the trouble not only to think about politics and power, but to acquaint himself with their machinery by active partici- pation – as early as 1961, through his personal association with Willy Brandt. That, of course, was only the beginning of an involvement that was to cost Grass more conflicts and bitter disappointments, all of which entered into the experience that shaped his imaginative works. If a writer is worried about the state of affairs in his own coun- try or elsewhere, Grass argued in the lecture, the best way, in a parlia- mentary democracy, is to do something about it not as an imaginative writer but as a citizen. As for his writing, if it is imaginative writing, he should resist every kind of extraneous pressure that would trans- form it into a vehicle or a weapon. 'Poems admit of no compromises; but we live by compromises. Whoever can endure this tension every day of his life is a fool and changes the world.'

Gottfried Benn, in his exchange of letters with Alexander Lernet- Holema of 1953, *Monologische Kunst*, had denied categorically that writers or artists can 'change the world'. Brecht had based all his practice on the assumption that they can. By insisting on the auton- omy of art – as Brecht, incidentally, had also done – *and* on the need to change the world by availing oneself of the traditional freedom of court fools, Grass proved a better dialectician than his Marxist oppo- nents. Grass had learned that in literature, as much as in practical politics or cooking, it is not a matter of this or that, but a little more of this rather than a little more of that; not of imagination or 'reality', of clowning or didacticism, of commitment or non-commitment, but of a particular blend of them all in every instance that makes for rightness and richness. Because he has borne this in mind at all times, in everything to which he has applied himself, Grass is not only an anti-specialist – the nearest thing to an all-round man the age allowed him to be, when even Goethe could be said by T. S. Eliot to have 'dabbled in' all the many activities he had tried to co-ordinate and synthesize in his mind – but an anti-ideologist. Even his theoretical pronouncements were nourished and sustained by his awareness of complexity, an awareness that he owes to first-hand experience. In his imaginative works, including his poems and his drawings, the mixture has not remained constant. Just as in his novels there has been a gradual shift away from subjective fantasy to observed realities – though never without an undercurrent of fantasy, fable or even myth – and that shift had its parallel in his plays written up to his 'German tragedy' about Brecht, *Die Plebejer Proben den Aufstand*

(1966), it was his first book of poems that showed Grass at his most exuberantly and uninhibitedly clownish. This is not to say that these early poems lack moral or metaphysical seriousness, but that the element of free play in them is more pronounced and more idiosyncratic than in the later poems, in which the clown had to defend his privilege of freedom both from his own scruples and the combined attack of opponents on the Right and Left.

It has become something of a commonplace in Grass criticism to note that his imagination and invention are most prolific where he is closest to childhood experience, by which I mean both his own, as evoked in the more or less autobiographical sections of his Danzig trilogy, or in the more or less autobiographical poem 'Kleckerburg', and childish modes of feeling, seeing and behaving. Almost without exception, the poems in Grass's first book owe their vigour and peculiarity to this mode of feeling, seeing and behaving. These early poems enact primitive gestures and processes without regard for the distinctions that adult rationality imposes on the objects of perception. (This freedom, rather than an influence, may account for the striking similarities between Grass's early poems and those of Hans Arp, whose principle of fortuitousness gave him a related freedom of association. Grass, who has generously acknowledged his indebtedness as a novelist to Alfred Döblin – even endowing a literary prize in his honour and name – has acknowledged no such debt to Arp for his poetry. Affinity is what matters, in any case, not influence.) Grass's early poems have their being in a world without divisions or distinctions, full of magical substitutions and transformations. Arp's eye and ear had the same mischievous innocence, giving a grotesque twist to everyday things and banal phrases; and Arp, too, was to adapt his unanchored images and metaphors to increasingly moral and social preoccupations, not to mention the metaphysical ones which, much like Grass, he had always combined with his comic zest. Surrealist practice, too, would be relevant as a precedent if Grass's early poems were not as realistic as they are fantastic, with a realism that seems fantastic only because it is true to the polymorphous vision of childhood.

Most of the poems in *Die Vorzüge der Windhühner* deal in unanchored images, like the 'eleventh finger' that cannot be tied down to any particular plane of meaning or symbolism, but owes its genesis and function to a complex of mainly personal associations. Such unanchored and floating images were also carried over into Grass's prose, especially in *Die Blechtrommel*, and some of them had such obsessive power over Grass's imagination that they recur with variations in his poems, prose narratives, plays and drawings. (Dolls, nuns, cooks and hens, snails and fish and mushrooms are a few of those. In many cases, these, in turn, are associated with processes and movements – such as flying, in the case of nuns – that are even more important to Grass than the thing, person or animal in itself.) The substitution practised by Grass in these poems also includes drastic synaesthesia, as in the many poems connected with music, orchestras or musical instruments. Sounds are freely transposed into visual impressions and vice versa, as in 'Die Schule der Tenöre' (The School for Tenors):

> Nimm den Lappen, wische den Mond fort,
> schreibe die Sonne, die andere Münze
> über den Himmel, die Schultafel.
> Setze dich dann.
> Dein Zeugnis wird gut sein,
> du wirst versetzt werden,
> eine neue, hellere Mütze tragen.
> Denn die Kreide hat recht
> und der Tenor der sie singt.
> Er wird den Samt entblättern,
> Efeu, Meterware der Nacht,
> Moos, ihren Unterton,
> jede Amsel wird er vertreiben.
>
> Den Bassisten, mauert ihn ein
> in seinem Gewölbe.
> Wer glaubt noch an Fässer
> in denen der Wein fällt?
> Ob Vogel oder Schrapnell,
> oder nur Summen bis es knackt,
> weil der Äther überfüllt ist
> mit Wochenend und Sommerfrische.
> Scheren, die in den Schneiderstuben
> das Lied von Frühling und Konfektion zwitschern, –
> hieran kein Beispiel.
>
> Die Brust heraus, bis der Wind seinen Umweg macht.
> Immer wieder Trompeten,
> spitzgedrehte Tüten voller silberner Zwiebeln.

Dann die Geduld.
Warten bis der Dame die Augen davonlaufen,
zwei unzufriedene Dienstmädchen.
Jetzt erst den Ton den die Gläser fürchten
und der Staub
der die Gesimmse verfolgt bis sie hinken.

Fischgräten, wer singt diese Zwischenräume,
den Mittag, mit Schilf gespiesst?
Wie schön sang Else Fenske, als sie,
während der Sommerferien,
in grosser Höhe daneben trat,
in einen stillen Gletscherspalt stürzte,
und nur ihr Schirmchen
und das hohe C zurückliess.

Das hohe C, die vielen Nebenflüsse des Mississippi,
der herrliche Atem,
der die Kuppeln erfand und den Beifall.
Vorhang, Vorhang, Vorhang.
Schnell, bevor der Leuchter nicht mehr klirren will,
bevor die Galerien knicken
und die Seide billig wird.
Vorhang, bevor du den Beifall begreifst.

· · · · · ·

Take your duster, wipe away the moon,
write the sun, that other coin
across the sky, the blackboard.
Then take your seat.
Your report will he a good one,
you will go up one class,
wear a new, brighter cap.
For the chalk is in the right
and so is the tenor who sings it.
He will unroll the velvet,
ivy, yard-measured wares of night,
moss, its undertone,
every blackbird he'll drive away.

The bass – immure him
in his vault.

Who now believes in barrels
in which the wine-level falls?
Whether bird or shrapnel
or only a hum till it cracks
because the ether is overcrowded
with weekend and seaside resort.
Scissors which in the tailor's workshops
twitter the song of springtime and haute couture –
this is no example.

Puff out your chest, till the wind takes its devious way.
Trumpets again and again,
conical paper bags full of silver onions.
After that, patience.
Wait till the lady's eyes run away,
two dissatisfied skivvies.
Only now that tone which the glasses fear
and the dust
that pursues the ledges until they limp.

Fishbones, who will sing these gaps,
sing noon impaled with rushes?
How well did Elsie Fenner sing
when, in the summer vacation
at a great height she took a false step,
tumbled into a silent glacier crevasse
and left nothing behind but
her little parasol and the high C.

The high C, the many tributaries of the Mississippi,
the glorious breath
that invented cupolas and applause.
Curtain, curtain, curtain.
Quick, before the candelabrum refuses to jingle,
before the galleries droop
and silk becomes cheap.
Curtain, before you understand the applause.

There is no need to go into an elaborate and solemn explication that
would amount to a translation of the poem into the terms of adult
rationality – terms irrelevant to the poem in any case. It is enough to
point out that its subject or gist is a sequence of kinetic gestures,

derived in the first place from a personal response to the singing of tenors, but proceeding by a series of free substitutions and transpositions. These substitutions and transpositions observe no distinction between one order of experience and another, between aural and visual or tactile phenomena, between what is physically possible and what is not. The world of childhood becomes a *motif* at the start, with the chalk and blackboard images given a cosmographic extension, and the school caps which in Germany used to mark membership of successive classes by their colours and are associated with progress, promotion and ascent, like the tenor voice. That, however, is a simile; and in Grass's poems metaphor is autonomous, a thing is not *like* another thing but is the other thing for the purpose and duration of the poem, as it is in children's games. Yet, although one thing in the poem leads to another, by associations that are astonishingly fluid, the poem is held together by an organization different from automatic writing in that the initial phenomenon is never quite left behind. Ingenuity and intellectual invention, too, are part of that organization, as in metaphysical or baroque poetry and its 'conceits'. Grass's love of the seventeenth century, its picaresque fiction and metaphysical wit, can be traced in his novels from *Die Blechtrommel* (1959; *The Tin Drum*) to *Das Treffen in Telgte* (1979; *The Meeting at Telgte*). Grass avails himself of the freedom of polymorphous childishness; but because he is not a child, and even his poems of innocence include his awareness of experience, wit serves him as a necessary mediator between the conscious and unconscious reservoirs that feed his art. The association of the bass voice, for instance, with a cellar, hence with wine and, most appropriately, with a wine-barrel or vat in which the fluid level falls, is so elementary as to be easily followed by anyone who has not lost all access to the sub-rational levels of his or her mind. The likening of a tenor voice to 'conical paper bags full of silver onions' is a little more far-fetched, a little more ingenious, but just as convincing; and so is all the play on light and darkness, bright and sombre sounds, leading to the dynamic analogy of cutting cloth and so to scissors, tailors and *haute couture*. Grass is at his most clownishly farcical in the passage introducing the woman singer who takes a false step, yet even her plunge into the crevasse is consistent with the whole poem's trans-sensory dynamism.

But for the wit and the more ingenious allusions in poems like 'The School for Tenors', they would belong to a realm of clown's and child's play that is amoral and asocial. Yet even in this poem satirical implications arise from references to historical phenomena like seaside resorts, shrapnel and, especially, to audiences in an opera house (which for upper class Germans had become a kind of secular, 'cultural' church). Grass makes fun of all those phenomena, as he was to make fun in his first novel even of the institutions that had shaped him in childhood and adolescence, the National Socialist Party and the Roman Catholic Church. The very short, almost epigrammatic pieces in the same first collection, though, introduce Grass the moralist looking over the shoulder of the clown and child, not least incisively in 'Familiar' (Family Matters), which compounds irony by judging the adult world from a child's point of view – a device most characteristic of the man who was to write *The Tin Drum* and later poems like 'Advent'. Incidentally, this poem is one of many reminders that Grass – a writer who has been accused of obscenity and blasphemy, has had his books burned and his house set on fire by the guardians of 'law and order' – was brought up as a Roman Catholic:

> In unserem Museum – wir besuchen es jeden Sonntag, –
> hat man eine neue Abteilung eröffnet.
> Unsere abgetriebenen Kinder, blasse, ernsthafte Embryos,
> sitzen dort in schlichten Gläsern
> und sorgen sich um die Zukunft ihrer Eltern.

> . . . . .

Family Matters

> In our museum – we always go there on Sundays –
> they have opened a new department.
> Our aborted children, pale, serious foetuses,
> sit there in plain glass jars
> and worry about their parents' future.

Here the grey, meticulous Muse of everyday life has taken over from the Muse of fantasy and dreams, as it was to do more consistently, though never completely, in Grass's second and third books of poems. Yet the didactic impact is made through fantasy – as in some of Arp's later poems – not through a consequential literalness, as practised by Brecht in short poems like the *Buckower Elegien* and by Brecht's many successors in the two German Republics. Like the opera house in 'Die Schule der Tenöre', the museum here has a specifically German connotation. It stands for the secular cult of self-improvement through art and education that tended to replace religious worship. That is why the museum is visited weekly, on Sundays. Abortion belongs to the same secularized order. His residual Catholicism – attested, not disproved, by his blasphemies – was to become another source of friction between Grass and the dogmatists of permissiveness.

Another early prose piece by Grass, his essay 'Die Ballerina' first published in 1956, not long after his marriage to Anna Schwarz, a ballet student, not only compares the ballerina with tenors, whose voices may demand that they grip the back of a chair or some other physical support, but brings out the traditionalism and conservatism – with a decidedly small 'c' – as essential to Grass as the freedom to innovate.

> The ballerina, like a nun, lives exposed to every temptation, in a state of the strictest asceticism. This analogy should not surprise you, since all the art come down to us has been the product of consistent restriction, never the immoderation of genius. Even if at times breakouts into the impermissible made and make us think that all is permitted in art, always even the most mobile of minds invented rules for itself, fences, forbidden rooms. So, too, our ballerina's room is restricted, surveyable, and permits changes only within the area available to her. The demands of the age will always require the ballerina to put on a new face, will hold exotic or pseudo-exotic masks in front of it. She will join in that decorative little game, knowing that every fashion suits her. The true revolution, though, will have to take place in her own palace.
>
> How similar it is in painting. How meaningless seem all attempts to see fundamental discoveries in the invention of new materials, in exchanging oil painting for a process of lacquer sprayed on to aluminium. Never will dilettantism, easily recognizable by its mannerisms, drive out the pertinacious flow of the skill that remains conservative even within its revolutions.

Grass, too, believed in the 'palace revolutions', fought out within oneself, that have to precede all general and outward change; and, as a graphic artist, he has remained outstanding for a minute and meticulous skill like that of the old masters, however grotesque the subjects and personal the vision of his drawings and etchings. Not only in politics, moderation and asceticism have always acted as a counter-weight to his exuberance and gusto. The two opposing tugs, with specific reference to the poems Grass was writing at the time, are designated once and for all in the next paragraph of the early prose piece:

The ballerina turns her mirror into an implacable implement of asceticism. Wide awake she trains in front of its surface. Her dance is not the dance with closed eyes. The mirror to her is nothing more than a glass that throws everything back, with exaggerated clarity, a merciless moralist she is commanded to believe. What liberties a poet takes with his mirror. What mystical, illegible postcards he drops into its baroque frame. To him the mirror is an exit, entrance, he searches like a still ignorant kitten behind the pane and, at best, finds a broken little box there, filled with buttons that do not match, a bundle of old letters he never expected to find again, and a comb full of hairs. Only at moments of irreversible transformation, when our bodies seem enriched or impoverished, do we stand in front of the mirror as she does, with eyes as awake. A mirror shows girls their puberty, no pregnancy escapes it, no missing tooth – should laughter try to provoke it. Perhaps a hairdresser, a taxi-driver, a tailor, a painter at his self-portrait, a prostitute who has furnished her little room with a number of these clarifying shards, have something in common with the ballerina. It is the anxious gaze of the craftsman, of a person who works with his or her body, it is the searching look into the mirror of conscience before confession.

The analogy of ballerina and nun could be censured as an instance of the very secularization that Grass had satirized in 'Family Matters'; but that would be to miss the point about Grass's residual Catholicism, which, to him, was not a Sunday religion. That aspect of the faith had been discredited for him by his up-bringing 'between the Holy Ghost and photographs of Hitler', as he put it in the autobiographical poem 'Kleckerburg', a conjunction of powers – formalized in the notorious Concordat – he was to lampoon in his prose fiction.

*   *   *

EVEN generically, Grass's first novel *The Tin Drum* (1959) is an amalgam of disparate types, including the German *Bildungsroman* – or its subcategory, the *Künstlerroman*, which traced the evolution of an artist's character – and the picaresque, particularly Grimmelshausen's *Der Abenteuerliche Simplicissimus* (1669/1671), the novel of the Thirty Years' War on which Brecht drew for his *Mutter Courage*.

Grimmelshausen offers a number of clues to the overall structure and meaning of Grass's novel, in so far as it has an overall structure and meaning; especially to the retrospective nature of the narrative, from the standpoint of a protagonist who has retired from the world, its follies and its evils. On another level, *The Tin Drum* forms part of an autobiographical trilogy set in Danzig, continued in the novella *Katz und Maus* (1961) and *Hundejahre* (1963; *Dog Years*) and it is in the evocation of this setting that Grass fused the utmost realism with his fantastic, fairy tale and grotesque inventions. After working on the novel in Paris from 1956 to 1958, Grass found it necessary to re-visit his home town, now the Polish city of Gdansk, mainly for a topographical documentation almost as thorough as that required by Uwe Johnson for the writing of his novels. As with Grass's poems, there is little point in puffing apart the many strands joined in Grass's prose or only in the invention of Oskar Mazerath, his tin drummer, who is a monster and a clown and a messianic figure; or in pointing out that this comic masterpiece is also a deeply serious and tragic work – more so even than Heinrich Böll's apotheosis of the clown or 'holy fool' figure in a later novel.

It is Grass's blasphemies that testify to the power over him of Roman Catholic dogma, as in the excursus 'Faith Hope Charity' at the end of Book I, culminating in the Association of Christ with the 'heavenly gasman' and the institution of the Church with the institution of the Nazi gas chambers; or the scene in the church, where Oskar substitutes himself for the infant Jesus. Oskar's refusal to grow up is his refusal to be part of the fallen world, which is that of adult society. His seeming amorality is that of innocence, though one that extends to the polymorphous sexuality of childhood.

Oskar's seeming amorality makes him a vehicle for the political de-demonization achieved by Grass in his rendering of lower middle class life in and around Danzig during the Third Reich. The opening episode, with its parody of the autobiographical and *Bildungsroman* prototype, sets the tone for the whole work. Oskar's maternal grandmother provides a refuge under her four skirts for an arsonist hunted by the police, and so establishes Oskar's pedigree (of original sin). The grandfather's small stature points forward to Oskar's arrested growth at the age of three, his pyromania to Oscar's anarchic nature and his ability to shatter glass with his voice, his compensatory gift and power, which is that of art. Oskar's dubious and divided paternity, too, is significant, since it corresponds to the German–Slav division at Danzig and Oskar's divided loyalty, which turns into impartial disloyalty, since both Germans and Poles are Nazified. (Both in poems and in the novel, Grass has celebrated the Polish national character in the personification Pan Quixote or 'Pan Kiehot'; but Oskar's 'Polish father', Bronski, is no more heroic or Quixotic than his German father Mazerath, both of whom belong to the fallen world.)

Oskar's arrested growth until the end of the war, when he gives up his drumming for a time and settles down to a more or less adult way of life as a short and misshapen, but no longer diminutive, citizen of West Germany, is one instance of the allegories woven into the picaresque, fantastic and realistic texture. The end of the war in itself is no redemption; and Oskar's attempt to accommodate himself to the post-war order leads only to his final renunciation of the world and his withdrawal from it into the 'home' that is a secular counterpart of the hermit's cell. It is there that he drums out his story, on the magical drum of art that can recapitulate and recall past events, but could also control or influence present ones, as when it broke up a Nazi meeting. The more adult Oskar of Book III has lost much of his zest because he has accepted his own fallen nature. That not only confronts him with moral choices, as when he decides to work as a mason's assistant rather than in the black market, but induces him to accept responsibility for a murder he did not commit. Politically, this *metanoia* has to do with the corporate guilt felt by Germans after the war; but the theological implications are weightier, once Oskar has lost his amoral innocence and begins to think about death.

Yet few readers will have paused in their passage through Books I and II of the novel to pick up hints about the destination. They will have been wholly absorbed by its rumbustious actions on the one hand, the subliminal effects of certain episodes and descriptions on the other. It is the physical and sensuous immediacy of Grass's writing that will have held their attention, unless they were incapable of the suspension of moral judgement that the child's eye view demands. What sticks in this reader's memory is the tenement block at Danzig and its ordinary, yet eccentric, if not monstrous, inhabitants, the cellars and shops, the topography of the city and its surroundings, the gruesome scene on the pier with the horse's head and the eels that produce a fatal trauma, the various erotic episodes and the aphrodisiac propensities of fizz, the ants that march across the floor while Oskar's German father swallows his party badge, and his Polish father's reluctant defence of the Post Office. In their own way, by the magnification and exaggeration of detail – as in Grass's drawings – these and other images build up a complex that amounts to the history of an era; and Grass's Danzig becomes a microcosm. Only the arrested innocence of an Oskar could have responded with sensuous immediacy to such a world, only his inhuman eye have registered such humanity as survived in it.

The novella *Katz und Maus*, originally written as part of a larger work, served Grass as a transition to the more adult perspective of *Dog Years*. The *novella* framework allowed him to confine it to a single level not of meaning – the theological implications of Mahlke's enlarged *Adam*'s apple, which becomes a mouse to the cat his school friend Pilenz set at his throat, are less escapable than those of *The Tin Drum* – but of narrative progression. Historically, it covers the same ground as Books II of that novel, whereas *Dog Years* returns to all the three periods to which its three Books correspond, the pre-war, war and post-war periods. Although the pivotal significance of the Adam's apple, like its transformation into a mouse, links the smaller work to Grass's characteristic imaginative procedures in earlier works, poems and plays as much as the first novel, the greater realism of *Katz und Maus* leaves little scope for clowning.

But for the change of tone and manner announced in *Katz und Maus*, Grass could hardly have undertaken another large-scale novel so soon after the first; and one set in the same place, in the same periods, and drawing on the same store of recollected experience. *The Tin Drum*, though, had been dominated by a single character, and much of its rich ambivalence had been due to Grass's imaginative self-identification with that character. *Dog Years* has two protagonists, Matern and Amsel, and three narrators. The two alsatian dogs Harras and Prinz (alias Pluto) carry so much of the symbolic load as to qualify as main characters also; but Grass does not identify to any comparable extent with any character in the book, human or canine. This in itself is a major difference. Grass could not have succeeded in writing an essentially different novel if he had not subordinated some of his picaresque and fairy-tale inventions to more sober concerns. It is pointless to regret that Matern and even Amsel – for all those exploits with scarecrows that do correspond to Oskar's magical and artistic faculties – lack the tin drummer's heroic and mythical dimension, without a compensating gain in finely differentiated sensibility. Even in *Dog Years*, personal relations remain somewhat crude and infantile, and both Matern and Amsel devote a great deal of energy in their mature years to the business of coming to terms with their youth. Just as the diminutive Oskar of the earlier periods was more vivid than the adult hunchback, both Matern and Amsel seem to become more shadowy as they grow older, their exploits less individual than representative, if not parabolic. This peculiarity is more striking in *Dog Years* because more weight falls on the later years, and because Oscar's arrested development has no parallel in the basic conception of the later novel. On the evidence of the Danzig trilogy alone, it looked very much as though Grass's imagination had remained fixed on his early years, as on the lost environment of his childhood and adolescence. Much of *Dog Years*, therefore, is sustained less by the exploration in depth and by the interaction of the principal characters than by their exploits and configuration; but though the action is not unified by a single protagonist, and even the narration is attributed to a staff of writers employed by Amsel (alias Brauxel) to chronicle the history of his scarecrow factory, all the seeming deficiencies of *Dog Years* are only the reverse side of Grass's minute recapitulation of the past and his devastating assault on the present. Among other things, the novel was the fullest and most convincing critique of Nazism yet achieved in fiction, when Oskar's monstrosity had tended to mythologize and demonize the phenomenon in the very act of de-mythologizing and de-demonizing it.

The exuberant fantasy and essential ambiguity of the first novel tended to blur its overall import. In *Dog Years* Grass managed to combine his humorous, often farcical, impartiality with a systematic deflation of Nazism. Not that the psychological ambivalences were eliminated. That would have been simplistic evasion. Matern is at once a Nazi and an anti-Nazi. Amsel, though half-Jewish and a victim of the régime, corrects the excesses of Matern's condemnation of the German national character. Yet these complexities can no longer be mistaken for an ambivalence on the author's part; they are facets of a reality which lie made more palpable than any other writer before him. I shall not try to list all the means used to attain this end; but the interweaving of the dog motif with the lives of Matern, Amsel, Tulla, Harry and many minor characters is at once the most subtle and the most effective. Tulla – also prominent in *Katz und Maus* – at one time chooses to share the kennel of Harras, the sire of Prinz who becomes Hitler's favourite dog; and it is Tulla who does her best to ruin the non-Nazis Amsel and Brunies. When Matern decides to poison Harras, what he has come to see in the dog is nothing less than the embodiment of Nazism. More layers are added to this complex when Hitler, just before the end of the war, launches a vast military action to recapture his dog Prinz, and this action is both conducted and reported in a vacuously mystifying code that parodies the terminology of Heidegger's philosophical writings. Prinz runs away to the West; and ironically it is Matern who becomes his new master, though he gives him the name of Pluto.

The scarecrow motif is another that unifies the whole work, though its final elaboration in Amsel's post-war factory, a kind of modern inferno, is almost too obtrusively allegorical. Like the dog motif and the prophetic meal-worms of Matern's father, the miller, Amsel's animated scarecrows connect the early Danzig chapters to the West Germany of the *Wirtschaftswunder*, which is shown to depend on the miller's financial predictions – and, ultimately, on worms. Matern's frustrated attempts to avenge himself on his former Nazi mentors and bosses after the war, with the help of names and addresses that appear miraculously in the public lavatory of the Cologne railway station, have the scurrilous abandon of many episodes in *The Tin Drum*, but their relevance to the larger satirical scheme is never left in doubt.

An especially gruesome form of revenge is to be carried out during confession on a Roman Catholic priest, but abandoned when the priest proves to turn a literally deaf ear to those who confess to him. The same confessional, though, serves Matern for an act of adultery with the wife of another 'war criminal', and Grass's love-hatred for the Church has lost none of its vehemence. Heidegger, whom Matern also wishes to confront, completely evades him in the funniest and most metaphysical of all these 'Materniads'.

The great Nazi atrocities are only hinted at, not described, for Grass was tactful enough to keep his de-demonizing within its proper limits. The brutal beating-up and rolling into a snowball of Amsel by a gang of masked S.A. men, one of whom is his best friend and 'blood brother' Matern, only costs him all his teeth and changes him from a fat boy into a thin man – an instance of those fairy-tale transformations that Grass could still reconcile with the most astringent realism elsewhere. Grass was wise to confine himself to what he knows and understands so well, the latent cruelty, malevolence and cowardice of children that can so easily be fostered and exploited by an adult world for its ostensibly adult purposes. Mahlke in *Katz und Maus* differs from Matern in his exceptional resistance to such pressures. Amsel does not resist them, but neutralizes them by parody, much as Grass has done as an imaginative writer, before choosing resistance as a citizen.

The circumstance that Matern is at once a 'good' and a 'bad' German not only makes his early relations with Amsel all the more convincing, but is crucial to the design of the whole novel. Matern has to be saved from his self-hatred and self-disgust as a German by his half-Jewish friend; but Amsel's Jewish father had been deeply influenced by the self-hatred and self-disgust of Otto Weininger, who claimed that 'the Jew has no soul. The Jew does not sing. The Jew does not play games.' The eagerness of Amsel's father to prove that the second and third of these assertions do not hold good for him – the first is harder to deal with – is a valid reflection on tendencies widespread among the assimilated German Jews. Eddi Amsel himself sings in the church choir and, with Matern's help, learns to hold his own in a fierce German ball game.

These are a few of the threads that make *Dog Years* more than a repeat performance. What the second novel has in common with the first is Grass's re-creation of a whole community and way of life, his retracing of the topography, folklore and vernacular of his native region; and, of course, his incomparable gift of getting inside the skins of children and adolescents, of presenting their barbarous rituals and codes as though they had been his only yesterday. *Dog Years* goes well beyond *The Tin Drum* in its combination of comic spontaneity with a serious and ambitious design.

*   *   *

GRASS's work on the prose trilogy, written within a mere six years and remarkable enough to establish his international fame, had not prevented him from publishing another book of poems, the collection *Gleisdreieck*, in 1960. 'Gleisdreieck' is the name of a Berlin rail junction and station; and it is the poems that touch on divided Berlin that show how fantasy had come to interlock with minute observation in Grass's work. The documentation that preceded the completion of

The Tin Drum is one instance of a development that can also be traced in the poems and drawings, from the high degree of abstraction in the drawings done for *Die Vorzüge der Windhühner* to the grotesque magnification of realistic detail in the drawings done for *Gleisdreieck*, and on to the hyper-realism of the clenched hand reproduced on the cover of the third collection, *Ausgefragt*. Grass's growing involvement in politics is bound up with that development. The clearance sale of the poem 'Ausverkauf' is a personal one, perhaps alluding to Grass's exploitation of his own life and memories in the prose trilogy, but it includes this unmistakable reference to East Berlin:

> Während ich alles verkaufte,
> enteigneten sie fünf oder sechs Strassen weiter
> die besitzanzeigenden Fürwörter
> und sägten den kleinen harmlosen Männern
> den Schatten ab, den privaten.
>
> .　　.　　.　　.　　.
>
> While I was selling it all,
> five or six streets from here they expropriated
> all the possessive pronouns
> and sawed off the private shadows
> of little innocuous men.

The underlying seriousness of Grass's clowning – as of all good clowning – is more apparent in *Gleisdreieck* than in the earlier collection. Without any loss of comic zest or invention, Grass could now write existential parables like 'Im Ei' (In the Egg) or 'Saturn', poems that take the risk of being open to interpretation in terms other than those of pure zany fantasy. One outstanding poem in *Gleisdreieck* has proved hard to translate, because its effect depends on quadruple rhymes and on corresponding permutations of meaning, for which only the vaguest equivalents can be found in another language. Grass himself has retained a special liking for this poem, the sinister nursery rhyme 'Kinderlied', perhaps because it achieved the most direct and the most drastic fusion in all his poetry of innocence and experience. This artistic fusion results from the confrontation of the freedom most precious to Grass, the freedom of child's play which is also the court fool's prerogative, with its polar opposite, the repression of individuality by totalitarian systems.

Wer lacht hier, hat gelacht?
Hier hat sich's ausgelacht.
Wer hier lacht, macht Verdacht,
dass er aus Gründen lacht.

Wer weint hier, hat geweint?
Hier wird nicht mehr geweint.
Wer hier weint, der auch meint,
dass er aus Gründen weint.

Wer spricht hier, spricht und schweigt?
Wer schweigt, wird angezeigt.
Wer hier spricht, hat verschwiegen,
wo seine Gründe liegen.

Wer spielt hier, spielt im Sand?
Wer spielt muss an die Wand,
hat sich beim Spiel die Hand
gründlich verspielt, verbrannt.

Wer stirbt hier, ist gestorben?
Wer stirbt, ist abgeworben.
Wer hier stirbt, unverdorben
ist ohne Grund verstorben.

       .   .   .   .   .

Who laughs here, who has laughed?
Here we have ceased to laugh.
To laugh here now is treason.
The laughter has a reason.

Who weeps here, who has wept?
Here weeping is inept.
To weep here now means too
a reason so to do.

Who speaks here or keeps mum?
Here we denounce the dumb.
To speak here is to hide
deep reasons kept inside.

Who plays here, in the sand?
Against the wall we stand

players whose games are banned.
They've lost, thrown in their hand.

Who dies here, dares to die?
'Defector!' here we cry.
To die here, without stain,
is to have died in vain.

Laughing, weeping, talking, keeping silent, playing and even dying are the spontaneous and uncalculated acts to which totalitarian repression attributes subversive motives, drowning 'the ceremony of innocence'. No other poem by Grass is at once so simple and so intricate, compacts so much meaning into so few words. One difficulty about the translation is that no single English word has the familiar and horrible connotations of a German word like 'angezeigt' – reported to the police or other authority for being ideologically suspect – or 'abgeworben' – the bureaucratic equivalent of being excommunicated, blackballed, expelled, deprived of civil rights, ceasing to exist as a member of a corporative order that has become omnipotent.

By the time his third book of poems, *Ausgefragt*, appeared in 1967, the politicization of West German literature and its author's commitment to the Social Democratic Party, for which he had undertaken a strenuous electioneering campaign in 1965, made its publication a political, rather than a literary, event. The collection does contain a high proportion of poems that respond directly – perhaps too directly in some cases – to political and topical issues. Some of them, like 'In Ohnmacht gefallen' (Powerless, with a Guitar), were bound to be read as provocations by the dominant radical Left:

Wir lesen Napalm und stellen Napalm uns vor.
Da wir uns Napalm nicht vorstellen konnen,
lesen wir über Napalm, bis wir uns mehr
unter Napalm vorstellen können.
Jetzt protestieren wir gegen Napalm.
    Nach dem Frühstück, stumm,
    Auf Fotos sehen wir, was Napalm vermag.
    Wir ziegen uns grobe Raster
    und sagen: Siehst du, Napalm.
    Das machen sie mit Napalm.
Bald wird es preiswerte Bildbände

mit besseren Fotos geben,
auf denen deutlicher wird,
was Napalm vermag.
Wir kauen Nägel und schreiben Proteste.
    Aber es gibt, so lesen wir,
    Schlimmeres als Napalm.
    Schnell protestieren wir gegen Schlimmeres.
    Unsere berechtigten Proteste, die wir jederzeit
    verfassen falten frankieren dürfen, schlagen zu Buch.
Ohnmacht, an Gummifassaden erprobt.
Ohnmacht legt Platten auf: ohnmächtige Songs.
Ohne Macht mit Guitarre, –
Aber feinmaschig und gelassen
wirkt sich draussen die Macht aus.

         ·   ·   ·   ·   ·

We read napalm and imagine napalm.
Since we cannot imagine napalm
we read about napalm until
by napalm we can imagine more.
Now we protest against napalm.
    After breakfast, silent,
    we see in photographs what napalm can do.
    We show each other coarse screen prints
    and say: there you are, napalm.
    They do that with napalm.
Soon there'll be cheap picture books
with better photographs
which will show more clearly
what napalm can do.
We bite our nails and write protests.
    But, we read, there are
    worse things than napalm.
    Quickly we protest against worse things.
    Our well-founded protests, which at any time
    we may compose fold stamp, mount up.
Impotence, tried out on rubber façades.
Impotence puts records on: impotent songs.
Powerless, with a guitar. –
But outside, finely meshed
and composed, power has its way.

Compared with his early poems, this one gave Grass little scope for playfulness. The moralist seems to have taken over even from the court fool. Yet the poem is not a polemic against political protest. The new gravity shows that Grass is quarrelling more with himself than with others, weighing up painful dilemmas that were his own. The old exuberance does re-assert itself elsewhere in the same collection, even in thematically related poems like 'Der Dampfkessel-Effekt' (The Steam Boiler Effect) that *are* primarily polemical. As for the trilogy 'Irgendwas machen' (Do Something), its centre piece 'Die Schweinekopfsülz' (The Jellied Pig's Head) was clearly intended to be a sustained political and satirical analogy, but somehow the cook in Grass seems to have gained the upper hand, deriving so much pleasure from his recipe in its own right that the reader, too, is carried away from the forum to the kitchen. Perhaps the happiest poem of all in *Ausgefragt* – happiest in two senses of the word – is 'Advent', since it blends social satire with the freedom and zest which, for Grass, appertain to the world of childhood. Even here, and in the autobiographical poem 'Kleckerburg', the tension has become extreme, because the amorality of childhood is at once re-enacted and judged in the light of mature social experience. 'Advent', in fact, juxtaposes the war games of children and those both of their parents and of nations. Moral judgement does not become explicit in this poem, and the implicit judgement seems to be in favour of the children who plan a family 'in which naughty is good and good, naughty' rather than of the parents 'who everywhere stand around and talk of getting children and getting rid of children.' What is certain about the poem is that Grass's new realism had not shut him off from the imaginative freedom and verbal play of his earlier work, though it is the realism that dominates even in poems about personal and domestic life like 'Ehe' (Marriage) and 'Vom Rest unterm Nagel' (Of the Residue under our Nails). The same realism underlay Grass's commitment to politics, his decision to 'defend the bad against the worse' within the framework of parliamentary democracy, rather than opt for the revolutionary utopias arrogantly demanded by fellow intellectuals who refused to dirty their hands in the business of practical politics. During the 1965 election campaign alone, Grass made 250 speeches all over West Germany.

In the midst of those activities and the controversies in which they never ceased to involve him, Günter Grass not only remained prolific

as an imaginative writer, but continued to uphold the personal free-
doms indispensable both to his practice and to that of his radical
opponents. Unlike the ideologists, Grass did not wish to carry politics
either into private life or into those artistic processes which they
censured and censored as 'individualistic'. Though public concerns
preponderate in the collection *Ausgefragt*, it also contains this short
poem, 'Falsche Schönheit':

Diese Stille,
    also der abseits in sich verbissne Verkehr
        gefällt mir,
und dieses Hammelkotelett,
    wenn auch kalt mittlerweile und talgig,
        schmeckt mir,
das Leben,
    ich meine die Spanne seit gestern bis Montag früh,
        macht wieder Spass:
ich lache über Teltower Rübchen
unser Meerschweinchen erinnert mich rosa,
Heiterkeit will meinen Tisch überschwemmen,
und ein Gedanke
    immerhin ein Gedanke,
        geht ohne Hefe auf;
            und ich freue mich,
                weil er falsch ist und schön.

     ·   ·   ·   ·   ·

Wrong Beauty

This quiet,
    that is, the traffic some way off, its teeth stuck into itself,
        pleases me,
and this lamb cutlet,
    though cold by now and greasy,
        tastes good,
life,
    I mean the period from yesterday to Monday morning,
        is fun again:
I laugh at the dish of parsnips,
our guinea pig pinkly reminds me,
cheerfulness threatens to flood my table,
and an idea,

an idea of sorts,
    rises without yeast,
        and I'm happy
            because it is wrong and beautiful.

The idea is one of those out of which Grass continued to make poems, drawings and prose books while applying himself to what would have been a full-time occupation for most men or women, his defence of the freedom to produce work that is 'wrong and beautiful'.

Grass's insistence on this freedom must be seen against the background of what was happening in West German literature, partly in response to the Vietnam War. While East German poets like Wolf Biermann and Reiner Kunze were desperately defending the individual from encroachments on his privacy on the part of an all-powerful collective, or of an all-powerful bureaucracy that claims to represent the collective, many West German writers were doing their best to deprive themselves of such liberties as they enjoyed – by self-censorship as much as by intolerance of any art they judged to be private or individualistic. In extreme cases, like that of Hans Magnus Enzensberger at one time, the conflict between social conscience and personal inclination could lead to the public renunciation of all imaginative writing, and such a renunciation, in that climate, turned into an interdict. It is true that to prescribe what could and could no longer be written had been a favourite pastime of German critics even before the politicization became extreme and dominant. Love poems were out, because love is a form of bourgeois self-indulgence; nature poems, because we live in a technological age; confessional poems, or poems of personal experience, because they are poems of personal experience; moon poems, because as Peter Rühmkorf argued well before the first moon landing – cosmonauts are better qualified to deal with the moon than poets. Needless to say, all those kinds of poems continued to be written, if in new ways, even before the tide turned and the 'new subjectivity' was proclaimed. Günter Grass openly defied those prescriptions and proscriptions, while setting definite limits to his own individualism by the very act of devoting himself to a political cause at the expense of his private life and his art.

His prodigious capacity to 'endure that tension' has been amply proved by his subsequent works. Even his book of political speeches and controversies, *Über das Selbstverständliche* (1968), is a collection so well-written, so forceful and so many-sided as to qualify as one of his literary works. Characteristically, the snail he adopted as an emblem of his political stance – evolution, as opposed to revolution – became one of those obsessive images that have nourished his imaginative work. Not only did it become his own left eye in a self-portrait of 1972 – while his right eye remained open to all kinds of other things – but it entered into other drawings and etchings, and became the nucleus of another prose book, *Aus dem Tagebuch einer Schnecke* (1972), in which even practical politics intermingle with childhood innocence and fantasy. If realistic and topical concerns are uppermost in the novel *Örtlich Betäubt* (*Local Anaesthetic*) of 1969, fairy tale and myth came back into their own in *Der Butt* (1977; *The Flounder*) a work on the same scale and of the same quality as the Danzig trilogy, written before Grass's political achievements and frustrations.

As for Grass's poetry, it became more and more bound up with his drawing and graphic work, and its later progress is best followed in the two books *Zeichnungen und Texte 1954–1977* (1982), and *Radierungen und Texte 1972–1982* (1984), in which the intimate interrelationship can be traced. (The snail reappears as late as 1982, in an etching called 'The Dream of a Place of One's Own', in which the home is a concrete bunker. This sums up Günter Grass's present commitment, less to a political party than to the causes of disarmament and conservation.) A self-portrait of 1982, 'With a glove, pensive', shows an older and sadder Grass, but one who has not given up fighting. That etching faces the text of his poem 'Müll unser':

Suchte Steine und fand
den überlebenden Handschuh
aus synthetischer Masse.

Jeder Fingerling sprach.
Nein, nicht die dummen Segelgeschichten
sondern was bleiben wird:

Müll unser
Strände lang.
Während abhanden wir
niemand Verlust sein werden.

. . . . .

Our refuse

Looked for stones and found
the surviving glove
made of synthetic pulp.

Every finger spoke.
No, not those inane yachtsmen's yarns
but of that which will last:

our refuse
beaches long.
Whereas we gone
will be a loss to no one.

In that reflection on our age and our prospects Günter Grass is at one again with most of his former associates in the *Gruppe 47*, though few of them are now militant or hopeful enough to give active support to his untiring campaigns. The German title of the poem, by placing the possessive pronoun after the noun, parodies the Lord's Prayer – a late instance of Grass's blasphemies, 'wrong beauty', and affronts to every kind of decorum. (In 1965, at the award of the Büchner Prize for Literature, he had chosen to deliver a political speech, 'Über das Selbstverständliche' [On That which Goes Without Saying], to the assembled members of a learned academy.) In the late poem, once more, the clown's prerogative and the moralist's compulsions have come together, in the absence of those courts whose authority could set limits to the destructive power games of would-be adults and so relieve Grass of the need to blaspheme. The dispensability of our species, of course, is another blasphemy against every religious, every secular, creed, but it is one committed every day by the players of those power games, in their commercial exploits and their planning of wars. In both his capacities, and over the decades, Grass has made it his consistent business to fling back such blasphemies into the bland faces of those who live by them. [...]

From THE POETRY OF SURVIVAL

[Hans Magnus Enzensberger]

... ELOQUENCE and elegance have always distinguished the work of Hans Magnus Enzensberger, a pioneer not only of the politicization of West German literature but also of those ecological preoccupations that have superseded it; not Jens's classicizing eloquence of balanced and supple periods, it is true – although lately Enzensberger has indulged in archaisms like 'Brosame' for 'crumb' – but an eloquence and elegance due to mastery of the vernacular, as of the specialized terminologies inaccessible and repulsive to most poets. In his mastery of both, as a poet and polemical essayist, Enzensberger was so fluently up-to-date as to be always ahead of his time, simply because no one else was as well-informed, as perspicacious and intelligent. When his first book of poems, *Verteidigung der Wölfe*, appeared in 1957, he was seen as the West German poet best fitted to take over the function of Brecht (who had died in the previous year) as a socially and politically committed poet; that is, as one who had taken the trouble to inform himself about the issues that his poems raised. In retrospect, it would seem that Enzensberger had less in common with Brecht than with Auden, whose positive commitments, too, are much harder to pin down than his up-to-dateness, his elegance, and his verbal skill. Both poets may have excelled at social comment and social criticism; but if constant commitments can be traced in either's work, these are more likely to be moral than strictly ideological. Enzensberger, of course, knew his Marx, as Auden knew his; but the Marx of his poem in *Blindenschrift* (1964) is a 'gigantic bourgeois' and 'gigantic traitor' to his own class, betrayed in turn by his followers and disciples, ending up as 'the iron mask of freedom'. It is a human study, above all, like some of Auden's 'potted biographies' in verse, bringing out both the irony and the pathos of Marx's life, rather than the celebration of an exemplary creed; and if a message can be extracted from the poem, it is: 'only your enemies/remained what they were' – as they undoubt-edly have remained, to this day. When the simplists of the class war became dominant in West Germany, a few years after Enzensberger's poem was published, they challenged his commitment and turned against him, as they turned against T. W. Adorno or anyone else who presumed to think for himself, as Marx had done. Enzensberger's commitment could not be pinned down by simplists of the class war on either side.

Like all comparisons, though, that of Enzensberger to Auden should not be pushed very far. Being knowledgeable, *au fait*, and imperturbably poised was only Enzensberger's outward guise. Behind it there was a passion, a vehemence quite unlike anything in Auden. This came out in the hyperbole that flawed some of the poems in his first book, but also in the bitter eloquence of its 'sad poems' and its 'wicked poems', like the title poem defending the wolves against the lambs, because it is the lambs in every age that keep the wolves going; or the manifesto poem 'Ins Lesebuch für die Oberstufe' (For a Senior College Textbook), with its exhortation to read not odes but railway timetables, because they are more accurate. This anticipates Enzensberger's notorious renunciation of poetry some ten years later, his purging at one time of his own library of most of its *belles lettres* sections in favour of reference books, sociological books and scientific books of many kinds, and his editorship of the review *Kursbuch* (Railway Timetable!), devoted less to *belles lettres* than to the most rigorous contributions to those other disciplines. This, in turn, was only one extremity of a love-hate relationship to poetry. Enzensberger also worked as the editor of a whole series of books that made known the work of outstanding foreign poets of this century in bilingual selections, as well as of his important anthology relegating those same poets to a museum, but presenting them all the same, and another excellent one of nursery rhymes. He was also generous in his praise of fellow poets, like Nelly Sachs, whose work drew on sources quite different from railway timetables. The vehemence of his disgust with his own country was carried over into his second book, especially the longer poem 'Landessprache' – the title is a bitter travesty of a line of Hölderlin's that proclaims 'love' as the 'language of the country', Germany – and so, in places, was the hyperbole of his first book. As an essayist and editor, Enzensberger was in the forefront of those who conveyed a 'radical enlightenment' to generations of West Germans; and though his main emphasis did not fall on language or on experiment, like Heissenbüttel's, nor even on literature generally, like Walter Höllerer's, like them he was prepared to divert much of his energy from his own imaginative writing to the most various activities in the service of enlightenment and mediation. Since extremes meet, and all poets work within the same sphere of possibilities, often bumping their heads on the periphery and having to turn round, Enzensberger's anti-experimental and anti-formalist position did not prevent him from working with quotations, like Heissenbüttel, for what amounted to a *collage* or *montage* technique in his 'Sommergedicht'; and it was a poet classified as 'hermetic' and 'formalist', Paul Celan, whose later work drew on scientific knowledge, even of nuclear physics, in a way that accorded, but was not seen to accord, with Enzensberger's prescriptions and practices.

That Enzensberger's practices did not always accord with his prescriptions goes without saying, since he is a poet, and a poet does not do what he sets out to do, but what he can and must. It was Enzensberger's third collection, *Blindenschrift*, that showed the full range of his possibilities. The personal feelings reserved for love poems in the second collection and the ecological concerns anticipated there in the poem 'Das Ende der Eulen' (The End of the Owls), amongst others, had begun to fuse with his social and political themes. Self-knowledge and self-criticism had begun to both sharpen and moderate his quarrels with others, so that his eloquence was no longer marred by rhetorical excesses. Whereas in the past his longer poems had tended to be his weakest – because the sensuous data were most thinly spread – a new richness and allusiveness of texture was attained in his longer poem 'lachesis lapponica'. Here Enzensberger succeeded in co-ordinating and controlling tensions at once personal and existential, particular and general. The confrontation with solitude in bare Scandinavian landscapes served a necessary dialectical complement to the social involvement, while the social involvement itself remained intense.

How intelligent can a good poet afford to be – in, rather than behind, his poems? How variously well-informed? How tough-minded? There were times in Hans Magnus Enzensberger's writing life when these questions troubled some of his readers; and not only when Enzensberger himself posed them in his essays and statements. After his three early collections, published between 1957 and 1964, it seemed for a long time that he had no more use for the spontaneous, more personal lyricism that had balanced his public concerns; that the polemicist had taken over from the poet, deliberately and definitively. Apart from a few new poems added to his selection of 1971,

Gedichte 1955–1970, Enzensberger had kept silent as a poet until *Mausoleum* appeared in 1975; and, however intelligent, knowing, tough-minded, well-informed and accomplished, that sequence was not distinguished by lyricism. If those thirty-seven studies 'in the history of Progress' were ballads, as he called them, they were ballads that neither sang nor danced, but nailed down their subjects with a laboratory-trained efficiency, though one that could be delicate, even tender from time to time.

This development remained relevant to *Der Untergang der Titanic* (1978; *The Sinking of the Titanic*), though in fact Enzensberger had already returned to more personal and existential preoccupations in shorter poems not collected at that time, and the long sequence, too, is less rigorously held down to a single purpose and manner. Behind the poetic development – or anti-poetic development, some would say – lay an ideological one, from what had looked like a revolutionary commitment to 'the principle of hope' at least. In fact it had been utopian and independent enough to put no strictly ideological constraint on the poet, through an arduous grappling with the hard facts of economic, political and technological power structures – as examined in Enzensberger's brilliant essays even before his first collection of them in 1962, *Einzelheiten* – to a general disillusionment with every existing social system and any likely to materialize in the near future. (This disillusionment, bravely and elegantly borne, and by no means defeatist, became most apparent in the book of essays *Politische Brosamen* of 1982.)

One crucial stage in that development was Enzensberger's visit to Cuba in 1969. Not only was *The Sinking of the Titanic* conceived and begun there, but the Cuban experiences are worked into the broken narrative of the poem, like many other seeming interpolations, digressions, leaps in space, time, and even manner. Like most long or longer poems written in this century, it is not an epic, but a clustering of diverse, almost disparate, fragments around a thematic core. The main event of the poem, the going down of the *Titanic* in 1912, becomes a symbol and a microcosm, with extensions, parallels, repercussions on many different levels. The Titanic is also Cuba, East Berlin, West Berlin (where Enzensberger lived for many years, before returning to Bavaria, where he was born), an up-dated version of Dante's Hell, and many other places besides, including any place where any reader of the poem is likely to be. Not content with that much telescoping,

Enzensberger also includes flashbacks to the fifteenth, sixteenth and nineteenth centuries, all to do with doubts, self-doubts, about art and the relation of art to reality. Other interpolations are even more explicit in their questioning of the truthfulness and usefulness of poets and poetry. These also introduce Dante by name, though he is present in the whole poem, as a paradigm of what poetry can and cannot achieve.

I shall not attempt to list all the many theses and sub-theses ironically advanced in the poem – usually to be challenged or contradicted by others – since it is the business of poems to do that as succinctly as possible. Yet one brief quotation, from Enzensberger's own English version of his text, does seem to subsume the main message: 'We are in the same boat, all of us. But he who is poor is the first to drown.' Characteristically for Enzensberger, this assertion is supported by statistics of the passengers – first class, second class, steerage and crew – drowned and saved in the *Titanic* disaster. Much other material of that kind, including a menu, has been drawn upon. The most lyrical, that is, song-like, canto of the thirty-three in the book – not counting the numbered interpolations – is the twentieth, adapted from *Deep Down in the Jungle: Negro Narrative and Folklore from the Streets of Philadelphia*. Documentary collages have been one of Enzensberger's favoured devices in verse and prose, and they are prominent as ever here, as in the Thirteenth Canto, made up of snatches of miscellaneous hymns and popular songs. Another is the permutation of simple colloquial phrases into puzzles or tautologies not simple at all, but devastating, as in the interpolated 'Notice of Loss'. Yet the most impressive and re-assuring parts of the sequence, poetically, are those in which Enzensberger lets himself go again a little, relying less on his bag of tricks – a formidable one – than on imaginative penetration of specific experience, other people's and his own. A high-spirited, often comically cynical desperation are his peculiar contribution to the range of poetry. It becomes affirmative, if not joyful, in the concluding canto, a celebration of bare survival.

As for the other side of his gifts, his sheer accomplishment and adroitness, one instance of it is his success in translating so intricate and ambitious a sequence into a language not his own, English – one of several in which he is fluent. In earlier English versions of his own poems he had allowed himself the freedom of 'imitation'. This one is a very close rendering, with no loss of vigour or exuberance, and very little diminution of the idiomatic rightness of the German original.

In 1980 Enzensberger bridged a gap of sixteen years by publishing a new book of short poems, *Die Furie des Verschwindens*. As his later volume of collected poems, *Die Gedichte* (1983), was to show, he had never quite ceased to write such poems even during his self-imposed silence; but for his readers *Die Furie des Verschwindens* linked up with his *Blindenschrift* of 1964 as a continuation of the kind of poetry that springs from moments of intense experience – experience inevitably subjective up to a point, however objective the correlatives. By this I do not mean confessional' poems. Even the longest poem in the new collection, 'Die Frösche von Bikini', is a semi-dramatic monologue whose speaker cannot be identified with the person of the poet – except perhaps in passages like:

> Nein, auf Selbsterfahrung lege er keinen Wert,
> und Probleme habe er nicht,
> wenigstens keine 'eigenen'.

> . . . . .

> No, he did not care for self-knowledge
> and did not go in for problems,
> not at least of 'one's own'.

That longer poem is one of stock-taking, at once personal and impersonal, because not self-concerned enough to indulge in confessions. Most of the shorter poems, too, are character studies that achieve a new balance between social criticism and the spontaneity with which it had tended to conflict. By getting under the skin of a thirty-three-year-old woman, an uneasy male business executive, an equally uneasy employee on holiday in Spain – each a 'short history of the bourgeoisie', as another poem is called – Enzensberger presents a whole complex of delicate interactions in the fewest possible words, from the inside; and it no longer matters whether the social perceptions are subjective or objective, whether the inside is the poet's or another person's real or fictitious. The social criticism is more incisive and more searching than ever before, because Enzensberger has learned to dispense with the reformer's vantage point, as well as with the rhetorical bravura of his early verse. That, in turn, may well be because he has come to include himself among those – bourgeois or otherwise – whose prospects are summed up in the poem 'Unregierbarkeit' (Ungovernability):

Mit immer kürzer werdenden Beinen
watschelt die Macht in die Zukunft.

. . . .

On legs growing shorter and shorter
power is waddling into the future.

A group of predominantly topical poems, concerned with this situation, leads to up the many-faceted longer poem, hence to a second group of short poems that have less to do with specific power structures than with more generally existential disparities. One of them, 'Besuch bei Ingres', is a brilliantly comic exposure of those disparities between life and art that had so worried Enzensberger in *The Sinking of the Titanic*; but on that score, too, Enzensberger's inhibiting self-doubts seem to be nearer to a resolution. A spark of the old utopianism still glimmers beneath the gloom and worldly wisdom of Enzensberger's later poems – though it is a utopianism inherent in the human condition rather than one imposed on it by a poet's vision; and the vigour, precision and elegance of his manner are unimpaired. [...]

From *The Truth of Poetry* (1969)

Tensions in Modern Poetry from Baudelaire to the 1960s

THE TRUTH OF POETRY

THAT POETRY embodies or enacts truth of one kind or another has hardly ever been denied by poets themselves, even by poets who have gone further than Baudelaire in the search for a syntax liberated from prose usage, for an imagery not subservient to argument, or for a diction determined more by acoustic values than by semantic exigencies. It is an error to assert that poetry since Baudelaire's time has developed only in one of those directions. Different poets have explored different possibilities of development; and quite a number of considerable poets no less modern than those who would trace their descent from Mallarmé have taken none of those directions, but aspired to a bareness and directness of statement that far exceeds anything demanded by the strictest classical canons. To Dryden the words that make up a poem were 'the image and ornament' of the thought which it was the primary function of that poem to 'convey to our apprehension', though Dryden was writing about verse translation, and even his practice as a poet and translator of poetry does not always accord with so rigid a definition. The modern poets in question differ from Dryden in having no use for ornament, and no use for images or metaphors that are ornamental in the sense of merely adding grandeur or dignity to their thoughts. The important thing for the readers and critics of modern poems is not to expect too simple or constant an approach to the many kinds of truth which different kinds of poems are able to convey.

Reviewing Bonamy Dobrée's *The Broken Cistern* in 1954, Donald Davie quoted this well-known passage from A. E. Housman's 1933 lecture *The Name and Nature of Poetry*:

> Poems very seldom consist of poetry and nothing else; and pleasure can be derived also from their other ingredients. I am convinced that

most readers, when they think they are admiring poetry, are deceived by inability to analyse their sensations, and that they are really admiring, not the poetry of the passage before them, but something else in it, which they like better than poetry.

Davie went on to comment:

> I. A. Richards, in *Practical Criticism*, proved that this was so. Now Bonamy Dobrée argues that poetry nowadays has few readers of this sort; and this, too, though it cannot be proved, seems very likely. The surprising thing is that he thinks this is a pity. One would think that if the poet no longer has many readers of this sort he is well rid of them. But Professor Dobrée believes that poetry can be a civilizing influence even on people who read poems for something other than their poetry. This is, to say the least, highly questionable, for *Practical Criticism* seemed to prove also that if poetry was read in this wrong-headed way it was a debilitating influence, not civilizing at all.

It would be pleasant to be able to agree with Davie that 'poetry nowadays has few readers of this sort'; but quite a number of them are still to be met at public poetry readings, in university seminars and in other unlikely places. 'Poetry,' Housman said in the same lecture, 'is not the thing said, but a way of saying it. Can it then be isolated and studied by itself? For the combination of language with its intellectual content, its meaning, is a union as close as can well be imagined.' If critics as expert as Professor Dobrée insist on separating 'the thing said' from 'the way of saying it', or insist that poetry, after all, is 'the thing said', as Professor Heller has done, readers of that sort will most probably be met for a long time to come; and not only in those countries where any other sort of reader is considered ideologically suspect. Even after Symbolism, Imagism, Futurism, Expressionism, Surrealism, and the new Concrete poetry, not only critics and readers, but poets too, remain divided on those questions to which Baudelaire could not give an unequivocal answer; and the division, in many cases, remains an inner division, one of those quarrels with himself out of which a poet, as Yeats said, makes poetry.

Donald Davie himself once wrote an eloquent appeal for a kind of poetry that 'must reek of the human' and show no 'loss of faith in

---

* '. . . that Orphic interpretation of the earth, which is the poet's one task and the supreme literary game.'

conceptual thought'; and, as he argued at the time, in *Articulate Energy*, such a poetry would have to return to a syntax more logical than dynamic. Though his own position has probably changed since that time, his analysis of modern poetic syntax, and of the philosophical and psychological changes that led to its adoption, is still valid. Above all, he was right to stress the importance of poetic syntax:

> It is from that point of view, in respect of syntax, that modern poetry, so diverse in all other ways, is seen as one. And we can define it thus: *What is common to all modern poetry is the assertion or the assumption (most often the latter) that syntax in poetry is wholly different from syntax as understood by logicians and grammarians.* When the poet retains syntactical forms acceptable to the grammarian, this is merely a convention which he chooses to observe. But never before the modern period has it been taken for granted that all poetic syntax is necessarily of this sort. This is, surely, the one symbolist innovation that is at the root of all the technical novelties that the symbolist poets introduced. Later poets could refuse to countenance all the other symbolist methods and still, by sharing, consciously or not, the symbolist attitude to syntax, they stand out as post-symbolist.

In the same study Donald Davie quoted a comparison by Paul Valéry between Mallarmé's poetic syntax – a syntax, incidentally, which Mallarmé also succeeded in carrying over into prose – and the 'attitudes of men who in algebra have examined the science of forms and the symbolical part of the art of mathematics. This type of attention makes the structure of expressions more felt and more interesting than their significance or value.' Davie's conclusion was that 'the syntax of Mallarmé appeals to nothing but itself, to nothing outside the world of the poem.'

Yet Mallarmé has also been seen as the representative of a tradition as old as poetry itself. Elizabeth Sewell, from whose book *The Structure of Poetry* Davie quoted the remark by Valéry, has made just that connection in her later book, *The Orphic Voice*. There she cites Mallarmé's own reference to the Orphic tradition:* 'l'explication orphique de la terre, qui est le seul devoir du poète et le jeu littéraire

---

* 'Artistic abstraction, being incidental to a symbolical process that aims at the expression and knowledge of something quite concrete – the facts of human feeling, which are just as concrete as physical occurrences – does not furnish elements of genuine abstract thought. The abstractive processes in art would

par excellence'; and her book has the singular merit of relating the 'postlogic' of modern poetry – as exemplified in the syntactic developments analysed by Donald Davie – with developments in science and thought. She has no doubts at all about the capacity even of modern poetry to embody truth: 'Poetry puts language to full use as a means of thought, exploration and discovery, and we have so far just about made a beginning and no more on its potential usefulness.' The operative words are 'exploration' and 'discovery', since the crucial distinction between an expository syntax and the syntax of post-Symbolist poetry has to do with the later poets' readiness to explore truths rather than to assert them. Elizabeth Sewell shows that there is a precedent for the exploratory procedure not only in the poetry of all periods but also in philosophy and speculative science. Poetry, she suggests, has the same aim as religion, myth and science; and 'that is truth, taken in its most simple everyday sense.' This function of poetry has been summed up once and for all in the Preface to *Lyrical Ballads*: 'Poetry is the breath and finer spirit of all knowledge, carrying sensation into the midst of the objects of science itself.'

*   *   *

THE POETRY of Mallarmé and his successors carried sensation – image, music and gesture – into realms that were once considered accessible only to abstract thought and logical argument. Not many poets before them were as consistent or deliberate in working out a syntax close to 'the logic of consciousness itself', as Susanne K. Langer has put it, though Hölderlin's syntactical contractions, ellipses and suspensions are as daring as anything in Mallarmé and Hölderlin, too, quite consciously worked for a poetry as 'alive' as possible, in which the very processes of thinking and feeling and imagining are enacted.

Nevertheless, the quarrel is not over. What Susanne Langer calls the 'artistic interest' of poetry continues to clash with what she calls the 'propositional' – sometimes, indeed, within the work of a single poet or even within the structure of a single poem. One may accept

---

probably always remain unconscious if we did not know from discursive logic what abstraction is . . . For science moves from general denotation to precise abstraction; art, from precise abstraction to vital connotation, without the aid of generality.'

the view of an aesthetician like Susanne Langer that all art is 'abstract' – in a special sense which she defines* – and symbolic; that 'the relation of poetry to the world of facts is the same as that of painting to the world of objects; actual events, if they enter its orbit at all, are motifs of poetry, as actual objects are motifs of painting. Poetry, like all art, is abstract and meaningful.' Yet at the same time one may find oneself responding primitively to the 'propositional interest' of a line like Mallarmé's

La chair est triste, hélas! et j'ai lu tous les livres

or Yeats's

Man has created death

though both are excellent examples of pseudo-factual assertions whose meaningfulness is not detachable from their contexts. In the early, still somewhat Baudelairean poem by Mallarmé ('Brise marine'), as in the Yeats poem, the single line, because it is a syntactical unit, still makes a kind of appeal more characteristic of classical verse than of Mallarmé's later, more subtly organized poetry, in which every image and cadence is intricately related to every other, and even punctuation is discarded. Another way of putting it is that the Romantic convention of confessional poetry still dominates Mallarmé's early poems, as it did the poems of Baudelaire, to a degree that invites a 'propositional interest' rather than an artistic one. The proposition in Mallarmé's poem 'L'Azur', that 'Heaven is dead' ('Le ciel est mort'), can hardly fail to arouse a response akin to our response to Nietzsche's claim, made in prose, that 'God is dead.' Mallarmé's proposition does not fill a whole line; but the apostrophizing of 'matter' in the same line – 'Vers toi, j'accours! donne, ô matière . . .' – makes a link so important in the history both of thought and of art, so essential also to an understanding of Mallarmé's development as an artist, that it is difficult to resist an interpretation that would leave the context out of account. It was the realization that poets do not need to provide that kind of evidence – in this case, a variation of Nietzsche's discovery that the death of God makes 'art the last metaphysical activity within European nihilism', with the corollary that this modern art may have to be ultimately materialistic,

---

* 'L'Imagination, c'est la moisson d'avant les semailles. La raison, c'est de l'imagination qui a de la bouteille.'

however spiritual and quasi-religious the impulses behind it – which led Mallarmé and his successors to evolve a poetry no longer conducive to the literal interpretation of isolated lines or parts of lines.

This realization does not necessarily imply a 'loss of nerve' on the part of modern poets, as Donald Davie suggested in *Articulate Energy*, or an impoverishment of poetry, as Bonamy Dobrée regretted in *The Broken Cistern*. The ontological or psychological truths conveyed in statements like 'Man has created death' and 'Le ciel est mort' have not been taken out of poetry, even where poets have come to resist the temptation to formulate them directly. Poets still think, as well as feel and imagine; but the thinking and the feeling and the imagining have tended more and more to be rendered as the indivisible process which, intrinsically, they have always been. 'Imagination,' said the French poet Saint-Pol Roux, in 1923, 'is a reaping before the sowing. Reason is imagination that has gone stale.'*

What is hardly questionable is that the understanding of poems as poems has been hindered by nothing so much as by the direct assertions that could be detached from them – that is, by those passages in them that seem most immediately understandable. Some assertions of that order, like this notorious one glossed by W. H. Auden, have seemed to cry out to be detached because they are so quotable:

> If asked who said Beauty is Truth, Truth Beauty! a great many readers would answer 'Keats'. But Keats said nothing of the sort. It is what he said the Grecian Urn said, his description and criticism of a certain kind of work of art, the kind from which the evils and problems of this life, the 'heart high sorrowful and cloyed', are deliberately excluded. The Urn, for example, depicts, among other beautiful sights, the citadel of a hill town; it does not depict warfare, the evil which makes the citadel necessary.
>
> Art arises out of our desire for both beauty and truth and our knowledge that they are not identical.

Critics more inclined to Platonism or to Elizabeth Sewell's Orphic tradition would probably disagree with Auden's interpretation; and that precisely is the trouble with general assertions of that order. Auden is certainly right to point to the strictly poetic function of those words within that particular poem. But when he goes on to state that poets write out of the knowledge that beauty and truth are not identical, he is telling us something about poets like Auden, and not necessarily about poets like Keats, whose assertion or proposition remains controversial, a debating point for critics and aestheticians; and that, at best, is an incidental function of poetry.

*　　*　　*

W. H. AUDEN himself received only incidental mention in Hugo Friedrich's widely read study of the development of modern poetry, *Die Struktur der modernen Lyrik*; and once again we are reminded that there is no such thing as a single modern movement in poetry, wholly international, and progressing in a straight line from Baudelaire to the middle of this century (the period covered by Hugo Friedrich's book). Friedrich does tend to concentrate on a single line of development – that towards 'pure', 'absolute' or hermetic poetry – and his academic specialization is in the Romance languages, in which that line of development has been much stronger than in the Anglo-Saxon, Slavic or Scandinavian language areas. In English poetry especially, every step forward in the direction of pure or hermetic verse has been followed by at least two paces backwards, or by what used to be called a period of 'consolidation.' The history of Imagism – the most promising of the Anglo-Saxon varieties of modernism – is a case in point. Yet Baudelaire, as I have tried to show, was a moralist as well as an aesthete; and it is the moral concerns of the non-hermeticists that have brought them back again and again to modes of poetic utterance that diverge from the line of development traced by Hugo Friedrich. Characteristically, the mere passing reference to Auden is matched by a similar one to Bertolt Brecht, a poet not affected by Friedrich's linguistic specialization. If Baudelaire is to be taken as a starting point – and Friedrich does begin with Baudelaire – the dilemma inherent in modern poetry has to be taken into account. Baudelaire, after all, was one of the first poets to grapple with some of the realities of the modern megalopolitan scene; and the English-language poets from T. S. Eliot to Auden, from William Carlos Williams to Philip Larkin and Charles Tomlinson, have excelled at kinds of poetry that respond much more faithfully than Baudelaire's to specific localities and ways of life. The assimilation of experienced and observed realities into poetry, that is, into the diction, imagery and rhythmic structure of verse, is a process seemingly at odds with the trend towards abstraction, as understood by Susanne Langer, or towards the essential autonomy of art. Yet wherever major poetry has been written in the past century, or in any other, the two opposing impulses have met, imagination (or inwardness') has fused in some new way with outer experience.

Hugo Friedrich puts all the stress on what he calls the 'destruction of reality' in modern poetry, beginning with Baudelaire and his 'depersonalization of poetry, at least in as much as the lyrical word no longer proceeds from the unity of poetry with the empirical self.' Yet he grants that this unity was characteristic only of the confessional poetry of the Romantic period, so that Baudelaire's 'depersonalization' can be seen as a return to classical premisses. (That was how Eliot's advocacy of impersonality in literature linked up both with his modernism and with his preference for classicism.) With Rimbaud the thrust of imagination does assume a vehemence that warrants Friedrich's notion of a 'destruction of reality' by certain modern poets. He is also right to remark on the 'empty transcendentalism' of much modern poetry, citing Rimbaud's recourse to 'angels without God and without a message'. (A whole genealogy of such angels could be traced from Rimbaud to Stefan George, Rilke, Wallace Stevens and Rafael Alberti, and Friedrich does make the connection between Alberti's angels and those of Rimbaud.) In Rimbaud, too, Friedrich finds evidence of 'a process of dehumanization' characteristic of the development of modern poetry – but again, one must object, only of that line of development which Friedrich chooses to pursue. He quotes this line from Mallarmé's *Hérodiade*:

> Du reste, je ne veux rien d'humain

and claims that 'it could serve as a motto for Mallarmé's entire work'. But this is a poem in dialogue form, and it is Herodias who speaks, in a work by a poet who had severed 'the unity of poetry with the empirical self' much more thoroughly than Baudelaire. Friedrich himself quotes Mallarmé's famous remark to Degas that 'poems are made not of ideas but of words'. True, Friedrich also quotes this personal confession by Mallarmé in a letter to Cazalis of 1866: 'After I had found nothingness I found beauty'; and there is no denying that a profound nihilism underlies the extreme aestheticism of the late nineteenth and early twentieth centuries.

It is the one-sidedness of Friedrich's view of what constitutes modern poetry that allows him to make generalizations like the following: 'To call a thing by name means to spoil three quarters of one's pleasure in a poem ... this applies to Mallarmé, as to almost all the lyrical poetry after him'; or: 'The modern poem avoids acknowledging the objective existence of the objective world (including the inner one) by descriptive or narrative elements.' Yet elsewhere he admits that 'there is also a poetry crowded with things', though 'this abundance of things is subject to a new way of seeing and combining, to new stylistic devices; it is material for the lyrical subject's power to arrange it as he pleases'; and he speaks of Francis Ponge as a writer of 'a poetry that has no other content than things. ...' 'The subjects of his free verse poems are called bread, door, shell, pebble, candle, cigarettes. They are captured so factually that one critic (Sartre) has spoken of a "lyrical phenomenology". The ego that captures them is fictitious, a mere carrier of language. This language, however, is anything but realistic. It does not so much deform things as make them so inert, or impart so strange a vitality to things inert by nature, that a spooky unreality is created. But man is excluded.'

I have already suggested that man can never be excluded from poetry written by human beings, however impersonal or abstract; and of Francis Ponge's poems in particular one could equally well say that they render not things, but a way of looking at things and experiencing things. Ponge, it is true, has expressed severe misgivings about the anthropocentric view of a universe that has become 'nothing more than man's field of action, a stage on which to exercise his power'; but this, too, is a view of man. Elsewhere, in his book *Liasse* (1948), Ponge has written: 'People say that art exists for its own sake. This means nothing to me. Everything in art exists for men.' As for his approach to things – an attempt to put men back into the natural universe, and relate them to its phenomena – he has commented: 'My method most certainly is not one of contemplation in the strict sense of the word, but rather of one so active that the naming follows immediately; it is an operation with pen in hand, so that I see closer analogies in alchemy ... and quite generally in action, too (including political action), than in some sort of ecstasy that originates only in the individual and rather makes me laugh.'

As Werner Vortriede has shown, Symbolist practice rests on the assumption of a magical correspondence between the inner and outer worlds, an assumption which he traces back to Novalis and other theorists of German Romanticism. 'Psychologically speaking,' he remarks, Mallarmé's use of symbols and Symbolist practice generally is a 'secularized mysticism'; psychologically speaking, because the Symbolists were perpetually producing analogies of the poetic process itself. Yet at least in his earlier years, Mallarmé still spoke of 'understanding' poems, saying that our pleasure in a poem consists in our *gradual* understanding. The reader, therefore, is invited to participate in a process of exploration. Francis Ponge's reference to alchemy brings us up once more against the peculiar interchangeability of subject and object in so much modern poetry. Rilke's so-called 'thing poetry' in his *Neue Gedichte* is another striking instance. This has usually been seen as a highly subjective poet's attempt to emulate the practice of painters and sculptors in their concern with the visual and tactile qualities of the physical world. Rilke's 'Der Panther', one seeming triumph of poetic objectivity in that collection, is as much a poem about the poetic process as a poem about a panther: the caged animal's gaze, which encounters only images unrelated to the panther's true nature, images that enter the panther's eyes but 'cease to be' when they reach his heart, like the bars of the first stanzas, with no 'world' behind them – all these are analogies of the poet's alienated 'inwardness'. But that, too, is 'psychologically speaking', and there is no need for us to enquire into the psychological machinery. What makes the poem successful is that the poet has found a correspondence that works – Eliot's 'objective 'correlative' – and rendered it in such a way as not to distract us with allusions to his state of mind, Baudelaire's poem 'L'Albatros', psychologically speaking, is a similar poem, but Baudelaire still felt obliged to explain and resolve his analogy between the animal and the poet 'whose giant's wings prevent him from walking', much as Rilke's panther is a 'great will' paralysed by the lack of anything on which to exercise itself. Baudelaire's explanation turns his albatross into a metaphorical bird, less interesting in itself than Rilke's panther; and it allows the unsympathetic or literal-minded reader to object that poets, not being birds or angels, don't have wings, let alone giant's wings. The comparison detracts from both the bird and the poet, because even the most rigorously sustained simile always implies that the two things compared are not, in fact, identical. Whatever its psychological and philosophical premises, therefore, Mallarmé's recourse to freely floating, unanchored and unexplained images enriched the resources of poetry; artistically speaking – that is, in terms of effects rather than causes – it absolved later poets from the stale dichotomy of mind and things.

* * *

LANGUAGE itself guarantees that no poetry will be totally 'dehuman-
ized', regardless of whether a poet attempts to project pure inward-
ness outwards – as Rilke often did – or to lose and find himself in
animals, plants and inanimate things. The exact balance between the
expression of feeling and penetration of the world outside may be a
problem for poets when they are not writing poetry, as well as for
those of their critics whose main interests are psychological and
philosophical. If the poem succeeds, the problem is resolved in that
poem: within its bounds a magical correspondence does indeed
prevail. Something of this interchangeability seems to attach even to
the latest experiments in a kind of poetry that neither expresses nor
records anything at all, but makes words and their interrelationships
its only material; significantly enough, this kind of poetry has been
described both as 'abstract' and as 'Concrete' poetry.

William Carlos Williams is another poet whose work is crowded
with people, places and things. As in Ponge's work, this involvement
was an active one, based on the reciprocity of imagination and exter-
nal reality. It is usual to label Williams with the prescription 'no ideas
but in things', a parenthesis that occurs in his poem 'A Sort of Song':

> Let the snake wait under
> his weed
> and the writing
> be of words, slow and quick, sharp
> to strike, quiet to wait
> sleepless.
>
> – through metaphor to reconcile
> the people and the stones.
> Compose. (No ideas
> but in things) Invent!
> Saxifrage is my flower that splits
> the rocks.

To begin with, this is a dynamic poem of discovery; and the words
in brackets are not a prescription, but part of an experience – a part of
the experience, incidentally, which could not be rendered in terms of
the two 'images' or things dominant in the poem, the snake and the
saxifrage. In later poems Williams evolved a meditative style that no

The Truth of Poetry · 557

more excludes direct statement of ideas than does that of Eliot's *Four Quartets*; and even here he has to resort to the language of ideas in order to convey his purpose – akin to Ponge's opposition to the anthropocentric exploitation of the universe – 'through metaphor to reconcile the people and the stones.' A later poem, 'The Desert Music', adds a reflection on the character of Williams's involvement with the outside world:

> to imitate, not to copy nature, not
> to copy nature
>
> NOT prostrate to copy nature
> > but a dance . . . !

The line that follows carries us right back into the physical world, so that once more the lines quoted lose their prescriptive character and become part of an experience that is also a discovery. In both cases it is impossible, and irrelevant, to say whether Williams has written a poem about the poetic process or about people and things.

Nor is there any real inconsistency between the procedure in the earlier poem, 'A Sort of Song', and Williams's words in another, later poem, 'The Host' – words that have also been detached from their context and treated as a kind of manifesto:

> it is all
> > according to the imagination!
> Only the imagination
> > is real! They have imagined it
> > > therefore it is so

Here Williams is not even speaking primarily about poetry or art, but about religious belief – which to him, a non-believer, is imagination – and as always the general observation proceeds from his encounter with people, places and things, from a specific occasion which he does not so much narrate as dynamically re-enact in words that render both an inner and an outer experience.

Read out of context, 'Only the imagination is real' becomes a statement which one would be inclined to attribute not to Williams, but to his American contemporary who seems to represent the opposite pole of modern poetry, Wallace Stevens – a poet as self-contained as Williams was open to everything around him. Yet the diction and, above all, the syntax and metre of the immediate context – with that word 'they' which switches without transition from the general statement to the people of the poem, the 'tall negro evangelist', the 'two Irish nuns' and the 'white-haired Anglican' – bring us back at once to Williams and the urgency of immediate experience. Philosophically, Williams and Stevens meet in that passage, as extremes are apt to meet in modern poetry, since the possibilities of poetic expression are always being pushed to the limits. When such a limit has been reached, a poet may swing back to the other side. Yet the principle of imagination was no less present in the words on either side of the parenthesis in 'A Sort of Song', the words 'compose' and 'invent'. If there is a seeming contradiction between 'no ideas but in things' and 'Only the imagination is real' it has to do with language itself.

One thing that Williams had in common with Wallace Stevens, as with Ezra Pound and T. S. Eliot and almost every significant poet of his time, was a constant concern with the possibilities and limits of language, including the contradiction inherent in it as the material of poetry. In his profound and perceptive essay 'The Poet as Fool and Priest' the late Sigurd Burckhardt showed why language itself forbids total abstraction in poetry or prose:

> There can be no non-representational poetry; the very medium forbids. MacLeish's 'A poem should not mean but be' points to an important truth, but as it stands it is nonsense, because the medium of poetry is unlike any other. Words must mean; if they don't they are gibberish. The painter's tree is an image; but if the poet writes 'tree', he does not create an image. He *uses* one; the poetic image is one only in a metaphorical sense . . . Words already have what the artist first wants to give them – meaning – and fatally lack what he needs in order to shape them – body.

This fundamental, but easily overlooked, characteristic of language points to one of the limits that Williams came up against, as all the one-time Imagists did. Incidentally, it also disposes of Erich Heller's fears about the arrogance of those – like Mallarmé, Rilke or Stevens – who set themselves up as 'creator poets', and it modifies all definitions of the functions of poetry which – like Susanne Langer's – are based on a consideration of all the arts. Burckhardt goes on to explain why poets – and not only modern poets – have often gone out of their way to make their language 'difficult' (just as other poets, or the same poets at other times, have cultivated a simplicity of diction equally far removed from the literary or non-literary styles of discourse prevalent in their time):

> Ideally, the language of social intercourse should be as window-glass; we should not notice that it stands between us and the meaning 'behind' it. But when chemists recently developed a plastic coating which made the glass it was spread on fully invisible, the results were far from satisfactory: people bumped into the glass. If there were a language pure enough to transmit all human experience without distortion, there would be no need for poetry. But such a language not only does not, it cannot exist. Language can no more do justice to all human truth than law can to all human wishes. In its very nature as a social instrument it must be a convention, must arbitrarily order the chaos of experiences, allowing expression to some, denying it to others. It must provide common denominators, and so it necessarily falsifies, just as the law necessarily inflicts injustice. And these falsifications will be the more dangerous the more 'transparent' language seems to become, the more unquestionably it is accepted as an undistorting medium. It is not window-glass but rather a system of lenses which focus and refract the rays of an hypothetical unmediated vision. The first purpose of poetic language, and of metaphors in particular, is the very opposite of making language more transparent. Metaphors increase an awareness of the distortion of language by increasing the thickness and curvature of the lenses and so exaggerating the angles of refraction. They shake us loose from the comfortable conviction that a grave is a grave is a grave. They are semantic puns, just as puns are phonetic metaphors; though they leave words as sounds intact, they break their semantic identity.

Poetic language, then, resorts to what Brecht, in a very different connection, called 'alienation effects'. Metre and rhyme, Burckhardt shows, are such effects, until they become a 'binding convention of poetry' and lose their 'dissociative force'. Commenting on the song from *The Tempest*, 'Full fathom five . . .', he shows that in order to be rich the word in poetry 'must first become strange'. Dislocations of normal syntax, as in Mallarmé, are another device of that kind. 'A word that can function simultaneously as two or more different parts of speech, a phrase which can be parsed in two or more ways – to the despair of all grammar teachers – simply extends the pervasive incertitude of poetry from words to their connections into statements.'

Yet as soon as such things as rhyme, metre and inversion have become poetic conventions, poets may have to reverse the whole process in order to produce the necessary alienation. They may even try to do without metaphoric language of any kind, since non-poetic discourse, too, is full of metaphors. If poetic or discursive conventions tend towards formality and intricacy, they will explore the possibilities of simple colloquial language, as Blake and Wordsworth did in the eighteenth century, or as Williams did in ours.

In this context Burckhardt takes up William Empson's analysis of ambiguity and shifts 'the emphasis a little', as he puts it – a modest understatement on his part:

> He [Empson] made us aware that one word can – and in great poetry commonly does – have *many meanings*; I would rather insist on the converse, that many meanings have *one word*. For the poet, the ambiguous word is the crux of the problem of creating a medium for him to work in. If meanings are primary and words only their signs, then ambiguous words are false; each meaning should have its word, as each sound should have its letter. But if the reverse is true and words are primary – if, that is, they are the corporeal entities the poet requires – then ambiguity is something quite different: it is the fracturing of a pristine unity by the analytic conceptualizations of prose.

The distinction leads Burckhardt to his main contention that the nature of language itself forces poets into the dual rôles of fool and priest, since 'the poet's purpose is to tell truths – truths which escape the confines of discursive speech. And to do so he is committed to the word, even the negative, as in some sense physically present. How, then, can he express negations?' Burckhardt finds the answer in Shakespeare's 116th sonnet, though the function of negatives and negation in more recent poetry is a special one that will concern me in another chapter. For the present, Burckhardt's conclusion that 'the poet must always be half fool, the corrupter of words', is worth bearing in mind, just because it is his analysis of passages from Shakespeare that led to it. The contradictions inherent in language itself are not confined to poetry after Baudelaire, though modern poets have experienced them most acutely.

> The poet would be much safer [Burckhardt writes] if he did not commit himself to the Word, but in ironic detachment exploited the infinite ambiguities of speech. Or he could retreat to the safety of a sacro-religious order, give up his claim to verbal priesthood and turn 'mouthpiece'. Both roads have been taken – but they lead to self-abnegation. . . . Where the philosopher seeks certitude in the sign – the 'p' of propositional calculus – and the mystic in the ineffable – the 'OM' of

the Hindoos – the poet takes upon himself the paradox of the human word, which is both and neither and which he creatively transforms in his 'powerful rhyme'. This rhyme is his deed; it dissociates, dissolves the word into its components – mark and bark – but simultaneously fuses it into a new and now sacramental union.

*   *   *

THE PURPOSE of poets, then, is 'to tell truths', but in ways necessarily complicated by the 'paradox of the human word'. From Baudelaire onwards (and long before Baudelaire) poets have grappled endlessly with that basic paradox; and since the writing of poetry is a 'deed' – a process of exploration and discovery – the truths told are of a special kind. Certainly there have been times when, even in verse, the emphasis fell on the elegant and decorous exposition of truths that were already the common property of writer and reader; but those were periods of a cultural homogeneity – or of a cultural exclusiveness – unknown to any of the poets with whom I am concerned. 'One of the most difficult things in writing poetry,' Wallace Stevens remarked with a matter-of-fact dryness not really surprising in a poet active long after Mallarmé, 'is to know what one's subject is. Most people know what it is and do not write poetry, because they are so conscious of that one thing. One's subject is always poetry, or should be. But sometimes it becomes a little more definite and fluid, and the thing goes ahead rapidly.' In other words, it is the poem that tells the poet what he thinks, not *vice versa*; and Stevens remarks on just that peculiarity of poets – an aspect of what Keats called their 'negative capability' – in a later letter: 'Some people always know exactly what they think. I am afraid that I am not one of those people. The same thing keeps active in my mind and rarely becomes fixed. This is true about politics as about poetry.' Yet the thinking does crystallize – in poems; and Stevens could also write: 'It made me happy the other day to find that Carnap said flatly that poetry and philosophy are one. The philosophy of the sciences is not opposed to poetry any more than the philosophy of mathematics is opposed.'

Mallarmé, Valéry, Stevens and Jorge Guillén are some of the poets who have tried to think in purely poetic terms, much as a mathematician thinks in purely mathematical terms – without direct reference, that is, to concerns that may well have been theirs when they were doing other things. As Mallarmé wrote in 1867, he created his work 'only by *elimination*'. This elimination, active also in the work of later poets, is certainly akin both to the abstractions of mathematics and to the trend towards abstract forms in the visual arts that began with the post-Impressionists; but since words have meanings independent of the special functions that poetry lends to them, such analogies should never be taken too literally. Even Stevens combined elements of verbal clowning with his philosophical seriousness, which was priestly in the precise sense that Burckhardt defined. Stevens began with a belief in poetry for poetry's sake: 'What I am after in all this is poetry, and I don't think that I have ever written anything with any other objective than to write poetry.' It was only when he tried to explain this belief to himself and to others that he came to relate it to preoccupations that were by no means purely aesthetic.

It is the paradox inherent in language itself that makes the theories and occasional pronouncements of poets more confusing, more obscure and often more self-contradictory than their practice. Pierre Reverdy, for instance, wrote in 1948 that 'the poet has no subject at all. . . . His work is valuable just because it adduces no reason for its discontinuity and its process of fusing with incompatible things.' In a radio discussion with Francis Ponge and Jean Cocteau the same poet said that 'form is only the visible part of content – the skin.' The two statements seem to contradict each other, though both make sense when applied to Reverdy's poetry, or to that of many other poets of his time. In the first instance Reverdy was thinking of a subject that could be paraphrased in prose, translated or abstracted from its medium into that of logical discourse. In the second instance he was thinking not of that kind of subject, but of the peculiarly poetic thinking and feeling and imagining that do indeed determine the form of a poem, especially where that form is 'organic' or 'free'. Both statements, therefore, say something about the indivisibility of form and content in poetry, and both imply a distinction between content and subject.

Genuine differences between poets do arise over the value that each attributes to the public functions and implications of poetry – functions and implications that are very far from having been eliminated once and for all by Mallarmé's dictum that 'poems are made not of ideas but of words', or by MacLeish's 'a poem should not mean but be.' These, in any case, are half-truths, as Burckhardt argued, since words can never be totally severed from the connection with ideas and meaning. Nor does one need to be a Marxist to recognize that all poetry has political, social and moral implications, regardless of whether the intention behind it is didactic and 'activist' or not. Contrary to what Hugo Friedrich has asserted, a very good case could be made out for the special humanity of much modern poetry, a concern with humankind as a whole all the more intense for being 'depersonalized' as much Romantic poetry was not, because the more confessional of the Romantic poets were primarily interested in their own individuality and in those things that made them different from other people.

Quite apart from moral or political commitments as such – and I shall have more to say of these, as of the persistence of Romantic-Symbolist attitudes in poets otherwise modern – the mere practice of poetry as an art whose medium is language has social implications which have been given special prominence this century, as by the Austrian critic and aphorist Karl Kraus, all of whose copious writings on society and literature are based on the analysis of the many uses and abuses of language. If poets are writers whose use of language is necessarily critical, because whatever else a poem may be it cannot be a good poem unless every word in it has been weighed, they have an inescapable function that has been stressed even by a writer as much at odds with own society and its values as Ezra Pound: 'Has literature a function in the state, in the aggregation of humans, in the republic …? It has. … It has to do with the clarity and vigour of "any and every" thought and opinion. … When this work goes rotten – by that I do not mean when they express indecorous thoughts – but when the very medium, the very essence of their work, the application of word to thing goes rotten, i.e. becomes slushy and inexact, or excessive or bloated, the whole machinery of social and individual thought and order goes to pot.' That was also the view of Karl Kraus, who was far from sharing Ezra Pound's political enthusiasms at this time. These political enthusiasms have a great deal to do with the extent to which Pound remained rooted in the Romantic-Symbolist aesthetic; but, however limited his view of social realities, Pound was passionately concerned with them in a way that Mallarmé, for instance, was not: 'In proportion as his work is exact, i.e. true to human consciousness and to the nature of man, as it is exact in formulation of desire, so it is durable and so it is useful; I mean it maintains the precision, and clarity of thought not merely for the benefit of a few dilettantes and "lovers of literature", but maintains the health of thought outside literary circles and in non-literary existence, in general individual and communal life.' Nor is there any confusion about ideas and words, the meaning and the being of poetry, in Pound's definition of great literature, in the same work, as 'merely language charged with meaning to the utmost possible degree.'

'Human consciousness' and 'the nature of man' – these two concepts alone indicate why poetry can never exclude man, as long as it is written by human beings rather than machines (and even machines are designed and made by men). What poetry can exclude, especially where words are picked up at random, split up into their components or left to form visual or sonic patterns on the page, is individuality; but where those exercises are meaningful, they reveal something about language, and language brings us back to 'human consciousness and 'the nature of man'.

Octavio Paz has explained why 'poetry is a food which the bourgeoisie – as a class – has proved incapable of digesting.' Poetry, he argues, has tried in different ways to abolish 'the distance between the word and the thing', and this distance is due to the self-consciousness of civilized men and their separation from nature. 'The word is not identical with the reality which it names because between men and things – and, on a deeper level, between men and their being – self-consciousness interposes.' Modern poetry, according to Paz, moves between two poles, which he calls the magical and the revolutionary. The magical consists in a desire to return to nature by dissolving the self-consciousness that separates us from it, 'to lose oneself for ever in animal innocence, or liberate oneself from history.' The revolutionary aspiration, on the other hand, demands a 'conquest of the historical world and of nature.' Both are ways of bridging the same gap and reconciling the 'alienated consciousness' to the world outside.

Yet both tendencies may be at work within the same poet, and even within the same poem, just as a poet may combine the function of priest and fool, hater and lover of words. Octavio Paz, too, has written: 'What characterizes a poem is its necessary dependence on words as much as its struggle to transcend them.' The dependence has to do with the poet's involvement in history and society, the transcendence with the magical short cut back to nature and to the primitive unity of word and thing. Both correspond to general human concerns, though many people may be unaware of the tensions and complexities inherent in their relationship with words or with things. An extraordinary degree of alienation from language, even as a medium of simple communication, has become more and more widespread in 'advanced' societies, as one can see in television interviews with young people incapable of uttering a simple short sentence not helped out by 'sort of' and 'you know'. The causes of this non-articulation may well be closely connected with the 'word-scepticism' which underlies many of the practices of modern poets (and which Hofmannsthal attributed to a basic split between the conventions of language and the reality of particular things). The truth of poetry, and of modern poetry especially, is to be found not only in its direct statements but in its peculiar difficulties, short cuts, silences, hiatuses and fusions.

From A PERIOD LOOSE AT ALL ENDS

... THE DISTINCTION between public and private poetry is valid if we apply it not so much to subjects or themes as to the relationship between poet and reader posited by the very structure and texture of poems on any subject whatever. The very absence of subjects or theme in Surrealist poetry – or the impossibility of categorizing and rationalizing its subjects or themes – points back to its Romantic-Symbolist ancestry and to its essentially exploratory nature. That is why André Breton objected to the 'objective starting-point', which must also be an objective 'end-point', in Aragon's *Front-rouge*. Most of the English political' poetry of the thirties could make little use of Surrealist or other modernist innovations because its primary aim was not exploratory, but hortatory or descriptive; it posited a relationship between poet and reader based on common experience, common attitudes, common knowledge. (Its weaknesses often sprang from the circumstance that this community did not really exist, because the poets in question were divided and protected from most of those on whose behalf they would have liked to speak, by the barriers of class and education.) It was from the point of view of an exploratory poet that Ezra Pound could write in 1931: 'All the developments in English verse since 1910 are due almost wholly to Americans. In fact, there is no longer any reason to call it English verse, and there is no present reason to think of England at all.' Some thirty-five years later, in his Introduction to the revised *Faber Book of Modern Verse*, its American editor, Donald Hall, remarked: 'Sometimes I wonder if England ever came to modern art at all. While Stravinsky and Picasso and Henry Moore – to mention one Englishman at least – were inventing forms and techniques, W. H. Auden was "experimenting" with sonnets and off-rhyme and Anglo-Saxon metres.' Auden and Dylan Thomas are the only British-born poets represented in H. M. Enzensberger's international *Museum of Modern Poetry* (1960), as compared to ten American-born, sixteen French, five Polish and four Czechoslovak poets, to pick out a few of the nationalities represented there. Yet Britain would undoubtedly be well represented in any international anthology of the best poems written during the same period, if modernity were not the criterion; and Enzensberger himself has argued that the modern poetry exhibited in his 'museum' is a thing of the past, that it 'can be continued only as a conventional game.'

This brings us back to the difference between a primarily exploratory or experimental poetry and one primarily concerned with its function as a means of communication. It was an excellent American poet, Robert Frost, who formulated the basic premiss of those non-modernists whose work tends to be public in the sense suggested above: 'In literature it is our business to give people the thing that will make them say, "Oh yes, I know what you mean." It is never to tell them something they don't know, but something they know and hadn't thought of saying. It must be something they recognize.' Needless to say, too rigid an insistence on that principle would severely restrict the scope of twentieth-century poets, as it has restricted the scope of lesser poets than Robert Frost, even where no totalitarian programme for the arts enforced its extreme application. Robert Frost himself offered a corrective and acknowledged the degree to which all good poetry must be exploratory, when he wrote: 'For me the initial delight is the surprise of remembering something I didn't know I knew.'

The difference, then, is a difference of degree, and it has to do with what kind of inner and outer realities a poet considers himself free to explore. The Surrealists set no limit to their freedom, at least as far as inner realities, including the subconscious, are concerned; and Dylan Thomas too exercised that kind of freedom in his earlier poems, not only telling people something they didn't know, but telling them something he didn't know before the poem brought it to light. What Robert Frost forgot to include in his statement is that even the things which people don't know about themselves, or about anything else, can be recognized when they appear in a poem, though Frost implies as much when he speaks of the delight of 'remembering something I didn't know I knew.' That is why poets who cared as little as Dylan Thomas did about being understood, about speaking for others rather than for themselves, could awaken a wider and deeper response than other poets scrupulously conscious of what their readers might be expected to know and not to know.

However concerned with their moral and social functions, therefore, the best poets of the inter-war period achieved a balance between personal and public utterance, between exploration and reference, between the poem's freedom merely to 'be' and the inescapable tendency of words to convey or imply meaning. This is as true of Mayakovsky and Pasternak in Soviet Russia as of Montale and Ungaretti in Fascist Italy, though the greater the public pressure on poets to conform, the greater was their need to safeguard a little area of freedom by resorting to a 'hermetic' art. The cultural bureaucrats responded by assuming, quite rightly in most cases, that anything they could not understand must be subversive and heterodox. Even Bertolt Brecht, the most consistent theorist and practitioner of a politically committed poetry that was also modern and intelligent, availed himself of Chinese models in order to escape the conse-quences of living under a Communist régime, writing short poems whose imagery could not easily be translated into unambiguous state-ments; and Brecht had become a master of subterfuge long before he exposed himself to that danger.

*　　*　　*

IN THE MIDDLE twenties Brecht began to evolve a theory of poetry directly opposed both to Romantic-Symbolist conceptions of 'pure' or 'absolute' poetry and to the individualistic premises of early twen-tieth-century modernism. Like the theories of most poets, Brecht's were preceded by practice, by his own poems written since the end of the war, a representative selection from which was published in 1927 in his book *Hauspostille* (Manual of Piety). In the same year Brecht, who had been invited to act as judge for a poetry competition, reported on the work of some four hundred poets who had submitted entries, and refused to award a prize. In the report Brecht wrote that 'apart from my own productions I have never been especially inter-ested in lyrical poetry'; and he went on to declare that 'poetry undoubtedly ought to be something that can easily be assessed for its utility value. ... All great poems have a documentary value. They contain their authors' way of speaking, that of important men.' Brecht admitted that he thought little of the poetry of Rilke, Stefan George and Franz Werfel, three of the most widely read and imitated German poets of the time, a dislike substantiated in a much later note (1940): 'The poet now represents only himself. In George the pontifical line, under the mask of contempt for politics, becomes openly counter-revolutionary, i.e. not only reactionary, but an active and effective instrument of the counter-revolution.' In another comment on his report of 1927 Brecht insists that the poetry written under the influence of the three poets mentioned is neither useful nor beautiful.

> I don't wish to make Stefan George responsible for the World War. But I see no reason why he should isolate himself. I believe that this naïve sage wanted to show all those who share his opinions that he was incomparable and unique. After a brief examination of his aesthetic value I had to conclude that he was fit for police duties. And for a policeman an attitude of pure enjoyment in the midst of an intricate nexus of crimes is not the right one. It is not a policeman's business merely to register certain conflicting emotions on his face. . . . I go on to assert that almost all the poetry of the declining bourgeoisie, but certainly its representative part, shows too many class-war tendencies to have a purely aesthetic value.

Even in this radical application of Marxian principles to literary criticism (or polemics) Brecht pays lip service at least to considerations of beauty rather than utility; and it is important to bear in mind that Stefan George, Brecht's principle target here and elsewhere, did assume the active function of prophet and leader of a cultural élite, despite his early beginnings as a disciple of Mallarmé and his professions of a pure aestheticism. Nor does Brecht deny the value of poetry as the expression of personality, though his notions of what constitutes an 'important man' clearly differ from those of the 'declining bourgeoisie.' What his own notions were can be deduced from the 'proletarian' image of himself in the poem 'Of Poor B. B.' in *Hauspostille*. What is much more crucial, Brecht's definitive edition of the *Hauspostille*, prepared in the last decade of his life and published after his death, includes his three 'Psalms', prose poems whose free imagery derives from the visionary poems of Rimbaud and is close to Surrealist practice:

> 6. Das ist der Sommer. Scharlachene Winde erregen die Ebenen, die Gerüche werden Ende Juni masslos. Ungeheure Gesichte zähnefletschender nackter Männer wandern in grossen Höhen sudwärts. . . .

> 7. In den Hütten ist das Licht der Nächte wie Lachs. Man feiert die Auferstehung des Fleisches.

.   .   .   .   .

6. This is summer. Scarlet winds stir up the plains, the smells at the end of June grow boundless. Monstrous visions of teeth-gnashing naked men travel southwards at great heights. . . .

7. In cottages the nocturnal light is like salmon. The resurrection of the flesh is celebrated.

Other 'psalms' and poems written in the same manner, in 1920 and 1921, were collected posthumously in the second and eighth volumes of Brecht's *Gedichte*. In a note of 1938 Brecht mentions that he sang the psalms to a guitar accompaniment and defends himself against the charge of 'formalism.' 'Because I am an innovator in my field, some people keep on shouting that I'm a formalist. They do not find the old forms in my work, and, worse, they find new ones, and then they infer that it is the forms that interest me, but I have discovered that I'm rather inclined to deprecate the formal element. I have studied the old forms of poetry, story-telling, drama and theatre at various times and only given them up when they stood in the way of what I wanted to say.' As Brecht knew as well as anybody, contemporary poets not fortunate enough to be living and working outside Russia, as Brecht was, were simply not free to say what they wanted to say; and in the fifties Brecht became explicit about the need for new forms, though in a note not published in his lifetime: 'Only new contents permit new forms. Indeed they demand them. For if new contents were forced into old forms, at once you would have a recurrence of that disastrous division between content and form, because the form that is old would separate from the content that would be new. The life which is everywhere assuming new forms in our society, in which the foundations are being shifted, can be neither rendered nor influenced by a literature in the old form.' The same division between form and content, Brecht argues, is a characteristic of the 'bankruptcy of literature in the late capitalist epoch.' In the same way Brecht warned against the narrow interpretation of 'realism' that was cramping, and still cramps, Communist literature. As an example of social, if not socialist realism, *avant la lettre* he cites Shelley's *The Mask of Anarchy*, which he also translated – a striking instance of Brecht's ability to make use of the most diverse models, from ancient

---

* Permission to quote the text of this poem here was refused by the copyright holder.

Greek drama to Arthur Waley's translations from the Chinese, from Villon to Kipling, from Luther's Bible to jazz lyrics and cabaret songs. It was almost certainly with his own practices in mind that Brecht argued against the suppression of 'destructive and anarchistic poetry' by the State, which 'damages pro-State literature if it suppresses anti-State literature.' A retrospective note of 1940 on his own *Hauspostille* judges it to be not only anarchic but 'dehumanized', since in these poems 'beauty adheres to wrecks, rags become delicate. The sublime rolls in the dust, meaninglessness is saluted as a liberator. The poet has lost solidarity even with himself: risus mortis. But it's not without strength.'

Brecht's most revolutionary act as a poet was what he called his 'language-washing.' It was by stripping his diction of ornamental and sentimental accretions that he avoided the pitfalls of 'committed' verse, and so assumed an exemplary importance for so many younger poets after the Second World War. Although his extraordinarily varied poetic output – which fills some two thousand pages in the posthumous collected edition, with more poems likely to be added – includes a good deal of didactic political verse, he maintained his own freedom to say what he wanted to say. His theoretical statements, too, are truly dialectic. 'Art *is* an autonomous realm,' he wrote in 1940, 'though in no circumstances an autarchic one'; and this in connection with another Romantic poem of the 'bourgeois era', Wordsworth's 'She was a Phantom of Delight'. A note of 1944 on Arthur Waley's translations from the Chinese demonstrates that 'there is no difference between didacticism and entertainment. . . . In its didactic as in its other works, poetry succeeds in enhancing our enjoyment of life. It sharpens the senses and turns even pain into pleasure.'

By far the greater part of Brecht's poetry is designed to give people 'something they recognize'; but Brecht's directness could serve to make a point as devastating in its exposure of Communist smugness as so many of his other political poems are in their exposure of capitalist exploitation or Fascist militarism. His poem on the workers' uprising in East Berlin, 'Die Lösung', is a good example of Brecht's ability to say the unexpected thing about public affairs:*

The Solution

After the uprising on June 17th
The Secretary of the Authors' Union

Had leaflets distributed in the Stalinallee
Which said that the people
Had forfeited the government's confidence
And could only win it back
By redoubled labour. Wouldn't it
Be simpler in that case if the government
Dissolved the people and
Elected another?

This poem was not included in the selection from his *Buckower Elegien* which Brecht published in his *Versuche 13* of 1954, and Brecht's dealings with political authorities and powers of every kind are reminiscent of James Joyce's motto, 'Silence, exile and cunning.' Yet 'Die Lösung' is direct enough, making its point without recourse to metaphor, heightened language or formal prosody. From the *Hauspostille* onwards, effrontery had always been part of Brecht's poetic gesture. In late poems like 'Die Lösung' the effrontery is conveyed not by posturizing, strong words and forceful rhythms, but by the seeming laxity and randomness of the presentation. It is as though the poet could not be bothered to turn his prose into 'poetry'; but in their own way those lines answer almost all the demands of the *Imagist Manifesto*: 'To use the language of common speech, but to employ always the exact word, not merely the decorative word. To create new rhythms as the expression of new moods. To allow absolute freedom in the choice of subject. To present an image. We are not a school of painters, but we believe that poets should render particulars exactly and not deal with vague generalities. To produce poetry that is hard and clear, never blurred and indefinite. Finally, most of us believe that concentration is the very essence of poetry.' One could cavil about the fourth clause, 'to present an image', if the later practice of the Imagists themselves had not shown that lyrical verse is one thing, political verse another.

That Brecht was aware of the chief author of the *Imagist Manifesto*, Ezra Pound, is attested by a short poem written in the early forties, 'E. P. Auswahl seines Grabsteins', which takes issue not with Ezra Pound's later political affiliations but with the aestheticism which Brecht must have regarded as their premiss:

E. P. Auswahl seines Grabsteins

Die Herstellung von Versteinerungen
Ist ein mühsames Geschäft und
Kostspielig. Ganze Städte
Müssen in Schutt gelegt werden
Und unter Umständen umsonst
Wenn die Fliege oder der Farn
Schlecht plaziert wurde. Überdies
Ist der Stein unserer Städte nicht haltbar
Und auch Versteinerungen
Halten sich nicht sicher.

.   .   .   .   .

E. P. L'Election de Son Sépulchre

The production of petrifactions
Is an arduous business and
Expensive. Whole towns
Must be reduced to rubble
And at times in vain –
If the fly or the fern
Was badly placed. Furthermore
The stone of our towns is not lasting
And even petrifactions
Can't be relied on to last.

Here the satire is as cryptic and indirect as it is open and direct in 'The Solution', because the subject itself is comparatively esoteric, as well as being delicate. What is evidently implied is a dialectical relationship between art intended to be autarchic and the social conditions required to sustain it. 'Petrifaction' or fossilization stands for the process by which living organisms – including human lives – are transmuted by such an art into monuments. Brecht's implicit alternative is an art that transmutes as little as possible, insisting on the primacy of immediate human needs. With a number of blatant exceptions, due to his own political affiliations, Brecht's poetry avoided monumentalism and the 'production of petrifactions', because his social consciousness did not need to be projected ideologically, but informed his responses to every kind of experience, every phenomenon touched upon in his work. Although it is conceivable that the casualness which was his alternative to monumentalism will reduce much of his poetry to the order of occasional verse, his occasions remain relevant and crucial enough, his tone of voice distinctive enough behind all the stylistic masks and conventions of which he made use, to have justified his claim, 'I need no gravestone', until now.

Ich benötige keinen Grabstein

Ich benötige keinen Grabstein, aber
Wenn ihr einen für mich benötigt
Wünschte ich, es stünde darauf:
Er hat Vorschläge gemacht. Wir
Haben sie angenommen.
Durch eine solche Inschrift wären
Wir alle geehrt.

    . . . . .

I need no gravestone, but
If you need one for me
I wish the inscription would read:
He made suggestions. We
Have acted on them.
Such an epitaph would
Honour us all.

Only one other twentieth-century poet I can think of, William Carlos Williams, succeeded as well as Brecht in integrating his poetic and social selves to the extent of really overcoming the Romantic-Symbolist dichotomies. Both became masters of the seemingly off-hand, seemingly effortless manner that leaves no gaps between the thing said and the way of saying it, between what the poem enacts and the person who enacts it. Of the two, Williams was by far the more sensuous and visual poet, and he presented 'images' rather than moralities; but both poets made a new purity out of the very stuff which most of their predecessor poets had condemned in advance as impure, because it was ordinary and workaday. The similarity of tone is striking as soon as Williams addresses himself to the community, instead of applying himself to the individual people and things that constitute it. So in 'Tract':

No wreaths please –
especially no hot-house flowers.

Some common memento is better,
something he prized and is known by:
his old clothes – a few books perhaps –
God knows what! You realize
how we are about these things,
my townspeople –
something will be found – anything
even flowers if he had come to that.
So much for the hearse.

Because Brecht had to pass through a phase of individualistic revolt – that of his play *Baal* and the poems in *Hauspostille* – before becoming identified with ordinariness, Williams succeeded much better than he in the rendering of 'all trades, their gear and tackle and trim', and indeed of the 'pied beauty' celebrated by Gerard Manley Hopkins. Here Brecht was inhibited by his political preoccupations, his concern with those realities which could almost turn 'a conversation about trees' into a crime; and for a long time, gentleness and the kind of sympathy that flows freely into other persons and things seemed suspect to him, because of their associations with 'bourgeois' sentiment, the luxury of people whose feelings and energies are otherwise unemployed. Brecht did write poems in praise of people, things, places and – repeatedly – trees; and his poem 'Die Liebenden' (from his opera *Mahagonny*) is the most memorable of many in which harsh realities yield a tenderness of their own. Brecht's poem 'An die Nachgeborenen' (To Posterity) refers to the circumstances that make such poems stand out from the body of his work:

> ... Dabei wissen wir doch:
> Auch der Hass gegen die Niedrigkeit
> Verzerrt die Züge.
> Auch der Zorn über das Unrecht
> Macht die Stimme heiser. Ach, wir
> Die wir den Boden bereiten wollten für Freundlichkeit,
> Konnten selber nicht freundlich sein. . . .
>
>   .   .   .   .   .
>
> And yet we know well:
> Even hatred of vileness
> Distorts a man's features.
> Even anger at injustice

Makes hoarse his voice. Ah, we
Who desired to prepare the soil for kindness
Could not ourselves be kind.

*   *   *

THE HISTORICAL importance of Brecht's reversal of the dominant poetic trends since Baudelaire – and indeed since Romanticism – needs little emphasis. Most of his poetry is public to a degree reminiscent of classical eras, and much of it is popular without condescension, even where Brecht had deliberate recourse to media, like the ballad, sonnet and song, that seemed incapable of being truly revived and modernized. Unlike the poetry of William Carlos Williams, little of Brecht's is impersonal in the sense suggested by Pasternak when he wrote: 'In art the man is silent and the image speaks.' Brecht's personality, his wily intelligence and his moral toughness, are present even in poems that come close to being pastiche; but not obtrusively so in the later poems, because the personality itself has been stripped down to essentials.

Pasternak too had to revise his early reliance on the image and on the music of poetry. 'We drag everyday things into prose for the sake of poetry. We entice prose into poetry for the sake of music,' he wrote in *Safe Conduct* (1931), but also: 'Poetry as I understand it flows through history and in collaboration with real life.' The autonomous image and the music of poetry had to be reconciled with a historical consciousness that had become inescapable in the age of total politics. In an interview given shortly before his death, Pasternak said: 'In writing as in speaking the music of the word is never just a matter of sound. It does not result from the harmony of vowels and consonants. It results from the relation between the speech and the meaning. And meaning – content – must always lead.'

Except where poetry insulated itself against this historical consciousness, or was preserved from it by a continuity of traditions and institutions – in countries relatively undisrupted by war or revolution – the old dispute about the primacy of form or content assumed a new urgency and a new complexity. The question itself is rather like the one as to which came first, the chicken or the egg; but the answer in each individual case, the exact balance, to be struck by each poet between conscience and imagination, public and private concerns, communication and discovery, became truly difficult and problematic. National differences, too, asserted themselves with a vengeance after the international Futurism of 1912. In French, Italian and Spanish poetry, for instance, the primacy of 'form' was maintained much more stubbornly than in English, American, Russian and German poetry, for reasons not only social and political, but cultural and linguistic. Though the Surrealist movement broke up, Surrealist practice retained its hold on French poets up to the fifties and sixties – as in the work of Paul Éluard, Pierre Jean Jouve, Pierre Reverdy, Henri Michaux and René Char – while the public, popular and social poetry of Jacques Prévert was rarely taken as seriously by French critics as it was by critics outside France.

Dadaism, too, proved tenacious long after it had gone underground (to emerge after the Second World War). The sound poems of Kurt Schwitters set a precedent for much that seemed most new a decade after his death. Jean (or Hans) Arp, better known as a sculptor, wrote and published poems over a period of sixty years, beginning in 1903 with poems that anticipate Surrealism despite their *art nouveau* features. In his Dadaist poems proper, written from 1916 to shortly after the First World War, 'words, catchwords, sentences from daily newspapers and especially their advertisements became the basis for poetic constructions,' as Arp explained. Chance became an artistic principle, because Arp identified chance with reality and nature, as opposed to all that is willed and deliberate in conventional art. That principle, too, was to be revived by Concrete poetry, like Arp's use of verbal collage and his permutations of words and idioms. 'dada', Arp wrote in 1931 or 1932, 'is for nonsense that doesn't mean stupidity. dada is nonsensical like nature and life. dada is for nature and against art. dada like nature wants to give everything its essential place.' Most of those poems by Arp which he called 'unanchored', because their words and things are not tied down to a preconceived meaning, are untranslatable, because they play too freely with their material, which is language. But in the twenties some of Arp's poems began to reveal an anchor that could be metaphysical or social:

> während die einen mit ihrer rechten hand auf ihre linke hand
> und mit ihrer linken hand auf ihre rechte hand zeigen
> beide hände voll zu tun haben
> und dennoch auf keinen grünen zweig kommen
> wachsen die andern auf bäumen in den himmel

obwohl jemand da ist der dafür zu sorgen hat
dass die bäume nicht in den himmel wachsen . . .

. . . . .

while some point with their right hands to their left hands
and with their left hands to their right hands
have their hands full
and so can't get to the top of the tree
others grow on trees into the sky
although there is someone whose business it is to see
that trees don't grow up to the sky . . .

Even here Arp plays changes on German idioms in a way that
cannot be fully rendered; but the anchor is visible in any language, as
in this passage from the same sequence:

als ihm der boden unter den füssen fortgenommen wurde
heftete er sich mit seinen blicken an die decke
und sparte seine schuhe
so hing er regungslos wie ein scharadensack
und frönte dem abc des herrn-und damenlosen leibes
es drängte ihn nicht einen befiederten schabrackenhiatus
    zu wichsen
er strebte weder danach ein held des tages noch ein held der nacht
    zu werden . . .

. . . . .

when the ground was taken from under his feet
he attached himself to the ceiling with his eyes
and saved his shoes
like that he hung motionless like a charade sack
and served the abc of the masterless and mistressless body
he was not impelled to wax a plumed caparison hiatus
he did not aspire to become either a hero of the day or a hero of
    the night . . .

The anchoring of such poems is given away in the same sequence,
when Arp calls a shoe 'the emblem of senseless busyness.' By 1930,
when he wrote his sequence 'Das Tagesgerippe' (The Skeleton of
Day), the exuberant nonsense of the Dada period had yielded to a
more sober, elegiac and largely retrospective mood, and even the
verbal play had been discarded, as in Section 7:

wo sind die blätter
die glocken welken
es läutet nicht mehr in der erde
wo wir einst schritten
ist das licht zerrissen
die spuren der flügel führen ins leere
wo sind die lippen
wo sind die augen
grauenvoll zerschlug sich ihr herz zwischen den häuptern
der letzte atemzug fällt aus dem körper wie ein stein
wo wir einst sprachen flieht das blut aus dem feuer
und der gestaltlose kranz dreht sich im schwarzen grund
unsichtbar für immer ist die schöne erde
die flügel schweben nie mehr um uns

   . . . . .

where are the leaves
the bells wilt
no ringing is heard in the earth
where once we walked
the light is torn
the wakes of wings lead into the void
where are the lips
where are the eyes
their heart between heads was horribly dashed to pieces
the last breath drops from the body like a stone
where once we talked our blood flees from the fire
and the shapeless wreath turns in the blackness below
for ever invisible is our beautiful earth
never again will the wings hover around us

In the later poems, written in the next three decades, Arp's nonsense rarely lacks an ironic sting or an elegiac undertone. The principle of fortuitousness had lost most of its impact on people whose complacency was being thoroughly shaken up without the help of the arts, if it was not incapable of being shaken up by anything whatever. The sequence 'Blatt um Feder um Blatt' of 1951–2 contains an epigram that could not be more explicit:

Nun hat die Angst die meisten Menschen verlassen,
und die Unendlichkeit hat kein gutes Wort
kein ängstigendes Wort mehr für sie.
Gähnende Leeren wachsen neben gähnenden Leeren.

. . . . .

> Now fear has abandoned the greater part of men
> and infinity hasn't one kind word,
> one fearful word to say to them.
> Yawning voids grow next to yawning voids.

Yet in the same sequence Arp still writes that 'Chance frees us from the net of meaninglessness', and 'We take refuge in deeper games', a statement literally true of the poems he continued to write until shortly before his death in 1966.

Arp's insistence on chance has more in common with the Surrealist practice of 'automatic writing' than with the more rigorously 'scientific' experiments in verbal analysis, verbal patterning and verbal permutation of the Concrete poets. Another way of putting it is that Arp's reliance on chance gave the greatest possible scope to his imagination, as well as to his ingenuity, since his games with words and idioms did not exclude the free association of images. Just as William Carlos Williams's reliance on minutely observed realities did not prevent him from concluding that 'only the imagination is real', Arp's starting-point at the opposite end did not prevent him from anchoring many of his poems in recognizable realities; and even where Arp did not impose a preconceived meaning on his poems, the nature of language saw to it that meanings were released by his verbal structures.

Arp's identification of chance with nature implies a faith in meanings which our normal use of language cannot apprehend; and long before he became a master of comic nonsense Arp was a visionary poet of a more conventional kind. In a poem written in the late thirties, 'Lied des Roten', Arp recalls the artists in the Café Odéon of 'twenty years ago'. They vanish again and 'smoking eggs lie in their place.' The poem continues:

> wenn ich nicht acht gebe
> entsteht nun ein gedicht.
> trinken und singen fällt mir ein
> wir trinken und singen
> und die zeit vergeht.
> es singt und weht
> und wandert im licht.
> eines tages rascheln wir wie welke blätter fort

zerfallen zu staub
und werden wieder funken und sterne
und singen und trinken
und wandern selig in feurigen mänteln.

.   .   .   .   .

if I'm not careful now
I shall write a poem.
drinking and singing occur to me.
we drink and sing
and time goes by.
it sings and wafts
and walks in the light.
one day we all rustle off like dead leaves
crumble to dust
and turn again into sparks and stars
and sing and drink
and blissfully walk in our fiery mantles.

The subject of 'it sings and wafts' is not 'time'. The 'it' is impersonal, and its identity is not revealed. The cosmic and Biblical allusions in the poem point back to Arp's earliest, pre-modernist and pre-Dadaist, visions. Arp's 'nature' was never that of the naturalists, but a super-reality which words could not name but only let through when they had been shaken and broken up, as they were by Arp's nonsense. Despite the anchors, a concession to historical consciousness, Arp's use of language remained as different as possible from that of Brecht, who picked up his words and idioms where he found them and treated most of them as a solid, reliable currency. [...]

Select Bibliography

[Note: This bibliography lists mainly first editions of publications. Excerpts in this anthology may be taken from later editions.]

POETRY

Flowering Cactus, Hand and Flower Press, 1950
Poems 1950–1951, Hand and Flower Press, 1952
The Dual Site, Routledge and Kegan Paul, 1958
Weather and Season, Longmans, 1963
Travelling, Fulcrum Press, 1969
Travelling I–V, Agenda Editions, 1972
Ownerless Earth: New and Selected Poems, Carcanet Press, 1973
Real Estate, Carcanet Press, 1977
Variations, Carcanet Press, 1981
Collected Poems 1941–1983, Carcanet Press, 1984
Selected Poems, Carcanet Press, 1988
Roots in the Air, Anvil Press, 1991
Collected Poems 1941–1994, Anvil Press, 1995
Late, Anvil Press, 1997
Intersections, Anvil Press, 2000
From a Diary of Non-Events, Anvil Press, 2002
Wild and Wounded, Anvil Press, 2004
Circling the Square, Anvil Press, 2007

TRANSLATION

Poems of Hölderlin, Nicholson and Watson, 1943
Twenty Prose Poems of Baudelaire, Editions Poetry London, 1946
Ludwig van Beethoven, *Letters, Journals and Conversations*, Thames and Hudson, 1952
Georg Trakl, *Decline*, Latin Press, 1952
Hugo van Hofmannsthal, *Poems and Verse Plays* (with other translators), Routledge and Kegan Paul, 1961
Modern German Poetry 1910–60 (with Christopher Middleton), MacGibbon and Kee, 1962
Friedrich Hölderlin, *Poems and Fragments*, Routledge and Kegan

Paul, 1966. Second edition, Cambridge University Press, 1980. Third and fourth editions, Anvil Press, 1994, 2004

Günter Grass, *Selected Poems*, Secker and Warburg, 1966

Hans Magnus Enzensberger, *poems for people who don't read poems* (with Jerome Rothenberg), Secker and Warburg, 1968

Georg Trakl, *Selected Poems* (with others), Jonathan Cape, 1968

East German Poetry (ed.; with other translators), Carcanet Press, 1972

German Poetry 1910–1975, Carcanet Press, 1977

Helmut Heissenbüttel, *Texts*, Marion Boyars, 1977

Philippe Jaccottet, *Seedtime* (with André Lefevere), New Directions, 1977

Günter Grass, *In the Egg* (with Christopher Middleton), Secker and Warburg, 1978

Franco Fortini, *Poems*, Arc, 1978

Paul Celan, *Poems*, Carcanet Press, 1980. New editions from Anvil Press: *Poems of Paul Celan*, 1988; second edition, 1995; third edition, 2007

Rainer Maria Rilke, *An Unofficial Rilke*, Anvil Press, 1981. Reissued as *Turning-Point*, Anvil Press, 2003

Peter Huchel, *The Garden of Theophrastus*, Carcanet Press, 1983. New edition, Anvil Press, 2004

Goethe: *Poems and Epigrams*, Anvil Press, 1983. New edition: *Roman Elegies and Other Poems*, Anvil Press, 1996

Marin Sorescu, *Selected Poems*, Bloodaxe Books, 1983

Günter Eich, *Pigeons and Moles*, Skoob Books, 1991

Franz Baermann Steiner, *Modern Poetry in Translation*, New Series No. 2, King's College London, 1992

Hans Magnus Enzensberger, *Selected Poems*, Bloodaxe Books, 1994

Werner Dürrson, *The Kattenhorn Silence*, Cloud, 1995

Hans Magnus Enzensberger, *Kiosk*, Bloodaxe Books, 1997

Ernst Jandl, *Dingfest/Thingsure*, Dedalus Press, 1997

Günter Grass, *Selected Poems 1956–1993*, Faber and Faber, 1999

W. G. Sebald, *After Nature*, 2002

ESSAYS AND CRITICISM

Reason and Energy, Studies in German Literature, Routledge and Kegan Paul, 1957

From Prophecy to Exorcism, The Premisses of Modern German Literature, Longmans, 1965

The Truth of Poetry, Tensions in Modern Poetry from Baudelaire to the 1960s, Weidenfeld and Nicolson, 1969; Anvil Press, 1996

Art as Second Nature, Occasional Pieces 1950–74, Carcanet Press, 1975

A Proliferation of Prophets, Essays on German Writers from Nietzsche to Brecht, Carcanet Press, 1983

After the Second Flood, Essays on Post-War German Literature, Carcanet Press, 1986

Testimonies, Selected Shorter Prose 1950–1987, Carcanet Press, 1989

MEMOIRS AND INTERVIEW

A Mug's Game, Intermittent Memoirs 1924–1954, Carcanet Press, 1973

String of Beginnings, Intermittent Memoirs 1924–1954, Skoob Books, 1991

Michael Hamburger in Conversation with Peter Dale, Between the Lines, 1998